Barcode in Back

FOR REFERENCE ONLY
NOT TO BE TAKEN FROM THIS ROOM

HUMBER LIBRARIES LAKESHORE CAMPUS
3199 Lakeshore Blvd West
TORONTO, ON.   M8V 1K8

The Psychology of Teen Violence and Victimization

The Psychology of Teen Violence and Victimization

Volume 2: Prevention Strategies for Families and Schools

Michele A. Paludi, Editor

Foreword by Lisa Krenkel

 PRAEGER

AN IMPRINT OF ABC-CLIO, LLC
Santa Barbara, California • Denver, Colorado • Oxford, England

Copyright 2011 by Michele A. Paludi

All rights reserved. No part of this publication may be reproduced, stored in a retrieval system, or transmitted, in any form or by any means, electronic, mechanical, photocopying, recording, or otherwise, except for the inclusion of brief quotations in a review, without prior permission in writing from the publisher.

Library of Congress Cataloging-in-Publication Data

The psychology of teen violence and victimization / Michele A. Paludi, editor ; foreword by Lisa Krenkel.
　p. cm.
Includes bibliographical references and index.
ISBN 978-0-313-39375-4 (hardback: acid-free paper) — ISBN 978-0-313-39376-1 (ebk)
1. Children and violence. 2. Violence in children. 3. Youth–Crimes against. I. Paludi, Michele Antoinette.
HQ784. V55P79 2011
303.60835–dc23　　2011033276

ISBN: 978-0-313-39375-4
EISBN: 978-0-313-39376-1

15 14 13 12 11　1 2 3 4 5

This book is also available on the World Wide Web as an eBook.
Visit www.abc-clio.com for details.

Praeger
An Imprint of ABC-CLIO, LLC

ABC-CLIO, LLC
130 Cremona Drive, P.O. Box 1911
Santa Barbara, California 93116-1911

This book is printed on acid-free paper ∞

Manufactured in the United States of America

There can be no better measure of our governance than the way we treat our children, and no greater failing on our part than to allow them to be subjected to violence, abuse, or exploitation.

—*Jessica Lange*

It is my hope that these volumes of *The Psychology of Teen Violence and Victimization* will help parents, educators, activists, and legislators continue to advocate for and protect the rights of children and adolescents.

—*Michele A. Paludi*

Contents

Foreword by Lisa Krenkel ix

Acknowledgments xi

Introduction by Michele A. Paludi xiii

PART I. IMPACT OF TEEN VIOLENCE ON ADOLESCENTS, FAMILY, AND PEERS

Chapter One: Peer Victimization and Post-Traumatic Stress Disorder in Children and Adolescents 3
James Crosby

Chapter Two: Treatment of Adolescent Victims of Violence 17
Beth M. Housekamp, Marjorie Graham-Howard, Bethany Ashby, and Alice Fok-Trela

Chapter Three: Effects of Playing Violent Video Games 41
Craig A. Anderson and Sara Prot

Chapter Four: The Role of Victimization Experiences in Adolescent Girls and Young Women's Aggression in Dating Relationships 71
Katie M. Edwards, Christina M. Dardis, and Christine A. Gidycz

PART II. EDUCATIONAL RESPONSES TO TEEN VIOLENCE

Chapter Five: Educating Teens to Discriminate Abusive from Nonabusive Situations 89
Imelda N. Bratton, Christopher P. Roseman, and William E. Schweinle

Chapter Six:	Young People's Representations of Bullying Causes *Robert L. Thornberg*	105
Chapter Seven:	Desensitization to Media Violence *Kostas A. Fanti and Marios N. Avraamides*	121
Chapter Eight:	What We Do Matters: Making Shelter When Teachers Abuse Teens *Billie Wright Dziech*	135

PART III. COMMUNITY RESPONSES TO TEEN VIOLENCE

Chapter Nine:	Community Interventions: Providing Support for Adolescent Victims of Violence *Roseanne L. Flores*	163
Chapter Ten:	Adolescents and Firearms *Deanna L. Wilkinson, Ashley Hicks, and Shelly Bloom*	171
Chapter Eleven:	Delinquency and Violent Behavior in Girls: Prominent Risks and Promising Interventions *Ann Booker Loper, Emily B. Nichols, and Caitlin M. Novero*	199
Chapter Twelve:	Broadening the Frame of Violence Prevention through the Promotion of Youth Community Engagement *Jessica J. Collura, Brian D. Christens, and Shepherd Zeldin*	221
Chapter Thirteen:	Abusive Adolescent Boys in Adulthood *William E. Schweinle*	239

About the Editor and Contributors	251
Index	259

Foreword

Lisa Krenkel

> The solution of adult problems tomorrow depends in large measure upon the way our children grow up today. There is no greater insight into the future than recognizing that, when we save children, we save ourselves.
> *Margaret Mead*

The subject of teen violence in today's society is both volatile and controversial. Teenagers are the victims of violence, and the perpetrators are increasingly not only adults but also teens' own peers. As an attorney, I have seen the end result of this disturbing trend: a juvenile justice system that is overburdened, underfunded, outdated, and ill-equipped to deal with the onslaught of cases involving teenagers. Teenage victims are not often afforded the same resources as adult victims of physical abuse and sexual violence, and even when they are, the resources are designed to assist adult victims and are not tailored to the unique psychology of teens, who are often marginalized in our society. Ultimately this results in a resistance to treatment and assistance that can have life-threatening or lifelong consequences.

The statistics are staggering, and the solution is evasive. The violence is increasingly more violent in degree, and the age of the offender is younger and younger. Technology has quickly outpaced society's ability to codify many crimes such as sexting and child pornography. Sexual violence in schools and on school buses, bullying, and Internet crimes of harassment, humiliation, and intimidation are increasingly unmonitored, with devastating results.

Is the answer merely to treat these juvenile offenders as adults and absorb them into the adult criminal justice system? Should the adult laws of criminal intent and capacity be applied to teen offenders? Will adult concepts of punishment serve the same purpose when applied to teenagers? Can we help the teen victims in the same way that we try to help adult victims of violent crime?

In these two volumes, Dr. Paludi and her colleagues seek to examine the roots and causes of teen violence by exploring society's changing attitudes toward sex, gender, and violence and teenagers' precarious status within this paradigm. Dr. Paludi has dedicated her life to helping women and children. She is an educator, author, and expert witness and a psychological theoretician. In these volumes, she challenges us all to explore the difficult issues that affect children, specifically teenagers, in a time of technological advancement that is marked by social inequality and the marginalization of teenagers, who can neither defend nor empower themselves. As a litigator, I see the aftermath of the violence, its end result. Dr. Paludi and contributing authors explore the etiology of this violence as it manifests itself in an effort to change the pattern of violence and victimization that has besieged our nation's youths.

Acknowledgments

I have had the honor of knowing and working with individuals and organizations who have advocated for adolescents' rights, especially with respect to violence and victimization. I would like to acknowledge their work and the impact they have had in protecting our children and teens:

The American Association of University Women
Business and Professional Women's Club of Schenectady, New York
Governor Mario Cuomo's Task Force on Sexual Harassment
Florence L. Denmark
Susan Klein
Lisa Krenkel
Donna Linder and Child Find of America
Paula K. Lundberg-Love
Jennifer L. Martin
Kevin L. Nadal
Bernice Sandler
Nan Stein
Susan Strauss
Brittany Tarabour
United States Department of Education's Subpanel on the Prevention of Violence, Sexual Harassment, Alcohol and Other Drug Abuse in Higher Education
Women's Studies Program, Northeastern University

I also appreciate the caring and support of my sisters Rosalie Paludi and Lucille Paludi during the writing and editing of these volumes.

My sincere thanks to Debbie Carvalko and her colleagues at Praeger for knowing how much writing and editing books means to me. As Toni Morrison is quoted as saying, "If there's a book you really want to read but it hasn't been written yet, then you must write it." Debbie knows this about me!

Introduction

Michele A. Paludi

Adolescents and Hate Crimes

> Hate crimes are the scariest thing in the world because these people really believe what they're doing is right.
>
> Cher

During the writing of *The Psychology of Teen Violence and Victimization*, the following incidents received national attention:

March 2010: Massachusetts high school student Phoebe Prince committed suicide following bullying, verbal harassment, and physical abuse from peers at school.

May 2010: Cactus Grill Restaurant in Leawood, Kansas, was sued by the Equal Employment Opportunity Commission for sexually harassing an 18-year-old woman, including unwanted touching, sexual advances, and requests for sex.

July 2010: Cory Miller, a 16-year-old teen from Havana, Illinois, was attacked by bullies for the third time in two years. Cory was born with cerebral palsy and is confined to a wheelchair. The bullies had taunted and threatened him, violently kicked and beat him, spit on him, and broke his wheelchair and glasses. They left him lying in dirt.

August 2010: The Centers for Disease Control and Prevention High School Youth Risk Behavior Survey reported that Arkansas, Alaska, West Virginia, Kentucky, and Missouri were the five states with the highest percentages of girls being raped.

September 2010: Marco Gonzalez, a 15-year-old boy in Georgia, was abducted by individuals who stole his family car with him inside of it.

October 2010: Rutgers University student Tyler Clementi committed suicide after learning that his roommate and classmate had used a webcam to secretly broadcast Tyler's sexual relationship with another man.

> October 2010: Four teenagers in Staten Island, New York, were arrested for bullying a Muslim classmate, Kristian, for more than a year, which included spitting in his face, punching him in the groin, and calling him a terrorist.
>
> October 2010: Yale University fraternity Delta Kappa Epsilon paraded through the university campus shouting sexually offensive slogans against women, including "No Means Yes; Yes Means Anal."

Much violence against adolescents and committed by adolescents is a result of hate crimes (McConnell & Swain, 2000; Steinberg, Brooks, & Remtulla, 2003), as illustrated by the incidents listed above. A hate crime is a crime that in whole or in part is motivated by the offender's bias toward the victim's status. Hate crimes are intended to hurt and intimidate individuals because they are perceived to be different with respect to their sex, religion, race, color, national origin, sexual orientation, gender, or disability (Paludi, Ellens, & Paludi, 2010). While hate crimes are assaults against an individual, they are also assaults against everyone who shares the victim's status (e.g., Muslims, individuals with disabilities, African Americans, lesbians, gay males, females).

Legislation lists specific crimes that are identifiable as a hate crime, including murder; manslaughter; robbery; aggravated assault; burglary; motor vehicle theft; arson; forced and nonforced sex offenses; intimidation; destruction, damage, or vandalism of property; and other crimes involving injury to any person or property. When the behavior does not fall into one of the listed criminal categories identified above, hate offenses are referred to as bias-motivated incidents. These incidents may include cases of verbal slurs and may be precursors to more serious hate crimes (Paludi et al., 2010). Thus, violence against adolescents (as well as adults) exists along a continuum, from incivility and microaggressions to hate crimes, including assault and murder (Paludi, 2010; see also chapters 1 and 5, volume 1, and chapter 10, volume 2, of this book set).

A Closer Look at Gender-Based Hate Crimes

Gender-based hate crimes are the most prevalent type of hate crimes committed and experienced by teens. Gendered violence, or gender-based violence, has been defined as follows: "any act that results in, or is likely to result in, physical, sexual, or psychological harm or suffering to women, including threats of such acts, coercion or arbitrary deprivation of liberty, whether occurring in public or private life" (United Nations, 1995). This definition includes rape, stalking, intimate partner violence, and child sexual abuse. The terminology "gendered violence" is used, as highlighted by Russo and Pirlott (2006, p. 181), "because such violence is shaped by gender roles and status in society. . . . A complex mix of gender-related cultural values, beliefs, norms, and social institutions implicitly and even explicitly have supported intimate partner violence and provided little recourse for its victims."

Hate crimes against lesbians, gay men, and transgender individuals is gendered. Unlike other forms of hate crimes, however, gender-based hate crimes toward lesbian, gay, bisexual, and transgender youths are viewed as the most socially acceptable type of violence by adolescents (see chapter 1, volume 1, of this book set). Boys and men commit most of the violent crimes against gay males and lesbians (National Coalition of Anti-Violence Programs, 2009). The majority of murders of transgender individuals are perpetrated by nontransgender men; most victims are transgender women. Such violence has its roots in gender nonconformity (Schilt & Westbrook, 2009). The violence is fueled by anger as well as fear about gender nonconformity and feeling deceived by the individual's gender presentation (Schilt & Westbrook, 2009).

Adolescent girls are exposed to more violence than are adolescent boys (Flores, 2006; see also chapter 11, volume 2, of this book set). The National Survey on Drug Use and Health of the Substance Abuse and Mental Health Services Administration (2010) reported that from their sample of 33,091 girls aged 12 to 17, 18.6% got in a serious fight at school or work, 14.1% participated in a group-against-group fight, and 5.7% were violent toward others with an intent to hurt them. With respect to adolescent boys, this research found that 25.4% got into a serious fight at school or work, 17% participated in a group-against-group fight, and 9.3% attacked another person with the intent to harm that person.

Girls (and women) are most likely to be murdered by a romantic partner or ex-partner (Lundberg-Love & Wilkerson, 2006; McHugh, Livingston, & Frieze, 2008; Tan & Gregor, 2006). Ten percent of teen girls report that they have experienced physical violence in their own relationships, including hitting, shoving, throwing of objects, grabbing, and other physical force used with the intention to injure, harm, or kill another individual (McHugh et al., 2008; Ulloa, Castaneda, & Hokoda, 2010; see also chapter 2, volume 1, and chapter 4, volume 2, of this book set). A comparison of intimate partner violence rates in adolescents and adults indicates that teen girls are at a higher risk of intimate partner abuse (Silverman, Raj, Mucci, & Hathaway, 2001; see also chapter 11, volume 1, of this book set).

In addition, girls and women are more likely than males to experience stalking and sexual assault (see chapter 12, volume 1, of this book set). In fact, adolescent girls aged 16 to 19 are almost four times more likely than the general population to be victims of rape, with the majority of these girls experiencing date rape, not stranger rape (Gerber & Cherneski, 2006; Maxwell, Robinson, & Post, 2003).

Approximately 71% of school-aged females report being bullied (Chisolm, 2010; Martin, 2010; Paludi, 2010; see also chapter 6, volume 1, and chapter 6, volume 2, of this book set). Eighty percent of adolescents have been sexually harassed by a peer, including name calling, graffiti written about them in school bathrooms, offensive drawings disseminated about them, unwanted touching, cyberbullying, sexual rumors, and pressure for sex (see chapter 8, volume 1, and chapter 8, volume 2, of this book set).

As another example of gendered violence, approximately 30% of adolescent girls are victims of child sexual abuse (Lundberg-Love & Marmion, 2006; see also chapters 9 and 10, volume 1, of this book set).

Placing Gendered Violence into an Adolescent Developmental Context: Power Issues

> American boys must be protected from a culture of violence that exploits their worst tendencies by reinforcing and amplifying the atavistic values of the masculine mystique. Our country was not created so that future generations could maximize profit at any cost. It was created with humanistic, egalitarian, altruistic goals. We must put our enormous resources and talents to the task of creating a children's culture that is consistent with these goals.
>
> *Myriam Miedzian*

In the life cycle, adolescence is a transitional stage between childhood and adulthood (Newman & Newman, 2008). According to theories of adolescent development, one of the most important developmental tasks of adolescence is establishing an identity (Erikson, 1963). During adolescence, individuals begin to integrate the opinions of influential others (e.g., parents, teachers, music idols, actors) into their own likes and dislikes. The eventual outcome is people who have a clear sense of their values and beliefs, occupational goals, and relationship expectations. This normative developmental task can be disrupted by individuals manipulating the adolescents (Kroger, 2000).

Adolescents are establishing intimacy and self-esteem during this stage as well (Chisholm, 2010). During adolescence, girls and boys want to be seen as popular with their peer group (Hartup & Stevens, 1999). The functions of a peer group for teens include social support, emotional intimacy, fun, and understanding. Adolescents are more likely to behave in ways that are gender-role stereotypic when with their peer group than when alone (Doyle & Paludi, 1998). Because of the importance placed on the peer group, behavior that is gender-role stereotypic is intensified during adolescence in order for teens to fit in with their peers.

Among boys, the pressure to be tough is intensified during adolescence; teen boys are likely to engage in fights with their peers. They do so in order to gain status and popularity among other teens in their peer group (American Association of University Women, 2001). Teen boys are likely to participate in a crowd, that is, a large group of boys recognized by a few characteristics, such as involvement in athletics (Way & Pahl, 1999). In addition, Paludi, Martin, and Paludi (2007) and Giladi (2005) noted that boys act out of extreme competitiveness or fear that they will lose their position of power. Since they don't want to be viewed as less masculine or weak by their male peers, they engage in sexual victimization of girls. Thus, girls are the objects of the game to impress other boys.

De-individuation is common among adolescent boys; they discontinue self-evaluation and instead adopt group norms and attitudes. De-individuation causes group members to behave more aggressively than they would as individuals (Paludi, 2010).

In addition, Doyle and Paludi (1998) and DeSouza (2004) noted that the male-as-aggressor theme is so central to many adolescent boys' self-concept that it spills over to their relationships with girls. The California Coalition Against Sexual Assault (2002) reported that among 1,600 juvenile sexual assault offenders, 23.5% perceived sex as a way to feel power and control, 9.4% perceived sex as a way to dissipate anger, and 8.4% perceived sex as a way to punish girls. In addition, both abusers and victims attribute the responsibility for violent dating behavior to victims; for example, the girl provoked the violence because of her personality, the girl had a need for affection, or the girl was influenced by her peer group (Lavoie, Hebert, Tremblay, Vitaro, & McDuff, 2002). Equally disconcerting is research by Jackson, Cram, and Seymour (2000) indicating that 77% of girls and 67% of boys in high school endorse sexual coercion, including unwanted genital contact and sexual intercourse.

Hate Crimes, Violence, and Stereotypic Beliefs

During adolescence, teens rely on stereotypes about individuals and, in the case of hate crimes, act on these stereotypes (Morrison, Morrison, Pope, & Zumbo, 1999; Otis & Loeffler, 2006). Stereotypes refer to individuals' cognitions that typically do not correspond with reality (Fiske & Lee, 2008). Stereotypes occur when individuals are classified by others as having something in common because they are members of a particular group or category or are perceived to be a member of this group (e.g., gay men, Latinos, disabled, female).

Social science research has identified that stereotypes have the following characteristics (Fiske, 1993):

> Groups that are targeted for stereotypes are easily identified and relatively powerless. This misperception is difficult to modify even though individuals who hold stereotypes have interacted with individuals of the group who disconfirm the stereotypes.
>
> There is little agreement between the composite picture of the group and the actual characteristics of that group. This is the product of a bias in individuals' information-processing mechanisms.

Race/color stereotyping is a psychological process that describes individuals' structured set of beliefs about the personal attributes of individuals because of their actual or perceived race or because it is believed that this individual has a particular racial background (Feinberg, 2000). Gender stereotyping is a psychological process describing individuals' structured set of beliefs about the personal attributes of men and women (Kite, Deaux, & Haines, 2008). Sexual orientation stereotyping is a psychological process describing individuals' structured set of beliefs about personal attributes of others because of their perceived or acknowledged sexual orientation (Herek & Garnets, 2007).

Psychologists have identified an emotional component to stereotypic cognitions: prejudice as well as a behavioral component to individuals' cognitions involving discrimination, harassment, and violence, including hate crimes (Fiske, 1993). Individuals' statements and nonverbal gestures toward women and men and individuals' race/color and sexual orientation provide insight into their structured set of beliefs about individuals of different sexes, races, and sexual orientations (Reskin, 2000).

Negative attitudes and feelings about individuals' sex, race, and sexual orientation develop as a consequence of cognitive, motivational, and sociocultural processes (Paludi et al., 2010). The cognitive aspect refers to placing individuals in categories that activate gender stereotypes, race stereotypes, and sexual orientation stereotypes. The motivational aspect refers to the need for individual power, control, and status. The sociocultural aspect refers to viewing as normal negative attitudes and behavior toward individuals because of their sex, race, or sexual orientation (Fiske & Lee, 2008).

Characteristics such as English fluency, skin color, and accents are salient features that individuals use to categorize a person. Consequently, individuals activate stereotypical traits about these characteristics (Wigboldus,

Dijksterhuis, & vanKnippenberg, 2003). Stereotypes are not labels but instead are assumptions about personality traits and behaviors that people in the labeled categories are thought to possess (Kite, Deaux, & Haines, 2008). Stereotypes have negative effects; the categorization process causes people to emphasize differences between groups and similarities within groups. Thus, for example, Latinos are seen as radically different from White individuals (Fiske & Lee, 2008).

Out-Group Homogeneity Bias

Related to stereotyping is the out-group homogeneity bias (Judd, Park, Yzerbyt, Gordijn, & Muller, 2005; Mulvey, Hitt, & Killen, 2010). This is a process by which individuals view groups in which they are not a part (e.g., a sexual orientation or race different from their own) as more homogeneous than their own group (e.g., their own sexual orientation or race). Thus, stereotypes concerning members of out-groups are stronger than those of in-group members. According to Judd (cited in DeAngelis, 2001, p. 3), "people are more willing to ignore individuating information about members of out-groups, lumping them all into a single disliked category." In actuality, focusing on differences among protected categories ignores in-group variability. The overemphasis on differences provides confirmation of the stereotype that religions are opposite and that one's own beliefs are normative while others are a deviation from the norm (Judd et al., 2005).

Adolescents hold stereotypes about victims, for example, victims of sexual assault (Maxwell et al., 2003). Adolescents typically blame the victim for the assault, including the style of dress and walking in certain neighborhoods. Kershner (1996) noted that most students aged 14 to 19 stated that forced sexual intercourse is acceptable under certain circumstances. Marciniak (1998) found that gender role attitudes, attitudes, and cognitive development are important factors in sexual aggression and in accepting rape myths. The continuation of stereotyping in adolescence is explained by the role that stereotyping plays in perpetuating group identity, group norms, and exclusion (Killen, Sinno, & Margie, 2007).

Gendered Violence in the Media

> We must also be careful to avoid ingesting toxins in the form of violent TV programs, video games, movies, magazines, and books. When we watch that kind of violence, we water our own negative seeds, or tendencies, and eventually we will think and act out of those seeds.
>
> *Thich Nhat Hanh*

Violence against adolescents has been explained by adhering to stereotypes about unequal power relations and patriarchal values. As Russo and Pirlott (2006, p. 181) summarized with respect to gender-based violence, "gender roles and expectations, male entitlement, sexual objectification, and discrepancies in power and status have legitimized, rendered invisible, sexualized, and helped to perpetuate violence against women." In addition, factors embedded in the adolescent culture that influence as well as support violence include alcohol and drug use, religious influences, devaluation of subordinated groups, the sexualization of violence, and video games (Maxwell et al., 2003; see also chapter 3, volume 2, of this book set). A major catalyst for the incidence of hate crimes, including gender-based hate crimes and other forms of violence in the United States, is the frequency with which violence is portrayed in media, especially media consumed by adolescents (see chapter 3, volume 1, of this book set).

The Parents Television Council (2003) noted that in 2002 compared to 1998, violence on television was 41% more frequent during the 8:00 p.m. time slot and 134% more frequent during the 9:00 p.m. time slot. Kaufman (2004) noted that in January 2004, three continuous hours of violent television programs were aired on one station on Thursday evenings: *Cold Case, CSI,* and *Without a Trace.* Kaufman (2004, p. 2) cited research from the National Cable Television Association's National Television Violence Study indicating that "across the three years of this study, a steady 60% of TV programs contain violence . . . [and] much of the violence is glamorized, sanitized, and trivialized" (p. 2).

Beresin (2010) reported that television programs offer 812 violent acts per hour, with children's cartoons displaying approximately 20 violent acts hourly. Violence in music videos has been observed in between 56% and 76% of the videos and include hitting, shootings, stabbings, punching, and kicking (Baxter, De Reimer, Landini, Leslie, & Singletary, 1985; Sherman & Dominick, 1986; Greeson & Williams, 1986). The most violent music videos are rap, followed by rock. These videos also included alcohol use and smoking as part of the violence.

Beresin (2010) noted that by the time children are 18 years old, they will have watched 28 hours of television per week, viewed 200,000 acts of violence in the television programs, and seen more than 16,000 murders in these shows. Seventy-five percent of children and teens watch music videos, with 60% of them indicating that they view these videos pretty much or a lot (Henry J. Kaiser Family Foundation, 2007; van den Bulck & Beullens, 2005). Klein and colleagues (1993) and the Council on Communications and Media (2009) reported that teens aged 14 to 16 years old listen to music an average of 40 hours per week.

In violence portrayed in the media, girls and women are often portrayed as weak, objectified, submissive, and vulnerable (LaTouche, 2007). Pipher (1994) concluded that adolescent girls suffer psychologically from negative body image, lowered self-esteem, and achievement conflicts, all as a consequence of the culture's messages about young women's bodies needing to be protected, made more beautiful, and preserved. These messages are part of rock music videos, song lyrics, and television programs.

In contrast, the media portrays boys and men as aggressive and powerful. Violence is thus used to reinforce gender norms. Exposure to violence in media increases aggressive thoughts and a permanent hostility toward girls and women (Anderson & Bushman, 2002; Anderson, Carnagey, & Eubanks, 2003). Bretthauer, Zimmerman, and Banning (2007) noted that a review of "The Hot 100" list generated by Billboard Chart Research Services indicated that violence, especially violence against women, was prominent in music lyrics. They identified six themes in their review: men and power, sexual violence, objectification of women, sex as a main priority for men, women defined in terms of their relationships with men, and women not valuing themselves.

Armstrong (2001) found that gangsta rap music is identified with violent and misogynist lyric portrayals, including corporal punishment for women, hitting women with shoes, physically attacking women who refuse sex, rape, and murder. According to Armstrong (2001, p. 8), "the hegemonic dimension of gangsta rap music's narratives is immediate evidence of a rape culture. . . . In fact, gangsta rap music is a 'celebration' of rape culture and its most powerful contemporary voice."

Furthermore, exposure to violence in rock music videos has been linked to increased beliefs in stereotypes about sexuality, attractiveness, and violence. Adolescent boys who have been exposed to rock music videos have stated that they would engage in violence against women; boys who were not exposed to music videos did not endorse this view (Kaestle, Halpern, & Brown, 2007; Johnson, Adams, Ashburn, & Reed, 1995). Research by Malamuth and Check (1981) noted that when men who had never raped were exposed to depictions of sexual assault, they reported a heightened sexual arousal from the scenes and an increase in their rape fantasies. Thus, research suggests that most men find violence a stimulant to heighten or arouse their sexual feelings. Men find sexuality related at some level to an expression of aggression, and in turn aggression heightens their sexual fantasies or actual sexual behaviors (Doyle & Paludi, 1998).

Impact of Violence on Adolescents

The impact of violence has significant effects on adolescents. For example, teens (and children) who are exposed to violence on television will be provided with violent heroes to imitate and taught that violence is the way to resolve conflict with individuals, especially with dating partners (Beresin, 2010; Ward, 2002). Most of these adolescents have televisions in their own rooms, so they watch programs without parental supervision and editing (Beresin, 2010). Adolescents also use headphones, so their parents are not able to hear the lyrics to the music to which their teens are listening.

Bretthauer, Zimmerman, and Banning (2007) noted that music lyrics send relationship messages to listeners, who are predominantly adolescents. St. Lawrence and Joyner (1991) reported that adolescents' preference for heavy metal music is a significant marker for substance abuse, suicide risk, alienation, and risk-taking behaviors during adolescence (e.g., failure to use contraceptives, failure to use a seatbelt). Furthermore, according to Kaufman (2004, p. 3), "the hero of TV shows never gets in trouble for his/her violent actions. The hero is always 'justified' in one way or another when committing violent acts. . . . Television will never show a main character lose an arm, leg or get killed on screen. In reality, with as much gunplay that appears on TV, main characters should also get shot. . . . The hero can really be as violent as he/she wants."

Comstock and Paik (1991) identified four dimensions related to the way that violence is portrayed on television and that may heighten the likelihood of the influence of television: efficacy, normativeness, pertinence, and susceptibility. For example:

Violence is justified.
The perpetrator is similar to the viewer.
Violence is portrayed as real events, not events simulated for a television drama.
Violent acts leave the viewer in a state of unresolved excitement.

Research suggests a positive correlation between television violence and aggressive behavior (see chapter 7, volume 2, of this book set). Eron and Huesmann (1986) reported that there is a sensitive period between 8 and 12 years of age during which children are particularly susceptible to the impact of violence portrayed in the media. In addition, boys are more likely than girls to identify with a violent character and to subsequently model aggressive behavior.

Introduction xxiii

With respect to the impact of real-life violence on adolescents, including rape, intimate partner violence, sexual harassment, and bullying, several reports have documented the high cost of various forms of violence within three major perspectives: (1) psychological health, (2) physiological, and (3) education/work (e.g., Barron & Hebl, 2010; Contrada et al., 2000; Dansky & Kilpatrick, 1997; Katz, Joiner, & Kwon, 2002). Responses by adolescents to violence include headaches, sleep disturbances, disordered eating, gastrointestinal disorders, nausea, crying spells, scars, bruising, broken bones, absenteeism from school, decreased morale, decreased school satisfaction, performance decrements, damage to interpersonal relationships at school, and post-traumatic stress disorder (PTSD).

PTSD is a consequence of violence. Symptoms of PTSD include anxiety, physiological arousal, irritability, avoidance/denial, intrusion, repetitive nightmares, impaired concentration and memory, and acting-out behaviors. Immediately after the violent episode, individuals experience a sense of disbelief, shock, and psychological and physical numbing. A few days after the incident, individuals experience three different types of consequences:

1. Reexperiencing consequences (e.g., dreaming, flashbacks).
2. Withdrawal consequences (e.g., social withdrawal, absenteeism).
3. Other consequences (e.g., irritability, sleep disturbances, anger, exaggerated startle responses) (Avina & O'Donohue, 2002; see also chapters 1 and 2, volume 2, of this book set).

In addition, adolescents think about violence to themselves through self-injury (e.g., cutting) as well as suicide (see chapter 3, volume 1, of this book set). Furthermore, adolescents who have not had anyone intervene on their behalf to stop the violence learn to keep silent about future abuse because they believe that no one will ever help them (Paludi, 2010).

Present Volumes

Violence against adolescents has been recognized as a major public health and human rights issue that requires a coordinated response from parents, teachers, counselors, and providers (e.g., health care, mental health, rape crisis centers) in the teen's community (chapter 7, volume 1, and chapters 5, 9, and 12, volume 2). I wanted to edit these two volumes to highlight the following for parents, educators, guidance counselors, and adolescents themselves:

1. Implications of adolescence as a life stage for individuals learning to be violent and to accept violence.

2. Understanding the relationship among violence, powerlessness, and lack of access to resources with respect to adolescent victims of violence.
3. Types of violence common to adolescence (e.g., bullying, harassment, intimate partner violence, gang violence, rape).
4. Understanding the link between violence during adolescence and gender roles and gender-related life circumstances.
5. Strategies for prevention for parents, teachers, counselors, and case workers.

This two-volume set on the psychology of teen violence and victimization features scholarly research about individual, institutional, and societal influences on violence against adolescents and perpetrated by adolescents. Contributors discuss the impact of race on perceptions of teen sex offenders (chapter 4, volume 1); the role of adolescent victimization in women's aggression in their relationships, violent behavior in girls, schoolyard violence, bullying, teen relationship violence, adolescent stalking, educating teens to discriminate abusive from nonabusive situations (chapter 5, volume 2); adolescents, firearms, and violent video games (chapter 3, volume 2); and teen violence prevention (chapter 13, volume 2). We take a multicultural approach to teen violence. In addition, I offer readers resources on teen violence, including organizations concerned with teen violence and victimization.

My goal is that these chapters and resources stimulate additional research agendas on teen violence and victimization that make Tyler, Phoebe, Cory, Marco, Kristian, and other victims of violence central, not marginal and visible, not invisible to our research and advocacy. Marion Wright Edelman's sentiment is expressed throughout these volumes: "If we don't stand up for children, then we don't stand for much."

References

American Association of University Women. (2001). *Hostile hallways: The annual survey on sexual harassment in America's schools.* Washington, DC: Author.

Anderson, C., & Bushman, B. (2002). The effects of media violence on society. *Science, 295,* 2377–2379.

Anderson, C., Carnagey, N., & Eubanks, J. (2003). Exposure to violent media: The effects of songs with violent lyrics in aggressive thoughts and feelings. *Journal of Personality and Social Psychology, 84,* 960–971.

Armstrong, E. (2001). Gangsta misogyny: A content analysis of the portrayals of violence against women in rap music, 1987–1993. *Journal of Criminal Justice and Popular Culture, 8,* 96–126.

Avina, C., & O'Donohue, W. (2002). Sexual harassment and PTSD: Is sexual harassment diagnosable trauma? *Journal of Traumatic Stress, 15,* 69–75.

Barron, L., & Hebl, M. (2010). Sexual orientation: A protected and unprotected class. In M. Paludi, C. Paludi, & E. DeSouza (Eds.), *Praeger handbook on understanding and preventing workplace discrimination: Vol. 1. Legal, management and social science perspectives* (pp. 251–273). Westport, CT: Praeger.

Baxter, L., De Riemer, C., Landini, A., Leslie, L., & Singletary, M. (1985). A content analysis of music videos. *Journal of Broadcasting and Electronic Media, 29,* 333–340.

Beresin, E. (2010). The impact of media violence on children and adolescents: Opportunities for clinical interventions. *American Academy of Child and Adolescent Psychiatry.* Retrieved on November 8, 2010, from http://www.aacap.org/cs/root/developmentor/the_impact_of_media_violence_on_children_and_adolescents_opportunities_for_clinical_interventions.

Bretthauer, B., Zimmerman, T., & Banning, J. (2007). A feminist analysis of popular music. *Journal of Feminist Family Therapy, 18,* 29–51.

California Coalition Against Sexual Assault. (2002). *Research on rape and violence.* Retrieved on November 11, 2010, from http://www.calcasa.org/stat/CALCASA_Stat_2008.pdf.

Chisholm, J. (2010). Perils in cyberspace: Current trends in cyberbullying. In M. Paludi & F. Denmark (Eds.), *Victims of sexual assault and abuse: Resources and responses for individuals and families: Vol. 1. Incidence and psychological dimensions* (pp. 59–88). Westport, CT: Praeger.

Comstock, G., & Paik, H. (1991). *Television and the American child.* San Diego, CA: Academic.

Contrada, R., Ashmore, R., Gary, M., Coups, E., Egeth, J., Sewell, A., Ewell, K., Goyal, T., & Chasse, V. (2000). Ethnicity-related sources of stress and their effects on well-being. *Current Directions in Psychological Science, 9,* 136–139.

Council on Communications and Media. (2009). Impact of music, music lyrics, and music videos on children and youth. *Pediatrics, 124,* 1488–1494.

Dansky, B., & Kilpatrick, D. (1997). Effects of sexual harassment. In W. O'Donohue (Ed.), *Sexual harassment: Theory, research and practice.* Boston: Allyn & Bacon.

DeAngelis, T. (2001). Understanding and preventing hate crimes. *Monitor on Psychology, 32,* 1–7.

DeSouza, E. (2004, July). *Intercultural and intracultural comparisons of bullying and sexual harassment in secondary schools.* Paper presented at the Association for Gender Equity Leadership in Education, Washington, DC.

Doyle, J., & Paludi, M. (1998). *Sex and gender: The human experience.* New York: McGraw-Hill.

Erikson, E. (1963). *Childhood and society.* New York: Norton.

Eron, L. D., & Huesmann, L. R. (1986). The role of television in the development of prosocial and antisocial behavior. In D. Olweus, J. Block, & M. Radke-Yarrow (Eds.), *The development of antisocial and prosocial behavior: Research, theories and issues* (pp. 285–314). New York: Academic Press.

Feinberg, M. (2000). *Racism: Why we dislike, stereotype and hate other groups and what to do about it.* Washington, DC: American Psychological Association.

Fiske, S. (1993). Controlling other people: The impact of power on stereotyping. *American Psychologist, 48,* 621–628.

Fiske, S., & Lee, T. (2008). Stereotypes and prejudice create workplace discrimination. In A. Brief (Ed.), *Diversity at work*. New York: Cambridge University Press.

Flores, R. (2006). Adolescent girls speak about violence in their community. In F. Denmark, H. Krauss, E. Halpern, & J. Sechzer (Eds.), *Violence and exploitation against women and girls* (pp. 47–55). Boston: Blackwell.

Gerber, G., & Cherneski, L. (2006). Sexual aggression toward women: Reducing the prevalence. In F. Denmark, H. Krauss, E. Halpern, & J. Sechzer (Eds.), *Violence and exploitation against women and girls* (pp. 35–46). Boston: Blackwell.

Giladi, A. (2005, August). *Sexual harassment or play? Perceptions and observations of young children's experiences in kindergarten and early schooling in Israel*. Paper presented at the Conference of the International Coalition Against Sexual Harassment, Philadelphia, PA.

Greeson, L. E., & Williams, R. A. (1986, December). Social implications of music videos for youth: An analysis of the content and effects of MTV. *Youth and Society, 18*(2), 177–189.

Hartup, W., & Stevens, N. (1999). Friendships and adaptation across the life span: Current directions. *Psychological Science, 8*, 76–79.

Henry J. Kaiser Family Foundation. (2007). *Parents, children and media: A Kaiser Family Foundation Survey*. Menlo Park, CA: Henry J. Kaiser Family Foundation.

Herek, G., & Garnets, L. (2007). Sexual orientation and mental health. *Annual Review of Clinical Psychology, 3*, 53–75.

Jackson, S., Cram, F., & Seymour, F. (2000). Violence and sexual coercion in high school students' dating relationships. *Journal of Family Violence, 1*, 23–36.

Johnson, J., Adams, M., Ashburn, L., & Reed, W. (1995). Differential gender effects of exposure to rap music on African American adolescents' acceptance of teen dating violence. *Sex Roles, 33*, 597–605.

Judd, C., Park, B., Yzerbyt, V., Gordijn, E., & Muller, D. (2005). Attributions of intergroup bias and outgroup homogeneity to ingroup and outgroup others. *European Journal of Social Psychology, 35*, 677–704.

Kaestle, C. E., Halpern, C. T., & Brown, J. (2007). Music videos, pro-wrestling, and acceptance of date rape among middle school males and females: An exploratory analysis. *Journal of Adolescent Health, 40*, 185–187.

Katz, J., Joiner, T., & Kwon, P. (2002). Membership on a devalued social group and emotional well-being: Developing a model of personal self-esteem, collective self-esteem and group socialization. *Sex Roles, 47*, 419–431

Kaufman, R. (2004). *Filling their minds with death: TV violence and children*. Retrieved on November 8, 2010, from http://www.turnoffyourtv.com/healtheducation/violencechildren/violencechildren.html.

Kershner, R. (1996). Adolescent attitudes about rape. *Adolescence, 31*, 29–33.

Killen, M., Sinno, S., & Margie, N. (2007). Children's experiences and judgments about group exclusion and inclusion. In R. Kail (Ed.), *Advances in child development and behavior* (pp. 173–218). New York: Elsevier.

Kite, M., Deaux, K., & Haines, E. (2008). Gender stereotypes. In F. Denmark & M. Paludi (Eds.), *Psychology of women: A handbook of issues and theories* (2nd ed.). Westport, CT: Praeger.

Klein, J., Brown, J., Childres, K., Oliveri, J., Porter, C., & Dykers, C. (1993). Adolescents' risky behavior and mass media use. *Pediatrics, 92,* 24–31.

Kroger, J. (2000). *Identity development: Adolescence through adulthood.* Thousand Oaks, CA: Sage.

LaTouche, K. (2007). *Gender representation in BET's 106 & Park and Sucker Free on MTV: A content analysis.* Thesis submitted to the College of Communication for the degree of master of science.

Lavoie, F., Hebert, M., Tremblay, R., Vitaro, L., & McDuff, D. (2002). History of family dysfunction and perpetration of dating violence by adolescent boys: A longitudinal study. *Journal of Adolescent Health, 30,* 375–383.

Lundberg-Love, P., & Marmion, S. (2006). *Intimate partner violence against women: When spouses, partners or lovers attack.* Westport, CT: Praeger.

Lundberg-Love, P., & Wilkerson, D. (2006). Battered women. In P. Lundberg-Love & S. Marmion (Eds.), *Intimate violence against women* (pp. 31–45). Westport, CT: Praeger.

Malamuth, N., & Check, J. (1981). The effects of mass media exposure on acceptance of violence against women: A field experiment. *Journal of Research in Personality, 15,* 436–446.

Marciniak, L. (1998). Adolescent attitudes toward victim precipitation of rape. *Violence and Victims, 13,* 287–300.

Martin, L. (2010). Bullying and peer sexual harassment: A prevention guide for students, parents and teachers. In M. Paludi & F. Denmark (Eds.), *Victims of sexual assault and abuse: Resources and responses for individuals and families: Vol. 1. Incidence and psychological dimensions* (pp. 89–109). Westport, CT: Praeger.

Maxwell, C., Robinson, A., & Post, L. (2003). The nature and predictors of sexual victimization and offending among adolescents. *Journal of Youth and Adolescence, 32,* 465–477.

McConnell, S., & Swain, J. (2000, August). *Victim-offender mediation with adolescents who commit hate crimes.* Paper presented at the 108th Annual Conference of the American Psychological Association, Washington, DC.

McHugh, M., Livingston, N., & Frieze, I. (2008). Intimate partner violence: Perspectives on research and intervention. In F. L. Denmark & M. Paludi (Eds.), *Psychology of women: A handbook of issues and theories* (pp. 555–589). Westport, CT: Praeger.

Morrison, M., Morrison, T., Pope, G., & Zumbo, B. (1999). An investigation of measures of modern and old-fashioned sexism. *Social Indicators Research, 48,* 39–50.

Mulvey, K., Hitti, A. & Killen, M. (2010). The development of stereotyping and exclusion. *Cognitive Science, 1,* 597–606.

National Coalition of Anti-Violence Programs. (2009). *Lesbian, gay, bisexual, transgender and queer domestic violence in the United States in 2008.* Retrieved on November 9, 2011, from http://www.avp.org/documents/2008NCAVPLGBTQ DVReportFINAL.pdf.

Newman, B., & Newman, P. (2008). *Development through life: A psychosocial approach.* Belmont, CA: Wadsworth.

Otis, M., & Loeffler, D. (2006). Changing youths' attitudes toward difference: A community-based model that works. *Social Work with Groups, 28,* 41–64.

Paludi, M. (2010, October). *The continuum of campus violence: Applying "Broken Windows Theory" to prevent and deal with campus violence.* U.S. Department of Education National Meeting on Alcohol, Drug Abuse and Violence Prevention in Higher Education, National Harbor, MD.

Paludi, M., Ellens, H., & Paludi, C. (2010). Religious discrimination. In M. Paludi, C. Paludi, & E. DeSouza (Eds.), *Praeger handbook on understanding and preventing workplace discrimination: Vol. 1. Legal, management and social science perspectives* (pp. 157–182). Westport, CT: Praeger.

Paludi, M., Martin, J., & Paludi, C. (2007). Sexual harassment: The hidden gender equity problem. In S. Klein (Ed.), *Handbook for achieving gender equity through education* (2nd ed., pp. 215–229). Mahwah, NJ: Erlbaum.

Parents Television Council. (2003). *TV bloodbath: Violence on prime time broadcast TV.* Retrieved on November 11, 2010, from http://www.parentstv.org/ptc/publications/reports/stateindustryviolence/main.asp.

Pipher, M. (1994). *Reviving Ophelia: Saving the selves of adolescent girls.* New York: Ballantine.

Reskin, B. (2000). The proximate causes of employment discrimination. *Contemporary Sociology, 29,* 319–328.

Russo, N. F., & Pirlott, A. (2006). Gender-based violence: Concepts, methods, and findings. In F. Denmark, H. Krauss, E. Halpern, & J. Sechzer (Eds.), *Violence and exploitation against women and girls* (pp. 178–205). Boston: Blackwell.

Schilt, K., & Westbrook, L. (2009). Doing gender, doing heteronormativity: Gender normals, transgender people, and the social maintenance of heterosexuality. *Gender and Society* 23(4), 440–464.

Sherman, B., & Dominick, J. (1986). Violence and sex in music videos: TV and rock 'n' roll. *Journal of Communication, 36,* 79–93.

Silverman, J. G., Raj, A., Mucci, L. A., & Hathaway, J. E. (2001). Dating violence against adolescent girls and associated substance use, unhealthy weight control, sexual risk behavior, pregnancy, and suicidality. *Journal of the American Medical Association, 286,* 372–379.

St. Lawrence, J. S., & Joyner, D. J. (1991). The effects of sexually violent rock music on males' acceptance of violence against women. *Psychology of Women Quarterly, 15,* 49–63.

Steinberg, A., Brooks, J., & Remtulla, T. (2003). Youth hate crimes: Identification, prevention and intervention. *American Journal of Psychiatry, 160,* 878–989.

Substance Abuse and Mental Health Services Administration. (2010). *Factors affecting violent behavior in teen girls.* Retrieved on November 14, 2010, from http://www.teendrugabuse.org/mental-health/factors-affection-violent-behavior-in-teen-girls/.

Tan, J., & Gregor, K. (2006). Violence against pregnant women in northwestern Ontario. In F. Denmark, H. Krauss, E. Halpern, & J. Sechzer (Eds.), *Violence and exploitation against women and girls* (pp. 320–338). Boston: Blackwell.

Ulloa, E., Castaneda, D., & Hokoda, A. (2010). Teen relationship violence. In M. Paludi & F. Denmark (Eds.), *Victims of sexual assault and abuse: Resources and responses for individuals and families: Vol. 1. Incidence and psychological dimensions* (pp. 111–135). Westport, CT: Praeger.

United Nations. (1995). *Report of the Fourth World Conference on Women, Beijing, 4–5 September, 1995.* New York: United Nations.

van den Bulck, J., & Beullens, K. (2005). Television and music video exposure and adolescent alcohol use while going out. *Alcohol, 40,* 249–253.

Ward, R. (2002). Fan violence: Social problem or moral panic? *Aggression and Violent Behavior, 7,* 453–475.

Way, N., & Pahl, K. (1999). Friendship patterns among urban adolescent boys: A qualitative account. In M. Kopala & L. Suziki (Eds.), *Using qualitative methods in psychology* (pp. 145–161). Thousand Oaks, CA: Sage.

Wigboldus, D., Dijksterhuis, A., & vanKnippenberg, A. (2003). When stereotypes get in the way: Stereotypes obstruct stereotype-inconsistent trait inferences. *Journal of Personality and Social Psychology, 84,* 470–484.

PART I

Impact of Teen Violence on Adolescents, Family, and Peers

CHAPTER ONE

Peer Victimization and Post-Traumatic Stress Disorder in Children and Adolescents

James Crosby

Introduction

In recent years, peer victimization (PV) has become an increasing societal concern. Youths,[1] parents, teachers, community members, and the media have all increased dialogue on this topic, and myriad opinions have developed on its potential consequences and the appropriate methods of intervention. Of particular concern to many are the perceived outcomes of being bullied, including internalizing distress, suicidal ideation or behavior, and even school shootings. A recent cover of *People* magazine posed a chilling question regarding the suicide of a 15-year-old victim of bullying: "Bullied to Death?" (see Smolowe, Herbst, Weisensee, Rakowsky, & Mascia, 2010). This widely read popular media outlet mulled over concerns with which professionals and researchers grapple on a regular basis (e.g., the relation between PV and distress, as well as the criminalization of bullying due to its perceived negative outcomes).

Corresponding to growing concerns from adults and youths, the extant literature on PV is expanding at an unprecedented rate. Of particular interest are findings (e.g., Smith, Schneider, Smith, & Ananiadou, 2004) that seem to indicate somewhat less than satisfactory results from many schoolwide antibullying interventions. These data, coupled with the continuing empirical associations of PV and negative outcomes (e.g., internalized distress; see Davidson & Demaray, 2007), indicate a significant need for ongoing research and development in understanding the impact of bullying on victims, as well as for improved methods for reducing its incidence and consequences.

The focus of this chapter is to examine PV as a traumatic experience. Some adults (and youths) see PV as a normative experience. Further, these persons may be less likely to intervene if they perceive the behaviors of bullies as normative or relatively harmless. While the literature supports the hypothesis that PV can be traumatic for some youths, the data are even more compelling in light of the need for improvement in interventions and outcomes for individual victims.

A Brief Review of Peer Victimization

Although an increase in popular media coverage seems recent, PV has received attention in the professional literature for nearly four decades. As is noted in most PV literature reviews, much of the early interest and works were stimulated by Dan Olweus. In his book *Aggression in the Schools: Bullies and Whipping Boys,* Olweus (1978) reviewed the developmental history of bullying terminology as it relates to PV, citing the work of ethologist Konrad Lorenz on mobbing in animal packs and military populations. (The term "mobbing," based on the term "mob . . . [defined as] a group of individuals joined in some kind of activity" [Olweus, 1978, p. 2], remains in usage in some circles when discussing bullying behaviors, although more so in the United Kingdom and other areas of Europe than in North America.)

During the 1970s, Olweus extended these ideas of group-mobbing to research on individuals who were exposed to systematic aggression over time, initiating the first systematic study of PV. The results of this study were ultimately published in a Swedish text (Olweus, 1973; later published in English as Olweus, 1978). At that time (1973), there was scarcely any published research on this topic. Further, no clear definition of PV had been established in the (limited) extant literature. If PV research, assessment, and intervention were to advance, an operational definition was imperative.

Defining Peer Victimization

A victim of bullying is defined as someone who is subjected to intentionally negative acts by a more powerful individual repeatedly over time. Each of the components in the aforementioned definition are based on

Olweus's (1978) definition and are pervasively used in studies of PV across disciplines and locales. Further, PV may manifest in different forms, including physical (e.g., hitting, kicking), verbal (e.g., threats, name calling), relational (e.g., social exclusion), and cyberbullying (i.e., manifestations of verbal or relational PV via electronic means, such as text messaging or Web-based social networks). Further, Arsenault, Bowes, and Shakoor (2010) succinctly reviewed three groups who may be involved in bullying. First, bullies are the perpetrators of the negative acts, who may have a behavioral profile similar to children with general conduct problems. Second, victims are those in receipt of the negative acts. Finally, bully-victims represent a small group of individuals who could be classified as both bully and victim.

Additionally, it should be noted that bullying and PV are not synonymous terms.[2] Specifically, "bullying" refers to perpetrators' actions. "Peer victimization" (PV) refers to the experiences of victims of bullying and is the focus of this chapter.

Trauma in Children

As noted by Weaver (2000), post-traumatic stress disorder (PTSD) was originally an explanation for a range of symptoms associated with a catastrophic or traumatic event. PTSD (APA, 2000) is an anxiety disorder composed of symptoms in three main categories: (a) reexperiencing a traumatic event, (b) increased physiological arousal, and (c) avoidance of stimuli that are associated with the trauma or stressor. An important factor that distinguishes PTSD from other anxiety disorders is its association with a traumatic stressor.

As noted by Fairbank, Putnam, and Harris (2007), attempting to estimate the prevalence of PTSD in children is an arduous task. For example, child maltreatment data are often not collected due to mandatory reporting laws. In one large-scale survey of youth violence (Finkelhor, Ormrod, Turner, & Hamby, 2005), experiences of violence were pervasive. Specifically, more than half of the respondents had experienced some type of violent assault (not including bullying experiences) during the previous year. More than 20% of the sample had experienced physical bullying in the previous year. Further, more than 20% had experienced teasing or emotional bullying during the same period. Although not all such experiences will lead to the presentation of post-traumatic stress symptomatology, early identification and intervention are clearly critical. There are myriad long-term sequelae associated with early life PTSD, including a greater risk for traumatic reactions to stressors later in life and continuing internalizing problems (see Norris & Sloan, 2007, for an excellent review of the epidemiology of trauma and PTSD). Importantly, Norris and Sloan noted that violence is the single greatest cause of PTSD and that no other objective would aid in reducing the prevalence of PTSD as much as curbing violence.

Regarding exposure to a traumatic event, the American Psychiatric Association (2000) states that "the person [must have] experienced, witnessed, or [have been] confronted with an event or events that involved actual or threatened death or serious injury, or a threat to the physical integrity of self or others" (*DSM-IV-TR*; Criterion A1, p. 467). Further, the individual's response to the traumatic event must have involved "intense fear, helplessness, or horror" (p. 467). Additionally, some child-specific notes are listed in the diagnostic criteria for PTSD, including trauma-themed repetitive play, frightening dreams that do not necessarily have recognizable content, and trauma-specific reenactment.

One of the most pressing topics related to potential revisions of the PTSD diagnostic criteria in the pending *DSM-V* is related to the A1 criterion: describing and defining the features of the traumatic event. While multiple concerns have been raised about Criterion A1, some may be succinctly summarized as follows: The stressor should be thought of as subjectively perceived or experienced. That is, some individuals with PTSD may not have directly experienced the stressor. Rather, the mere threat of the stressor may result in PTSD symptomatology. If such a diagnostic adjustment were made, those persons who feel that there is a genuine threat to their life or to their physical integrity qualify (at least partially) for a diagnosis of PTSD. Further, as discussed below, researchers and practitioners should examine the expected nature of the traumatic event or stressor. That is, should these events or stressors be only life threatening or physical in nature?

Peer Victimization and Post-Traumatic Stress Disorder: A Plausible Relationship?

PV has been repeatedly related to internalizing distress (e.g., anxiety, social withdrawal, depression, etc.) in a variety of populations (e.g., see Crick & Bigbee, 1996; Davidson & Demaray, 2007; Grills & Ollendick, 2002; Hawker & Boulton, 2000). Additionally, Arsenault, Bowes, and Shakoor (2010) aptly weighed in on the issue of bullying and, broadly, mental health problems in youths with an excellent review of the literature. Among many other compelling findings, Arsenault and colleagues reported that both family factors (e.g., parental domestic violence) and individual characteristics (e.g., withdrawal behaviors, history of internalizing problems) can predict which children will become targets of bullying.

Further, considering evidence that victimization can be quite stable over time, the authors discussed literature (e.g., Barker et al., 2008) indicating that children who are chronically victimized are most at risk for developing detrimental outcomes and are more likely (than their nonvictimized peers) to display both internalized (e.g., anxiety) and externalized distress (e.g., aggression). Additionally, the experience of peer victimization seems to neurologically impact the effectiveness that youths can cope with stress (Vaillancourt et al., 2008).

While there are numerous studies supporting the hypothesis that PV and internalizing symptomatology are related, is it plausible that PV experiences could ultimately lead to PTSD? Given the long-term impact of early trauma experiences in individuals with PTSD, this is an essential question. If a behavior is considered a normal or developmentally appropriate experience for youths, then serious consideration and intervention are less likely. Further, if the different types of bullying (i.e., physical, verbal, relational) are perceived to be differentially severe, then the probability of intervention could differ across type.

First, the literature on PV and PTSD must be addressed. Interestingly, one of the earliest studies of the relation between PV and post-traumatic stress symptomatology was focused on adult samples and workplace bullying. Mikkelsen and Einarsen (2002) found that the majority of their sample of workplace bullying victims reported post-traumatic stress symptomatology. (Although a more detailed examination of workplace bullying is precluded here, it should be noted that this is an intriguing and fast-developing area of the literature.) In one of the earliest studies on youth-age PV and PTSD, Mynard, Joseph, and Alexander (2000) found a positive relationship between PTSD symptomatology and PV experiences in high school students in the United Kingdom. Further, Weaver (2000) examined a case in which an adolescent female was reported to exhibit the symptoms of PTSD, apparently as the result of PV experiences in school.

Storch and Esposito (2003) succinctly reviewed the PV/internalizing distress literature to date and reported that PV is associated with a number of outcomes, including acute anxiety, hypervigilance, helplessness, and powerlessness. Further, they directly examined the relationship between self-reported PV and the symptoms of PTSD in an urban sample of 205 fifth and sixth graders. Their results indicated significant positive relationships between PTSD symptomatology and both overt (i.e., physical victimization, as assessed by the authors) and relational victimization (i.e., $r = .37$ and $.33$, respectively).

In a similar study of the relationship between PV and PTSD symptomatology, Crosby, Oehler, and Capaccioli (2010) examined the self-reports of fifth- through eighth-grade students in rural schools. The examination of these variables in a rural locale, in part, addressed some concerns expressed by Storch and Esposito (2003) that participants in their urban sample may have been exposed to other traumatic events that could have also influenced the results of their study. Additionally, participants in the rural sample were asked about verbal victimization and PTSD symptomatology via items that were specifically oriented to PV experiences. The results of Crosby and colleagues supported those of Storch and Esposito and others, indicating a positive relationship between PTSD symptomatology and PV. Specifically, the data in an examination of the relationship between PV and PTSD symptomatology revealed significant positive correlations between physical ($r = .62$), verbal ($r = .65$), and relational victimization ($r = .63$). Additionally, female participants reported higher levels of PTSD symptomatology and relational victimization than did male participants. No other significant differences were found between genders on victimization type.

Weaver (2000) intriguingly queried readers as to whether or not posttraumatic stress disorder can be diagnosed in adolescence without a catastrophic stressor. (As discussed below, this is a critical question when considering a diagnosis of PTSD for a victim of bullying.) Weaver reported a pattern of symptomatology in his case study, which closely matches a PTSD symptom presentation, and observed that some researchers and diagnosticians may not consider peer victimization to be life threatening. Therefore, he elaborated, some may consider an adjustment disorder to be a more appropriate diagnosis, due to a potentially prevailing assumption (even in some professional circles) that peer victimization is a relatively common experience and is not considered catastrophic, per se. In essence, Weaver presented the PV-PTSD question to professionals and researchers and called for further examination of the diagnostic criteria and additional research. Fortunately, researchers have made progress in this area of the literature.

Arguably, PV has been associated with a much broader and more severe range of sequelae than adjustment disorders alone. As previously mentioned, many of these studies indicate a variety of internalizing problems, including anxiety. As PTSD is categorized as an anxiety disorder (APA, 2000), it is plausible that such an outcome (i.e., PTSD) could result from repeated exposure to physical violence (for example) from peers. After all, it is certainly reasonable to question a conceptualization of youth-based chronic abuse (i.e., peer victimization) as being within the range of normal experiences.

Further, there are certainly data to support a hypothesis that all types of PV (including verbal and relational victimization) are associated with post-traumatic stress symptomatology (e.g., see Crosby et al., 2010, and Storch & Esposito, 2003). Based on the previous discussion of including the notion of threats of trauma to the definition of traumatic stressor, some types of verbal victimization (e.g., being threatened with physical harm) seem to be a reasonable fit, conceptually.

Relational victimization, however, may be more problematic. Although the literature seems to indicate that relational victimization can also result in traumatic stress, adults often perceive this type as less harmful than its more direct counterparts (e.g., physical aggression). Further, if the diagnostic criterion (i.e., A1) is constructed to require only real or threatened physical experiences (thereby implicitly excluding other types of [indirect] experiences), then relational victimization would be out of the realm of possibility for conceptualization as a traumatic stressor. Clearly, this is an undesirable scenario. The data support a relation between all types of victimization, not only those that include real or threatened physical victimization experiences.

In sum, the extant literature seems to indicate that PV experiences and post-traumatic stress symptomatology are related. Topographically, the behaviors experienced by victims (e.g., repeated physical violence, etc.) are quite similar to the experiences of other youths who would perhaps be more readily considered for a PTSD diagnosis (e.g., chronic physical abuse by a parent). Although, the literature on PV and PTSD is still somewhat limited in quantity, the relationship between these two variables is quite plausible and well supported by the data that are available. More research, including data on how victims attempt to cope with their PV experiences, is certainly warranted.

Trauma and Ecology

These aforementioned findings (e.g., Crosby et al., 2010; Storch & Esposito, 2003; Weaver, 2000) are striking, and their implications must be examined in the context of student ecology and adult (i.e., teacher, parent, etc.) perceptions of PV and their likelihood to intervene. As discussed by Bauman and Del Rio (2006), most bullying occurs in schools, and teachers and other school personnel are often in the best position to intervene. It is imperative that teachers and other school personnel be committed to effective bullying intervention and that they understand the topography and potential severity of all types of bullying (i.e., physical, verbal, relational, cyberbullying, etc.). Specifically, what are adults' views on PV and how do these views relate to the likelihood that they will intervene? If, in fact, adults do perceive the types of victimization as differentially severe and are differentially likely to intervene on the types, then some youths may be more likely to suffer negative outcomes.

Adult Perceptions of Peer Victimization

Although somewhat limited (both in number and methodology), the extant literature on teachers' perceptions of the severity of the different types of bullying seems to support a disparity. That is, teachers may be more likely to perceive some forms of bullying as more severe (or harmful) than others and to intervene based on their perceptions of severity (e.g., see Bauman & Del Rio, 2006, with a preservice teacher sample). Other than perceptions of severity, perceptions of ambiguity (i.e., not being able to accurately recognize or define certain bullying behaviors) are also problematic. Relational bullying, for example, is much more difficult to observe, and there is some evidence to indicate that youths are less likely to report this type of victimization to adults (Birkinshaw & Eslea, 1998, as cited in Bauman & Del Rio). Furthermore, some teachers may view bullying as a normal experience and are less likely to intervene based on these beliefs (Kochenderfer-Ladd & Pelletier, 2008).

Additionally, some studies have indicated that teachers and students disagree about what constitutes bullying. In a large-scale study of perceptual differences (on bullying and peer victimization) between students and staff in one district, Bradshaw, Sawyer, and O'Brennan (2007) found that staff members across elementary and secondary levels significantly underestimated the number of students who are victimized on a frequent basis. Interestingly, some evidence indicates that teachers may not intervene as often as they think they do (Newman & Murray, 2005) and that youths perceive staff assistance as either unhelpful or even harmful (Rigby & Bagshaw, 2003).

How Might Social Support Relate to the Experience of Peer Victimization?

Alarmingly, there is some evidence to suggest that adults may be present when PV is occurring. For example, Crosby and colleagues (2010) found that 35% of the victims in their sample reported that adults were present at least "sometimes" when they were being victimized. Further, of the total sample, 66% reported that they had watched someone being victimized in the past two months, and 21% reported that they had been a bystander to victimization in the past week. This finding is quite unfortunate and indicates some problems with the viability of social support as a protective factor (for this sample).

Clearly, the usage of social support for victims must be examined more closely in future research. Davidson and Demaray (2007) defined social support "as knowledge that a person is cared for, is esteemed, and belongs to a large network of concerned people" (p. 384). Most parents, teachers, and other professionals would agree that social support should be a protective factor for victims of bullying. Davidson and Demaray, for example, found that social support from teachers and peers did moderate the relationship between PV and internalized distress. However, Hunter and Boyle (2004) found that children who are bullied persistently use social support less than those who experience victimization over shorter time periods.

It is also possible that the importance that victims place on social support may play a key role in coping strategy usage (Davidson & Demaray, 2007). That is, some victims who place a higher importance (or value) on social support may experience more significant distress than those who value social support less. This is indeed an intriguing hypothesis. Consider school systems and campuses that encourage seeking social support as the sole method of reducing victimization (e.g., "Just tell the teacher."). In settings such as those examined by Crosby and colleagues (2010), students reported that adults are sometimes present when they are victimized. In light of the common suggestion to seek social support for victimization, one wonders how victims may process the presence of these (passive or active) adult onlookers. That is, some victims of bullying may (understandably) view social support as a nonviable option when there are so many onlookers—particularly when adults are present. Others may perceive social support as quite important yet use it progressively less as they find it ineffective. Such dissonance between perceptions of importance and actual viability could be quite distressing. While this has not been sufficiently explored, it is plausible that continued unsuccessful attempts at eliciting social support from adults (who are occasional unwitting onlookers or may not perceive the victimization as severe enough to warrant intervention) may actually result in even higher levels of distress.

Conclusions and Implications for Intervention

The extant literature reviewed in this chapter lends support to the hypothesis that PV experiences can lead to PTSD. Of primary importance, however, is the validation of all types of PV as genuine threats to the mental health of some youths and a potential traumatic experience. As has been discussed, some parents and teachers perceive the various types of PV as differentially harmful. Specifically, physical victimization is the easiest to observe (or to view evidence of) and is perceived by adults as the most harmful. Verbal victimization, although direct, may present difficulties in gathering irrefutable evidence of its occurrence unless it is directly observed. Relational (or social) victimization is even more difficult to observe, as it involves more complex social structures and covert behaviors. Verbal and relational victimization often fall behind in perceptions of harmfulness and may be less likely to be viewed as legitimate victimization. The topography of each of these types must be included in psychoeducational programming for both adults and youths.

Further, each of the types of victimization can result in internalizing (and externalizing) distress. Therefore, parents, educators, and community members must be not only educated about the typology of PV but also informed that negative psychological sequelae are associated with all types. These sequelae may not occur for all students, especially for those that possess effective support networks and active coping strategies. However, for those who do not possess such protective factors and skills, the sequelae may range from milder internalizing distress to post-traumatic distress or even suicidality. Psychoeducation seems to be an excellent (and certainly underused) component of systemic intervention and dissemination of information.

Although the development of adaptive problem-solving skills seems to be quite important, it seems even more important that adults recognize that youths must also have absolute access to adult social support. The notion that intervention should focus predominantly on the development of problem-solving skills in the victim misses one key component of the definition of bullying: a power differential. In some cases, although not all, the power imbalance may be so great that problem solving (i.e., acting independently to reduce the victimization) could be nearly impossible. In these cases, social support may be the final option for victims. Norris and Sloan (2007) noted that although humans play a role in causing violence, they can also play a significant role in preventing violence. If victims perceive adults as unhelpful (e.g., being passively present when victimization occurs [see Crosby et al., 2010]), then it is little wonder that significant amounts of traumatic stress may occur. Surely, prevention efforts and vigilance from adults (i.e., those responsible for the safety and well-being of youths) should be a primary focus for reducing PV in schools and communities.

Adults must be educated and empowered to intervene on behalf of victims of bullying. First, however, seeking (at least adult) social support must be a viable option for all students. The clear establishment of a support network is, perhaps, one of the best ways to address this need for the viability of social support in a system. In some systems, this may be as simple as the appointment of a school counselor and/or a small group of teachers who could be approached as needed by youths who are being victimized. Individuals in these networks could mobilize supports for the student(s), including notifying parents (if necessary) and intervening as appropriate. Although the point seems apparent, psychoeducational approaches should clearly employ a view that victims should not be required to assume sole responsibility for their own safety.

Notes

1. Throughout this chapter, the term "youths" refers to children and adolescents.
2. This differentiation is not applied widely in the literature. I distinguish these terms in this fashion to clarify particular perspectives.

References

American Psychiatric Association (APA). (2000). *Diagnostic and statistical manual of mental disorders* (Rev. 4th ed.). Washington, DC: Author.

Arsenault, L., Bowes, L., & Shakoor, S. (2010). Bullying victimization in youths and mental health problems: "Much ado about nothing"? *Psychological Medicine, 40,* 717–729.

Barker, E. D., Bolvin, M., Brendgen, M., Fontaine, N., Arsenault, L., Vitaro, F., Bissonnette, C., Tremblay, R. E. (2008). The predictive validity and early predictors of peer victimization trajectories in preschool. *Archives of General Psychiatry, 65,* 1185–1192.

Bauman, S., & Del Rio, A. (2006). Preservice teachers' responses to bullying scenarios: Comparing physical, verbal, and relational bullying. *Journal of Educational Psychology, 98,* 219–231.

Birkinshaw, S., & Eslea, M. (1998, September). *Teachers' attitudes and actions toward boy v girl and girl v boy bullying.* Paper presented at the annual conference of the Developmental Section of the British Psychological Society, Lancaster University, Lancaster, England.

Bradshaw, C. P., Sawyer, A. L., & O'Brennan, L. M. (2007). Bullying and peer victimization at school: Perceptual differences between students and school staff. *School Psychology Review, 36,* 361–382.

Crick, N. R., & Bigbee, M. A. (1996). Relational aggression, gender, and social psychological adjustment. *Child Development, 66,* 710–722.

Crosby, J. W., Oehler, J., & Capaccioli, K. (2010). The relationship between peer victimization and post-traumatic stress symptomatology in a rural sample. *Psychology in the Schools, 47,* 297–310.

Davidson, L. M., & Demaray, M. K. (2007). Social support as a moderator between victimization and internalizing-externalizing distress from bullying. *School Psychology Review, 36,* 383–405.

Fairbank, J. A., Putnam, F. W., Harris, W. H. (2007). The prevalence and impact of child traumatic stress. In M. J. Friedman, T. M. Keane, & P. A. Resick (Eds.), *Handbook of PTSD: Science and practice* (pp. 229–251). New York: Guilford.

Finkelhor, D., Ormrod, R., Turner, H., & Hamby, S. L. (2005). The victimization of children and youth: A comprehensive, national survey. *Child Maltreatment, 10,* 5–25.

Grills, A. E., & Ollendick, T. H. (2002). Peer victimization, global self-worth, and anxiety in middle school children. *Journal of Clinical Child and Adolescent Psychology, 31,* 59–68.

Hawker, D., & Boulton, M. J. (2000). Twenty years' research on peer victimization and psychosocial maladjustment: A meta-analytic review of cross-sectional studies. *Journal of Child Psychology and Psychiatry, 41,* 441–455.

Hunter, S., & Boyle, J. (2004). Coping and appraisal in victims of school bullying. *British Journal of Educational Psychology, 74,* 83–107.

Kochenderfer-Ladd, B., & Pelletier, M. E. (2008). Teachers' views and beliefs about bullying: Influences on classroom management strategies and students' coping with peer victimization. *Journal of School Psychology, 46,* 431–453.

Mikkelsen, E., & Einarsen, S. (2002). Basic assumptions and symptoms of post-traumatic stress among victims of bullying at work. *European Journal of Work and Organizational Psychology, 11,* 87–111.

Mynard, H., Joseph, S., & Alexander, J. (2000). Peer-victimization and post-traumatic stress in adolescents. *Personality and Individual Differences, 29,* 815–821.

Newman, R. S., & Murray, B. J. (2005). How students and teachers view the seriousness of peer harassment: When is it appropriate to seek help? *Journal of Educational Psychology, 97,* 347–365.

Norris, F. H., Sloan, L. B. (2007). The epidemiology of trauma and PTSD. In M. J. Friedman, T. M. Keane, & P. A. Resick (Eds.), *Handbook of PTSD: Science and practice* (pp. 78–98). New York: Guilford.

Olweus, D. (1973). *Hackkycklingar och oversittare. Forskning om skolmobbning.* Stockholm: Almqvist & Wiksell.

Olweus, D. (1978). *Aggression in the schools: Bullies and whipping boys.* Washington, DC: Hemisphere Publishing.

Rigby, K., & Bagshaw, D. (2003). Prospects of adolescent students collaborating with teachers in addressing issues of bullying and conflict in schools. *Educational Psychology, 23,* 535–546.

Smith, J. D., Schneider, B. H., Smith, P. K., & Ananiadou, K. (2004). The effectiveness of whole school antibullying programs: A synthesis of evaluation research. *School Psychology Review, 33,* 547–560.

Smolowe, J., Herbst, D., Weisensee, E., Rakowsky, J., & Mascia, K. (2010). Bullied to death? *People, 73,* 66–70.

Storch, E. A., & Esposito, L. E. (2003). Peer victimization and posttraumatic stress among children. *Child Study Journal, 33,* 91–98.

Swearer, S. M., Grills, A. E., Haye, K. M., & Cary, T. (2004). Internalizing problems in students involved in bullying and victimization: Implications for intervention. In D. L. Espelage & S. M. Swearer (Eds.), *Bullying in American schools: A social-ecological perspective on prevention and intervention* (pp. 63–83). Mahwah, NJ: Lawrence Erlbaum Associates.

Vaillancourt, T., Duku, E., Decatanzaro, D., Macmillan, H., Muir, C., & Schmidt, L. A. (2008). Variation in hypothalamic-pituitary-adrenal axis activity among bullied and non-bullied children. *Aggressive Behavior, 34,* 294–305.

Weaver, A. (2000). Can post-traumatic stress disorder be diagnosed in adolescence without a catastrophic stressor? A case report. *Clinical Child Psychology and Psychiatry, 5,* 77–83.

CHAPTER TWO

Treatment of Adolescent Victims of Violence

Beth M. Housekamp, Marjorie Graham-Howard, Bethany Ashby, and Alice Fok-Trela

Adolescents worldwide are exposed to a number of traumatic events, including sexual abuse, physical abuse, partner abuse, school violence, war, and witnessing violence in their place of residence or community. The numbers of potential adolescent victims of violence are staggering. For example, in 2005 over 3.6 million children and adolescents were referred for child welfare services in the United States, and 899,000 of these child abuse and neglect cases were substantiated (U.S. Department of Health and Human Services, Administration on Children, Youth, and Families, 2007). The National Center for Victims of Crime (2010) reports the following recent statistics: In 2007, teens ages 12 to 19 experienced nearly 1.6 million violent crimes; this figure includes 179,056 robberies and 57,511 sexual assaults and rapes; during this same one-year period, 47% of youths ages 14 to 17 had experienced a physical assault, 16% had been sexually victimized, 17% had experienced abuse or neglect, 13% had been exposed to online sexual solicitations, 32% had reported being bullied at school and 173,600 teens were victims of serious violent crimes at school.

In the United States, adolescents who do not come from the majority culture have even greater risk of being a victim of violence. For example, from 1993 through 2003, Black youths ages 17 or younger were 5 times as likely as White youths to be homicide victims. American

Indian and Alaskan Native teens and young adults suffer the highest violent victimization of any age category in any racial group. Victims ages 18 to 24 make up almost one-third of all American Indian and Alaskan Native violent crime victims and have a violent victimization rate of 1 in 4. In addition, 18% of hate and bias incidents against lesbian, gay, bisexual, transgender, queer, or questioning (LGBTQ) victims reported to the National Coalition of Anti-Violence Programs recently were against victims ages 18 and younger, and from 1995 to 2008, 23 teens were murdered as a result of their gender identity or expression (National Center for Victims of Crime, 2010).

Socially marginalized adolescents have often experienced multiple forms of psychological trauma, as they suffer sustained exposure to an invalidating social environment, such as poverty, community violence, or other deprivation, as well abuse or neglect within their own interpersonal situation. As Briere and Lanktree (2008) note in their summary of the research literature on multiple impacts of trauma, "social and economic deprivation, as well as racism, sexism, homophobia, and homelessness, not only produce their own negative effects on children and adults they also increase the likelihood of trauma exposure and may intensify the effects of such victimization" (p. 2). Adolescents from homes and communities with less social stature are also more likely to be a victim of violence such as child abuse, sexual and physical assault, gang or community violence, drive-by shootings, robbery, sexual exploitation through prostitution, trauma associated with refugee status, witnessing domestic violence, and loss associated with the murder of a family member or friend (Briere & Lanktree, 2008).

Although estimates of the rate of post-traumatic stress disorder (PTSD) among youths who have experienced traumatic events vary, most studies have found prevalence rates around 15% (Cuffe et al., 1998; Stewart et al., 2004). As noted above, Briere and Lanktree recognize that when someone has experienced trauma within a setting where additional traumas are present (such as lower SES environments, residential treatment facilities, or juvenile justice settings), the psychological results are often multiple and severe, a phenomenon they identify as complex post-traumatic disturbance:

> Complex trauma can be defined as a combination of early and late-onset, multiple, and sometimes highly invasive traumatic events, usually of an ongoing, interpersonal nature. In most cases, such trauma includes exposure to repetitive childhood sexual, physical, and/or psychological abuse, often (although not always) in the context of concomitant emotional neglect and harmful social environments. (Briere & Lanktree, 2008)

Children and adolescents with complex PTSD also frequently have other comorbid symptoms, including anxiety, dissociation, depression, and externalizing disorders. In addition, adolescents who experience complex post-traumatic symptoms often self-mutilate or are violent toward others, abuse substances, have eating disorders, exhibit susceptibility to revictimization, and suffer traumatic bereavement due to the loss of significant others through violent circumstances (Briere & Lanktree, 2008; Carrion, Weems, Ray, & Reiss, 2002). In addition, those treating adolescent victims of violence note that adolescents may not meet full PTSD criteria but may still suffer from the same degree of functional impairment as those who have full-blown symptoms (Carrion et al., 2002).

Given the multiple traumas that adolescent victims of violence may experience and the complex symptomatology that may arise from exposure to violence within different settings, particularly socially marginalizing settings, it is critical to be aware of the impact of both the adolescent's home environment as well as the settings in which treatment may occur. In addition, assessment of the adolescent victim of violence must occur within a developmental framework that recognizes societal impacts as well as the need for appropriate test selection. Finally, treatment of PTSD and other complex traumatic disturbances arising from exposure to violence must recognize the individual circumstances of the type(s) of violence the adolescent has experienced. In providing an overview of assessment and treatment of adolescent victims of violence, this chapter focuses on each of these broad areas.

Types of Treatment Settings for Adolescent Victims of Violence

Mental health professionals work with adolescent victims of violence in a variety of settings, including schools, psychiatric treatment facilities, residential facilities, medical hospitals, the juvenile justice system, as well as traditional outpatient clinics and private practice settings. Each of these settings require an awareness of the systemic structure and impacts, the various legal and ethical obligations within the different settings, and alternative treatment options present depending on the setting where one is working with the adolescent.

Providing Treatment within School Settings

One common setting where counselors work with adolescent victims of violence is public or private schools. With increased concern about children and adolescents experiencing bullying or violence at school, schools have introduced both systemic, curriculum-based approaches to treating violence and individual counselors and others to provide support for individual victims of bullying and violence. Generally, programs may be either curriculum based or peer led. They may focus on social skills or on restorative justice (i.e., forgiveness). Programs may focus specifically on the participants involved, or they may involve the entire school.

The development of systemic interventions began with Dan Olweus, who was the first to suggest the integration of common elements; his work culminated into what has now become the standard in antibullying programs. The goal of such programs is to teach students social skills that will allow them to create healthy relationships (Substance Abuse and Mental Health Services Administration, 2009b). These programs focus not only on the perpetrators and the victims, but also on the students who are bystanders. By doing so, they strive to change the social dynamics in the peer groups and the roles played by adults in shaping the students' school experiences.

Adolescent Victims in Short- or Long-Term Psychiatric Hospital Settings

Adolescents are occasionally treated in short- or long-term hospital settings or in residential facilities that specialize in the treatment of substance abuse, severe acting out behaviors, or family-related issues. The trend for hospital stays, consistent with the norm for all developmental groups, is for short periods of initial stabilization and follow-up through partial day treatment programs or outpatient services provided on site at the hospital. During an initial 3- to 5-day hospitalization, the most severe presenting symptoms and crisis issues can be addressed. This may include psychotic symptoms, depression and suicidal ideation, conduct disorder and impulsive acting-out behaviors, homicidal risk, self-injurious behaviors, and substance abuse. Treatment focuses on reducing immediate risk of harm to self and others and on rapidly stabilizing symptoms with medication and therapy. Once the teen is no longer an imminent risk, she can be released home with follow-up care. Family and group therapy are provided both while the adolescent is in the hospital and upon her release.

Medical Centers and Hospitals

A medical setting is often the first place traumatized adolescents, particularly those who have been assaulted, go to seek treatment. They present in emergency departments or at their primary care providers' office for treatment of physical injuries, testing for sexually transmitted infections, and documentation of abuse. In addition, because many adolescents have good relationships with their primary care providers and these visits are confidential, the initial disclosure of abuse and trauma is often made to their physician. Often, primary care providers have known these adolescents and their families for years. They are invested in their patients' physical and emotional well-being, and many recommend that their patients seek mental health services. When patients are referred by their primary care providers, it is important for mental health professionals to include these physicians in their treatment and disposition planning, as physicians will continue to interact with adolescents and their families long after therapy is terminated.

Residential Treatment Settings

Some adolescents (including adolescent victims of violence) present with psychological needs that cannot be adequately addressed in either an outpatient or inpatient setting. Eating disorders, substance abuse, self-injurious behaviors, and severe conduct disorder may all require an out-of-home placement in a residential treatment facility. Teens who have been removed from the home by a social services agency due to family neglect and abuse issues may also reside in group homes, foster homes, and long-term residential placement settings. While some of these adolescents are newly removed from the home, many were initially placed as young children and are essentially being raised in residential environments. When working with adolescent victims who are in such residential settings, it is critical to work closely with the treatment team, the agencies, case manager, and others who are interacting with the adolescent on a regular basis. Often those members of the team who are responsible for assisting the adolescent in managing his or her daily life are those who are most aware of the adolescent's struggles in coping and also are often on the receiving end of the adolescent's anger, fear, anxiety, and other emotional and behavioral symptoms.

The Juvenile Justice System

Adolescent victims of abuse who then go on to commit crimes and become involved with the juvenile justice system are another group in need of treatment. While awaiting trial or the disposition of their criminal case, these adolescents may be housed in a secure juvenile detention center. If the juvenile is facing serious charges, he or she may remain in a custody setting for weeks or even months before the criminal case is heard. Additionally, if the court deems that the youth represents a risk for future criminal acts, the minor may be ordered to a boot camp, placement, or secure facility. Many states have provisions that allow teens who are of a certain age and have committed certain categories of violent crimes to be transferred to the adult criminal court system. When this happens, the youth may be sentenced to adult prison or a juvenile correctional facility. Adolescents in the juvenile justice system have various treatment needs that may include amelioration of mental health symptoms, treatment for their own trauma history, substance abuse treatment, and sex offender treatment.

When providing treatment to an adolescent victim of violence who is also incarcerated because he or she is an offender, it is important to be aware of unique legal and ethical issues. Specifically, teens that have been ordered to treatment by the court do not have the same confidentiality rights that exist in an ordinary outpatient setting. Treatment that is court ordered may require the practitioner to provide regular feedback and clinical information to the court documenting the teen's progress and adjustment. Even for youths who are not mandated into treatment, the probation department or supervisory agency may require information from the mental health professional as part of the probationary plan. To complicate this further, since adolescents in the juvenile justice system are not yet adults, parental rights for information and consent are still required in many jurisdictions. It will therefore behoove the practitioner providing treatment services in the juvenile justice system to familiarize herself with the specifics of the legal and ethical issues and reporting requirements for her specific jurisdiction.

Assessment of Adolescent Victims of Violence

The appropriate assessment of the adolescent is the necessary first step or precursor to any treatment that is subsequently offered, regardless of setting, type of trauma experienced, or specific psychological or behavioral impact. The adolescent's symptom presentation depends on multiple factors, including age and developmental level at the time of the trauma, the nature and duration of the trauma, and social support following the traumatic event (Steiner, Carrion, Plattner, & Koopman, 2003). Research has demonstrated that severity of exposure to trauma correlates with severity of PTSD symptoms—the more extreme the trauma (such as being exposed to potentially deadly gunfire or other life-threatening violence), the longer the exposure to the traumatic situation (such as long-term abuse in the home), the age of the adolescent at the time of the severe trauma, and the more discrete types of severe trauma the adolescent experiences, the more likely he or she is to develop either PTSD or complex post-traumatic disturbance. Complex trauma is also more likely to develop if an infant or child is exposed to danger that is unpredictable, as the child must devote resources that are normally dedicated to growth and development to survival (Houskamp, Scott, Neumann, & McDonald, 2010; Briere & Lanktree, 2008). In addition, treatment is also impacted by where the adolescent is residing. If the adolescent is living in a setting that is unsafe, on the streets for instance, assessing the impact on the adolescent and finding a safe residence for him or her is a prerequisite of effective treatment.

Assessment, as conceptualized as an aide in treatment, can be broadly defined to include not only traditional psychology testing and specialized tests but also clinical interviewing, behavioral observations, and third-party interviews. The goal of assessment is to obtain, as quickly as possible, the necessary information that can guide and inform treatment. To this end, the assessment is conducted at the beginning of the treatment phase and is viewed as a part of the overall therapeutic process with the teen in need. The treating clinician can obtain this information in one or two sessions at the beginning of treatment and use the assessment as a way to begin establishing rapport, therapeutic alliance, and connection with the client. However, assessment is also an ongoing, dynamic piece of the treatment planning process and should be threaded through the entire process of therapy.

Depending on the specific treatment goals and needs of the client, the assessment should start with a thorough clinical interview. The focus of the assessment is to receive information regarding the teen's chief psychological symptoms or problems. However, other information, including the child's developmental history, family and social history, educational history, substance abuse history, criminal history, and prior mental health history, may also be necessary. The assessment should include a full evaluation of the trauma exposure history (Briere & Lanktree, 2008), including any history of exposure to child abuse, emotional neglect, assaults by peers, community violence, witnessing violence, traumatic loss, exposure to accidents and disasters, and serious medical illness or injury. This information can be obtained through either open-ended questioning or a structured interview protocol.

Use of standardized psychological testing may assist in the assessment process. For adolescents, it may be useful to obtain a brief measure of current cognitive functioning to rule out any developmental or cognitive limitations that may be a barrier to treatment. The Wechsler Abbreviated Scale of Intelligence (WASI) is a useful screening measure for intelligence, and if needed, the clinician can then administered either the WASI-IV or WISC-IV if more information is required. Personality inventories and symptoms checklists may also be helpful. The Child Behavioral Checklist (Achenbach, 1991) has a self-report, parent and teacher form. The MMPI-A (Butcher et al., 1992), PAI-A (Morey, 2008), and MACI (Millon, 1993) can all be filled out by the adolescent to provide information about current psychological functioning and symptoms. If more specific information is needed about a certain cluster of symptoms, the CDI, BDI, or BAI can also be chosen.

Specific trauma-specific measures are also available, and many were developed for specific age groups within the adolescent population. These may include the Trauma Symptom Checklist for Children, Trauma Symptom Inventory, Detailed Assessment of Posttraumatic Stress, and UCLA PTSD Index for DSV-IV (Briere & Lanktee, 2008). The advantage of these measures is to gather data on the specific trauma history of the adolescent and use this data as a framework for specific treatment intervention. The practitioner can obtain this information from either self-report or report by the caregiver, though many researchers suggest that obtaining information from both may provide the most comprehensive assessment (Briere & Lanktree, 2008).

Finally, for teens that have been exposed to a specific trauma unique to that population, the treating mental health professional may use trauma-specific inventories that were initially developed as research measures but have been proven to have clinical utility. For example, when working with adolescents who have been exposed to community or gang violence, mental health professionals may use the Community Violence Exposure Survey (Saltzman, Pynoos, Layne, Steinberg, & Aisenberg, 2001), which is a 25-item self-report inventory adapted from the more widely used Survey of Exposure to Community Violence.

Treating Adolescent Victims of Childhood Physical and Sexual Abuse and Assault

Maltreatment of children is a relatively common occurrence in the United States, particularly maltreatment and abuse by family members. For example, according to national statistics recently compiled, a report of child abuse is made every 10 seconds. Ninety percent of child sexual abuse victims know the perpetrator in some way and 68% are abused by family members. We also know that child abuse occurs at every socioeconomic level, across ethnic and cultural lines, within all religions, and at all levels of education. And the impact of child abuse for adolescents and adults is staggering. For example, 31% of women in prison in the United States were abused as children; over 60% of people in drug rehabilitation centers report being abused or neglected as a child; and approximately 80% of 21-year-olds that were abused as children were found to meet criteria for at least one psychological disorder. Abused children are also 25% more likely to experience teen pregnancy, and abused teens are three times less likely to practice safe sex, putting them at greater risk for STDs (Childhelp, 2010).

A wide range of significant immediate and longer-term psychological symptoms have been found to be associated with physical, sexual, or psychological abuse by a family member, close relative, or other trusted person. In particular, experiences of being abused as a child predispose one for difficulties such as anxiety, depression, post-traumatic stress disorder, substance abuse, and externalizing behaviors. In addition to these well-known traumatic responses, those who have a history of having been abused in childhood may also struggle with impaired self-disturbance. Impaired self-capacities comprise at least three separate but related types of disturbance: problems in one's ability to access and maintain a stable sense of identity or self (identity disturbance), an inability to regulate and/or tolerate negative emotional states (affect dysregulation), and difficulties in forming and sustaining meaningful relationships with others (relational disturbance). Briere and Rickards (2007) in a study assessing self-disturbance found that impaired self-capacities appear particularly associated with adverse interpersonal events (i.e., those within families or among adults close to the child). In addition, impairment in these areas was found primarily in those who had a history of being maltreated or abused as a child, in particular emotional abuse, emotional nonsupport, and sexual abuse when one was young.

Adolescent Victims of Physical and Sexual Assault

Perpetrators of assaults on adolescents may include same-age peers or adults, including adults in positions of authority and trust, such as teachers, coaches, religious leaders, neighbors, and other adults who come into contact with adolescents regularly and may abuse this power. At times, the adolescent may be both the perpetrator and victim of violence, as occurs in situations involving gang or community violence. Additionally, an earlier history of child sexual or physical abuse may make the youth more vulnerable to later assaults.

Sexual assaults on adolescents are prevalent, with some authors noting that adolescents have the highest rates of rape and other sexual assaults of any age group (American Academy of Pediatrics, Committee on Adolescence, 2001). Teens may be victims of sexual assault, molestation, rape, acquaintance or date rape, and statutory rape. The incidence of date rape in the adolescent population is high. A study conducted by Jackson, Cram, and Seymour (2000) found that 77% of female and 67% of male high school students endured some form of sexual coercion occurring in dating relationships. Statutory rape, which includes sex between a youth below the legal age to give consent and an older adolescent or adult, is also common. One study that analyzed crime report data found that 25% of sex crimes committed against minors involved statutory rape (Troup-Leasure & Snyder, 2005). With the spread of the Internet and teens having increasing exposure to social networks and chat groups, victimization by adults who meet and interact with adolescents online also occurs, though not as often as portrayed by the media. In a recent study, Wolak, Finkelhor, Mitchell, and Ybarra (2010) found that of the number of nationally reported statutory rape claims, approximately 7% was attributed to Internet-initiated sex crimes.

The psychological impact of sexual assault on adolescents has been studied extensively. Consistent with literature that has examined the effects of rape on adult women, teens that are sexually assaulted are more likely to develop PTSD and to be at greater risk for comorbid diagnoses, including depression, substance abuse, and other anxiety disorders (Hanson, 2002). Adolescent rape victims are more likely to have problems with low self-esteem, panic episodes, sleep problems, disordered eating, sexual problems, and social functioning (Vickerman & Margolin, 2009). Moreover, these ill effects, if left untreated, may continue to impact the adolescent adversely well into adult life.

Integrative Treatment of Complex Trauma for Adolescents (ITCT)

John Briere and Cheryl Lanktree (2008) developed the Integrative Treatment of Complex Trauma for Adolescents (ITCT) approach to assist adolescents who are struggling with the impacts of multiple traumas in their families and communities. The ITCT recognizes the cultural setting of the adolescent. Briere and Lanktree note that their approach, presented in a comprehensive manual, is a semi-structured approach that can be adapted on a case-by-case basis by the therapist to meet the specific needs of the adolescent, including attention to his or her cultural/ethnic background, developmental level, and psychological functioning. The core components of the ITCT approach to working with adolescent trauma survivors include:

- Assessment-driven treatment, with standardized trauma-specific measures administered at 2- to 4-month intervals to identify symptoms requiring special clinical attention.

- Attention to complex trauma issues, including post-traumatic stress, attachment disturbance, behavioral and affect dysregulation, interpersonal difficulties, and identity-related issues.
- Use of multiple treatment modalities, potentially including cognitive therapy, exposure therapy, mindfulness/meditation training, and relational treatment in individual and group therapy, based on the specific symptomatology of the youth. This approach also attempts to involve family members for family therapy sessions and parenting support and collateral sessions for caregivers.
- Early attention to immediate trauma-related issues such as acute stress disorder, anxiety, depression, and post-traumatic stress in order to increase the capacity of the client to explore more chronic and complex trauma issues. In some clients, this may include the use of psychiatric medication.
- Skills development in building emotional regulation and also problem-solving capacities.
- Advocacy and interventions at the system level (e.g., family, forensic/protection, and school) to establish healthier functioning and to address safety concerns.
- Allowance for a flexible time-frame for treatment, since the multiproblem nature of complex trauma sometimes precludes short-term therapy. (Briere & Lanktree, 2008)

Other treatments have also been developed focusing specifically on treating adolescent victims of sexual and physical assault. Evidence-based treatment of adolescent rape victims has generally employed a cognitive-behavioral approach. The overarching goals of treatment are to reduce anxiety, panic, and distress symptoms, assist the survivor in constructing a holistic narrative of the trauma, and use exposure to allow reprocessing and prevent the development of PTSD and other mental health disorders. Some of the more common treatment modalities have included stress inoculation training, prolonged exposure therapy, and cognitive processing therapy (Vickerman & Margolin, 2009), which have been adapted for use with the adolescent victim. Stress inoculation training focuses on using Meichenbaum's anxiety management procedures with rape victims through psychoeducation, in vivo exposure targeting rape-related phobias, and training with coping strategies. Prolonged exposure therapy focuses on decreasing anxiety associated with the rape memory through imagined reexposure to the assault in treatment and homework assignments. Cognitive processing therapy relies on psychoeducation, exposure, and cognitive techniques.

A particular focus of treatment with adolescent sexual assault victims is on the distorted cognitions that may occur as a result of the rape trauma. Self-blame and self-devaluation are a common effect of rape and may interact with social rape myths in such a way to impact negatively the trauma survivor's overall psychological functioning. Moor (2007) advocates a treatment that specifically addresses the rape victim's tendency to blame herself and to engage in negative self-appraisal, which prevents the formation of a healing narrative. The therapist uses therapeutic empathy, reality testing, reframing, and the provision of corrective information, which challenges the distorted myths and beliefs that the adolescent rape victim may hold.

A specific developmental concern that may arise when treating the adolescent victim of sexual assault is to prevent the disruption of normal developmental pathways in terms of sexual identity, sexuality, and interpersonal relationships. Since many teens have limited sexual experiences, a sexual assault may have the additional impact of disrupting the development of a healthy sexual identity. Therefore, in addition to addressing the distress symptoms, the treatment must also focus on resolving residual impacts of sexual trauma on the emerging and developing sense of a sexual self.

Adolescent Intimate Partner Violence

The prevalence of intimate partner violence (IPV) in adolescent dating relationships ranges from 30% to 80% (Hickman, Joycox, & Arnoff, 2004). The disparities in prevelance rates are likely due to how IPV is defined and the age of participants, among other factors. IPV is generally defined broadly and includes both verbal aggression, such as name calling and swearing, and physical aggression, such as throwing objects and shoving. Recent research estimates the prevalence of serious dating violence, including sexual and physical assault or drug/alcohol facilitated rape, at 2.7% of adolescent girls and .6% of adolescent boys (Wolitzky-Taylor et al., 2008). Given that a significant percentage of adolescents have been engaged in dating violence, adolescent therapists would do well to consider the potential of IPV, and its subsequent impact, in their work with clients.

Those most at risk for IPV are adolescents with histories of maltreatment as children. Some studies suggest that victims of child maltreatment are 3.5 times more likely to be involved in violent dating relationships as adults as compared to those children without histories of abuse (Coid, Petruckevitch, Chung, Richardson, Moorey, & Feder, 2003). More specific risk factors for victimization vary by gender. For girls, in addition to maltreatment, other risk factors include age, African American ethnicity, low parent education, delinquent behavior, sex with partner, alcohol use, having a friend who is a victim of IPV, and depression (Buzy et al., 2004; Foshee et al., 2004; Foster, Hagan, & Brooks-Gunn, 2004). Less is known about specific risk factors for boys. However, sex with partner, low self-esteem, and physical fighting with peers have been associated with male victimization (Foshee et al., 2004; Kaestle & Halpern, 2005).

Adolescent males and females are victimized by dating violence at similar rates (Graves, Sechrist, White, & Paradise, 2005; White & Smith, 2004), although recent studies of college students document more women engaging in physical aggression than men. However, although the prevalence of IPV is similar among males and females, it is important to note that the outcomes of the perpetration vary by gender (Wolfe, Scott, & Crooks, 2005). According to White (2009), "similar prevalence rates are not indicative of women's and men's partner violence being the same. The meaning and motives are different" (p. 3). Girls are more likely to be injured or experience psychological distress as compared to boys (Frieze, 2005; Williams and Frieze, 2005), and up to 10% of intentional injuries to girls are due to IPV (Griffin & Kossn, 2002). Girls are also more likely to be victims of sexual assault (Swan & Snow, 2006).

The presence of intimate partner violence has been correlated with multiple mental health issues. Suicidal ideation, substance use, depression, and post-traumatic stress disorder are all associated with intimate partner violence during adolescence (Callahan, Tolman, & Saunders, 2003; Silverman, Raj, Mucci, & Hathaway, 2001). Therefore, when IPV is present, it is critical for therapists to assess for other comorbid diagnoses. Further, adolescents with a history of IPV have poorer mental health outcomes as compared to adolescents who have not been victimized (Brown et al., 2009). Given the significant relationship between child maltreatment and IVP, in addition to addressing safety issues in the dating relationship, therapists may also need to assess safety issues at home.

Most of the treatment literature on adolescent IPV focuses on prevention and there is little empirical support for these interventions. The only evidenced-based intervention specifically targeted at reducing, in addition to preventing, adolescent IPV is the Safe Dates Program (Foshee et al., 1996; Foshee et al., 1998). The Safe Dates Program is a curriculum-based program that was developed for use with middle and high school age students. The major components include a 10-session curriculum on IPV; a play about dating abuse; a poster contest; and parent materials, including a letter, newsletter, and the Families for Safe Dates Program. There is also an evaluation questionnaire. The program is designed to be used in multiple settings, including psychoeducation groups and other treatment settings. Research evaluating the effectiveness of the program indicates that adolescents who participate experience 56–92% less physical, serious physical, and sexual IPV victimization and perpetration than nonparticipating adolescents and that these results were maintained over a three-year period (Foshee et al., 2005).

Interventions for Bullying and School Violence

School violence can take many forms. The most common forms of violence include fighting, verbal conflict, disruptive behavior, and bullying (Wilson & Lipsey, 2005). It is important to take note of and address these relatively milder forms of aggression, as research has shown that they can escalate into more overt violence (Wilson & Lipsey, 2005).

There are great costs to the individuals involved in incidents of bullying and school violence. These negative impacts are seen in many arenas of functioning: psychological, behavioral, emotional, physical, academic, and social. The Substance Abuse and Mental Health Services Administration of the U.S. Department of Health and Human Services reported that those who are victimized often experience psychological distress, poor self-esteem, and internalizing and externalizing behaviors (Substance Abuse and Mental Health Services Administration, 2009a). Emotions such as anger, sadness, frustration, and stress were expressed. Students reported physical difficulties as well, including headaches, vomiting, sleep disturbance, enuresis, abdominal pains, and increased medication use. Academically, victimized students had higher levels of absenteeism, negative school attitudes, and lowered academic achievement. Socially, these students reported social isolation and poor peer relationships. In terms of mental health and illness, there was a greater prevalence of major depressive disorder, anxiety disorders, suicidality, substance abuse, self-injurious behaviors, and trauma symptoms, as well as a greater vulnerability to psychosis. Students who were the victims of repeated occurrences of school violence became trapped in abusive relationships (Substance Abuse and Mental Health Services Administration, 2009b). Negative effects were also apparent with the aggressors, who learned how to use power and aggression to control others (Substance Abuse and Mental Health Services Administration, 2009b). Overall, school violence and bullying have costly effects on the educational system and lasting effects on the individuals, both on the perpetrators and the victims of the violence.

Common Elements in School Violence Prevention Programs

While research is lacking regarding the efficacy of school-based programs (Smith, Ryan, & Cousins, 2007), several common elements have been proposed for school violence prevention programs and antibullying programs. Recommended elements include:

1. Providing a definition of bullying.
2. Creating awareness of the various forms of bullying.
3. Addressing the specific issues of each school (for example, social skills training [Hymel, Schonert-Reichl, & Miller, 2006] or the notion of justice and fairness).
4. Teaching students how to develop healthy relationships, as compared to the bullying dynamic.
5. Training from a systemic perspective, including teachers, students, parents, and school staff, and providing training materials.
6. Using multimodal delivery of information (e.g., including school-wide education, routine interventions built into school policy, and intensive individual interventions) (Vreeman & Carroll, 2007).
7. Using peer processes to address bullying and encourage prevention.
8. Creating a systemic, fully integrated, and ongoing program that involves parents, students, classes, school staff, and the community (Tutty et al., 2005).
9. Providing interventions to students who are bullied and students who bully.
10. Developing protocols to report bullying incidents that minimize fear of retribution.
11. Providing systematic, periodic evaluation of the program.
12. Providing safe intervention programs for bystanders.
13. Developing and improving students' social behavior by promoting a positive school climate, which includes elements such as warm relationships and high standards for behaviors (Orpinas & Horne, 2006; Smokowski & Kopasz, 2005).

Effectiveness of Interventions

Overall, research indicates mixed results regarding school-based educational approaches to preventing school violence (Hunt, 2007). However, research studies are suggesting that there are certain common elements and themes in successful programs. Wilson and Lipsey (2005) examined 219 studies on the efficacy of different school-based interventions. The researchers found that the following were common elements of effective interventions:

- More effective programs had greater session frequency per week.
- Shorter programs were more effective than longer programs.

- Larger treatment effects were found with higher-risk students, especially with elementary school students.
- Different modalities are equally effective (e.g., social skills training, cognitive-behavioral programs, counseling).

Interestingly, a school climate that is based on restorative justice (which views school violence as a violation of relationships) tends to be more effective than a school climate that involves punitive policies (which views school violence as a violation of rules) (Smith, 2008). Because of this, zero tolerance policies and punitive discipline strategies have not been shown to be effective in increasing school safety and decreasing school violence (Stinchcomb, Bazemore, & Rienstenberg, 2006). Overall, researchers have found that successful interventions involve comprehensive, systematic interventions, specific moment-to-moment interventions, adult leadership, and student involvement and leadership (Pepler, Jiang, & Craig, 2006; Smokowski & Kopasz, 2005). School-based violence prevention programs, in general, have also been found to be effective. On average, bullying decreased by 20–23% and victimization by 17–20% following the implementation of school-based programs (Farrington & Ttofi, 2009).

Treatment for Individuals

Individual treatment is comprised of two types: treatment for the aggressor and treatment for the victim. Treatments that have been found to be effective with victims of school violence are usually consistent with trauma and grief-focused interventions. One modality is school-based group therapy, developed by Saltzman, Pynoos, Layne, Steinberg, and Aisenberg (2001). This treatment has five foci: (a) the traumatic experience, (b) reminders of trauma and loss, (c) the interplay of trauma and grief, (d) post-trauma adversities, and (e) developmental progression. This treatment is specially designed to screen for trauma exposure in students, reduce distress in trauma-related outcomes, and improve academic performance.

Cognitive-behavioral therapy has also been suggested to help victims reduce their anxiety regarding attending school following an incident of school violence. Some researchers have suggested the use of exposure by encouraging the child gradually to face increasingly anxiety-provoking situations and events while practicing relaxation techniques and cognitive-behavioral techniques designed to reduce anxiety (Silverman, 2010).

Treatment for aggressors involves building more adaptive social skills. These are often similar to the programs developed as part of school curriculum. However, the individual or small group format of delivering the training allows the training to be tailored to the individuals in the group.

Community Violence

Another adolescent group in need of treatment includes teenagers who have been victims of community violence. Community violence has been variously defined in the literature, and one of the criticisms is the lack of a consensus definition (Guterman, Cameron, & Staller, 2000). Some authors define community violence as the presence of violence and violence-related events within an individual's proximal environment (Seiger, Rojas-Vilches, McKinnney, & Renk, 2004). Other have defined community violence as instances in which individuals are assaulted by persons other than family members or partners while in the community (Denson, Marshall, Schell, & Jaycox, 2007). This may include direct exposure to violence through physical assault, fighting, or gang violence or through witnessing violent acts in one's home, neighborhood, or school. Also included are witnessing gang assaults, finding victims, exposure to weapons, and living in an unsafe neighborhood with high incidents of crime.

There is considerable evidence to suggest adolescents exposed to this type of violence are at risk for a variety of difficulties, including reduced academic achievement; aggressive, delinquent, or high-risk sexual behaviors; substance use and dependence; and trauma reactions, including PTSD, anxiety, and depressive symptoms (Saltzman et al., 2001). Moreover, traumatic death may be a result of community violence, resulting in the teen being forced to reconcile grief and loss issues in tandem with post-traumatic stress reactions. Unfortunately, teens that have witnessed or been victims of community violence appear to be an overlooked treatment group who rarely seek services independently and may actively deny or minimize such traumatic exposure when talking to parents, educators, and treatment providers (Saltzman et al., 2001).

Treatment interventions for adolescents who have been exposed to community violence are generally of two types: preventive interventions to decrease the likelihood of developing more severe psychopathology and interventions to decrease post-traumatic distress and accompanying risk factors. School-based approaches are particularly popular, and interventions have advocated either a group-based or an individually focused set of interventions.

Research on adolescent survivors of community violence has determined that although many survivors experience a stress reaction in the face of exposure to community violence, only a small subset of individuals display full symptoms of PTSD. Denson and colleagues (2007) conducted a longitudinal study of male Hispanic survivors of community violence and found acute symptom severity, measured five days after the initial trauma exposure, was the biggest predictor of later development of PTSD. In light of this research, many treatment programs have focused on the ability to prevent and reduce psychological sequelae after exposure to gang or community violence. If offered treatment shortly after exposure to the traumatic event, the chances of developing a post-traumatic stress reaction may be sharply reduced.

Treatment of adolescent community violence victims has extended to include other group-based therapeutic approaches with a trauma focus. One such approach focused on middle school adolescents who were exposed to community violence (Saltzman et al., 2001). After receiving an initial screening and survey, students who met criteria for group inclusion were offered group therapy. Twenty sessions focused on five modules (building group cohesion, therapeutic processing of selected traumatic experiences, management of the interplay between trauma, loss, and complicated bereavement, and problem-solving current adversaries to restore normal developmental progression). Group participation was associated with improvements in post-traumatic stress, grief symptoms, and academic performance.

Since adolescents and their parents are often exposed to the same community violence events, treatment should include a family therapy or parent education component. While the family may serve a protective function in ameliorating distress symptoms, parents underestimate the rates at which their children are exposed to community violence (Hill & Jones, 1997) and may be too distressed themselves to recognize the need for treatment. Seiger and colleagues (2004) recommend family-based interventions that focus on reestablishing a sense of order and routine, providing the teen with a developmentally appropriate explanation of the event, and improving overall parent-child relationships. They note that it may be difficult to intervene when the parents are more traumatized than the youth and may overreact by sharply curtailing the amount of time that the teen is allowed to spend outside of the home.

Summary

Adolescents are victims of severe, often multiple types of violence, including verbal abuse and severe teasing, bullying, physical assault, and sexual assault and incest. While research on the impacts and treatment of child abuse, including physical abuse and assault, has increased extensively over the last 30 to 40 years, we have only more recently begun to attend to difficulties such as the level of potential bullying that adolescents experience at school and over the Internet and the impact of trauma as it occurs within settings that are edges of society, such as homeless adolescents, those living in violent neighborhoods, or LGBTQ adolescents who are victims of bullying, assault, or even murder because of their sexual identity.

Adolescents who reside in communities where there is significant violence surrounding them are at risk for developing complex post-traumatic symptoms that must be addressed adequately in order for the adolescents to move beyond their current situations. Adolescents who have a less stable living environment for multiple reasons, whether because the severity of their symptoms requires psychiatric hospitalization, their behavior has put them within the context of the juvenile justice system, or they reside within the foster care or residential treatment system, are particularly at risk and require the best from those of us who provide treatment to them.

Mental health clinicians and researchers have recognized that adolescents who are victims of violence are ripe for intervention and assistance from those adults who develop caretaking, counseling, or mentoring roles with them. The adolescents who receive support and services, including effective evidence-based treatments, have an opportunity to break a cycle of violence and live a good life. The tools surveyed in this chapter can help all of us as we work with these adolescents and give them hope for a better future.

References

Achenbach, T. M. (1991). *Manual for the child behavior checklist/4–18 and 1991 profile*. Burlington: University of Vermont, Department of Psychiatry.

Aisenberg, E., & Mennen, F. (2000). Children exposed to community violence: Issues for assessment and treatment. *Child and Adolescent Social Work Journal, 17*, 341–360.

American Academy of Pediatrics, Committee on Adolescence. (2001). Care of the adolescent sexual assault victim. *Pediatrics, 107*, 1476–1479.

Briere, J., & Lanktree, C. B. (2008). *Integrative treatment for complex trauma in adolescents (ITCT-A): A guide for the treatment of multiply-traumatized youth*. Long Beach, CA: MCAVIC-USC Child and Adolescent Trauma Program, National Child Traumatic Stress Network, Substance Abuse and Mental Health Services Administration, U.S. Department of Health and Human Services.

Briere, J., & Rickards, S. (2007). Self-awareness, affect regulation, and relatedness: Differential sequels of childhood versus adult victimization experiences. *Journal of Nervous and Mental Disease, 195*, 497–503.

Brown, A., Cosgrave, E., Killackey, E., Purcell, R., Buckby, J., & Yung, A. (2009). The longitudinal association of adolescent dating violence with psychiatric disorders and functioning. *Journal of Interpersonal Violence, 24,* 1964–1979.

Butcher, J. N., Williams, C. L., Graham, J. R., Archer, R. P., Tellegen, A., Ben-Porath, Y. S., & Kaemmer, B. (1992). *MMPI-A (Minnesota Mutliphasic Personality Inventory—Adolescent): Manual for administration, scoring, and interpretation.* Minneapolis: University of Minnesota Press.

Buzy, W. M., McDonald, R., Jouriles, E. N., Swank, P. R., Rosenfield, D., Shimek, J. S., & Corbitt-Shindler, D. (2004). Adolescent girls' alcohol use as a risk factor for relationship violence. *Journal of Research on Adolescence, 14,* 449–470.

Callahan, M. R., Tolman, R. M., & Saunders, D. G. (2003). Adolescent dating violence victimization and psychological well-being. *Journal of Adolescent Research, 18,* 664–681.

Carrion, V. G., Weems, C. F., Ray, R., & Reiss, A. L. (2002). Toward an empirical definition of pediatric PTSD: The phenomenology of PTSD symptoms in youth. *Journal of the American Academy of Child and Adolescent Psychiatry. 41,* 166–173.

Childhelp. (2010). Retrieved on December 2, 2010, from http://www.childhelp.org/pages/statistics.

Coid, J., Petruckevitch, A., Chung, W., Richardson, J., Moorey, S., & Feder, G. (2003). Abusive experiences and psychiatric morbidity in women primary care attenders. *British Journal of Psychiatry, 183,* 332–339.

Cuffe, S. P., Addy, C. L., Garrison C. Z., Waller, J. L., Jackson, K. L., McKeown, R. E., & Chilappagari, S. (1998). Prevalence of PTSD in a community sample of older adolescents. *Journal of the American Academy of Child and Adolescent Psychiatry, 37,* 147–154.

Denson, T. F., Marshall, G. N., Schell, T. L., & Jaycox, L. H. (2007). Predictors of posttraumatic distress one year after exposure to community violence: The importance of acute symptom severity. *Journal of Consulting and Clinical Psychology, 75,* 683–692.

Farrington, D. P., & Ttofi, M. M. (2009). *School-based programs to reduce bullying and victimization.* Campbell Systematic Reviews. Oslo: Campbell Corporation.

Foshee, V. A., Bauman, K. E., Arriaga, X. B., Helms, R. W., Koch, G. G., & Linder, G. F. (1998). An evaluation of safe dates, an adolescent dating violence prevention program. *American Journal of Public Health, 88,* 45–50.

Foshee, V. A., Bauman, K. E., Ennett, S. T., Linder, G. F., Benefield, T., & Suchindran, C. (2004). Assessing the long-term effects of the safe dates program and a booster in preventing and reducing adolescent dating violence victimization and perpetration. *American Journal of Public Health, 94,* 619–624.

Foshee, V. A., Bauman, K. E., Ennett, S. T., Suchindran, C., Benefield, T., & Linder, G. F. (2005). Assessing the effects of the dating violence prevention program "safe dates" using random coefficient regression modeling. *Prevention Science, 6,* 245–258.

Foshee, V. A., Linder, G. F., Bauman, K. E., Langwick, S. A., Arriaga, X. B., Heath, J. L., McMahon, P. M., & Bangdiwala, S. (1996). The safe dates project: Theoretical basis, evaluation design, and selected baseline findings. *American Journal of Preventive Medicine, 12,* 39–47.

Foster, H., Hagan, J., & Brooks-Gunn, J. (2004). Age, puberty, exposure to intimate partner violence in adolescence. In J. Devine, J. Gilligan, K. Miczek, R. Shaikh, & D. Pfaff (Eds.), *Youth violence: Scientific approaches to prevention* (pp. 151–156). New York: New York Academy of Sciences.

Frieze, I. H. (2005). *Hurting the one you love: Violence in relationships.* Belmont, CA: Wadsworth/Thomson Learning.

Graves, K., Sechrist, S., White, J. W., & Paradise, M. J. (2005). Intimate partner violence perpetrated by college women within the context of a history of victimization. *Psychology of Women Quarterly, 29,* 278–289.

Griffin, M. P., & Kossn, M. P. (2002). Clinical screening and intervention in cases of partner violence. *Online Journal of Issues in Nursing, 7,* 1–11.

Guterman, N. B., Cameron, M., & Staller, K. (2000). Definitional and measurement issues in the study of community violence among children and youth. *Journal of Community Psychology, 28,* 571–587.

Hanson, R. F. (2002). Adolescent dating violence: Prevalence and psychological outcomes. *Child Abuse and Neglect, 26,* 449–453.

Hickman, L. J., Joycox, L. H., & Arnoff, J. (2004). Dating violence among adolescents: Prevalence, gender distribution, and prevention program effectiveness. *Trauma, Violence, and Abuse, 5,* 123–142.

Hill, H. M., & Jones, L. P. (1997). Children's and parents' perceptions of children's exposure to violence in urban neighborhoods. *Journal of the National Medical Association, 89,* 270–276.

Houskamp, B. M., Scott, S. T., Neumann, D. A., & McDonald, L. (2010). Assessing and treating battered women: An integrated model for helping victims of severe violence. In M. Paludi & F. A. Denmark (Eds.), *Victims of sexual assault and abuse: Resources and responses for individuals and families: Vol. 2. Resources for individuals and families: Criminal justice, community, therapeutic, educational and advocacy responses* (pp. 291–318). Westport, CT: Praeger.

Hunt, C. (2007). The effect of an education program on attitudes and beliefs about bullying and bullying behaviour in junior secondary school students. *Child and Adolescent Mental Health, 12,* 21–26.

Hymel, S., Schonert-Reichl, K. A., & Miller, L. D. (2006). Reading, 'riting, 'rithmetic and relationships: Considering the social side of education. *Exceptionality Education Canada, 16,* 149–192.

Jackson, S. M., Cram, F., & Seymour, F. W. (2000). Violence and sexual coercion in high school students' dating relationships. *Journal of Family Violence, 15,* 23–36.

Kaestle, C. E., & Halpern, C. T. (2005). Sexual intercourse precedes partner violence in adolescent romantic relationships. *Journal of Adolescent Health, 36,* 386–392.

McWhirter, P., & McWhirter, J. J. (2010). Community and school violence and risk reduction: Empirically supported prevention. *Group Dynamics: Theory, Research and Practice, 14,* 242–256.

Millon, T. (1993). The Millon Adolescent Personality Inventory and the Millon Adolescent Clinical Inventory. *Journal of Counseling and Development, 71,* 570–593.

Moor, A. (2007). When recounting the traumatic memories is not enough: Treating persistent self-devaluation associated with rape and victim-blaming rape myths. *Women and Therapy, 30,* 19–33.

Morey, L. C. (2008). *Personality Assessment Inventory—Adolescent (PAI-A).* Lutz, FL: Psychological Assessment Resources.

National Center for Victims of Crime (2010). *Teen Victims.* Retrieved on December 2, 2010, from http://www.ncvc.org/ncvc/main.aspx?dbName=DocumentViewer&DocumentID=38721.

Orpinas, P., & Horne, A. M. (2006). School social competence development and bullying prevention model: The school. In P. Orpinas & A. M. Horne (Eds.), *Bullying prevention: Creating a positive school climate and developing social competence* (pp. 79–105). Washington, DC: American Psychological Association.

Pepler, D., Jiang, D., & Craig, W. (2006, July). *Who benefits from bullying prevention programs: A mixed model analysis.* Paper presented at the Biennial Meeting of the International Society for the Study of Behavioural Development. Melbourne, Australia.

Saltzman, W. R., Pynoos, R. S., Layne, C. M., Steinberg, A. M., & Aisenberg, E. (2001). Trauma and grief-focused intervention for adolescents exposed to community violence: Results of a school-based screening and group treatment protocol. *Group Dynamics, Therapy, Research, and Practice, 5,* 291–303.

Seiger, K., Rojas-Vilches, A., McKinney, C., & Renk, K. (2004). The effects and treatment of community violence in children and adolescents: What should be done? *Trauma, Violence, and Abuse, 5,* 243–259.

Silverman, J. G., Raj, A., Mucci, L. A., & Hathaway, J. E. (2001). Dating violence against adolescent girls and associated substance use, unhealthy weight control, sexual risk behavior, pregnancy, and suicidality. *Journal of the American Medical Association, 286,* 572–579.

Silverman, W. K. (2010). *Child anxiety: Signs and symptoms of problematic reactions.* Retrieved on December 2, 2010, from http://www.teachsafeschools.org.

Smith, D. (2008). Promoting a positive school climate: Restorative practices for the classroom. In D. Pepler & W. Craig (Eds.), *Understanding and addressing bullying: An international perspective* (PREVNet Series Vol. 1, pp. 132–143). Bloomington, IN: Authorhouse.

Smith, J. D., Ryan, W., & Cousins, J. B. (2007) Antibullying programs: A survey of evaluation activities in public schools. *Studies in Educational Evaluation, 33,* 120–134.

Smokowski, P. R., & Kopasz, K. H. (2005). Bullying in school: An overview of types, effects, family characteristics, and intervention strategies. *Children and Schools, 27,* 101–110.

Steiner, H., Carrion, V., Plattner, B., Koopman, C. (2003). Dissociative symptoms in posttraumatic stress disorder: Diagnosis and treatment. *Child and Adolescent Psychiatric Clinics of North America, 12,* 231–249.

Stewart, A. J., Steiman, M., Cauce, A. M., Cochran, B. N., WhiteBeck, L. B., & Hoyt, D. R. (2004). Victimization and posttraumatic stress disorder among homeless adolescents. *Journal of the American Academy of Child and Adolescent Psychiatry, 43,* 325–331.

Stinchcomb, J. B., Bazemore, G., & Rienstenberg, N. (2006). Beyond zero tolerance: Restoring justice in secondary schools. *Youth Violence and Juvenile Justice, 4,* 123–147.

Substance Abuse and Mental Health Services Administration, U.S. Department of Health and Human Services. (2009a). *Psychosocial problems and bullying.* Retrieved on December 12, 2010, from http://www.prevnet.ca/Downloads/tabid/192/language/en-US/Default.aspx.

Substance Abuse and Mental Health Services Administration, U.S. Department of Health and Human Services. (2009b). *Bullying: Definitions.* Retrieved on December 2, 2010, from http://www.prevnet.ca/Downloads/tabid/192/language/en-US/Default.aspx.

Swan, S. C., & Snow, D. L. (2006). The development of a theory of women's use of violence in intimate relationships. *Violence Against Women, 12,* 1026–1045.

Troup-Leasure, K., & Snyder, H. N. (2005, August). Statutory rape known to law enforcement. *Juvenile Justice Bulletin.* Retrieved on October 13, 2010, from the National Criminal Justice Reference Service, http://www.ncjrs.gov/pdffiles1/ojjdp/208803.pdf.

Tutty, L., Bradshaw, C., Thurston, W. E., Barlow, A., Marshall, P., Tunstall, L., et al. (2005). *School-based violence prevention programs: A resource manual to prevent violence against girls and young women.* [Revision]. Calgary, Alberta, Canada: RESOLVE.

U.S. Department of Health and Human Services, Administration on Children, Youth, and Families. (2007). *Child maltreatment 2005.* Washington, DC: U.S. Government Printing Office.

Vickerman, K. A., & Margolin, G. (2009). Rape treatment outcome research: Empirical findings and state of the literature. *Clinical Psychology Review, 29,* 431–448.

Vreeman, R. C., & Carroll, A. E. (2007). A systematic review of school based interventions. *Archives of Pediatric Adolescent Medicine, 161,* 78–88.

White, J. W. (2009). A gendered approach to adolescent dating violence: Conceptual and methodological issues. *Psychology of Women Quarterly, 33,* 1–15.

White, J. W., & Smith, P. H. (2004). Sexual assault perpetration and reperpetration: From adolescence to young adulthood. *Criminal Justice and Behavior, 31,* 182–202.

Williams, S. L., & Frieze, I. H. (2005). Patterns of violent relationships, psychological distress, and marital satisfaction in a national sample of men and women. *Sex Roles, 52,* 771–784.

Wilson, S. J., & Lipsey, M. W. (2005). *The effectiveness of school-based violence prevention programs for reducing disruptive and aggressive behavior.* Retrieved on December 2, 2010, from http://www.ncjrs.gov/pdffiles1/nij/grants/211376.pdf.

Wolak, J., Finkelhor, D., Mitchell, K. J., & Ybarra, M. L. (2010). Online predators and their victims: Myths, realities, and implications for prevention and treatment. *Psychology of Violence, 1,* 13–35.

Wolfe, D. A., Scott, K. S., & Crooks, C. (2005). Abuse and violence in adolescent girls' dating relationships. In D. J. Bell, S. L. Foster, & E. J. Mash (Eds.), *Handbook of behavioral and emotional problems in girls* (pp. 381–414). New York: Kluwer Academic/Plenum.

Wolitzky-Taylor, K., Ruggiero, K. J., Danielson, C. K., Resnick, H. S., Hanson, R. F., Smith, D. W., et al. (2008). Prevalence and correlates of dating violence in a national sample of adolescents. *Journal of the Academy of Child and Adolescent Psychiatry, 47,* 755–762.

CHAPTER THREE

Effects of Playing Violent Video Games

Craig A. Anderson and Sara Prot

Introduction

Video games are extremely popular among children, teens, and adults. A wide spectrum of games is available on consoles (such as the Wii, XBox, and PlayStation), handheld players (such as Nintendo DS or an iPod), and cell phones. A recent study of media use among American youths done on a sample of more than 2,000 children and teens showed that there has been a significant increase in video gaming over the past five years (Rideout, Foehr, & Roberts, 2010). On any given day, 60% of young people play video games, spending an average of about 1 hour at the controller. Video game playing peaks among 11- to 14-year-olds, who average 1.5 hours per day. Boys continue to play more than girls (1 hour 37 minutes compared to 49 minutes).

Ten years ago, over 85% of games contained some violence, and about half included serious violent actions (Children Now, 2001). Violence in video games is often portrayed as justified, fun, and without negative consequences (Funk, Baldacci, Pasold, & Baumgardner, 2004). A majority of children prefer playing violent games over nonviolent ones (Funk et al., 2004).

It is a worrying fact that only 30% of children and teens report that their parents have rules about which video games they can play and how much time they can spend playing (Rideout et al., 2010). Research shows that parents often aren't familiar with the content of their children's favorite video games and underestimate their children's exposure to violence while playing (Funk, Hagan, & Schimming, 1999).

In response to congressional pressure, the Entertainment Software Rating Board (ESRB) was founded in 1994 by the game industry in order to aid consumers in determining a game's content and suitability for children and adolescents. The ESRB rates video games and displays age-based rating symbols and content descriptors on the game box. The rating system should, in theory, aid parents in controlling the kind of video game content to which their children are exposed. However, despite some improvements over the years, the existing rating system is flawed in multiple ways (Gentile, 2008). For example, almost 50% of T-rated games ("Teen," appropriate for persons 13 years or older) include potentially objectionable content that was not described on the box (Haninger & Thompson, 2004). Many parents don't understand the ratings. Only 19% of adolescents report that their parents have ever used the ratings to keep them from getting a game (Gentile, Lynch, Linder, & Walsh, 2004). Most adolescents play games rated as inappropriate for their age.

Furthermore, a recent analysis of ESRB ratings found that 31% of E games (Everyone), 91% of E10+ games (Everyone 10 and older), 91% of T games (Teens ages 13 and over), and 89% of M games (Mature, ages 17 and older) contained violence (Gentile, 2008). Because such a large number of children, teens, and adults play video games and because such a large proportion of games include violent content, it is important to understand the short-term and long-term effects that violent video games have on players.

This chapter describes a theoretical framework for understanding effects of playing violent video games, gives a short explanation of research designs and scientific causality, and then describes the current knowledge of violent video game effects. Effects of violent video games on aggression and related variables are described in detail. Effects of violent video games on prosocial behavior are briefly described, as are effects of video games on attention and cognitive control, school performance, and video game addiction.

Theoretical Frameworks

Several early and recent social cognitive models can provide useful contexts for understanding effects of exposure to violent media. Bandura's Social Learning Theory and Social Cognitive Theory (Bandura, 1973, 1983) proposes that children can learn behavioral responses by observing behaviors of others and by observing the outcomes of those behaviors. Classical experiments by Bandura and his colleagues using the Bobo doll paradigm showed that children can learn aggressive behavior through observation of both actual and filmed aggression (Bandura, Ross, & Ross, 1961, 1963a). Children are more likely to imitate a witnessed behavior if that behavior is rewarded and less likely to imitate the behavior if it is punished (e.g., Bandura, 1965; Bandura, Ross, & Ross, 1963b).

Huesmann (1986, 1998) proposed that people's behavior is guided by the acquisition, internalization, and application of behavioral scripts. Scripts are sets of highly associated concepts that guide perception of social events and enactment of social behavior. Children who are exposed to a lot of media violence are more likely to acquire behavioral scripts that contain aggression and violence. An aggressive script can become chronically accessible through repeated rehearsal. Numerous aspects of script theory have been empirically confirmed, both within the aggression domain as well as in other domains. For example, playing a violent video game increases the amount of aggressive content in a story completion task (Bushman & Anderson, 2002).

Two recent relevant models are the General Aggression Model (GAM; e.g., Anderson & Bushman, 2002; Anderson & Carnagey, 2004; Anderson & Huesmann, 2003; Barlett & Anderson, in press) and the General Learning Model (GLM) (Buckley & Anderson, 2006; Gentile et al., 2009; Swing & Anderson, 2008). GAM integrates social learning theory, script theory, and a host of other models, including cognitive-neoassociation theory (Berkowitz, 1984), cultivation theory (Comstock & Scharrer, 2007), desensitization theory (Carnagey, Anderson, & Bushman, 2007), and social information processing theory (Crick & Dodge, 1994). GLM extends the basic processes underlying GAM to other domains of social behavior.

An overview of the General Aggression Model is shown in Figure 3.1. GAM is a biosocial-developmental model that describes the personal and situational factors and processes that influence an individual's aggressive behavior in a social episode. It also provides a way to understand how biological factors interact with environmental factors to yield behavior in context (Raine, Brennen, Farrington, & Mednick, 1997).

GAM describes two sets of processes that influence the probability that a person will respond aggressively in a particular social encounter: distal factors and proximate factors. Distal factors (displayed in the upper part of Figure 3.1) are developmental factors that have helped shape an individual's personality. Distal factors operate by increasing proximate factors that facilitate aggression or by decreasing proximate factors that

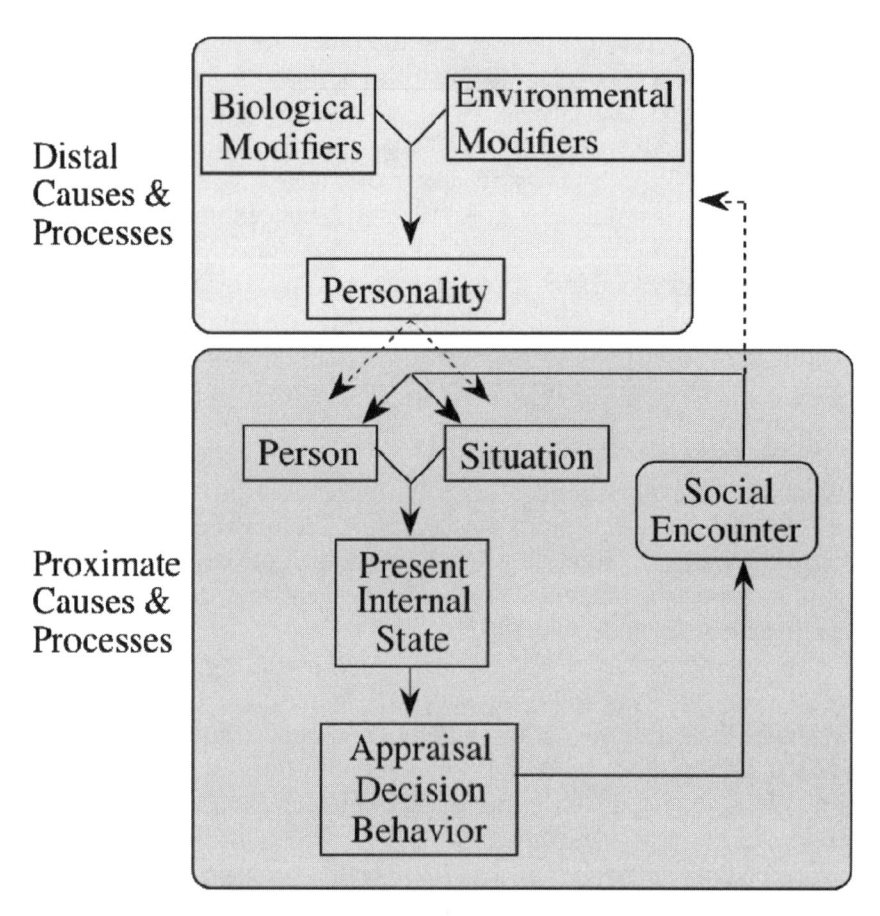

Figure 3.1 The General Aggression Model: Overall view.
From Anderson & Carnagey, 2004.

inhibit aggression. Distal factors that influence aggression include biological modifiers (e.g., low arousal levels, low serotonin, ADHD, hormonal imbalances; Anderson & Carnagey, 2004) and environmental modifiers (e.g., harsh or inconsistent parenting practices, cultural influences, poverty; Anderson & Carnagey, 2004).

Proximate factors (displayed in the lower part of Figure 3.1) are person and situation variables that are present and active in the current social episode. Situational factors that have been shown to influence aggression include exposure to media violence (Anderson et al., 2003), provocation (Bettencourt & Kernahan, 1997), heat (Anderson, 1989), and ostracism (Warburton, Williams, & Cairns, 2006). Person factors that influence aggression include trait aggression (Bushman, 1995), psychoticism (Markey & Scherer, 2009), trait hostility (Kirsh, Olczak, & Mounts, 2005), and anger (Berkowitz, 1984). Numerous person and situation factors influence the individual's present internal state—cognitions, affect, and arousal. These internal state variables influence one another and affect the probability of aggressive behavior.

The contents of one's present internal state influence appraisal and decision processes. Appraisals can be made automatically, resulting in an impulsive behavior. If the individual has the time and resources to reappraise the situation and if the outcome is important and unsatisfying, a thoughtful behavior is likely to occur. Both impulsive and thoughtful behaviors can be aggressive or nonaggressive.

The ensuing behavior influences the ongoing social encounter. In return, the results of the social encounter influence the situational input factor. Thus, GAM includes a feedback loop that can lead to a violence escalation cycle (Barlett & Anderson, in press; Anderson, Buckley, & Carnagey, 2008).

The long-term effects of any repeated episodic encounter (such as bullying, rejection), including the repeated play of violent video games, are illustrated in Figure 3.2. Long-term consumers of violent media can become more aggressive in outlook and can develop hostile perceptual biases, attitudes, beliefs, and behavior. Development, automatization, and reinforcement of aggression-related knowledge structures can lead to long-term personality changes (Carnagey & Anderson, 2003; Bartholow, Sestir, & Davis, 2005).

It is important to keep in mind that the learning processes described by GAM are general processes that cognitive, developmental, and social psychologists have studied for decades. Therefore, they can be applied not only to aggression but also to other kinds of behavior—for example, learning prosocial behavior (Gentile et al., 2009). The General Learning Model (GLM; Barlett & Anderson, in press; Buckley & Anderson, 2006; Gentile et al., 2009; Swing & Anderson, 2008) is an extension of GAM that illustrates how long-term attitudes and knowledge structures are formed with continued exposure to any type of repeated social encounter (including media). Short-term processes described by GLM are similar to those in GAM—situational and personality factors influence one's internal state (cognitions, affect, and arousal). Internal state variables influence appraisal and decision processes that lead to different types of behavior. In turn, one's behavior influences the situational input factor. GLM also predicts long-term changes that result from repeated learning. The main difference between GAM and GLM is that the latter

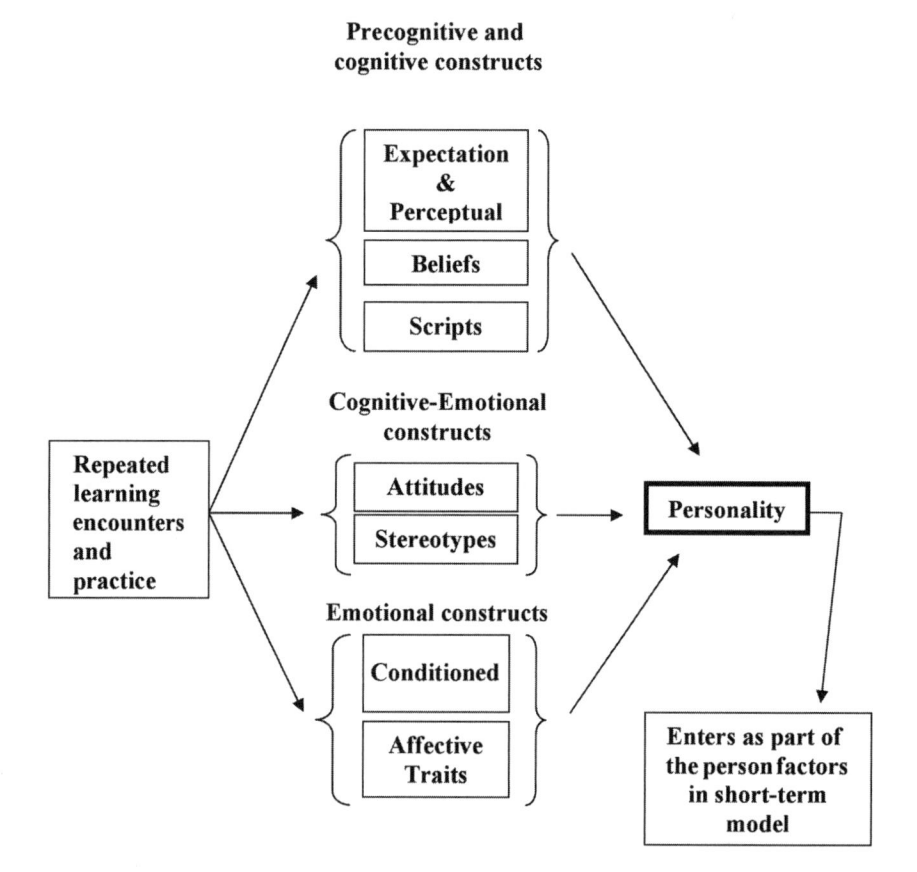

Figure 3.2 The General Learning Model. Extension of GAM to nonviolent contexts: Long-term processes.

From Barlett & Anderson, in press.

explicitly states that the same learning processes apply to all types of social behavior. In addition, the most recent version of GLM categorizes the outcome of long-term effects in a somewhat different way, as illustrated in Figure 3.2.

As applied to media effects, GLM (Barlett & Anderson, in press) notes that repeated exposure to any type of media influences personality through the development of precognitive and cognitive constructs (perceptual schemata, beliefs, and behavioral scripts), cognitive-emotional constructs (attitudes and stereotypes), and emotional constructs (conditioned emotions and affective traits). Considerable support for GLM comes from research exploring prosocial media influences on prosocial behavior (e.g., Gentile et al., 2009; Greitemeyer, 2009; Greitemeyer & Osswald, 2009, 2010).

Types of Studies in Video Game Research

Empirical researchers generally use three basic types of studies: experimental studies, cross-sectional correlational studies, and longitudinal studies (Anderson & Bushman, 2001; Swing & Anderson, 2010). Each study type has advantages and drawbacks and each is appropriate for certain kinds of research problems. Results obtained from different kinds of studies complement each other and allow researchers to get a complete picture of media violence effects.

In experimental studies, researchers manipulate exposure to media violence and view the short-term results of brief exposure. Participants are randomly assigned to different conditions (e.g., playing a violent or nonviolent video game). With all other factors controlled, a difference between two groups in, for example, aggression establishes a causal link between violent media and subsequent aggression. A potential disadvantage of experimental research is that certain types of more extreme physical aggression cannot ethically be used in such studies. For example, one cannot randomly assign children to play a violent or nonviolent video game and then give each of them a gun to see which group more frequently attempts to shoot other people. The best field experiments use measures of real physical aggression in natural settings, such as hitting, pushing, and fighting on the playground. The best laboratory experiments use well-validated paradigms to test important hypotheses. In general, experimental research in the aggression domain has shown high generalizability (Anderson & Bushman, 1997).

Cross-sectional correlational studies test for positive or negative relationships among theoretically relevant variables (e.g., a relationship between violent video game exposure and aggressive affect). The strengths of good correlational studies include the ability to measure more extreme forms of aggression, to test specific alternative explanations, and to suggest new hypotheses about causal relationship. However, the main disadvantage is that the results of a single correlational study (or of several) cannot establish cause and effect because the variables are measured at the same single point in time. Nonetheless, such studies are relevant to testing causal hypotheses because they provide an opportunity for falsification of the causal hypothesis, can test alternative hypotheses (and thus rule them out or support them), and allow the research to control for extraneous variables by statistical procedures.

In a longitudinal study researchers collect data on the same group of people at two or more points in time. This allows stronger causal statements than cross-sectional correlation studies because of the temporal relations among the variables. For example, one can assess media habits and aggressive behavior tendencies both early and late in a school year and then test whether amount of media violence exposure at Time 1 predicts aggressive behavior at Time 2 after statistically controlling for Time 1 behavior tendencies. Longitudinal studies have allowed researchers to document the real-life consequences of repeated exposure to large amounts of media violence. The main disadvantages of longitudinal studies are that they are time-consuming and expensive.

Each research design has its place in the study of media violence, and strong causal conclusions depend on consistent results across each of these designs (Abelson, 1995; Swing & Anderson, 2010). Meta-analytic procedures can be used to combine results of several studies and draw conclusions from integrated data. The most comprehensive meta-analysis of all three types of violent video game studies yielded consistent evidence that violent video game play causes an increase in the likelihood of physical aggression and a decrease of prosocial behavior (Anderson et al., 2010).

Probabilistic Causality and the Risk Factor Approach

To understand how violent video games influence players, it is important to understand the concept of probabilistic causality. Modern scientific causality is probabilistic, rather than "necessary and sufficient." That is, a variable X causes an increase in the likelihood of an outcome Y (Anderson, 2004). For example, saying that "smoking causes lung cancer" means that repeated smoking increases the likelihood that one will contract lung cancer. It does not mean that all smokers get lung cancer (a violation of sufficient causality). Also, in some cases nonsmokers get lung cancer (a violation of necessary causality). Similarly, saying that "violent video games cause aggression" does not mean that any person who plays violent video games will become aggressive or that any aggressive act is a product of violent video game play. It means that exposure to violent video games causes an increase in the likelihood of aggression.

Probabilistic causality is a result of the fact that human behaviors (such as aggression or prosocial behavior) are multi-causal. They are influenced by a large number of interacting factors, and exposure to violent media is just one of those factors. No one causal factor can explain more that a small proportion of the variance of that behavior. This same modern view of causality applies in numerous other scientific domains as well, medical science being an obvious example (heart disease, cancer).

A useful approach for understanding how multiple causes determine behavior is the risk and resilience approach (Gentile & Sesma, 2003). This approach focuses on life experiences (biological, environmental, social) that may put people at risk for future maladaptation (risk factors) and those factors that serve to protect from this risk exposure (protective factors). Within this approach, violent media are viewed as a risk factor for aggression. Other risk factors for aggression include genetic predispositions (Hudziak et al., 2003), poor parenting practices (Patterson, 1995), poverty (Ewart & Suchday, 2002), and having been bullied (Osofsky & Osofsky, 2001), among many others. Protective factors that decrease the risk of aggression include being female (Archer, 2004), having a positive family environment (Estévez López, Pérez, Ochoa, & Ruiz, 2008), and high empathy (Björkqvist, Österman, & Kaukiainen, 2000), among others.

Effects of risk and protective factors are cumulative—each additional risk factor increases the likelihood of aggression and each protective factor decreases it. No single factor alone is sufficient to elicit more extreme forms of aggression, but each is relevant and steps could be taken to minimize them (Anderson, Gentile, & Dill, in press). One nonobvious implication of this approach is that from a practical standpoint, we, as parents and as members of society, cannot allow exposure to violent video games (or any other single risk factor) to be used as a completely exonerating excuse for violence. Several key aggression-inhibiting factors rely on the individual's belief that he or she is responsible for his or her own behavior and will be held responsible by others.

Violent Video Game Effects

Short- and Long-Term Effects on Aggression and Related Variables

Effects of violent video games on aggression are a topic that has received a lot of attention and has been much discussed, both by researchers and by the general public. A large body of research papers has been published on the subject, as well as several review papers (Barlett, Anderson, & Swing, 2009; Bensley & Van Eenwyk, 2001; Dill & Dill, 1998; Emes, 1997; Griffiths, 1999) and meta-analyses (Anderson, 2004; Anderson & Bushman, 2001; Anderson, et al., 2004; Sherry, 2001).

The most recent and most comprehensive meta-analysis in this domain (Anderson et al., 2010) combined a total of 136 research papers with 381 effect size estimates involving over 130,000 participants. This is a much larger sample than in previous meta-analyses, both because of the rapid expansion of violent video game research in the past few years and because of the inclusion of previously unavailable studies from Japan.

Six outcome variables were included in the meta-analysis: aggressive behavior, aggressive cognition, aggressive affect, physiological arousal, desensitization/low empathy, and prosocial (helping) behavior. Results reported in this chapter are based on the sample of studies whose methodology met all best practices criteria (the "Best Raw" sample in Anderson et al., 2010). The "Best Raw" sample includes 221 effect sizes and a total of 61,000 participants. Both the best practices sample and the full sample yielded the same results—violent video games had significant affects on all six outcome variables, proving that video game violence is indeed a risk factor for increased aggression and decreased prosocial behavior. The main findings of the meta-analyses are shown in Figure 3.3. Results according to type of research design are displayed in Table 3.1.

Are the effect sizes large enough to be considered important? Because aggressive behavior is determined by a large number of factors (e.g., genetic predispositions, parental practices, cultural influences, personality, arousal

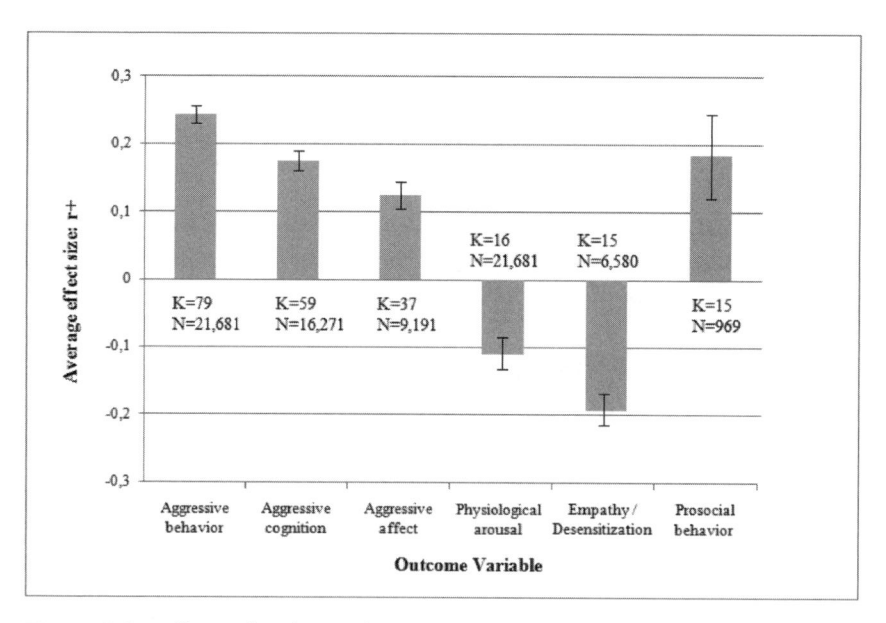

Figure 3.3 Effects of violent video games on aggressive behavior, aggressive cognition, aggressive affect, physiological arousal, empathy/desensitization, and prosocial behavior (results from the "Best Raw" sample, Anderson et al., 2010). K = number of effects. N = total sample size. Vertical capped bars are the upper and lower 95% confidence intervals.

Table 3.1 Average effect size of violent video game play.

Design	Total N	K	Ave. Effect (r+)	Z
Aggressive Behavior				
Experimental	2,513	27	.210	10.512**
Longitudinal	4,526	12	.203	13.787**
Cross-Sectional	14,642	40	.262	32.291**
Aggressive Cognition				
Experimental	2,887	24	.217	11.695**
Longitudinal	3,408	8	.115	6.728**
Cross-Correlational	9,976	27	.183	18.445**
Aggressive Affect				
Experimental	1,454	21	.294	11.289**
Longitudinal	2,602	5	.075	3.836**
Cross-Correlational	5,135	11	.101	7.227**
Physiological Arousal				
Experimental	633	4	−.182	−4.599**
Longitudinal	2,778	5	−.114	−6.022**
Cross-Correlational	3,495	7	−.093	−5.506**
Desensitization and Empathy				
Experimental	249	1	−.138	−2.175*
Longitudinal	2,421	4	−.184	−9.147**
Cross-Correlational	3,910	10	−.203	−12.845**

* $p < .05$ ** $p < .001$
Total N is the total number of participants in all of the summarized studies. K is the number of different studies. The average effect (r+) is the weighted average effect size, expressed as an r-value. Z is the Z-test of whether the effect is significantly different from zero.
Source: Results from the "Best Raw" data (Anderson et al., 2010).

levels, etc.; Anderson & Huesmann, 2003), no single factor can explain more than a small proportion of the individual differences in aggression. However, even small effect sizes can have important practical consequences. If large portions of the population are exposed to a risk factor and if effects accumulate across time, the risk factor can significantly influence the individual and society (Anderson et al., 2010). In fact, the obtained effect size of violent video games on aggression compares favorably to such risk factors as substance abuse, abusive parents, and poverty (U.S. Department of Health and Human Services, 2001).

Aggressive behavior. The notion that playing violent video games causes aggressive behavior has been supported by substantial research evidence. The consistency of the results from experimental, cross-correlational, and longitudinal studies demonstrate that violent video game play is a causal risk factor for physical aggression. This effect occurs in short-term and long-term contexts, across gender and culture, and to children and adolescents.

For example, in an experimental study by Konijn, Bijvank, and Bushman (2007), adolescent boys played a violent or a nonviolent video game. Next, the boys competed with a supposed partner, and the winner could blast the loser with loud noise through headphones (the aggression measure). The boys who had played a violent video game were more prone to behave aggressively, and especially so if they had identified with the violent characters in game. Identification with violent characters in the virtual world influenced the adolescents to behave more aggressively against others in the real world.

In a correlational study, adolescents exposed to greater amounts of video game violence were more likely to be involved in physical fights than those with lesser exposure (Gentile et al., 2004). The link between exposure to video game violence and physical aggression remained significant even when gender and trait hostility were statistically controlled.

A two-year-long longitudinal study tracked children's exposure to violent media and their violent and delinquent behavior between the ages of 12 and 14 years (Hopf, Huber, & Weib, 2008). Exposure to violent video games at the age of 12 was a significant predictor of violence ($b = .18$) and delinquency ($b = .29$) at the age of 14, even after controlling for earlier violence and delinquency and several other important variables. That is, violent video game play led to a relative increase in violent and deliquent behavior over time.

Perhaps the most persuasive evidence that video game violence is a significant risk factor for physical aggression is provided by the new meta-analysis cited earlier and displayed in Figure 3.3 and Table 3.1. This effect was significant regardless of the type of research design. The overall average effect size for best practices studies was $r+ = .244$, $p < .01$. The significant effect found in longitudinal studies ($r+ = .203$, $p < .01$) shows that playing violent video games can increase aggression over time. The relationship between violent video game play and aggressive behavior was moderated neither by sex nor by culture. It seems that effects of violent video games on aggression are robust, affecting both men and women and individuals from Western and Eastern cultures. A marginally significant age effect was found, suggesting that children might be more susceptible than adults. However, more research is needed to clarify this question (Anderson et al., 2010).

Aggressive cognition. Exposure to violent video games can have a number of cognitive consequences that can, in turn, lead to aggressive behavior. GAM predicts that violent video game exposure will have both short-term and long-term effects on cognition. In the short term, media violence can prime aggressive thoughts, making them more accessible (Anderson & Huesmann, 2003). Repeated exposure to virtual violence activates and strengthens aggression-related knowledge structures, such as perceptual and expectation schemas and behavioral scripts. It also reinforces normative beliefs that aggression is an appropriate response in a particular situation (Bushman & Huesmann, 2006; Carnagey & Anderson, 2003). These predictions have been confirmed by experimental, cross-sectional correlational, and longitudinal research.

An experimental study by Kirsh (1998) showed that playing violent video games can lead to the development of a hostile attribution bias. In this experiment, children who had played a violent video game were more prone to attribute malevolent intent to the wrongdoer in an ambiguous provocation story. The tendency to interpret ambiguous behaviors of others as malevolent can increase the likelihood that children will respond to real-life ambiguous provocation situations with aggression. Similar findings have been reported in other experimental studies (e.g., Bushman & Anderson, 2002).

A correlational study by Funk and colleagues (2004) explored the possibility that media presentations of justified violence may change the belief that violent behavior is wrong, encouraging the development of proviolence attitudes. Indeed, exposure to video game violence was positively associated with proviolent attitudes ($r = .30, p < .01$) and with diminished empathy ($r = -.24, p < .01$). Similar findings have occurred in numerous studies (e.g., Anderson et al., 2004).

A longitudinal study by Möller and Krahé (2009) tracked adolescents' violent video game usage, endorsement of aggressive norms, hostile attribution bias, and aggression over a period of 30 months. Results show that exposure to violent video games at the first time of measurement influenced physical aggression 30 months later via an increase of aggressive norms and hostile attribution bias. Similar findings have been reported in the other major longitudinal studies (e.g., Anderson, Gentile, & Buckley, 2007).

The meta-analysis by Anderson and colleagues (2010) has shown that exposure to violent video games is significantly related to higher levels of aggressive cognition, regardless of research design. The average effect size was $r+ = .175$, $p < .01$. Perhaps the most important finding is the significant longitudinal effect of violent video games on aggressive cognition. Together with the findings of experimental and cross-sectional studies, the data provide strong evidence that violent video game play is a significant causal risk factor for both short-term and long-term increases in aggressive thinking (Anderson et al., 2010). Furthermore, several of the longitudinal studies show that these changes in aggressive thinking at least partially mediate the long-term effects of violent video games on physical aggression.

Aggressive affect. Violent media increase aggression, at least in part, by producing feelings of anger and hostility (Swing & Anderson, 2010). Short-term effects of violent video game play on mood dissipate quickly (Barlett, Branch, Rodeheffer, & Harris, 2009), but repeated exposure to violent media can lead to the development of a hostile personality (e.g., Bartholow, Sestir, & Davis, 2005; Bushman & Huesmann, 2006).

An experimental study by Markey and Scherer (2009) on a sample of late adolescents and young adults showed that playing a violent video game caused the participants to feel more hostile. The relationship between exposure to video game violence and ensuing hostility was moderated by trait psychoticism—the negative effect of violent video games on mood was greater for individuals with high psychoticism scores. This finding is consistent with other research showing that persons with high trait aggression (Bushman, 1995) and high trait hostility (Kirsh, Olczak, & Mounts, 2005) might be more susceptible to some effects of violent media. Other studies, however, have found that brief exposure to violent video games increases the hostile affect of game players regardless of aggressive personality (e.g., Anderson & Carnagey, 2009, Experiment 2).

In a cross-sectional study, Bartholow, Sestir & Davis (2005) found that hostility mediated the relationship between habitual violent video game exposure and physical aggression ($z = 2.26$, $p < .05$). Numerous correlational studies have found positive correlations between video game violence and aggressive affect (e.g., Gentile et al., 2004). These findings suggest that increased hostility provides one pathway through which exposure to video game violence influences aggression.

The abovementioned two-year-long longitudinal study by Hopf, Huber, and Weib (2008) showed that both media-stimulated and real experiences of aggressive emotions associated with the motive for revenge are core risk factors for later violent behavior and delinquency. The authors conclude that continued exposure to real and virtual violence can lead to long-term emotional consequences. The Anderson and colleagues (2010) meta-analysis found that the average effect size for best practices studies of the violent video game effect on aggressive affect was $r+ = .124, p < .01$. These effects were statistically significant in experimental, cross-correlational, and longitudinal studies.

Physiological arousal. Playing video games, both violent and nonviolent ones, tends to produce physiological arousal (Swing, Gentile, & Anderson, 2009). Arousal can be measured in experimental studies using indicators such as heart rate, blood pressure, or skin conductance. The average effect size of violent video games on physiological arousal found in the meta-analysis by Anderson and his colleagues (2010) was $r+ = .184, p < .01$.

Aggression can be influenced by arousal in several ways. Heightened arousal strengthens the dominant action tendency, including aggressive tendencies. If a person is provoked to aggress while highly aroused, the result is a higher likelihood of aggression (Geen & O'Neal, 1969). According to excitation transfer theory, arousal can increase aggression if arousal from one source (e.g., exercise) is mislabeled as anger resulting from provocation (Zillmann, 1983). For example, arousal from viewing an erotic film can increase provoked aggression (Zillmann, 1971).

Research suggests that several features of video games can influence the amount of arousal they generate. Violent video games tend to produce more arousal that nonviolent ones (e.g., Fleming & Rickwood, 2001). Playing a realistic violent video game has been shown to stimulate more arousal and more aggressive thoughts than playing an unrealistic violent video game (Barlett & Rodeheffer, 2009). The presence of blood in a violent video game can lead to higher arousal, as well as more hostile feelings and cognitions (Ballard & Wiest, 1996; Farrar, Krcmar, & Nowak, 2006; Barlett, Harris, & Bruey, 2008).

How long do these effects last? A study by Barlett, Branch and colleagues (2009) shows that heightened arousal immediately after game play lasts between 4 and 9 minutes. Aggressive feelings and thoughts may last as few as 4 minutes. However, authors suggest that these short-term changes can start aggression-promoting processes that last much longer than 4 to 9 minutes.

Desensitization and empathy. Exposure to violent media can lead to desensitization—a reduction in emotion-related physiological reactivity to violence (Carnagey, Anderson, & Bushman, 2007). Although lessening anxiety can be a positive outcome in many contexts (e.g., treatment of phobias or PTSD), desensitization of children and other civilians to violent stimuli can have several harmful consequences. Anxiety associated with violence can serve to inhibit violent behaviors, so desensitization to violence could be expected to lead to disinhibition of aggression. This kind of emotional blunting may also lead to an underestimation of the seriousness of observed violence and reduce the likelihood of helping a victim (Carnagey & Anderson, 2003).

Empathy refers to the degree to which a person subjectively identifies and commiserates with a victim and feels emotional distress (Anderson et al., 2010). One of the predicted consequences of desensitization is a decrease in empathy for violence victims (Carnagey, et al., 2007). The fact that viewing violent films can lead to desensitization to violence and decreased empathy for victims has been shown by a body of empirical research (e.g., Dexter, Penrod, Linz, & Saunders, 1997; Mullin & Linz, 1995). The hypothesis that violent video games can have those same effects have also received empirical support from experiments, correlational studies, and longitudinal studies.

For example, in an experimental study (Carnagey et al., 2007) participants played a violent or a nonviolent game for 20 minutes and then watched a videotape containing scenes of real-life violence. Their physiological reactions while viewing violence were measured by monitoring their heart rate galvanic skin response (GSR). Participants who had played a violent video game had a lower heart rate and GSR, showing evidence of physiological desensitization to violence.

Evidence of chronic desensitization to violence through playing video games also exists. A study by Bartholow, Bushman, and Sestir (2005) shows that habitual violent game players have reduced amplitudes of the P300 component of the event-related brain potential while viewing violent images. P300 is associated with activation of the aversive motivational system. This reduced brain response while viewing violence predicted increased aggressive behavior in a later competitive task.

The previously mentioned study by Bartholow, Sestir & Davis (2005) showed that both short-term and long-term exposure to violent video games are associated with increased aggression. Mediators in the relationship between long-term exposure to violent video games and aggressive behavior were variables related to desensitization (decreased empathy, hostile perceptions, and hostile personality).

Although there are only a few high quality studies in this domain, meta-analytic results (Anderson et al., 2010) confirm that violent video game play is related to decreased empathy and desensitization. The average effect size for best practices studies was $r+ = -.194, p < .01$.

Helpful and Prosocial Behavior

Prosocial behavior can be defined as behavior involving helping or rewarding others, especially when this behavior brings no benefit to the helper (Barlett, Anderson, & Swing, 2009). The same learning processes that link violent video games to aggressive behavior could also be expected to suppress and interfere with prosocial behavior, at least in some contexts. In fact, several studies have documented reduced prosocial behavior in response to violent game play.

An experimental study by Bushman and Anderson (2009) showed that violent video game play can decrease helping a victim. Participants played a violent or nonviolent video game for 20 minutes. Afterward, while completing a lengthy questionnaire, they heard a loud fight outside the lab in which one person was injured. Participants who had previously played a violent game were less likely to notice the fight, perceived the fight as less serious, and took longer to help the injured victim. The authors suggested that people exposed to media violence may become "comfortably numb" to the pain and suffering of others and are consequently less helpful.

A correlational study by Gentile and colleagues (2009) assessed video game habits of a large sample of Singaporean children, along with several prosocial measures. Playing prosocial video games was shown to be positively related to helping, empathy, and cooperation. In contrast, violent video game play was negatively related to helping behavior.

A longitudinal study by Anderson, Gentile, & Buckley (2007) monitored children's violent media exposure, aggression, and prosocial behaviors two times during a school year. High exposure to video game violence at Time 1 significantly predicted a relative decrease in prosocial behavior (as rated by teachers and peers) at Time 2 (explaining 8% of the variance in prosocial behavior, $t = -5.14, p < .001$).

Results of the meta-analysis by Anderson and colleagues (2010) confirm that exposure to violent video games is significantly related to lower levels of prosocial behavior. The average effect size was $r+ = -.110$, $p < .01$. The effect was significant in experimental, cross-correlational, and longitudinal studies.

It is also important to note that prosocial and antisocial behaviors are not simply opposite sides of the same coin. People can be high in both aggressive and prosocial behaviors—for example, hostile toward enemies and helpful toward friends (Gentile et al., 2009). Prosocial and aggressive measures tend to be negatively correlated, but not strongly so.

Effects on Attention and Cognitive Control

Benefits to visuospatial attention. A number of correlational and experimental studies show that video game play can have beneficial effects on a wide array of visual and spatial skills (e.g., Castel, Pratt, & Drummond, 2005; Feng, Spence, & Pratt, 2007; Green & Bavelier, 2003, 2006).

Habitual video game players outperform nonplayers on several different visual tasks—for example visual enumeration, useful field of view, and target localization (Green & Bavelier, 2003, 2006). Nonplayers trained on action video games show improvements in such skills. For example, in an experiment by Feng, Spence, and Pratt (2007), participants substantially improved their spatial attention and mental rotation after only 10 hours of training with an action video game. Women benefited more than men, and so playing the action game reduced gender differences in spatial cognition.

In their review of video game effects on visual skills, Achtman, Green, and Bavelier (2008) conclude that action video games can be effectively used to train visual skills. Action video games offer a new way of rehabilitation for different patient groups (e.g., stroke patients with visual field deficits).

Interestingly, these beneficial effects on visuospacial processing have been found only for action games, not all video games in general (Green, Li, & Bavelier, 2010). Many action games include violent content, which shows that one video game can have both positive effects (improved visuospatial skills) and negative effects (increased aggression). However, both violent and nonviolent games have been associated to spatial-cognitive gains (e.g., Barlett, Branch, et al., 2009; De Lisi & Wolford, 2002). Therefore, players do not need to use a violent video game in order to achieve the spatial-cognitive benefits of video game exposure.

Attention deficits. The beneficial effects of video games on visuospatial skills have sometimes been misinterpreted as a claim that video games enhance attention in general. However, an emerging line of research suggests that video games may also have disruptive effects on attention and cognitive control.

Television viewing has been linked with greater subsequent attention problems in childhood (e.g., Landhuis, Poulton, Welch, & Hancox, 2007; Levine & Waite, 2000; Mistry, Minkovitz, Strobino, & Borzekowski, 2007). Researchers propose that, because most television programs involve high excitement and rapid changes of focus, exposure to television may harm children's abilities to sustain focus on less exciting tasks and shorten their attention spans (Christakis, Zimmerman, DiGiuseppe, & McCarty, 2004). Because many video games share these characteristics, it can be expected that they have the same type of negative effects on attention.

Several studies have found a higher prevalence of attention-related problems and/or ADHD/ADD diagnoses among habitual video game players (Bioulac, Arfi, & Bouvard, 2008; Gentile, 2009; Mistry et al., 2007). Swing, Gentile, Anderson, and Walsh (2010) conducted the first longitudinal study to explore the effects of violent video games on attention.

School-aged children were assessed over a 13-month period. More frequent game play and television viewing over this period of time each led to more teacher-reported attention problems. These results were significant even when effects of previous attention problems and gender were partialled out. Furthermore, the video game effect was stronger than the TV effect. This study provides the strongest evidence yet that the association between video game play and attention problems may be causal, not merely coincidental. Note that this study did not distinguish between violent and nonviolent media.

Swing and colleagues (2010) also reported a correlational study on a sample of late adolescents/early adults. The associations of exposure to screen media and attention problems found on this sample were similar to those found on the middle childhood sample, suggesting that adolescents are still vulnerable to these effects.

Disruption of cognitive control. Evidence from a small number of studies shows that video game experience may also be negatively related to cognitive control—the ability to maintain goal-directed information processing in the face of distraction or competing response alternatives (Bailey, West, & Anderson, 2010). Cognitive control can be measured using the Stroop interference task. In one version of this task, participants are shown a series of words and are asked to name the color. The words can be printed in either congruent colors (the word "red" printed in red) or incongruent colors (the word "red" printed in blue). The reaction time for naming the color of congruent words is faster than for incongruent ones, which is known as the Stroop effect.

Kronenberger and colleagues (2005) showed that adolescents who spent a lot of time viewing violent media (both television and video games) performed more poorly on the Stroop task than those who rarely consumed violent media. The association between violent video games and attention problems remained significant even after the level of exposure to violent television was controlled, showing that there is a unique effect of video game exposure on attention.

A study by Mathews and colleagues (2005) measured neural recruitment using functional magnetic resonance imaging (fMRI) while individuals performed a counting Stroop task. In low gamers, a typical pattern of neural recruitment was observed, which reflected greater activation of the anterior cingulated and lateral frontal cortex for incongruent blocks of trials relative to neutral blocks of trials. In contrast, high gamers failed to activate these brain structures while performing the incongruent trials.

Bailey and colleagues (2010) explored the effect of video game experience on proactive and reactive cognitive control. Proactive control represents a future-oriented form of control that serves to optimize task preparation. Reactive control represents a just-in-time form of control that serves to resolve conflict within a trial (Braver, Gray, & Burgess, 2007). Participants with extended versus limited experience with playing video games performed the Stroop task while event-related brain potentials were recorded. The results showed that the conflict adaptation effect (a behavioral measure of proactive control) was poorer in high gamers relative to low/no gamers when there was a long delay between trials. This effect was associated with attenuation of the ERP indicators of medial frontal negativity and frontal slow wave (ERP indices of proactive control) in high gamers. There was no difference between high gamers and low/no gamers in reactive cognitive control. This suggests that video game experience has a negative effect on proactive but not reactive cognitive control. These correlational findings complement evidence of an association between playing video games and attention deficits/hyperactivity and lead to the suggestion that video game experience may have a selective effect on proactive cognitive control processes that allow one to maintain optimal goal-directed information processing (Anderson et al., in press).

Additional experimental and longitudinal research is required to establish the existence of a causal relationship between video game experience and cognitive control. However, these results constrain the claims that playing video games improves attention in general (e.g., Green & Bavelier, 2006).

School Performance

A number of studies have found a significant negative association between the amount of screen time (video game play and television viewing) and school performance of children, adolescents, and college students (Anderson & Dill, 2000; Anderson, Gentile, & Buckley, 2007; Chan & Rabinowitz, 2006; Cordes & Miller, 2000; Gentile, 2009; Gentile et al., 2004; Rideout, Foehr, & Roberts, 2010; Sharif & Sargent, 2006). For example, a longitudinal study of elementary schoolchildren found that screen time (the amount of time spent on television and video games combined) was a significant negative predictor of children's grades (Anderson et al., 2007).

Gentile and colleagues (2004) explored gaming habits of adolescents and the level of parental monitoring of adolescent video game use. A significant negative correlation was found between the amount of video game play and grades. Parental involvement acted as a protective factor, showing a positive association with school performance.

One explanation of this relationship is the displacement hypothesis. Regardless of content, the amount of play could affect grades negatively by displacing time spent in other educational activities (such as reading, homework, etc.; Gentile et al., 2004). The displacement hypothesis has received some empirical support. A study on a large nationally representative sample of youths showed that gamers spent 30% less time reading and 34% less time doing homework than nongamers, indicating that video game play is a distraction from school-related activities (Cummings & Vandewater, 2007). Rideout, Foehr, and Roberts (2010) found that nearly half (47%) of heavy media users get poor grades, compared to 23% of light media users.

However, further research is needed to establish whether mechanisms other than displacement might also be involved in the association of media exposure and school performance (Barlett, Anderson, & Swing, 2009). It also might be true that children who have trouble at school seek to play games to feel a sense of mastery, or that attention problems cause both poor school performance and an attraction to games (Gentile, 2009).

Gaming Addiction

There is growing concern among researchers, educators, and parents about the addictive potential of video games. Most researchers studying the pathological use of video games have defined it similarly to how pathological gambling is defined—based on damage to family, social, school, occupational and psychological functioning (Anderson et al., in press). This approach appears to be valid, since both pathological video game use and pathological gambling are types of behavioral addictions (Griffiths, 2000; Tejeiro Salguero & Bersabé Morán, 2002). Games, like gambling, are initially played as a form of entertainment, because they are stimulating and produce positive emotions. At first this activity isn't pathological, but it can become so for some people when it begins to produce serious negative life consequences (Gentile, 2009).

Video game addiction has not yet been included in the *Diagnostic and Statistic Manual of Mental Disorders* (*DSM*) as a formal diagnosis. In the draft for the *DSM-V,* which is due to be published in 2013, the American Psychiatric Association proposed a category of addictionlike behavioral disorders. Gambling disorder has been moved into this category, and other addictionlike behavioral disorders such as Internet addiction will be considered as potential additions to this category as research data accumulate (American Psychiatric Association, 2010). Before Internet addiction and video game addiction can be accepted as a recognized mental health disorders, more research is needed to discover how large a problem this is, who is most at risk, the etiology of the disorder, how long it lasts, what the outcomes are, whether treatment is needed, and what types of treatment are most effective. Researchers have started gathering knowledge on these topics.

Gentile (2009) investigated video-gaming habits of a large nationally representative sample of American youths (aged 8 to 18 years). This study found that about 8% of video game players in this sample exhibited pathological patterns of play. Pathological gamers spent twice as much time playing than nonpathological gamers and received poorer grades. Pathological gaming also showed comorbidity with attention problems. In a large European sample, 11.9% of gamers fulfilled diagnostic criteria of addiction concerning their gaming behavior (Grusser, Thalemann, & Griffiths, 2007). A considerable prevalence of gaming addiction was found in samples from other parts of the world, for example Korea (Kim, Namkoong, Ku, & Kim, 2008) and Taiwan (Hsu, Wen, & Wu, 2009). Researchers have also started exploring the predictors and risk factors of video game addiction. Online game addiction has been associated with lower self-control, aggression, and narcissistic personality traits (Kim et al., 2008) and a preference for virtual life (Liu & Peng, 2009). It seems that gaming addiction is a problem affecting a considerable number of people worldwide and that additional research in this area is needed (Anderson et al., in press).

Conclusions

The recent explosion in video game research has helped improve our understanding of how video games in general and violent video games in specific affect players. A wealth of research now shows that playing violent video games is a causal risk factor for aggression and several aggression-related variables. One common mechanism for both the short- and long-term increases in aggressive behavior is increased accessibility of aggressive cognitions. The recent comprehensive meta-analysis yielded theoretically and empirically consistent findings, including significant effects of violent video game exposure on aggressive behavior, cognition, affect, and arousal, as well as negative effects on empathy/desensitization and prosocial behavior. These effects were similar across experimental, cross-sectional, and longitudinal designs; for males and females; for children, adolescents, and young adults; and for individuals from both Eastern and Western cultures (Anderson et al., 2010). Useful frameworks for understanding media effects on aggression as well as other types of learning (e.g., prosocial behavior) are provided by the General Aggression Model and the General Learning Model.

A smaller but not insignificant number of studies demonstrate that violent video games also have significant effects on attention and cognitive control. Some of these effects are positive—action games can improve some visual and spatial skills (e.g., Green & Bavelier, 2003, 2006). However, there also is growing evidence that video games may have negative effects on proactive cognitive control (e.g., Bailey et al., 2010) and are linked to attention deficits (e.g., Swing et al., 2010). Another reason for concern is the negative relation between time spent playing video games and school performance (e.g., Gentile et al., 2004; Sharif & Sargent, 2006). A growing number of studies are investigating the phenomenon of gaming addiction (e.g., Gentile, 2009).

To sum up, violent video games have been shown to have some limited positive effects (benefits to visuospatial functioning) and a host of negative effects. Although these effects aren't huge, they also are not trivial in size. Considering that a large number of children, adolescents, and adults play violent video games, the accumulation of these effects can have a significant impact on individuals and on our society.

References

Abelson, R. P. (1995). *Statistics as principled argument.* Hillsdale, NJ: Lawrence Erlbaum Associates.

Achtman, R. L., Green, C. S., & Bavelier, D. (2008). Video games as a tool to train visual skills. *Restorative Neurology and Neuroscience, Special Issue on Visual System Damage and Plasticity, 26,* 435–446.

American Psychiatric Association. (2010). *DSM-V Development.* Retrieved on September 3, 2010, from http://www.dsm5.org/Pages/Default.aspx.

Anderson, C. A. (1989). Temperature and aggression: Ubiquitous effects of heat on occurrence of human violence. *Psychological Bulletin, 106,* 74–96.

Anderson, C. A. (2004). An update on the effects of violent video games. *Journal of Adolescence, 27,* 113–122.

Anderson, C. A., Berkowitz, L., Donnerstein, E., Huesmann, L. R., Johnson, J., Linz, D., Malamuth, N., & Wartella, E. (2003). The influence of media violence on youth. *Psychological Science in the Public Interest, 4,* 81–110.

Anderson, C. A., Buckley, K. E., & Carnagey, N. L. (2008). Creating your own hostile environment: A laboratory examination of trait aggression and the violence escalation cycle. *Personality and Social Psychology Bulletin, 34,* 462–473.

Anderson, C. A., & Bushman, B. J. (1997). External validity of "trivial" experiments: The case of laboratory aggression. *Review of General Psychology, 1,* 19–41.

Anderson, C. A., & Bushman, B. J. (2001). Effects of violent video games on aggressive behavior, aggressive cognition, aggressive affect, physiological arousal, and prosocial behavior: A meta-analytic review of the scientific literature. *Psychological Science, 12,* 353–359.

Anderson, C. A., & Bushman, B. J. (2002). Human aggression. *Annual Review of Psychology, 53,* 27–51.

Anderson, C. A., & Carnagey, N. L. (2004). Violent evil and the general aggression model. In A. Miller (Ed.), *The social psychology of good and evil* (pp. 168–192). New York: Guilford.

Anderson, C. A., & Carnagey, N. L. (2009). Causal effects of violent sports video games on aggression: Is it competitiveness or violent content? *Journal of Experimental Social Psychology, 45,* 731–739.

Anderson, C. A., Carnagey, N. L., Flanagan, M., Benjamin, A. J., Eubanks, J., & Valentine, J. C. (2004). Violent video games: Specific effects of violent content on aggressive thoughts and behavior. *Advances in Experimental Social Psychology, 36,* 199–249.

Anderson, C. A., & Dill, K. E. (2000). Video games and aggressive thoughts, feelings, and behavior in the laboratory and in life. *Journal of Personality and Social Psychology, 78,* 772–791.

Anderson, C. A., Gentile, D. A., & Buckley, K. E. (2007). *Violent video game effects on children and adolescents: Theory, research, and public policy.* New York: Oxford University Press.

Anderson, C. A., Gentile, D. A., & Dill, K. E. (in press). Prosocial, antisocial, and other effects of recreational video games. In D. G. Singer & J. L. Singer (Eds.), *Handbook of children and the media* (2nd ed.). Thousand Oaks, CA: Sage.

Anderson, C. A., & Huesmann, L. R. (2003). Human aggression: A social-cognitive view. In M. A. Hogg & J. Cooper (Eds.), *Handbook of social psychology* (pp. 296–323). London: Sage Publications.

Anderson, C. A., Shibuya, A., Ihori, N., Swing, E. L., Bushman, B. J., Sakamoto, A., Rothstein, H. R., & Saleem, M. (2010). Violent video game effects on aggression, empathy, and prosocial behavior in Eastern and Western countries. *Psychological Bulletin, 136,* 151–173.

Archer, J. (2004). Sex differences in aggression in real-world settings: A meta-analytic review. *Review of General Psychology, 8,* 291–322.

Bailey, K., West, R., & Anderson, C. A. (2010). A negative association between video game experience and proactive cognitive control. *Psychophysiology, 47,* 34–42.

Ballard, M. E., & Wiest, J. R. (1996). Mortal Kombat™: The effects of violent videogame play on males' hostility and cardiovascular responding. *Journal of Applied Social Psychology, 26,* 717–730.

Bandura, A. (1965). Influence of models' reinforcement contingencies on the acquisition of imitative responses. *Journal of Personality and Social Psychology, 1,* 589–595.

Bandura, A. (1973). *Aggression: A social learning analysis.* Englewood Cliffs, NJ: Prentice-Hall.

Bandura, A. (1983). Psychological mechanisms of aggression. In R. G. Geen & E. Donnerstein (Eds.), *Aggression: Theoretical and empirical reviews* (pp. 1–40). New York: Academic Press.

Bandura, A., Ross, D., & Ross, S. A. (1961). Transmisssion of aggressions through imitation of aggressive models. *Journal of Abnormal and Social Psychology, 63*, 575–582.

Bandura, A., Ross, D., & Ross, S. A. (1963a). Imitation of film-mediated aggressive models. *Journal of Abnormal Social Psychology, 66*, 3–11.

Bandura, A., Ross, D., & Ross, S. A. (1963b). Vicarious reinforcement and imitative learning. *Journal of Abnormal Social Psychology, 67*, 601–607.

Barlett, C. P., & Anderson, C. A. (in press). Examining media effects: The general aggression and general learning models. In E. Scharrer (Ed.), *Media effects/media psychology*. New York: Blackwell-Wiley.

Barlett, C. P., Anderson, C. A., & Swing, E. L. (2009). Video game effects confirmed, suspected, and speculative: A review of the evidence. *Simulation and Gaming, 40*, 377–403.

Barlett, C. P., Branch, O. L., Rodeheffer, C. D., & Harris, R. H. (2009). How long do the short-term violent video game effects last? *Aggressive Behavior, 35*, 225–236.

Barlett, C. P., Harris, R. J., & Bruey, C. (2008). The effect of the amount of blood in a violent video game on aggression, hostility, and arousal. *Journal of Experimental Social Psychology, 44*, 539–546.

Barlett, C. P., & Rodeheffer, C. (2009). Effects of realism on extended violent and nonviolent video game play on aggressive thoughts, feelings, and physiological arousal. *Aggressive Behavior, 35*, 213–224.

Bartholow, B. D., Bushman, B. J., & Sestir, M. A. (2005). Chronic violent video game exposure and desensitization to violence: Behavioral and event-related brain potential data. *Journal of Experimental Social Psychology, 42*, 283–290.

Bartholow, B. D., Sestir, M. A., & Davis, E. (2005). Correlates and consequences of exposure to video game violence: Hostile personality, empathy, and aggressive behavior. *Personality and Social Psychology Bulletin, 31*, 1573–1586.

Bensley, L., & Van Eenwyk, J. (2001). Video games and real life aggression: Review of the literature. *Journal of Adolescent Health, 29*, 244–257.

Berkowitz, L. (1984). Some effects of thoughts on anti- and prosocial influences of media events: A cognitive-neoassociation analysis. *Psychological Bulletin, 95*, 410–427.

Bettencourt, B. A., & Kernahan, C. (1997). A meta-analysis of aggression in the presence of violent cues: Effects of gender differences and aversive provocation. *Aggressive Behavior, 23*, 447–456.

Bioulac, S., Arfi, L., & Bouvard M. P. (2008). Attention deficit/hyperactivity disorder and video games: A comparative study of hyperactive and control children. *European Psychiatry, 23*, 134–141.

Björkqvist, K., Österman, K., & Kaukiainen A. (2000). Social intelligence – empathy = aggression? *Aggression and Violent Behavior, 5*, 191–200.

Braver, T. S., Gray, J. R., & Burgess, G. C. (2007). Explaining the many varieties of working memory variation: Dual mechanisms of cognitive control. In A. Conway, C. Jarrold, M. Miyake, & J. Towse (Eds.), *Variation in working memory* (pp. 76–106). Oxford: Oxford University Press.

Buckley, K. E., & Anderson, C. A. (2006). A theoretical model of the effects and consequences of playing video games. In P. Vorderer & J. Bryant (Eds.), *Playing video games—Motives, responses, and consequences* (pp. 363–378). Mahwah, NJ: Lawrence Erlbaum Associates.

Bushman, B. J. (1995). Moderating role of trait aggressiveness in the effects of violent media on aggression. *Journal of Personality and Social Psychology, 69,* 950–960.

Bushman, B. J., & Anderson, C. A. (2002). Violent video games and hostile expectations: A test of the general aggression model. *Personality and Social Psychology Bulletin, 28,* 1679–1686.

Bushman, B. J., & Anderson, C. A. (2009). Comfortably numb: Desensitizing effects of violent media on helping others. *Psychological Science, 20,* 273–277.

Bushman, B. J., & Huesmann, L. R. (2006). Short-term and long-term effects of violent media on aggression in children and adults. *Archives of Pediatrics and Adolescent Medicine, 160,* 348–352.

Carnagey, N. L., & Anderson, C. A. (2003). Theory in the study of media violence: The general aggression model. In D. Gentile (Ed.), *Media violence and children* (pp. 87–106). Westport, CT: Praeger.

Carnagey, N. L., Anderson, C. A., & Bushman, B. J. (2007). The effect of video game violence on physiological desensitization to real-life violence. *Journal of Experimental Social Psychology, 43,* 489–496.

Castel, A. D., Pratt, J., & Drummond, E. (2005). The effects of action video game experience on the time course of inhibition of return and the efficiency of visual search. *Acta Psychologica, 119,* 217–230.

Chan, P. A., & Rabinowitz, T. (2006). A cross-sectional analysis of video games and attention deficit hyperactivity disorder symptoms in adolescents. *Annals of General Psychiatry, 5,* 16.

Children Now. (2001). *Fair play? Violence, gender, and race in video games.* Los Angeles: Children Now.

Christakis, D. A., Zimmerman, F. J., DiGiuseppe, D. L., & McCarty, C. A. (2004). Early television exposure and subsequent attentional problems in children. *Pediatrics, 113,* 708–713.

Comstock, G., & Scharrer, E. (2007). *Media and the American child.* San Diego, CA: Academic Press.

Cordes, C., & Miller, E. (2000). *Fool's gold: A critical look at computers in childhood.* College Park, MD: Alliance for Childhood.

Crick, N. R., & Dodge, K. A. (1994). A review and reformulation of social information processing mechanisms in children's adjustment. *Psychological Bulletin, 115,* 74–101.

Cummings, H. M. M., & Vandewater, E. A. P. (2007). Relation of adolescent video game play to time spent in other activities. *Archives of pediatric and adolescent medicine, 161*(7), 684–689.

De Lisi, R., & Wolford, J. L. (2002). Improving children's mental rotation accuracy with computer game playing. *Journal of Genetic Psychology, 163,* 272–282.

Dexter, H. R., Penrod, S. D., Linz, D., & Saunders, D. (1997). Attributing responsibility to female victims after exposure to sexually violent films. *Journal of Applied Social Psychology, 27,* 2149.

Dill, K. E., & Dill, J. (1998). Video game violence: A review of the empirical literature. *Aggression and Violent Behavior, 3,* 407–428.

Emes, C. E. (1997). Is Mr. Pac Man eating our children? A review of the effect of video games on children. *Canadian Journal of Psychiatry, 42,* 409–414.

Estévez López, E., Pérez, S. M., Ochoa, G. M., & Ruiz, D. M. (2008). Adolescent aggression: Effects of gender and family and school environments. *Journal of Adolescence, 31,* 433–445.

Ewart, C. K., & Suchday, S. (2002). Discovering how urban poverty and violence affect health: Development and validation of a neighborhood stress index. *Health Psychology, 21,* 254–262.

Farrar, K. M., Krcmar, M., & Nowak, K. L. (2006). Contextual features of violent video games, mental models, and aggression. *Journal of Communication, 56,* 387–405.

Feng, J., Spence, I., & Pratt, J. (2007). Playing an action video game reduces gender differences in spatial cognition. *Psychological Science, 18,* 850–855.

Fleming, M. J., & Rickwood, D. J. (2001). Effects of violent versus nonviolent video games on children's arousal, aggressive mood, and positive mood. *Journal of Applied Social Psychology, 31,* 2047–2071.

Funk, J. B., Baldacci, H. B., Pasold, T., & Baumgardner, J. (2004). Violence exposure in real-life, video games, television, movies, and the Internet: Is there desensitization? *Journal of Adolescence, 27,* 123–139.

Funk, J. B., Hagan, J. D., & Schimming, J. L. (1999). Children and electronic games: A comparison of parent and child perceptions of children's habits and preferences in a United States sample. *Psychological Reports, 85,* 883–888.

Geen, R. G., & O'Neal, E. C. (1969). Activation of cue-elicited aggression by general arousal. *Journal of Personality and Social Psychology, 11,* 289–292.

Gentile, D. A. (2008). The rating systems for media products. In S. Calvert & B. Wilson (Eds.), *The handbook of children, media and development* (pp. 527–551). Malden, MA: Blackwell.

Gentile, D. A. (2009). Pathological video game use among youth 8 to 18: A national study. *Psychological Science, 20,* 594–602.

Gentile, D. A., Anderson, C. A., Yukawa. S., Ihori, N., Saleem, M., Ming, L. K., Shibuya, A., Liau, A. K., Khoo, A., & Sakamoto, A. (2009). The effects of prosocial video games on prosocial behaviors: International evidence from correlational, experimental, and longitudinal studies. *Personality and Social Psychology Bulletin, 35,* 752–763.

Gentile, D. A., Lynch, P. J., Linder, J. R., & Walsh, D. A. (2004). The effects of violent video game habits on adolescent aggressive attitudes and behaviors. *Journal of Adolescence, 27,* 5–22.

Gentile, D. A., & Sesma, A. (2003). Developmental Approaches to Understanding Media Effects on Individuals. In D. Gentile (Ed.), *Media violence and children* (pp. 87–106). Westport, CT: Praeger.

Green, C. S., & Bavelier, D. (2003). Action video game modifies visual selective attention. *Nature, 423,* 534–537.

Green, C. S., & Bavelier, D. (2006). Effect of action video games on the spatial distribution of visuospatial attention. *Journal of Experimental Psychology: Human Perception and Performance, 32,* 1465–1468.

Green, C. S., Li, R., & Bavelier, D. (2010). Perceptual learning during action video games. *Topics, 2,* 202–216.

Greitemeyer, T. (2009). Effects of songs with prosocial lyrics on prosocial behavior: Further evidence and a mediating mechanism. *Personality and Social Psychology Bulletin, 35,* 1500–1511.

Greitemeyer, T., & Osswald, S. (2009). Prosocial video games reduce aggressive cognitions. *Journal of Experimental Social Psychology, 45,* 896–900.

Greitemeyer, T., & Osswald, S. (2010). Effects of prosocial video games on prosocial behavior. *Journal of Personality and Social Psychology, 98,* 211–221.

Griffiths, M. (1999). Violent video games and aggression: A review of the literature. *Aggression and Violent Behavior, 4,* 203–212.

Griffiths, M. (2000). Does Internet and computer "addiction" exist? Some case study evidence. *CyberPsychology and Behavior, 3,* 211–218.

Grusser, S. M., Thalemann, R., & Griffiths, M. D. (2007). Excessive computer game playing: Evidence for addiction and aggression? *Cyberpsychology and Behavior, 10,* 290–292.

Haninger, K., & Thompson, K. M. (2004). Content and ratings of teen-rated video games. *Journal of the American Medical Association, 291,* 856–865.

Hopf, W. H., Huber, G. L., & Weib, R. H. (2008). Media violence and youth violence: A two-year longitudinal study. *Journal of Media Psychology: Theories, Methods, and Applications, 20,* 79–96.

Hsu, S. H., Wen, M., & Wu, M. (2009). Exploring user experiences as predictors of MMORPG addiction. *Computers and Education, 53,* 990–999.

Hudziak, J. J., van Beijsterveldt, C. E. M., Bartels, M., Rietveld, M. J. H., Rettew, D. C., Derks, E. M., et al. (2003). Individual differences in aggression: Genetic analyses by age, gender, and informant in 3-, 7-, and 10-year-old Dutch twins. *Behavior Genetics, 33,* 575–589.

Huesmann, L. R. (1986). Psychological processes promoting the relation between exposure to media violence and aggressive behavior by the viewer. *Journal of Social Issues, 42,* 125–139.

Huesmann, L. R. (1998). The role of social information processing and cognitive schema in the acquisition and maintenance of habitual aggressive behavior. In R. Geen & E. Donnerstein (Eds.), *Human aggression: Theories, research, and implications for policy* (pp. 73–109). New York: Academic Press.

Kim, E. J., Namkoong, K., Ku, T., & Kim, S. J. (2008). The relationship between online game addiction and aggression, self-control, and narcissistic personality traits. *European Psychiatry, 23,* 212–218.

Kirsh, S. J. (1998). Seeing the world through Mortal Kombat–colored glasses: Violent video games and the development of a short-term hostile attribution bias. *Childhood, 5,* 177–184.

Kirsh, S. J., Olczak, P. V., & Mounts, J. R. W. (2005). Violent video games induce an affect processing bias. *Media Psychology, 7,* 239–250.

Konijn, E. A., Bijvank, N. M., & Bushman, B. J. (2007). I wish I were a warrior: The role of wishful identification in effects of violent video games on aggression in adolescent boys. *Developmental Psychology, 43,* 1038–1044.

Kronenberger, W. G., Matthews, V. P., Dunn, D. W., Wang, Y., Wood, E. A., Giauque, A. L., Larsen, J. L., Rembusch, M. E., Lowe, M. J., & Li, T. Q. (2005). Media violence exposure and executive functioning in aggressive and control adolescents. *Journal of Clinical Psychology, 61,* 725–737.

Landhuis, C. E., Poulton, R., Welch, D., & Hancox, R. J. (2007). Does childhood television viewing lead to attention problems in adolescence? Results from a prospective longitudinal study. *Pediatrics, 120,* 532–537.

Levine, L. E., & Waite, B. M. (2000). Television viewing and attentional abilities in fourth and fifth grade children. *Journal of Applied Developmental Psychology, 21,* 667–679.

Liu, M., & Peng, W. (2009). Cognitive and psychological predictors of the negative outcomes associated with playing MMOGs (massively multiplayer online games). *Computers in Human Behavior, 25,* 1306–1311.

Markey, P. M., & Scherer, K. (2009). An examination of psychoticism and motion capture controls as moderators of the effects of violent video games. *Computers in Human Behavior, 25,* 407–411.

Mathews, V. P., Kronenberger, W. G., Wang, Y., Lurito, J. T., Lowe, M. J., & Dunn, D. W. (2005). Media violence exposure and frontal lobe activation measured by functional magnetic resonance imaging in aggressive and nonaggressive adolescents. *Journal of Computer Assisted Tomography, 29,* 287–292.

Mistry, K. B., Minkovitz, C. S., Strobino, D. M., & Borzekowski, D. L. (2007). Children's television exposure and behavioral and social outcomes at 5.5 years: Does timing of exposure matter? *Pediatrics, 120,* 762–769.

Möller, I., & Krahé, B. (2009). Exposure to violent video games and aggression in German adolescents: A longitudinal analysis. *Aggressive Behavior, 35,* 75–89.

Mullin, C. R., & Linz, D. (1995). Desensitization and resensitization to violence against women: Effects of exposure to sexually violent films on judgments of domestic violence victims. *Journal of Personality and Social Psychology, 69,* 449–459.

Osofsky, H., & Osofsky, J. (2001). Violent and aggressive behaviors in youth: A mental health and prevention perspective. *Psychiatry: Interpersonal and Biological Processes, 64,* 285–295.

Patterson, G. (1995). Coercion as a basis for early age of onset for arrest. In J. McCord (Ed.), *Coercion and punishment in long-term perspectives* (pp. 81–105). New York: Cambridge University Press.

Raine, A., Brennen, P. A., Farrington, D. P., & Mednick, S. A. (Eds.). (1997). *Biosocial bases of violence.* London: Plenum Press.

Rideout, V. J., Foehr, U. G., & Roberts, D. F. (2010). *Generation M²—Media in the lives of 8- to 18-year-olds.* Menlo Park, CA: Kaiser Family Foundation.

Sharif, I., & Sargent, J. D. (2006). Association between television, movie, and video game exposure and school performance. *Pediatrics, 118,* 1061–1070.

Sherry, J. L. (2001). The effects of violent video games on aggression: A meta analysis. *Human Communication Research, 27,* 409–431.

Swing, E. L., & Anderson, C. A. (2008). How and what do video games teach? In T. Willoughby & E. Wood (Eds.), *Children's learning in a digital world* (pp. 64–84). Oxford, UK: Blackwell.

Swing, E. L., & Anderson, C. A. (2010). Media violence and the development of aggressive behavior. In M. DeLisi & K. M. Beaver (Eds.), *Criminological theory: A life-course approach* (pp. 87–108). Sudbury, MA: Jones and Bartlett.

Swing, E. L., Gentile, D. A., & Anderson, C. A. (2009). Violent video games: Learning processes and outcomes. In R. E. Ferdig (Ed.), *Handbook of research on effective electronic gaming in education* (Vol. 2, pp. 876–892). Hershey, PA: Information Science Reference.

Swing, E. L., Gentile, D. A., Anderson, C. A., & Walsh, D. A. (2010). Television and video game exposure and the development of attention problems. *Pediatrics, 126,* 214–221.

Tejeiro Salguero, R. A., & Bersabé Morán, R. M. (2002). Measuring problem video game playing in adolescents. *Addiction, 97,* 1601–1606.

U.S. Department of Health and Human Services. (2001). *Youth violence: A report of the surgeon general.* Rockville, MD: U.S. Department of Health and Human Services, Centers for Disease Control and Prevention; National Center for Injury Prevention and Control; Substance Abuse and Mental Health Services Administration, Center for Mental Health Services; and National Institutes of Health, National Institute of Mental Health. Retrieved on September 3, 2010, from http://www.surgeongeneral.gov/library/youthviolence/chapter4/sec3.html.

Warburton, W. A., Williams, K. D., & Cairns, D. R. (2006). When ostracism leads to aggression: The moderating effects of control deprivation. *Journal of Experimental Social Psychology, 42,* 213–220.

Zillmann, D. (1971). Excitation transfer in communication-mediated aggressive behavior. *Journal of Experimental Social Psychology, 7,* 419–434.

Zillmann, D. (1983). Arousal and aggression. In R. Geen & E. Donnerstein (Eds.), *Aggression: Theoretical and empirical reviews* (Vol. 1, pp. 75–102). New York: Academic Press.

CHAPTER FOUR

The Role of Victimization Experiences in Adolescent Girls and Young Women's Aggression in Dating Relationships

Katie M. Edwards, Christina M. Dardis, and Christine A. Gidycz

Overview

Dating violence—which includes physical, sexual, and psychological abuse—is a major public health problem with far-reaching consequences to both victims and society. Much of the dating violence research has focused on girls and women as victims and boys and men as perpetrators. However, there is a burgeoning body of literature demonstrating that girls and young women engage in aggressive behaviors toward their dating partners. In a meta-analysis, Archer (2002) reported that women were slightly more likely than men to perpetrate physical aggression toward heterosexual partners. Data derived from adolescent samples suggest similar findings. Across studies of adolescents, 28% to 44% of girls report engaging in physical aggression toward a dating partner, whereas 11% to 39% of boys report engaging in similar behaviors (see Hickman, Jaycox, & Aronoff, 2004, for a review). Magdol and colleagues (1997) found that among young adults in New Zealand, 22% of men and 37% of women reported perpetrating physical aggression in dating relationships during the past 12 months and 86% of men and 95% of women reported perpetrating psychological aggression in dating relationships during the past 12 months. Similarly, Edwards, Desai, Gidycz, and VanWynsberghe (2009) found that 12% of college women reported perpetrating physical aggression, and 74% reported perpetrating psychological aggression (broadly defined) over a brief two-month follow-up period. Importantly, however, research with both adolescents and young adults suggests that the vast majority of sexual assaults, including those that occur within the context of dating relationships, are perpetrated by boys and young men (Fisher, Cullen, & Turner, 2000; Foshee, 1996; Hickman et al., 2004).

Although adolescent girls and young women appear to engage in similar rates of physical and psychological aggression toward dating partners as boys and young men, there are several caveats to this data: (a) adolescent girls' and young women's aggression is often motivated by fear and self-defense, whereas adolescent boys' and young men's use of aggression is often motivated by power and control; (b) adolescent boys and young men often engage in more serious forms of perpetration than adolescent girls and young women; and (c) adolescent girls and young women report greater injury, fear, and psychological consequences to dating violence victimization than do male victims of dating violence (Archer, 2000; Foshee, 1996; Molidor & Tolman, 1998; O'Keefe & Treister, 1998; Swan et al., 2008; Tjaden & Thoennes, 2000).

Additionally, there are gender differences in risk factors for perpetration of dating violence. In particular, research demonstrates that victimization experiences are a stronger and more consistent predictor of adolescent girls' and young women's engagement in aggression than adolescent boys' and young men's engagement in aggression (Follette & Alexander, 1992; Graves, 2007; Luthra & Gidycz, 2006; Magdol et al., 1997; O'Keefe, 1998). Indeed, there is a growing consensus in the literature that adolescent girls' and young women's experiences of perpetrating dating violence must be considered within the context of their own victimization experiences in childhood, adolescence, and young adulthood (Edwards et al., 2009; Graves, Sechrist, White, & Paradise, 2005; Swan & Snow, 2002; Zahn, 2007). Accordingly, the purpose of this chapter is to provide an overview of research that has assessed the relationship between adolescent girls' and young women's experiences of victimization and their own use of aggression in dating relationships. Additionally, theoretical explanations for these relationships and implications for gender-sensitive prevention efforts are discussed. Of note, although there are factors other than victimization experiences (e.g., socioeconomic status, antisocial behavior, association with delinquent peer group) that affect adolescent girls' and young women's use of aggression in dating relationships, they are beyond the scope of this review and discussed elsewhere (e.g., Graves, 2007). Further, given that the vast majority of dating violence research has been conducted with heterosexual adolescents and young adults, adolescent girls' and young women's perpetration of same-sex dating violence is not addressed in this review, although this is an important area for future research (for a review, see Murray & Mobley, 2009).

Research Evidence

There are a number of studies that have assessed the role of victimization experiences in adolescent girls' and young women's use of aggression in dating relationships. Much of this research focuses on the role of childhood abuse and exposure to domestic violence and young women's subsequent use of aggression in adolescence and young adulthood. Although there is some conflicting evidence in the research literature (Foo & Margolin, 1995; Graves et al., 2005; O'Keefe, 1997), most data support the general finding that childhood abuse and/or exposure to domestic violence in childhood increases adolescent girls' and young women's risk for perpetrating dating violence (Follete & Alexander, 1992; Kaura & Allen, 2004; Luthra & Gidycz, 2006; O'Keefe, 1998). For example, in a sample of adolescent girls, O'Keefe (1998) found that among females who witnessed high levels of interparental violence, having additionally experienced child abuse increased the likelihood of both perpetrating and receiving dating violence. In a college sample, Crawford and Wright (2007) found that childhood sexual, physical, and emotional abuse predicted subsequent perpetration of dating aggression (generally defined as physical, verbal, and/or sexual aggression). Similarly, Magdol, Moffitt, Caspi, and Silva (1998) found that harsh punishment in childhood (including items consistent with physical and verbal abuse) was significantly correlated with young women's subsequent perpetration of both verbal and physical abuse in their dating relationships. Moreover, research generally suggests that childhood abuse perpetrated by fathers is more predictive of subsequent dating violence perpetration than childhood abuse perpetrated by mothers (Edwards et al., 2009; Kaura & Allen, 2004; Luthra & Gidycz, 2006). A possible explanatory mechanism for these findings is that paternal abuse is often more severe than maternal abuse (Paterson, Fairbairn-Dunlop, Cowley-Malcolm, & Schluter, 2007) and causes children to feel more helpless and defenseless than maternal abuse (Miller, Downs, & Testa, 1993; Paterson et al., 2007).

Despite the importance of early abusive experiences, there is a growing body of research demonstrating that more recent victimization experiences in adolescence and/or young adulthood are more predictive of adolescent girls' and young women's use of aggression than childhood experiences. Research with adolescent girls documents that dating violence perpetration is strongly associated with dating violence victimization during this time period (Cano, Avery-Leaf, Cascardi, & O'Leary, 1998; O'Keefe, 1997). For example, O'Keefe (1997) found that, among predictors of dating violence including attitudes toward dating violence, childhood experiences with violence, dating violence conflict, and alcohol or drug use, the strongest predictor of inflicting dating violence for adolescent girls was having received past physical violence from a dating partner. This pattern progresses into young adulthood. For example, Luthra and Gidycz (2006) found that women who reported paternal abuse in childhood were three times more likely to report physical dating violence perpetration than women who did not report paternal abuse histories. However, a much stronger relationship was found between physical dating violence victimization in adolescence and college women's reports of physical dating violence victimization; in fact, women who reported being the victim of physical dating violence in adolescence or young adulthood were 103 times more likely to engage in physical dating violence perpetration than women without histories of physical dating violence victimization.

Research using longitudinal, prospective designs provide further evidence that childhood experiences are often less predictive of dating violence perpetration than victimization experiences that occur in the context of dating relationships (Edwards et al., 2009; Graves et al., 2005; Magdol et al., 1997). For example, using a prospective design, Edwards and colleagues (2009) found that reports of childhood abuse at the first survey session were unrelated to women's reports of perpetrating physical and psychological aggression over a 2-month interim period. In fact, results from the two prospective, longitudinal regression analyses suggested that verbal victimization over the interim predicted women's reports of verbal perpetration over the interim and that physical victimization over the interim predicted women's reports of physical perpetration over the interim. The Edwards and colleagues (2009) study also showed that sexual victimization in adolescence/young adulthood increases young women's likelihood of perpetrating dating violence during this same time period. These findings are consistent with other research showing that women who are sexually victimized by a dating partner are more likely to reciprocate with physical or verbal aggression rather than sexual aggression (DiLillo, Giuffre, Tremblay, & Peterson, 2001). Further, this supports the notion that women likely match their conflict resolution and resistance strategies to those being used by their dating partner (Abel, 2001; Gidycz, McNamara, & Edwards, 2006; Ullman, 1998). However, future research that assesses the temporal sequencing in abusive dating interactions is needed to better document the extent to which adolescent girls' and young women's aggression occurs in response to adolescent boys' and young men's threatening behaviors.

In another prospective study of college women, Graves and colleagues (2005) found that although childhood abuse was unrelated to women's reports of physical perpetration in adolescence, physical dating violence victimization in adolescence predicted women's reports of physical dating violence perpetration in adolescence and subsequent physical dating violence perpetration in college. Additionally, in a longitudinal study that followed a New Zealand birth cohort for 20 years, results showed that women physically victimized by partners were 10 times more likely to perpetrate physical aggression than women not victimized by partners; abusive experiences in childhood were generally not as predictive of dating violence perpetration as more recent victimization experiences (Magdol et al., 1997). These studies are consistent with the hypothesis that the effects of family-of-origin violence may attenuate over time, and concurrent factors, such as being victimized within the context of a relationship, become stronger predictors of dating aggression. Similarly, it has also been suggested that childhood abuse increases adolescent girls' and young women's risk for subsequent victimization in these later developmental periods, which in turn increases their propensity to use aggression against a dating partner (Edwards et al., 2009; Swan et al., 2008). Thus, future work is needed to explore the extent to which earlier family-of-origin abuse indirectly affects subsequent perpetration by placing one at risk for abuse in intimate relationships that occur beginning in adolescence.

Theoretical Explanations

The theories that are used most commonly to explain the relationship between adolescent girls and young women's victimization experiences and use of aggression in dating relationships are self-defense, social learning theory, and developmental traumatology theory. Although other theories have been provided to explain dating violence perpetration, these three theories are reviewed because they (unlike other theories) have victimization as the central, explanatory variable.

Self-Defense

Much prior research has postulated that adolescent girls and women perpetrate intimate partner violence out of self-defense (Abel, 2001; Dasgupta, 1999; Hamberger & Guse, 2002; Swan et al., 2008), whereas for men issues of power and control are prominent (Dasgupta, 2002; Rennison & Welchans, 2000). O'Keefe's (1997) study of high school students found that adolescent girls were significantly more likely than adolescent boys to use violence for reasons of self-defense. Noonan and Charles (2009) also found that self-defense was a key motivator for girls slapping boyfriends among middle school youths. In a study of 14- to 18-year-olds, Molidor and Tolman (1998) found that 36% of girls reported that they defended themselves when physically assaulted by male partners. The idea that women are not the likely initiators of violence is supported by empirical research, as 70% of adolescent girls report that their male partner initiated violence in their relationships (Molidor & Tolman, 1998). Further, Foshee and colleagues (2007) found that 39% of aggressive acts reported by girls were either in self-defense or retaliatory in response to patterns of violence committed by the male partner and that an additional 17% of aggressive acts were perpetrated in a situation in which it was the first time a girl's partner aggressed against her. The study by Foshee and colleagues (2007) underscores that adolescent girls and young women may use aggression toward a partner out of self-defense in the immediate presence of danger or days or even months following their victimization or a pattern of violence. This latter type of response is termed retaliatory aggression (as opposed to self-defense) in which adolescent girls and young women aggress against their partners in response to a pattern of violent victimization in the relationship, even if not in the immediate presence of danger (Dasgupta, 1999; Faith, 1993; Fiebert & Gonzalez, 1997; Follingstad, Wright, Lloyd, & Sebastian, 1991). However, it could be argued that it is difficult to distinguish retaliatory aggression and aggression for self-defense purposes.

Social Learning Theory and Intergenerational Transmission of Violence Theory

According to social learning theory (Bandura, 1977) and the intergenerational transmission of violence theory (Widom, 1989), children who witness and/or experience parent-to-child or parent-to-parent violence within their families are more likely to adopt and imitate these behaviors within their dating relationships; they view it as an appropriate means for resolving conflict. In support of this theory, Riggs and O'Leary (1996) found that positive attitudes about dating aggression were related to having witnessed parental aggression and experiencing child abuse. Further, positive attitudes toward dating aggression, having a history of aggressive behavior, and high levels of conflict in one's relationship predicted female perpetration of dating violence. Although some studies (e.g., Riggs & O'Leary, 1996; Magdol et al., 1997; Tontodonato & Crew, 1992) have found empirical support for the social learning theory in understanding dating violence perpetration, other studies have failed to document relationships among childhood abuse, positive attitudes toward dating violence, and dating violence perpetration (Follette & Alexander, 1992; O'Keefe & Treister, 1998; Schwartz, O'Leary, & Kendziora, 1997).

In addition to the relationship between previous victimization experiences and subsequent perpetration of dating violence, exposure to a partner's attitudes, beliefs, and/or behaviors regarding violence can affect the other partner's attitudes about violence and their own use of violence (Sellers, Cochran, & Branch, 2005), which is consistent with social learning theory. For example, the chance of physical aggression toward one's partner becomes greater when the other partner endorses and displays the behavior himself/herself (Riggs & O'Leary, 1989; O'Keefe & Treister, 1998). Further, interdependence theory (Thibaut & Kelley, 1959) suggests that close others influence adolescent behavior, and because adolescents have not had extensive relationship experiences, it is posited that adolescents form standards based on observation of close others (e.g., friends, parents). Standards of acceptable interaction can shape perpetration or victimization interactions. In support of this theory, adolescents with peers who are perpetrators or victims of dating violence are more likely to experience dating violence in their own relationships (Arriaga & Foshee, 2004; Gwartney-Gibbs, Stockard, & Bohmer, 1987).

Thus, the social learning theory posits that perpetration of aggression is both a product of childhood experiences of abuse as well as the abuse experienced within intimate relationships. And while research generally supports the tenets of the social learning theory, not all studies find relationships between victimization experiences in childhood and subsequent perpetration of dating violence (Foo & Margolin, 1995; Graves et al., 2005; O'Keefe, 1997). Further, not all adolescent girls and young women who grow up in abusive households perpetrate dating violence, and some females who perpetrate dating violence come from households in which they did not experience violence. Given the limitations of the social learning theory and its exclusive focus on victimization, Riggs and O'Leary (1989) expanded on this theory by proposing that a history of victimization and other background factors (e.g., aggressive personality characteristics, arousability, psychopathology) interact with situational factors (e.g., interpersonal conflict, substance abuse, relationship satisfaction, problem-solving skills, communication styles) to determine whether or not an individual will engage in dating violence. Several studies have found empirical support for this theory in predicting the perpetration of violence among both adolescent girls and boys and young women and men (Luthra & Gidycz, 2006; Magdol et al., 1997; Riggs & O'Leary, 1996).

Developmental Traumatology Theory and Affect Theory

According to developmental traumatology theory (DeBellis & Putman, 1994), trauma-related symptomatology mediates the relationship between a history of maltreatment and subsequent maladaptive outcomes (which could include dating violence perpetration) due to stress-induced neurobiological changes. For example, stress during child abuse could lead to structural and functional brain changes, resulting in a variety of potential maladaptive outcomes, including higher episodic responses to traumatic cues. Similarly, affect theory posits that individuals characterized by affective profiles including hostility, anxiety, and depression are more likely to engage in violent behavior generally (Starzomski & Nussbaum, 2000) and interpersonal violence specifically (Magdol et al., 1997) and that these profiles can occur due to child maltreatment. This theory is supported by the fact that young women tend to experience sexual abuse over extended periods of time and at younger ages than young men, putting women at a higher risk for trauma symptom development (Simkins & Katz, 2002).

Thus, researchers postulate that violence may provide an outlet for the emotional distress experienced by females who have traumatic experiences such as child maltreatment and prior dating violence (Simkins & Katz, 2002; Swan & Snow, 2002). In support of this theory, Capaldi and Crosby (1997) found that among 18-year-old women with abuse histories, those young women who reported both depression symptoms and low self-esteem were more likely to commit violence against their dating partners than those without such symptomtology. A study of adolescent dating violence similarly found that females with a history of child maltreatment were more than seven times as likely to have clinically significant difficulties with anger and depression and more than nine times as likely to experience clinically significant levels of anxiety and PTSD than those without a maltreatment history and that such women were marginally more likely to perpetrate abuse than women who were not as severely traumatized (Wolfe, Scott, Wekerle, & Pittman, 2001). Further, Wolfe, Wekerle, Scott, Straatman, and Grasley (2004) studied high school students longitudinally, finding that child maltreatment was related to trauma-related anger at Time 1, which prospectively predicted dating violence perpetration. In this study, trauma symptoms were the only variable that predicted an increase in violent perpetration longitudinally, whereas attitudes toward violence, self-efficacy, and empathy were not related to perpetration of violence over time, suggesting a unique role of post-traumatic stress symptoms above and beyond relationship factors and attitudes toward violence. Thus, victimization experiences in childhood, adolescence, and adulthood may predict dating violence perpetration through negative affective states.

Conclusion and Implications

The purpose of this chapter was to review the literature on adolescent girls' and young women's use of aggression in dating relationships. Although this is a relatively new area of research, overall studies suggest that adolescent girls and young women engage in similar rates of physical and psychological dating aggression as do adolescent boys and young men (Hickman et al., 2004; Magdol et al., 1997). Nevertheless, research shows that there are important gender differences in the risk factors, developmental trajectories, motivations, functions, manifestations, and consequences of dating violence (Archer, 2000; Foshee, 1996; Molidor & Tolman, 1998; O'Keefe & Treister, 1998). In this chapter, we focused specifically on how experiences of victimization relate to adolescent girls' and young women's use of physical and psychological dating aggression. Although a number of studies have documented relationships between childhood abuse and exposure to domestic violence and subsequent dating violence perpetration, victimization experiences in adolescence and young adulthood are generally more salient predictors of dating violence perpetration than childhood experiences (Cano et al., 1998; O'Keefe, 1997). Indeed, there is a growing consensus in the literature that among adolescent girls and young women concurrent factors (e.g., dating violence victimization) are stronger predictors of dating aggression than family-of-origin violence (O'Keefe, 1997; Luthra & Gidycz, 2006). Theoretical explanations for these relationships draw on self-defense, social learning, intergenerational transmission of violence, developmental traumatology, and affect theories (Dasgupta, 1999; DeBellis & Putnam, 1994; Hamberger & Guse, 2002; Riggs & O'Leary, 1996).

Given the endemic rates of dating violence and the negative consequences of dating violence to victims and society, there have been increasing efforts aimed at the primary prevention of dating violence. A number of dating violence prevention programs have been developed for adolescents and young adults. Whereas some programs are guided by feminist theory and/or social learning theory, other programs adapt a more skills-based and gender-neutral approach (for reviews, see Hickman et al., 2004; Whitaker et al., 2006). In fact, most dating violence prevention programs target mixed-gender audiences and do not take into account gender differences in dating violence perpetration. Furthermore, only a small number of studies have used rigorous methodologies to assess the effects that dating violence programming has on participants' attitudes and, most importantly, reduction in aggressive dating behaviors (Hickman et al., 2004; Whitaker et al., 2006). Indeed, only two programs (Safe Dates and Youth Relationships Project) that have undergone controlled evaluations have demonstrated actual reductions in dating violence (although these reductions do not always remain consistent over time) (Foshee, 1996; Foshee et al., 1996, 1998, 2000, 2004; Wolfe et al., 2001, 2003). Both Safe Dates and Youth Relationships Project employ intensive, multi-session curricula with mixed-gender, adolescent audiences. However, the target audiences for these two programs are somewhat different: Safe Dates is a school-based program that targets all youths, whereas the Youth Relationships Project is a community-based program that targets high-risk youths with histories of maltreatment. Interestingly, although the effects of the Safe Dates program did not vary by gender (Foshee et al., 2004), the effects of the Youth Relationships Project were stronger for girls than for boys (Wolfe et al., 2003).

Preliminary findings from outcome evaluation studies of dating violence prevention programs underscore the importance of potential gender differences in program effectiveness. Accordingly, it has been suggested that gender-specific programming may be more effective in presenting dating violence and sexual assault than mixed-gender programming (Edwards et al., 2009; Gidycz, Orchowski, & Edwards, in press; Graves, 2007), especially in light of the fact that most evaluations of these programs find null results (Gidycz et al., in press; Hickman et al., 2004; Whitaker et al., 2006). Given the documented gender differences in dating violence, and consistent with proposed theoretical explanations of adolescent girls' and young women's aggression, it is presumable that programming grounded in female-specific socialization experiences and experiences of past victimizations will be more effective than gender-neutral programming (Edwards et al., 2009; Graves, 2007; Zurbriggen, 2009). Whereas some programming efforts are critical for both sexes (e.g., definitions of dating violence, identification of risky dating situations, healthy conflict resolution strategies, changing norms associated with dating violence, decreasing bystander behavior), some gender-specific information (e.g., coping with past trauma, self-defense strategies) might best be delivered in single-gender programs. Ultimately, it is an empirical question about whether mixed- or single-gender programs are most effective in reducing dating violence.

In the past decade, our understanding of adolescent girls and young women's perpetration of dating violence has increased. However, more research is needed in order to better understand the gender variations in risk factors for and theoretical explanations of dating violence. Although research demonstrates that many adolescent girls and young women aggress in response to men's aggression, there is clearly a subset of women who are initiators and primary perpetrators of aggression in relationships, which warrants further empirical investigation. We also need to develop a better understanding of the temporal sequencing of violence within adolescent relationships as well as the role of peer norms and substance abuse in dating violence (and if gender moderates any of these relationships). As our understanding of gender variations in dating violence increases, this information can be used to refine, develop, and evaluate dating violence prevention programs in schools and communities while advocating for broader institutional and societal changes to promote healthy dating relationships.

References

Abel, E. M. (2001). Comparing the social service utilization, exposure to violence, and trauma symptomatology of domestic violence female "victims" and female "batterers." *Journal of Family Violence, 16,* 401–420. doi:10.1023/A:1012276927091

Archer, J. (2000). Sex differences in aggression between heterosexual partners: A meta-analytic review. *Psychological Bulletin, 126,* 651–680. doi:10.1037/0033-2909.126.5.651

Archer, J. (2002). Sex differences in physically aggressive acts between heterosexual partners: A meta-analytic review. *Aggression and Violent Behavior, 7,* 313–351. doi:10.1016/S1359-1789(01)00061-1

Arriaga, X. B., & Foshee, V. A. (2004). Adolescent dating violence: Do adolescents follow in their friends', or their parents', footsteps? *Journal of Interpersonal Violence, 19,* 162–184. doi:10.1177/0886260503260247

Bandura, A. (1977). *Social learning theory.* Englewood Cliffs, NJ: Prentice-Hall.

Cano, A., Avery-Leaf, S., Cascardi, M., & O'Leary, K. (1998). Dating aggression in two high school samples: Discriminating variables. *Journal of Primary Prevention, 18,* 431–446. doi:10.1023/A:1022653609263

Capaldi, D. M., & Crosby, L. (1997). Observed and reported psychological and physical aggression in young, at-risk couples. *Social Development, 6,* 184–206. doi:10.1111/1467-9507.00033

Capaldi, D. M., & Gorman-Smith, D. (2003). The development of aggression in young male/female couples. In P. Florsheim (Ed.), *Adolescent romantic relations and sexual behavior: Theory, research, and practical implications* (pp. 243–278). Mahwah, NJ: Lawrence Erlbaum Associates.

Crawford, E., & Wright, M. O. (2007). The impact of childhood psychological maltreatment on interpersonal schemas and subsequent experiences of relationship aggression. *Journal of Emotional Abuse, 7,* 93–116. doi:10.1300/J135v07n02_06

Dasgupta, S. D. (1999). Just like men? A critical view of violence by women. In M. F. Shepard & E. L. Pence (Eds.), *Coordinating community responses to domestic violence: Lessons from Duluth and beyond* (pp. 195–222). Thousand Oaks, CA: Sage.

Dasgupta, S. D. (2002). A framework for understanding women's use of non-lethal violence in intimate heterosexual relationships. *Violence Against Women, 8,* 1364–1389. doi:10.1177/107780102762478046

DeBellis, M. D., & Putnam, F. W. (1994). The psychobiology of childhood maltreatment. *Child and Adolescent Psychiatric Clinics of North America, 3*(4), 663–678.

DiLillo, D., Giuffre, D., Tremblay, G. C., & Peterson, L. (2001). A closer look at the nature of intimate partner violence reported by women with a history of child sexual abuse. *Journal of Interpersonal Violence, 16,* 116–132. doi:10.1177/088626001016002002

Edwards, K. E., Desai, A. D., Gidycz, C. A., & VanWynsberghe, A. (2009). College women's aggression in relationships: The role of childhood and adolescent victimization. *Psychology of Women Quarterly, 33,* 255–265. doi:10.1111/j.1471-6402.2009.01498.x

Faith, K. (1993). *Unruly women: The politics of confinement and resistance.* Vancouver, Canada: Press Gang.

Fiebert, M. S., & Gonzalez, D. M. (1997). College women who initiate assaults on their male partners and the reasons offered for such behavior. *Psychological Reports, 80,* 583–590.

Fisher, B. S., Cullen, F. T., & Turner, M. G. (2000). *The sexual victimization of college women* (NCJ 182369). Washington, DC: U.S. Department of Justice.

Follette, V. M., & Alexander, P. C. (1992). Dating violence: Current and historical correlates. *Behavioral Assessment, 14,* 39–52.

Follingstad, D. R., Wright, S., Lloyd, S., & Sebastian, J. (1991). Sex differences in motivations and effects in dating violence. *Family Relations, 40,* 51–57. doi:10.2307/585658

Foo, L., & Margolin, G. (1995). A multivariate investigation of dating violence. *Journal of Family Violence, 10,* 351–377. doi:10.1007/BF02110711

Foshee, V. A. (1996). Gender differences in adolescent dating abuse prevalence, types, and injuries. *Health Education Research, 11,* 275–286. doi:10.1093/her/11.3.275-a

Foshee, V. A., Bauman, K. E., Arriaga, X. B., Helms, R. W., Koch, G. G., & Linder, G. F. (1998). An evaluation of Safe Dates, an adolescent dating violence prevention program. *American Journal of Public Health, 88*(1), 45–50. doi:10.2105/AJPH.88.1.45

Foshee, V. A., Bauman, K. E., Ennett, S. T., Linder, G. F., Benefield, T., & Suchindran, C. (2004). Assessing the long-term effects of the Safe Dates program and a booster in preventing and reducing adolescent dating violence victimization and perpetration. *American Journal of Public Health, 94,* 619–624. doi:10.2105/AJPH.94.4.619

Foshee, V. A., Bauman, K. E., Greene, W. F., Koch, G. G., Linder, G. F., & MacDougall, J. E. (2000). The Safe Dates program: 1-year follow-up results. *American Journal of Public Health, 90*(10), 1619–1622. doi:10.2105/AJPH.90.10.1619

Foshee, V. A., Bauman, K. E., Linder, F., Rice, J., & Wilcher, R. (2007). Typologies of adolescent dating violence: Identifying typologies of adolescent dating violence perpetration. *Journal of Interpersonal Violence, 22,* 498–519. doi:10.1177/0886260506298829

Foshee, V. A., Linder, G. F., Bauman, K. E., Langwick, S. A., Arriaga, X. B., Heath, J. L., et al. (1996). The Safe Dates project: Theoretical basis, evaluation design, and selected baseline findings. *American Journal of Preventive Medicine, 12,* 39–47.

Gidycz, C. A., McNamara, J. R., & Edwards, K. E. (2006). Women's risk perception and sexual victimization: A review of the literature. *Aggression and Violent Behavior, 11*(5), 441–456. doi:10.1016/j.avb.2006.01.004

Gidycz, C. A., Orchowski, L. M., & Edwards, K. M. (in press). Sexual violence: Primary prevention. In J. White, M. Koss, & A. Kazdin (Eds.), *Violence against women and children: Consensus, critical analysis, and emergent priorities.* Washington, DC: American Psychological Association.

Graves, K. N. (2007). Not always sugar and spice: Expanding theoretical and functional explanations for why females aggress. *Aggression and Violent Behavior, 12,* 131–140. doi:10.1016/j.avb.2004.08.002

Graves, K. N., Sechrist, S. M., White, J. W., & Paradise, M. J. (2005). Intimate partner violence perpetrated by college women within the context of a history of victimization. *Psychology of Women Quarterly, 29,* 278–289. doi:10.1111/j.1471-6402.2005.00222.x

Gwartney-Gibbs, P. A., Stockard, J., & Bohmer, S. (1987). Learning courtship aggression: The influence of parents, peers, and personal experiences. *Family Relations, 36,* 276–282. doi:10.2307/583540

Hamberger, L. K., & Guse, C. E. (2002). Men's and women's use of intimate partner violence in clinical samples. *Violence Against Women, 8,* 1301–1331. doi:10.1177/107780102762478028

Hickman, L. J., Jaycox, L. H., & Aronoff, J. (2004). Dating violence among adolescents: Prevalence, gender distribution, and prevention program effectiveness. *Trauma, Violence, and Abuse, 5,* 123–142. doi:10.1177/1524838003262332

Kaura, S. A., & Allen, C. M. (2004). Dissatisfaction with relationship power and dating violence perpetration by men and women. *Journal of Interpersonal Violence, 19,* 576–588. doi:10.1177/0886260504262966

Luthra, R., & Gidycz, C. A. (2006). Dating violence among college men and women: Evaluation of a theoretical model. *Journal of Interpersonal Violence, 21,* 717–731. doi:10.1177/0886260506287312

Magdol, L., Moffitt, T. E., Caspi, A., Newman, D. L., Fagan, J., & Silva, P. A. (1997). Gender differences in partner violence in a birth cohort of 21-year-olds: Bridging the gap between clinical and epidemiological approaches. *Journal of Consulting and Clinical Psychology, 65*, 68–78. doi:10.1037/0022-006X.65.1.68

Magdol, L., Moffitt, T. E., Caspi, A., & Silva, P. A. (1998). Developmental antecedents of partner abuse: A prospective longitudinal study. *Journal of Abnormal Psychology, 107*, 375–389. doi:10.1037/0021-843X.107.3.375

Miller, B. A., Downs, W. R., & Testa, M. (1993). Interrelationships between victimization experiences and women's alcohol use. *Journal of Studies on Alcohol and Drugs, 11*, 109–117.

Molidor, C., & Tolman, R. M. (1998). Gender and contextual factors in adolescent dating violence. *Violence Against Women, 4*, 180–195. doi:10.1177/1077801298004002004

Murray, C. E., & Mobley, A. K. (2009). Empirical research about same-sex intimate partner violence: A methodological review. *Journal of Homosexuality, 56*(3), 361–386. doi:10.1080/00918360902728848

Noonan, R. K., & Charles, D. (2009). Developing teen dating violence prevention strategies: Formative research with middle school youth. *Violence Against Women, 15*, 1087–1105. doi:10.1177/1077801209340761

O'Keefe, M. (1997). Predictors of dating violence among high school students. *Journal of Interpersonal Violence, 12*, 546–568. doi:10.1177/088626097012004005

O'Keefe, M. (1998). Factors mediating the link between witnessing interparental violence and dating violence. *Journal of Family Violence, 13*, 39–57. doi:10.1023/A:1022860700118

O'Keefe, M., & Treister, L. (1998). Victims of dating violence among high school students. *Violence Against Women, 4*, 195–223. doi:10.1177/1077801298004002005

Paterson, J., Fairbairn-Dunlop, P., Cowley-Malcolm, E., Schluter, P. (2007). Maternal childhood parental abuse history and current intimate partner violence: Data from the Pacific Islands Families Study. *Violence and Victims, 22*, 474–488.

Rennison, C. M., & Welchans, S. (2000). *Intimate partner violence*. Washington, DC: U.S. Department of Justice, Bureau of Justice Statistics.

Riggs, D. S., & O'Leary, D. K. (1989). A theoretical model of courtship aggression. *Violence in dating relationships: Emerging social issues*. New York: Praeger Publishers.

Riggs, D. S., & O'Leary, D. K. (1996). Aggression between heterosexual dating partners: An examination of a causal model of courtship aggression. *Journal of Interpersonal Violence, 11*, 519–540. doi:10.1177/088626096011004005

Schwartz, M., O'Leary, S. G., & Kendziora, K. T. (1997). Dating aggression among high school students. *Violence and Victims, 12*, 295–305.

Sellers, C. S., Cochran, J. K., & Branch, K. A. (2005). Social learning theory and partner violence: A research note. *Deviant Behavior, 26*, 379–395. doi:10.1080/016396290931669

Simkins, S., & Katz, S. (2002). Criminalizing abused females. *Violence Against Women, 8*, 1474–1499. doi:10.1177/107780102237966

Starzomski, A., & Nussbaum, D. (2000). The self and the psychology of domestic homicide-suicide. *International Journal of Offender Therapy and Comparative Criminology, 44*(4), 468–479. doi:10.1177/0306624X00444005

Swan, S. C., Gambone, L. J., Caldwell, J. E., Sullivan, T. P., & Snow, D. L. (2008). A review of research on women's use of violence with male intimate partners. *Violence and Victims, 23*, 301–314. doi:10.1891/0886-6708.23.3.301

Swan, S. C., & Snow, D. L. (2002). A typology of women's use of violence in intimate relationships. *Violence Against Women, 8*, 286–319. doi:10.1177/107780120200800302

Thibaut, J. W., & Kelley, H. (1959). *The Social Psychology of Groups.* New York: Wiley.

Tjaden, P., & Thoennes, N. (2000). Prevalence and consequences of male-to-female and female-to-male intimate partner violence as measured by the National Violence Against Women Survey. *Violence Against Women, 6*, 142–161. doi:10.1177/10778010022181769

Tontodonato, P., & Crew, B. (1992). Dating violence, social learning theory, and gender: A multivariate analysis. *Violence and Victims, 7*, 3–14.

Ullman, S. E. (1998). Does offender violence escalate when rape victims fight back? *Journal of Interpersonal Violence, 13*, 179–192. doi:10.1177/088626098013002001

Whitaker, D. J., Morrison, S., Lindquist, S., Hawkins, S. R., O'Neil, J. A., Nesius, A. M., et al. (2006). A critical review of interventions for the primary prevention of perpetration of partner violence. *Aggression and Violent Behavior, 11*, 151–166. doi:10.1016/j.avb.2005.07.007

Widom, C. W. (1989). The cycle of violence. *Science, 244*(April), 160–244.

Wolfe, D. A., Scott, K., Wekerle, C., & Pittman, A.-L. (2001). Child maltreatment: Risk of adjustment problems and dating violence in adolescence. *Journal of the American Academy of Child and Adolescent Psychiatry, 40*(3), 282–289. doi:10.1097/00004583-200103000-00007

Wolfe, D. A., Wekerle, C., Scott, K., Straatman, A., & Grasley, C. (2004). Predicting abuse in adolescent dating relationships over one year: The role of child maltreatment and trauma. *Journal of Abnormal Psychology, 113*, 406–415.

Wolfe, D. A., Wekerle, C., Scott, K., Straatman, A., Grasley, C., & Reitzel-Jaffe, D. (2003). Dating violence prevention with at-risk youth: A controlled outcome evaluation. *Journal of Consulting and Clinical Psychology, 71*, 279–291.

Zahn, M. A. (2007). The causes of girls' delinquency and their program implications. *Family Court Review, 45*, 456–465. doi:10.1111/j.1744-1617.2007.00161.x

Zurbriggen, E. L. (2009). Understanding and preventing adolescent dating violence: The importance of developmental, sociocultural, and gendered perspectives. *Psychology of Women Quarterly, 33*, 30–33. doi:10.1111/j.1471-6402.2008.01471.x

PART II

Educational Responses to Teen Violence

CHAPTER FIVE

Educating Teens to Discriminate Abusive from Nonabusive Situations

Imelda N. Bratton, Christopher P. Roseman, and William E. Schweinle

Research on How Adolescents Experience Abuse

Over the past 30 years, there has been an increase in media attention on scientific research into the abuse that adolescents experience. Makepeace (1981) originally noted this phenomenon, which eventually lead to awareness that adolescent abuse and abusiveness are a serious public health issue. For instance, the most current data from the National Child Abuse and Neglect Data System (U.S. Department of Health and Human Services, Administration on Children, Youth, and Families, 2010) found that 772,000 children (1 to 17 years of age) were victims of child abuse or neglect in 2008. Approximately 71.1% experienced neglect; 16.1% experienced physical abuse; 9.1% experienced sexual abuse; and 7.3% experienced emotional or psychological maltreatment.

Other research estimates place overall rates from 9% to 80% (e.g., Boney-McCoy & Finkerlhor, 1995; Ely, Dulmus, & Wodarski, 2002; Hickman, Joycox, & Arnoff, 2004; O'Keefe & Treister, 1998; Perry & Fromuth, 2005; Roberts & Klein, 2003). Variance between the different reported results tends to depend on how the researchers operationally define the word "abuse." Regardless, these findings do suggest that abuse occurs to at least roughly 1 in 10 teens.

The majority of abuse research has focused on physical abuse and has identified an association between teenagers' experience of abusive situations and mental health issues. For example, teens who experience dating violence have an increased rate of depression, eating disorders, and suicidal thoughts or ideation, as well as diminished mental and physical well-being (Ackard & Neumak-Sztainer, 2002; Coker et al., 2000). Furthermore, females who experience dating violence encounter more psychological abuse than males (Ely et al. 2002; Foshee, 1996; Fredland et al., 2005; Hamby & Sugarman, 1999; Molidor & Tolman, 1998; Simons, Lin, & Gordon, 1998).

Psychological abuse is common among teenagers and serves to intimidate or control the victim. The prevalence of psychological abuse between teens has been estimated at 20% to 96% (James, West, Deters, & Armijo, 2000; Jezl, Molidor, & Wright, 1996; Molidor, 1995). Foshee (1996) identified threatening behaviors, behavior monitoring, personal insults, and emotional manipulation among various types of psychological abuse used by teenagers. Although both male and female teens exhibit these behaviors, adolescent females are more likely than adolescent males to use emotional abuse. Additionally, Kasian and Painter (1992) reported an association between the use of psychological abuse in relationships and the risk of physical relationship violence.

Learning requires the ability to focus and concentrate, which can be difficult for students who have other things (e.g., abuse) on their mind. Although adolescents frequently experience abusive situations, there are few studies examining the academic effects of these abusive experiences. However, some studies offer important insight. For instance, Luster, Small, and Lower (2002) found that girls and boys who experienced abuse from an adult had lower grade-point averages. More recently, Banyard and Cross (2008) replicated these results and emphasized the importance of social support in moderating the effect of abuse on students' academic performance. Specifically, Banyard and Cross found that abused male teens who perceived that they had neighborhood support had better grades, while abused female teens who perceived that they had parental and neighborhood support reported only a reduced frequency of suicidal thoughts. It is clear then, that abuse, whether from adults or from peers, does negatively affect students' school performance.

Adolescents' Attitudes toward Abuse

The ability to recognize abuse can be difficult for adults. It can be especially difficult for inexperienced teenagers. For instance, among teenagers abuse is not easy to distinguish from "just kidding around" or rough play (Sears, Byers,

Whelan, & Saint-Pierre, 2006). These distinctions are especially ambiguous in the complex social and developing intra- and interpersonal worlds of adolescents.

The inability to make this important distinction could be related to the developmental stages of adolescence. And teen relationships are typically unstable, which can increase the likelihood of violence. Foshee, Bauman, Linder, Rice, and Wilcher (2007) found that adolescents who initially reported they had perpetrated acts of violence toward their dating partners were actually referring to playful—but perhaps inappropriate or inept—flirting. More specifically, Foshee and colleagues found that among both male and female adolescents, slapping, pushing, or hitting others is a common occurrence in various relationships and does not signify an act of violence. This plausibly explains, at least in part, why adolescents may have a difficult time identifying an abusive situation.

Several studies have examined the possibility that parental violence is a factor leading to acceptance of abuse in future peer relationships (Foshee, Ennett, Bauman, Benefield, & Suchindran, 2005; Lichter & McCloskey, 2004; White & Smith, 2009). For instance, Fredland and colleagues (2005) conducted a qualitative study exploring the perspectives of adolescents. Fredland et al. identified several personal experiences in adolescents' home environment that impacted the acceptance of abuse in their friendship or dating relationships. Although the adolescents in the study recognized that violence is not part of a healthy relationship, they were not surprised that it can be present in relationships. Some adolescents even described the need to assault their partners when talking does not solve relationship issues. Males listed the following physical acts as examples: slapping, hitting, kicking, etc. Additionally, some of the male participants argued that it was acceptable to strike a female if the female initiated the physical altercation, or that it was fine to strike a female partner but not in the face. These "rules" describing when it is acceptable to strike females shows that young men know they should not generally use violence with females. However, the boys appeared to be confused about whether violence against one's female partner is never acceptable. Overall, Fredland and colleagues found that both male and female adolescents viewed violence as acceptable in relationships.

In the past, it has been assumed that males were typically perpetrators of partner abuse. However, emerging research indicates that males and females may initiate adolescent violence equally (Arriaga & Foshee, 2004; Gray & Foshee, 1997; Ozer, Tschann, Pasch, & Flores, 2004; Rennison, 2002; Tjaden and Thoennes, 2000).

Teenagers are often reluctant to intervene in peer violence situations (Weisz & Black, 2008). This could be due to the belief that it is not their business or responsibility, though it is possible that they simply do not know how to intervene effectively. Females in the Weisz and Black study reported concern about negative consequences for intervening and expressed fear that the violence may be turned toward them. This is a realistic concern, as the majority of teenagers reported to Weisz and Black they had either experienced or perpetrated violence within 6 months of the study. Other theories speculate that teenagers are hesitant to intervene because they like to think that they could take care of their own issues and do not want someone else to intercede in their relationship conflicts. On the other hand, teenagers are more likely to intervene in someone else's relationship abuse if they know either the perpetrator or victim of abuse (Black & Weisz, 2005; Tisak & Tisak, 1996).

Immaturity, lack of experience, fear, and previous abuse experience may lead teenagers into and keep them in abusive situations. While friendships and dating relationships are a natural part of the social development process, abuse should not be so easily accepted in this process. Still, emerging research indicates that teenagers have a high rate of abuse in their relationships, do not interact with clear or correct definitions of abuse, have an overall accepting view of abusive situations, and are generally hesitant to intervene in abusive situations between their peers.

Abuse in the Literature

One of the critical issues in researching and in adjudicating abuse is operationally defining "*abuse.*" Among academic literature, the law, advocacy organizations, and researchers, one can find various views on how abuse should be defined. Although some definitions are somewhat similar, there are distinct differences. Initially, definitions of abuse tended to reflect the legal definition, which included only behaviors that resulted in physical harm or included the threat of physical harm to another person. However, more recent definitions have expanded on this and take into consideration some of the contextual issues surrounding potentially abusive behavior. For example, several authors consider dating violence to include physical, sexual, and/or psychological aggression or threats in an unmarried relationship (Glass et al., 2003; Herrman, 2009). The inclusion of sexual and psychological aggression greatly expands on the scope of older research, as well as on clinical and legal definitions of abuse. Furthermore, there has been a variety of terms used to denote violence in teenagers' relationships (e.g., dating violence, intimate partner violence, and partner abuse). This has also inhibited a clearer definition and understanding of abuse.

This definitional variance is further evident in the differences between specific state laws, which define abuse in forensic settings. Although statutes may vary from state to state, the more broad definition of abuse does not. Lawyers and courts typically consult *Black's Law Dictionary* for descriptions and meanings of terms in legal preparations and proceedings. *Black's Law Dictionary* defines abuse as "physical or mental maltreatment, often resulting in mental, emotional, sexual, or physical injury." In addition, violence is defined as "the use of physical force, usually accompanied by fury, vehemence, or outrage; physical force unlawfully exercised with the intent to harm . . . violence between members of a household . . . the infliction of physical injury, or the creation of a reasonable fear that physical injury or harm will be inflicted, by a parent or a member or former member of a child's household, against a child or against another member of the household." These common definitions are used when lawyers prepare for custody, abuse/neglect hearings, and protection orders.

There are many national and state advocacy organizations devoted to the prevention of abuse and domestic violence of children, adolescents, and adults. These organizations publish valuable information related to abuse and violence, which can usually be accessed through the Internet. This information generally includes a definition of abuse or violence, checklists of examples of abuse or violence, how to get help, and contact information for local and national resources. For instance, the Advocacy Center and the Domestic Abuse Project (2010) define domestic violence and emotional abuse as "behaviors used by one person in a relationship to control the other. Partners may be married or not married; heterosexual, gay, or lesbian; living together, separated, or dating." Importantly, this definition encompasses the notion of power and control over the victim. In 2010, the Advocacy Center and Domestic Abuse Project definition was expanded by the National Center for Victims of Crime to include "willful intimidation."

Both of these organizations consider emotional, sexual, and physical acts as components of abuse or violence. The National Council on Child Abuse and Family Violence is unique by specifying gender in their definition: "domestic violence includes physical abuse, sexual violence, psychological and/or emotional abuse of a woman by her mate or companion" (Domestic Abuse Project, 2010). These are only a few of the definitions of abuse and violence that are used by various advocacy organizations nationwide. However, the operating definitions used by advocacy organizations concur in continuing to broaden their definitions of abuse and in their consideration of the contexts and outcomes of behaviors that could be considered abusive.

In the past, researchers commonly operationally defined abuse or violence for participants in surveys or qualitative interviews. Two definitions generally employed by researchers were "the use or threat of physical force or restraint carried out with the intent of causing pain or injury to another" (Sugarman & Hotaling, 1991) and "any attempt to control or dominate another person physically, sexually, or psychologically, causing some level of harm" (Wolfe et al., 1996). These definitions were frequently used interchangeably or in conjunction with one another to describe the type of incident(s) being investigated.

More recently, researchers have revisited the definitions of abuse and violence. The growing body of research literature indicates that abuse is bidirectional (e.g., Straus, 2008) and that the assumption that males are the only ones who perpetrate is sexist (Ross & Babcock, 2010). Interestingly, Ross and Babcock question who the victim is in bidirectional violence. Historically, men have been typically blamed for initiating violence, though this assumption is not categorically accurate. Although some women react in self-defense, other women instigate and perpetrate violence. Some couples are mutually violent. Furthermore, assuming the male is solely at fault prohibits the study of female-initiated perpetration, which has been an area that is relatively unresearched. Ultimately, this is disadvantageous for both female and male partners, as researchers have not developed the necessary understanding of this phenomenon to intervene effectively when females are violent.

A majority of feminist researchers agree that violence needs to be considered in context. Consistent with the introduction of new ideas, researchers are debating the most appropriate method to contextualize violence. Researchers have used instruments such as the Conflict Tactics Scales, the Revised Conflict Tactics Scales, the National Crime Victimization Survey, and the Women's Experiences of Battering to obtain data. Langhinrichsen-Rohling (2010) recently explored how researchers and practitioners can effectively measure partner violence. Based on her findings, she recommends that practitioners and researchers assess injuries, experienced fear, motivation behind the violence, and antecedents to the violence, as well as the cultural context of each individual involved in the violent situation. Obtaining the "big picture" of violence may allow researchers to gain richer data that can yield better understanding in this research area. Effective early adolescent prevention strategies can be developed based on this data, as can unique intervention techniques for males and females.

Langhinrichsen-Rohling (2010) reviewed the work of various dyadic researchers and functional typologies to differentiate subtypes of intimate partner violence. The typologies do not include a gender focus, which makes them generalize to homosexual and heterosexual relationships and allow for the possibility that males or females or both partners could perpetrate violent acts. Langhinrichsen-Rohling included a call to researchers to arrive at some consensus that there are different subtypes of intimate partner violence perpetrators (which is applicable for both males and females). Variables such as severity of violence, generalization of violence, motivation for violence, and extent of alcohol or drug use should be established to differentiate subtypes of perpetrators. Langhinrichsen-Rohling argued that the use of typologies in research would allow for a better understanding of etiology, intervention, and treatment strategies, as well as expand research focused on women's use of violence.

However, Langhinrichsen-Rohling's controversial perspective on intimate partner violence has received some criticism from her colleagues. For instance, although Ross and Babcock (2010) supported Langhinrichsen-Rohling's view that females are perpetrators of violence and that the field lacks knowledge of female perpetration, and although they agreed that female-instigated/perpetrated violence should be researched (and raised the question of who the victim actually is in cases of bidirectional abuse), they did not concur with applying typologies to couples who experience violence. Ross and Babcock argue that not all perpetrators fit into categories. And, based on this premise, Ross and Babcock recommended the use of a dimensional approach, in which abuse can be evaluated using one or more oblique and orthogonal continua, which results in a profile of a given abusive behavior rather than a discrete category. Ross and Babcock suggest that researchers should identify and develop measures for these continuous abuse-related dimensions and establish evidence-based links to possible interventions.

Stark (2010) concurred with the argument that both males and females participate in violence. Stark also suggested that clinicians may be able to use a form of typology in clinical work with abusive partners. He defined abuse as having the following components. It is: non-voluntary, characterized by exercising authority over another and reallocating opportunities that will benefit the abuser. Stark recommended examining acts of violence in their historical context by exploring subjective information from the victim and taking into consideration whether the victim experienced fear or psychological trauma. Additionally, Stark argued that viewing abuse in historical contexts supports research and victims' reports that abuse can be a continuous "process" rather than one or more isolated categorical events. It is important to note here that the additive outcomes of long-term abuse may be substantially more detrimental to victims than any single incident. However, minor abuse is generally minimized in the courts, which treat minor abusive episodes as uniquely occurring misdemeanors. Unlike Langhinrichsen-Rohling, Stark supported the continued research of male-dominated abuse, arguing that males who are assaulted by females do not desire or need additional assistance, support, or protection.

Based on his research, Johnson (2010) created a control-based typology. Types include intimate terrorism, violent resistance, and situational couple violence. Intimate terrorism is the use of violence, along with other tactics, to gain control over the partner. Violent resistance is the use of violence to resist being controlled. Johnson also reported that males for the most part perpetrate violence. Partners who are in intimate terrorism relationships can also employ and experience violent resistance. Johnson argued on the basis of data collected from advocacy agencies that these are *the* two main types of violence. Johnson further argued that this is the case because intimate terrorism occurs continuously over the length of the relationship. This also concurs with Starks's assertion that abuse should be viewed in context. The third type of abuse, situational couple violence, refers to disputes that escalate into verbal and physical aggression. Situational couple violence is not ongoing, does not have a control motive, and is perpetrated by both males and females.

Johnson further argued that situational violence dominates general research data and declared that the differences between sources of data, agencies, and researchers are what have led to historically inconsistent frequency estimates and research findings about intimate partner violence. Johnson suggested that data from agencies is truly representative of violence and that general research data does not accurately represent violence. He adds that there is a higher level of male than female violence perpetration and intimate terrorism.

Clearly, as this brief literature review reveals, defining abuse is difficult. And, based on the current legal, political, advocacy, and scientific debates revolving around the definition(s) of partner abuse, it appears that more debate, and hopefully more research, will help better clarify this issue. However, for the time being, abuse can be defined as an amalgam of the different definitions we have discussed above.

> Abuse is the threat to act or action that leads to physical, psychological, or sexual harm to a person.

Involvement in Abusive Relationships

For both the perpetrator and the victim, tendencies toward abusive relationships may begin to reveal themselves before full adulthood. These tendencies are often a manifestation of formative childhood experiences, such as having been the victim of parental abuse or having witnessed abusive behavior between parents (see Dutton, 2007, for a thorough review of these predisposing and related personality factors). For instance, a child's observation and subsequent perception of patterns of abusive behavior or the child's observation of a victim's willingness to remain in an abusive relationship may be mirrored in the child's early romantic relationships. This is why it is valuable to identify warning signs of abusive tendencies and educate teenagers at these early stages. For both perpetrator and victim, intervention may have invaluable long-term implications. We thus direct the focus of our current discussion toward recognized and recognizable abuse tendencies in teenage relationships.

Teenage romantic engagement is a particularly powerful emotional time in life. Both boys and girls struggle to understand their complex feelings of attachment, their sexual desires, and the social and ethical nuances of dating. This is already a tumultuous period in one's psychosocial development, even without any significant abuse or neglect in a teenager's life. For teens who also struggle with childhood trauma, or who simply are prone to wild mood swings, violence, and abusive behavior, the furor of the dating world is likely to encourage a number of inappropriate to severely dysfunctional responses toward an intimate partner. Similarly, for those who struggle with low self-esteem, insecurity, and difficulty establishing a sound personal identity, there may be a tendency to enter into and remain in almost any relationship, including an abusive one. The discussion hereafter will consider the dynamic between a teenager's desire to engage in healthy, appropriate relationships and recognizing both signs and situations that lend themselves to abuse in teenage relationships.

Recognizing Abusive Situations

As discussed earlier in this chapter, the first task in addressing the phenomenon of abuse in teenage relationships is defining abuse and framing it as something recognizable. According to Eckhardt, Jamison, and Watts (2002), there is a clear connection between one's anger arousal, management of that anger, and the likelihood of violence. They compared the scores of nonviolent (NV) men to men who have committed acts of dating violence (DV) on two formally endorsed modes of anger testing: the

State-Trait Anger Expression Inventory (STAXI) and the articulated thoughts during simulated situations (ATSS) instruments. Following these tests, Eckhardt and colleagues coded the participants' articulated thoughts for anger-related affect, other negative emotions, and aggressive verbalizations. Relative to NV men, the DV men scored significantly higher on STAXI Trait Anger, Anger In, and Anger Out scales. The DV men also scored lower on STAXI Anger Control. Finally, the DV men articulated more aggression during ATSS anger arousal than the NV men did (Eckhardt et al., 2002).

The results of the Eckhardt and colleagues (2002) study indicate that nonviolent men generally have a greater ability to manage their emotions and, simultaneously, are able to recognize their emotional interactions with greater accuracy. By contrast, violent men tend to interpret a majority of events as motivated or designed to invoke their anger. The apparent differences underscore either an emotional management deficiency among the violent men or a greater appetite for violence in their relationships. These findings are useful in recognizing abuse patterns or tendencies among potential partners.

When members of a peer group or adults see an adolescent who is quick to anger irrationally, it may seem reasonable, or even imperative, for the adult or peer member to intervene. The need to seek out interventions may be particularly important when this anger tends to be expressed toward a relationship partner. While poor anger control or an extreme appetite for violence may not inherently predict a violent or abusive relationship, these characteristics should be seen as evidence that there may be an underlying emotional dysfunction present in the relationship.

This prompts consideration of the scientific obstacles to effective evaluation of the causes of intimate partner violence (IPV). Specifically, clinical research has documented a myriad of behaviors that would be clinically perceived as abuse. For example, Bell and Naugle (2008) argue that many theories provide conceptual explanations for IPV. Each of these theories is supported by empirical findings. However, these theories offer only limited explanation of IPV episodes and are not explanatory enough to have a good impact on IPV treatment and prevention programs. This lack of understanding makes it difficult for clinical and lay observers to predict and intervene in violence—especially in teenage relationships.

The repeated emphasis throughout most research is on the tendency of men to be the perpetrators and women the victims of IPV. Many studies have focused investigative inquiry on illuminating and understanding the characteristics exhibited by abusive men. It is here that such personality assessment tools as the MMPI come into consideration. Eckhardt, Samper, and Murphy (2008) identified characteristics such as (a) having experienced abuse during the formative childhood years, (b) having scored higher on psychopathology measures, and (c) having substance abuse problems as contributing to male tendencies toward IPV. Eckhardt and colleagues conclude that most partner-abusive men do not appear to have anger-related personality issues. However, teen anger problems may be indicative of personality traits that can enable IPV and that may make treatment difficult.

Again, these precursors are useful for identifying patterns of abuse. That stated, the findings by Langhinrichsen-Rohling (2010) also require us to question the primacy of male-centered abuse observation and consider that many other forms of abuse go unreported. Langhinrichsen-Rohling suggests that this represents a core problem for researchers and clinicians who work at trying to identify and predict abuse. She further argues that data from broader samples, including information about uni- and bidirectional abuse, need to be aggregated and analyzed. These arguments suggest that in attempting to identify patterns of abuse in teenage relationships, it is necessary to look for all varieties of abusive behavior and contexts, rather than simply those that appear to be modal.

Teenage/Adolescent Patterns of Abuse

In teenage romantic relationships, it is important to identify patterns of abuse. Research findings indicate that the incidence of dating violence and abusiveness in teenage relationships is on the rise and that there is a problematic tendency toward acceptance of these behaviors among teenage peer groups. Accordingly, there is pressure on peers, parents, teachers, counselors, and religious leaders to notice the signs of abuse and possibly to intervene. Moreover, there is a need to make young individuals who are entering romantic relationships for the first time aware of the warning signs of abuse, which are not always unambiguous and/or immediately evident.

Young men who (a) tend to lose their temper quickly, (b) show a proclivity toward unpredictable moodiness, (c) are unable to process personal feelings of distress, and/or (d) are inclined to assign blame to those closest to them when faced with difficulties are more likely to abuse their relationship partner, but the abuse may not occur early in the relationship. The same may be true of young men who are inherently overprotective, demanding, jealous, or insecure within the context of a romantic relationship.

Abusive Behaviors Checklist

Abusive relationships can sometimes occur in this evolving fashion; it reinforces the compelling need for techniques or approaches of differentiating between abusive and nonabusive relationships. It often falls on caring friends and a strong support system to help individuals recognize and leave abusive situations. Therefore, the checklist below is directed at teenagers, their friends, their parents, and their teachers. It is intended to serve as a resource by which they might identify patterns of abuse in relationships among adolescents. While this list not all-inclusive, it is based on similar checklist models currently available. Observing any combination of two of the following conditions justifies concern about the possibility of abuse:

Visual signs of unexplained injury

Evidence of abusive verbal behavior by one or both partners

Pushing, shoving, or signs of physical confrontation in front of others

Depression or mood swings in one or both partners

Tendencies toward social withdrawal and isolation from friends or family

Reduced interest in previous hobbies or activities

Isolation within the relationship and a tendency to avoid interaction with other couples

Showing signs of fear over upsetting or angering partner

Possessiveness, jealousy, or insecurity of one or both partners

Frequently making excuses or apologies for partner's behavior

Sudden tendencies toward substance abuse

References

Ackard, D. M., & Neumak-Sztainer, D. (2002). Date violence and date rape among adolescents: Associations with disordered eating behaviors and psychological health. *Child Abuse and Neglect, 26,* 455–473.

Arriaga, X., & Foshee, V. (2004). Adolescent dating violence: Do adolescents follow in their friends', or their parents', footsteps? *Journal of Interpersonal Violence, 19,* 162–184.

Banyard, V., & Cross, C. (2008). Consequences of teen dating violence: Understanding intervening variables in ecological context. *Violence Against Women, 14,* 998–1013.

Bell, K., & Naugle, A. (2008). Intimate partner violence theoretical considerations: Moving toward a contextual framework. *Clinical Psychology Review, 28,* 1096–1107.

Black, B. M., & Weisz, A. N. (2005). Dating violence: A qualitative analysis of Mexican-American youths' views. *Journal of Ethnic and Cultural Diversity in Social Work, 13,* 69–90.

Boney-McCoy, S., & Finkerlhor, D. (1995). Psychosocial sequelae of violent victimization in a national youth sample. *Journal of Consulting and Clinical Psychology, 61,* 726–736.

Coker, A., McKeown, R., Sanderson, M., Davis, K., Valois, R., & Huebner, S. (2000). Severe dating violence and quality of life among South Carolina high school students. *American Journal of Preventive Medicine, 19,* 220–227.

Domestic Abuse Project. (2010). Retrieved on July 11, 2010, from http://www.domesticabuseproject.org/definitions_of_abuse.asp.

Dutton, D. (2007). *The abusive personality: Violence and control in intimate relationships.* New York: Guilford.

Eckhardt, C., Jamison, T. R., & Watts, K. (2002). Anger experience and expression among male dating violence perpetrators during anger arousal. *Journal of Interpersonal Violence, 17,* 1102–1114.

Eckhardt, C., Samper, R., & Murphy, C. (2008). Anger disturbances among perpetrators of intimate partner violence: Clinical characteristics and outcomes of court-mandated treatment. *Journal of Interpersonal Violence, 23,* 1600–1617.

Ely, G., Dulmus, C., & Wodarski, J. (2002). Adolescent dating violence. In L. A. Rapp-Paglicci, A. R. Roberts, & J. S. Wodarski (Eds.), *Handbook of violence* (pp. 33–53). New York: Wiley.

Foshee, V. (1996). Gender differences in adolescent dating abuse prevalence, types and injuries. *Health Education Research, Theory, and Practice, 11,* 275–286.

Foshee, V., Bauman, K., Linder, F., Rice, J., & Wilcher, R. (2007). Typologies of adolescent dating violence: Identifying typologies of adolescent dating violence perpetration. *Journal of Interpersonal Violence, 22,* 498–518.

Foshee, V., Ennett, S., Bauman, K., Benefield, T., & Suchindran, C. (2005). The association between family violence and adolescent dating violence onset: Does it vary by race, socioeconomic status, and family structure? *Journal of Early Adolescence, 25,* 317–344.

Fredland, N., Ricardo, I., Campbell, J., Sharps, P., Kub, J., & Yonas, M. (2005). The meaning of dating violence in the lives of middle school adolescents: A report of a focus group study. *Journal of School Violence, 4,* 95–114.

Glass, N., Fredland, N., Campbell, J., Yonas, M., Sharps, P., & Kub, J. (2003). Adolescent dating violence: Prevalence, risk factors, health outcomes, and implications for clinical practice. *Journal of Obstetrical, Gynecological, and Neonatal Nursing, 32,* 227–238.

Gray, H., & Foshee, V. (1997). Adolescent dating violence: Differences between one-sided and mutually violent profiles. *Journal of Interpersonal Violence, 12,* 136–141.

Hamby, S., & Sugarman, D. (1999). Acts of psychological aggression against a partner and their relation to physical assault and gender. *Journal of Marriage and the Family, 61,* 959–970.

Herrman, J. (2009). There's a fine line . . . Adolescent dating violence and prevention. *Pediatric Nursing, 35,* 164–170.

Hickman, L., Joycox, L., & Arnoff, J. (2004). Dating violence among adolescents: Prevalence, gender distribution, and prevention program effectiveness. *Trauma, Violence, and Abuse, 5,* 123–142.

James, W., West, C., Deters, K., & Armijo, E. (2000). Youth dating violence. *Adolescence, 35,* 455–465.

Jezl, D., Molidor, C., & Wright, T. (1996). Physical, sexual, and psychological abuse in high school dating relationships: Prevalence rates and self-esteem issues. *Child and Adolescent Social Work Journal, 13,* 69–87.

Johnson, M. (2008). *A typology of domestic violence: Intimate terrorism, violent resistance, and situational couple violence.* Boston: Northeastern University Press.

Johnson, M. (2010). Langhinrichsen-Rohling's confirmation of the feminist analysis of intimate partner violence: Comment on "controversies involving gender and intimate partner violence in the United States." *Sex Roles, 62,* 212–219.

Kasian, M., & Painter, S. (1992). Frequency and severity of psychological abuse in a dating population. *Journal of Interpersonal Violence, 7,* 350–364.

Langhinrichsen-Rohling, J. (2010). Controversies involving gender and intimate partner violence in the United States. *Sex Roles, 62,* 179–193.

Lichter, E., & McCloskey, L. (2004). The effects of childhood exposure to marital violence on adolescent gender-role beliefs and dating violence. *Psychology of Women Quarterly, 28,* 344–357.

Luster, T., Small, S., & Lower, R. (2002). The correlates of abuse and witnessing abuse among adolescents. *Journal of Interpersonal Violence, 17,* 1323–1340.

Makepeace, J. M. (1981). Courtship violence among college students. *Family Relations, 30,* 97–102.

Molidor, C. (1995). Gender differences of psychological abuse in high school dating relationships. *Child and Adolescent Social Work Journal, 12,* 119–133.

Molidor, C., & Tolman, R. M. (1998). Gender and contextual factors in adolescent dating violence. *Violence Against Women, 4,* 180–194.

O'Keefe, M., & Treister, L. (1998). Victims of dating violence among high school students. *Journal of Interpersonal Violence, 12,* 195–223.

Ozer, E., Tschann, J., Pasch, L., & Flores, E. (2004). Violence perpetration across peer and partner relationships: Co-occurrence and longitudinal patterns among adolescents. *Journal of Adolescent Health, 34,* 64–71.

Perry, A., & Fromuth, M. (2005). Courtship violence using couple data: Characteristics and perceptions. *Journal of Interpersonal Violence, 20,* 1078–1095.

Rennison, C. (2002). *Criminal victimization 2001: Changes 2000–01 with trends 1993–2001* (NCJ Publication No. NCJ 104610). Washington, DC: U.S. Government Printing Office.

Roberts, T. A., & Klein, J. (2003). Intimate partner abuse and high-risk behavior in adolescents. *Archives Pediatric Adolescent Medicine, 157,* 375–380.

Ross, J., & Babcock, J. (2010). Gender and intimate partner violence in the United States: Confronting the controversies. *Sex Roles, 62,* 194–200.

Sears, H. A., Byers, E. S., Whelan, J. J., & Saint-Pierre, M. (2006). "If it hurts you, then it is not a joke": Adolescents' ideas about girls' and boys' use and experience of abusive behavior in dating relationships. *Journal of Interpersonal Violence, 21,* 1991–1207.

Simons, R., Lin, K-H., & Gordon, L. C. (1998). Socialization in the family of origin and male dating violence: A prospective study. *Journal of Marriage and the Family, 60,* 467–478.

Stark, E. (2010). Do violent acts equal abuse? Resolving the gender parity/asymmetry dilemma. *Sex Roles, 62,* 201–211.

Straus, M. A. (2008). Dominance and symmetry in partner violence by male and female university students in 32 nations. *Children and Youth Services Review, 30,* 252–275.

Sugarman, D., & Hotaling, G. (1991). Dating violence: A review of contextual and risk factors. In L. B. Levy (Ed.), *Dating violence: Young women in danger* (pp. 100–118). Seattle, WA: Seattle Press.

Tisak, M. S., & Tisak, J. (1996). Expectations and judgments regarding bystanders' and victims' responses to peer aggression among early adolescents. *Journal of Adolescence, 19,* 383–392.

Tjaden, P., & Thoennes, N. (2000). *Full report of the prevalence, incidence, and consequences of violence against women: Findings from the National Violence Against Women survey.* U.S. Department of Justice, Office of Justice Programs.

Troubled Teen Issues (TTI). (2009). Abusive teen relationships and teen dating violence. *Troubled Teen 101.* The National Center for Victims of Crime. Retrieved on December 15, 2010, from http://www.ncvc.org/ncvc/main.aspx?dbName=DocumentViewer&DocumentID=32347.

U.S. Department of Health and Human Services, Administration on Children, Youth, and Families. (2010). *Child maltreatment, 2008.* Washington DC: U.S. Government Printing Office. Retrieved on July 11, 2010, from http://www.acf.hhs.gov/programs/cb/pubs/cm08/index.htm.

Weisz, A. N., & Black, B. M. (2008). Peer intervention in dating violence: Beliefs of African American middle school adolescents. *Journal of Ethnic and Cultural Diversity in Social Work, 17,* 177–196.

White, J., & Smith, P. (2009). Co-variation in the use of physical and sexual intimate partner aggression among adolescent and college-age men: A longitudinal analysis. *Violence Against Women, 15,* 24–43.

Wolfe, D., Gough, R., Reitzel-Jaffe, D., Grasley, C., Pittman, A., & Stumpf, J. (1996). *Youth relationship manual: A group approach with adolescents for the prevention of woman abuse and the promotion of healthy relationships.* Thousand Oaks, CA: Sage.

CHAPTER SIX

Young People's Representations of Bullying Causes

Robert L. Thornberg

Bullying is a complex phenomenon and therefore has to be investigated and understood by several theoretical and methodological positions. Nevertheless, in the growing body of bullying research, investigating children's and teenagers' own perspectives on why bullying occurs is still a rather overlooked issue. At the same time, social psychological and social developmental theories, such as the social information processing (SIP) models (Crick & Dodge, 1994; Dodge, Coie, & Lynam, 2006) and symbolic interactionism (Blumer, 1969; Charon, 2007), claim that the way in which children and teens interpret and make sense of social situations and people (including themselves) in these situations affects and guides their behavior. For example, in Crick and Dodge's (1994) SIP model, children's and adolescents' cognitive processes of social information for solving social problems include a variety of constructs from the online processing of current social stimuli to latent knowledge structures or social schemas in their memory (see also Dodge, Coie, & Lynam, 2006). Children's and teens' assumptions and conceptions of social situations and the people involved in these situations influence how they process social information and thus how they respond and act in these social situations (Crick & Dodge, 1994; Gifford-Smith & Rabiner, 2004). Their social cognitions, at least in part and as a complement to situational or contextual factors such as social influence, cultural constructions, and reinforcements, can explain why they act as bullies or take on different bystander roles in bullying situations.

This chapter reviews research in which children's or adolescents' representations of bullying causes have, at least in part, been investigated. Whereas most of these studies have used qualitative methods (e.g., Hamarus & Kaikkonen, 2008; Horowitz et al., 2004; Swart & Bredekamp, 2009; Teräsahjo & Salmivalli, 2003), others have made use of a combination of qualitative and quantitative methods, so-called mixed methods (e.g., Frisén, Holmqvist, & Oscarsson, 2008; Thornberg & Knutsen, in press), and a few have operated with quantitative methods (e.g., Erling & Hwang, 2004; Hoover, Oliver, & Hazler, 1992). The review of this literature indicates that typical themes in children's and young people's representations of bullying causes are: (a) the deviant victim, (b) the struggle for status, power, and friendship, (c) the disturbed bully, (d) having fun and avoiding boredom, (e) group pressure, and (f) mindless bullying. This chapter describes these themes and then concludes by specifically examining research on bullying causes from the bullies' point of view.

The Deviant Victim

Research has shown that a common explanation among children and teens about why bullying occurs is that the victim is different, odd, or deviant in some way (Bosacki, Marini, & Dane, 2006; Buchanan & Winzer, 2001; Burns, Maycock, Cross, & Brown, 2008b; Erling & Hwang, 2004; Frisén et al., 2008; Frisén, Jonsson, & Persson, 2007; Hamarus & Kaikkonen, 2008; Hazler & Hoover, 1993; Hoover, Oliver, & Hazler, 1992; Teräsahjo & Salmivalli, 2003; Thomson & Gunter, 2008; Thornberg, 2010; Varjas et al., 2008). For instance, according to Buchanan and Winzer's (2001) interview study, the most commonly reported characteristic that could lead to being bullied was being different in some way. In Teräsahjo and Salmivalli's (2003) focus group study with 10- to 12-year-old students, the most common reason for bullying that came up in their conversations was the deviance of the children being bullied. Teräsahjo and Salmivalli labeled this "the odd student repertoire." According to a survey study in which 207 students participated (Hoover et al., 1992), "didn't fit in" was one of the highest ranked items of possible factors motivating bullying. Other very highly rated items were "physically weak," "short tempered," "the clothes," "facial appearance," "cried/was emotional," "overweight," and "good grades," which can all be interpreted as expressions of being "different" or "deviant."

Erling and Hwang (2004) conducted a survey study in which 960 children participated. The most frequent answers concerning why some students get bullied were that these students have a different appearance (43%) or are deviant in other ways than by appearance (31%). In Thornberg's (2010) interview study with 10- to 13-year-old students, 82% of them used reaction to deviance as at least one of their explanations why bullying occurs in school. In their focus group study with 11- to 14-year-old middle school students, Horowitz and colleagues (2004) found that "being different in any way" was the core theme underlying students' explanations why a peer becomes a victim of bullying or teasing. This theme permeated four major categories that emerged from their data analysis process: (a) physical appearance, (b) personality and behavior, (c) family and environment, and (d) school-related factors.

Examples of deviancy or differentness, according to school students, that make people more prone to being bullied are wearing "weird," wrong, or "non-cool" clothes (Bosacki et al., 2006; Buchanan & Winzer, 2001; Frisén et al., 2008; Hoover et al., 1992; Horowitz et al., 2004; Thornberg, 2010), having a different or deviant appearance (Frisén et al., 2007; Frisén et al., 2008; Hoover et al., 1992; Horowitiz et al., 2004; Teräsahjo & Salmivalli, 2003; Thomson & Gunter, 2008; Thornberg, 2010), being ugly or not looking good (Bosacki et al., 2006; Cranham & Carroll, 2003; Frisén et al., 2007; Frisén et al., 2008; Horowitz et al., 2004), being nerds, dorks, or geeks (Buchanan & Winzer, 2001; Burns et al., 2008b; Horowitz et al., 2004; Owens, Shute, & Slee, 2000; Thomson & Gunter, 2008; Thornberg, 2010), being quiet, shy, or socially insecure (Buchanan & Winzel, 2001; Burns et al., 2008b; Cranham & Carroll, 2003; Frisén et al., 2007; Frisén et al., 2008; Hamarus & Kaikkonen, 2008; Horowitiz et al., 2004; Thornberg & Knutsen, in press), not being good at sports (Buchanan & Winzer, 2001; Hazler & Hoover, 1993; Horowitz et al., 2004), being fat or overweight (Frisén et al., 2007; Frisén et al., 2008; Hoover et al., 1992; Horowitz et al., 2004; Swart & Bredekamp, 2009; Thomson & Gunter, 2008; Thornberg, 2010), being thin (Frisén et al., 2007; Swart & Bredekamp, 2009; Thornberg, 2010), being childish (Hamarus & Kaikkonen, 2008; Thornberg, 2010), belonging to a minority, different, or "wrong" culture, race, or ethnic group (Frisén et al., 2007; Frisén et al., 2008; Hamarus & Kaikkonen, 2008; Horowitz et al., 2004; Teräsahjo & Salmivalli, 2003; Thomson & Gunter, 2008), talking too much (Horowitz et al., 2004), having weird or strange speech (Erling & Hwang, 2004; Frisén et al., 2007; Thornberg, 2010), being provocative or annoying or saying annoying things (Burns et al., 2008b; Frisén et al., 2008; Hoover et al., 1992; Owens et al., 2000; Thornberg & Knutsen, in press), having a disability or a physical handicap (Horowitz et al., 2004; Thornberg, 2010), being "too stupid" (Hamarus & Kaikkonen, 2008; Horowitz et al., 2004; Thornberg, 2010), displaying academic or social shortcomings (Hazler & Hoover, 1993; Hoover et al., 1992), being "too smart" in class (Burns et al., 2008b; Horowitz et al., 2004), being a teacher's pet (Hazler & Hoover, 1993; Hoover et al., 1992; Horowitiz et al., 2004), acting too much like the other sex (Horowitz et al., 2004), playing with peers of the opposite sex (Thornberg, 2010), being hyperactive (Horowitz et al., 2004), behaving clumsy (Thornberg, 2010), being emotional, oversensitive, or short tempered (Frisén et al., 2008; Hoover et al., 1992), acting "gay" (Horowitz et al., 2004), having nonaccepted, "weird," or different friends (Hoover et al., 1992; Horowitz et al., 2004), not having any friends (Frisén et al., 2007; Frisén et al., 2008; Horowitz et al., 2004; Owens et al., 2000; Thornberg & Knutsen, in press), or having aspects of one's family, neighborhood, or housing that do not meet with peer group approval (Frisén et al., 2008; Hazler & Hoover, 1993; Horowitz et al., 2004; Thornberg, 2010).

In a mixed-methods study conducted by Frisén and colleagues (2008), 877 students (13 years old) filled out a questionnaire regarding bullying. An open-ended question about why they thought children were bullied was included in the questionnaire and the teens' responses were analyzed qualitatively and then statistically. According to their findings, 36% of the teens attributed bullying to victims' appearance (e.g., ugly, fat, or looking different), 21% reported that bullying occurs because victims are different in ways that are not explained (e.g., they stand out in a crowd, are simply "wrong" or different), 19% attributed bullying to the victims' behavior (e.g., strange, different, or ridiculous behavior, or are provocative or rude in some way), 19% attributed bullying to the victims' clothes (e.g., wear ugly or "wrong" clothes, have an ugly haircut, or wear glasses that are out of fashion), 10% explained bullying as a result of being a lonely or socially insecure victim, and 8% attributed bullying to victims' backgrounds (e.g., they come from a different country, their parents' occupations are unusual, or they have low socioeconomic status). Furthermore, they found that adolescents who had not been bullied were more likely than adolescents who had been bullied to report victims' appearance as well as victims' behavior.

In Hamarus and Kaikkonen's (2008) study, 85 teenagers (13–15 years old) were asked to write essays about their own experiences of bullying. In addition, 10 of them, who had admitted bullying others, were interviewed individually. Qualitative analysis revealed that difference was at the core of the teenagers' perceptions of bullying. This was claimed as one reason for bullying. "The qualities relating to the 'differences' of the pupil being bullied were considered to be negative characteristics within the youth culture, and respectively their opposites were culturally desired and appreciated. Quietness, shyness, being timid, sensitivity and being unfashionable, sickness/illness, race, stupidity, childishness, or exaggerated swottishness or religiosity are opposites of the cultural ideals represented by the students" (Hamarus & Kaikkonen, 2008, p. 337). According to the findings from a minor qualitative study in which 10 students aged 14–16 years old were interviewed (Cranham & Carroll, 2003), students' understanding and interpretation of what ensures an individual's popularity as well as the risk of being bullied and isolated in school was heavily determined by aspects of social rules of the school. In order to be popular and to avoid being bullied, individual students have to understand and comply with the subtle and complex rules that have been developed within the social framework in the school by the students and to understand the subtleties of social constructs and dynamic processes within friendships. Deviance from peer norms and standards was associated with being socially excluded and bullied.

In a mixed-methods study (Thornberg & Knutsen, in press), in which 176 students (15–16 years old) responded to a questionnaire and wrote down their explanations for bullying, 42% of them operated with victim attributing as at least one of their bullying explanations. Victim attributing refers to attributing the cause of bullying to the victim. The most common one was the account of the deviant victim (37%), and then accounts of the irritable victim (9%), the weak victim (8%), and the mean victim (4%). Furthermore, the statistical analysis revealed that significantly more male students attributed causes of bullying to the victim compared to female students. This confirmed previous research findings showing that boys blamed the victims more than girls in hypothetical bullying situations (Gini, 2008) and in self-reports regarding bullying experiences (Hara, 2002). In contrast, many more teenage girls attributed causes of bullying to the bully compared to teenage boys (Frisén et al., 2008; Thornberg & Knutsen, in press). However, in a qualitative study in which teenage girls participated, the girls tended to blame the victims as a result of doing something annoying or irritating, starting a conflict, or being indiscreet in some way ("usually they do something to bring it on themselves"; Owens et al., 2000).

The Struggle for Status, Power, and Friendship

Another significant theme found in many studies investigating children and adolescents' representations of bullying causes is the struggle for status, power, and friendship (Erling & Hwang, 2004; Hazler & Hoover, 1993; Owens et al., 2000; Phillips, 2003; Swart & Bredekamp, 2009; Teräsahjo & Salmivalli, 2003; Thornberg, 2010; Thornberg & Knutsen, in press; Varjas et al., 2008). For example, in Owens and colleagues (2000), teenage girls often explained peer harassment among girls as a result of a desire to be part of the group and have close friendships. Bullying was then linked to (a) attention seeking ("Hey, notice me. I'm important!"), and (b) group inclusion ("I'm in and you're out"). Being accepted by the peer group was crucial, and once accepted, girls made great efforts to retain their position within the group. Hence, girls participated in the group's spreading of rumors and ostracizing others in order to protect themselves and their position within the group.

Varjas and colleagues (2008) showed that many students attribute the motive of becoming a higher status person as a cause of bullying behavior. Some of the students in Erling and Hwang (2004) reported that they thought bullying happens because the bullies think they are cool or want to show that they have power. Whereas both boys and girls explained bullying as status positioning and power positioning, only girls attributed bullying to friendship positioning.

Teräsahjo and Salmivalli (2003) relate this issue to what they called "girls talk." In girls talk, friendship, fights, and bullying seemed to be strongly connected. Teräsahjo and Salmivalli (2003) concluded that, "from the point of view of this repertoire, the most crucial meaning of bullying is closely related to fear of losing important friends and their acceptance" (p. 150). Phillips (2003) conducted interviews with 31 female college students (aged 16–22 years old) about their secondary school and college experiences as victims, witnesses, and perpetrators of aggressive and violent behavior. According to these students, abusing others allowed the bully to show how "hard" she was and to boost her reputation and strengthen her position within the social hierarchy of the school.

In Thornberg and Knutsen (in press), 32% of the teens argued that bullying occurs because those who bully others want to manifest, maintain, or boost their power, status, or popularity (e.g., "Some people want to show off as 'popular.' They think they are so cool, and really want to show that by bullying someone else," "You want power"), or they try to protect themselves from social exclusion, harassment, or bullying (e.g., "They want to prove that they are 'tough' so nobody else bullies them back"). Many students in Swart and Bredekamp (2009) felt that there was a hierarchy at their school, and according to these students, the social hierarchy supported the formation of cliques and the culture of bullying. Cullingford and Morrison (1995) interviewed young offenders aged between 16 and 21. One of the most enduring memories of school among the participants was the general atmosphere of bullying and aggression that pervaded life in school. "Bullying and fighting are part of the general ethos of the school and are accepted by children as normal aspects of school life" (p. 550). Hence, these young people attributed bullying to the overall atmosphere of aggression in the school.

Frisén and her colleagues have found that some teens reasoned that bullying occurs because the bullies want to feel tough or cool (Frisén et al., 2007; Frisén et al., 2008), want to impress others (Frisén et al., 2007), or bully others to avoid being bullied themselves (Frisén et al., 2008). Twenty-six percent of the teenagers in Frisén and colleagues (2007) claimed that some children and adolescents bully others because they feel cool. In Phillips (2003), the female students reported a social order of girls at school with the majority of girls falling between the two extremes. At the top of the hierarchy was the "in-group," and according to the reports, the in-group established and maintained their powerful position by bullying other girls, especially those in a lower position in the hierarchy. Even girls in the middle of the pecking order could use the same tactics to harass similarly ranked girls or those at the bottom of the hierarchy. The girls in the study also reported that those who were at the bottom of the hierarchy were vulnerable to victimization, particularly from the in-group. Hence, bullying among girls was explained by referring to this "pecking order" process. In addition, in many studies, some children and teens also attributed bullying to jealousy (Bosacki et al., 2006; Frisén et al., 2007; Hazler & Hoover, 1993; Thornberg, 2010; Thornberg & Knutsen, in press)—a psychological motive that might explain at least some positioning behavior.

The Disturbed Bully

Another bullying explanation among children and teens is attributing bullying as a result of a "disturbed bully"; in other words, bullying takes place because the bully is a person who has low self-confidence, malicious personality, is mean, lacks empathy, or is insecure, and so on. According to Hazler and Hoover (1993), the students had a variety of ideas about why bullies bullied others, but they generally agreed that most bullying is the result of the bully's own lack of self-esteem. In Frisén and colleagues (2008), some adolescents explained that bullying occurs because the bullies have low self-confidence, are sad, or have pent-up anger, which they need to vent. All in all, 36% of the teens in the study attributed bullying to the bullies' personality, background, or motives (including social positioning motives). Teens who had been bullied were more likely than teens who had not been bullied to mention the bullies' personality, background, and motives.

In Frisén and colleagues (2007), 28% of the teens thought that bullies bully others because they have low self-esteem; 15% thought it happens because bullies have problems; and 4% thought it happens because the bullies are also victims. According to Thornberg (2010), 36% of the schoolchildren in the study expressed a social representation of bullying causes in terms of the "work of a disturbed bully." The bully is regarded as a child who has a bad temper, an angry or bad personality, ADHD, or poor self-esteem; feels insecure; feels bad; or does not know what to do with all his or her pent-up anger. Bullying is then explained as a result of these kinds of personal problems or characteristics in the bully. Some of the students connect the work-of-a-disturbed-bully explanation with family problems—the bully has been "disturbed" because there are a lot of quarrels or problems in his or her family, such as aggressive parents or siblings, alcoholism or drug problems, divorce, or bad or negligent parents.

In Thornberg and Knutsen (in press), 32% of the teens attributed bullying to the bully's inner flaws, which means that they reasoned that bullying occurs because the bully feels "bad" or insecure, has poor self-confidence, low self-esteem, psychological problems, or a weak mind, which causes him or her to bully others (e.g., "The reasons why they bullied us were their problems with self-esteem and self-confidence"). Another related category of bully attributing found in their study was explaining bullying in terms of boosting their sense of well-being. Sixteen percent of the teens explained that the bully torments others to feel better or enhance his or her self-confidence or self-esteem. Furthermore, Thornberg and Knutsen (in press) coded teens' explanations that attributed bullying to a problematic family of bullying (e.g., poor parenting, lots of quarrelling or conflicts, divorce, abuse, or harsh or nonloving parents) as a separate category and found that 14% of the teens used this attribution as at least one of their bullying explanations. Eight percent of the teens explained bullying in terms of the bully's "bad" personality. In other words, they reasoned that the bully is a bad, immoral, unempathic, or mean person, and thus he or she starts bullying others.

According to some students in Bosacki and colleagues (2006), instrumental motives (e.g., "He wants her lunch/money") as well as psychological motives (e.g., "It makes him feel better about himself if the other feels bad") within the bully could cause his or her bullying behavior. According to Buchanan and Winzer (2001), one of the most common responses given by the students why some children become bullies was a poor home environment.

Having Fun and Avoiding Boredom

Another reason that teenagers associate with initiating and maintaining bullying is to have some fun (Hamarus & Kaikkonen, 2008; Hazler & Hoover, 1993; Thornberg & Knutsen, in press) or to create excitement

(Owens et al., 2000) and to break the boredom of everyday life in school (Hamarus & Kaikkonen, 2008; Owens et al., 2000; Thornberg & Knutsen, in press). In Thornberg and Knutsen (in press), 8% of the teens used the account of doing it for fun, meaning that bullying occurs because the bullies think it is a funny or amusing thing to do and they just want to have some fun, as at least one bullying explanation. In addition, 5% of the teens expressed that bullying occurs because students have nothing to do or are bored as a result of the school life or structure as at least one of their bullying explanations.

According to Owens and colleagues (2000), this was the most common explanation among the girls who participated in their study. Some of the young participants in Cullingford and Morrison (1995) expressed a view that some children verbally bully others in order to have fun and without any hurtful intentions. Among the younger students in Thornberg (2010), the explanation of bullying as an amusing game, in other words, that bullying takes place because the bullies are amused by it in some way, was reported by 21% as at least one of their bullying explanations. Some of them reasoned that children may act like this because they have nothing else to do or are bored at school. Others reasoned that it was the reaction of the victim that was perceived as amusing or funny by the bullies, and then they picked victims based on how they react. According to some children, bullying is sometimes just intended as a joke and not with any intention to harm the victim seriously. Others reasoned that bullying takes place because bullies think it is fun to be naughty or mean. Finally, the amused response of the audience was viewed as a bullying motivating factor.

Group Pressure

Thirteen percent of the teens in Thornberg and Knutsen (in press) explained bullying as a consequence of group pressure as at least one of their bullying explanations. Group pressure as an explanation of bullying was also found among younger students in Thornberg (2010). For example, a victim in the study reported how classmates who could be nice and kind to her became mean and began to bully her when they got together as a group.

> Well, I know that when they are here at school, and perhaps they are with me or with others, they are really nice and kind, but when they come together, they maybe want to be much tougher in order to avoid being seen as a nerd. And I have really noticed that they want to be very tough when they are all together. (12-year-old girl, in Thornberg, 2010, p. 318)

This particular student and others used an explanation repertoire in which they blamed the group and explained bullying as the result of group pressure. Fear of becoming a new bullying target and fear of social exclusion could motivate peers to conform to the group pressure and join in bullying, some of them reasoned. According to some, peers in such groups think, "If I don't bully that kid too, then maybe I will be frozen out of the group." In Erling and Hwang (2004), 7% of the children used peer pressure as an explanation why students are bullied. According to Frisén and colleagues (2007), 9% of the teenagers in the study thought children and adolescents bully others because of peer pressure. In their study, Hamarus and Kaikkonen (2008) noted that, even those who do not actively participate in bullying do not want to be with the victim because of group pressure. According to Buchanan and Winzer (2001), one of the most common responses given by the students as to why some children become bullies was peer pressure.

Mindless Bullying

In Thornberg (2010), 14% of the students used "bullying as a thoughtless happening" or so-called "mindless bullying" as at least one of their bullying explanations, meaning that the bullies do not think at all about what they are doing and why they are doing it; it just happens. The bullies do not see the consequences of their behavior and they do not realize that they are actually being bullies, these students reasoned (e.g., "And then they say something and then maybe the other person becomes upset, and perhaps they say something everyday without thinking about it, and then it becomes bullying"). According to this explanation, the thoughtlessness among bullies causes and perpetuates bullying. Some students in Teräsahjo and Salmivalli (2003) constructed an argument in their talks about bullying that describes bullying as harmless interaction. By representing the parties not as victims and bullies but more as participants in the game, "this talk's function is not only to construct the interaction itself but also to underestimate the appearance of bullying" (p. 144). This repertoire of underestimation was very commonly used among the students. Whereas the young offenders in Cullingford and Morrison (1995) viewed physical bullying as harmful and intentional, verbal bullying was often viewed as harmless, unintentional, and normal during their school life.

Bullying Causes from Bullies' Point of View

A few studies have investigated how bullies explain bullying and why bullying takes place, according to them. In an interview study with students who bullied others (Burns, Maycock, Cross, & Brown, 2008a,

2008b), perceived provocations, peer group, and school factors emerged as key themes when they discussed reasons for initiating and persisting with bullying behavior. The subtheme "peer group" was associated with belonging and enhancing group status, which emphasizes the need to maintain inclusion within the peer group. Furthermore, according to the findings, "several students suggested that students bullied others because once they had started and became known as a 'bully,' or were involved in the group who bullied, it was difficult to stop" (Burns et al., 2008a, p. 1712), indicating a labeling process. "If their label provides status and power it might be difficult to relinquish that title. In addition, if students are likely to think of themselves in terms of someone who others think of as 'tough' or 'not to challenge,' they are more likely to act in ways that are consistent with the label" (Burns et al., 2008a, p. 1712). Not joining in with bullying was also related to a potential loss of social status within the group. Furthermore, Burns and colleagues (2008b) found that all the students used perceived provocation as a justification for bullying that they or others conducted. The perceived provocation was either direct or indirect. Direct perceived provocation refers to reaction to perceived aggression, especially in terms of being bullied in the first place and as a reaction to that, teasing, calling names, or hitting back or seeking out other students to bully. Indirect perceived provocation refers to being provoked by annoying or "different" students, which in turn incited aggressive acts. Both types of perceived provocation were used to justify bullying behavior.

Some of the young offenders in Cullingford and Morrison (1995) had also bullied others during their school life. They often saw taunting other children as an acceptable, even normal, part of social behavior and something that takes place within an overall atmosphere of aggression in school. Hence, to a great extent, they explained bullying or intimidation as a result of the school ethos. They also viewed certain types of bullying as "harmless" or "harmless fun," without any consideration for the point of view of the victim. Hence, based on these findings, Cullingford and Morrison concluded that the traditional emphasis on intentionality of harm in the concept of bullying is misleading, "in so far as it leaves out the point of view of many 'bullies.' . . . What may seem like harmless fun can be extremely distressing to the victim" (p. 551). Furthermore, some of the former bullies perceived themselves as powerless to control their own aggressive impulses or the difficulty of resisting the temptation to tease people in "fun." Although the participants in Cullingford and Morrison (1995) spoke openly about their involvement in fighting, they never defined their own actions in terms of bullying. In their own eyes, they did not bully others but just had some harmless fun, retaliated to provocation, or showed off and proved they could "look after themselves."

Thornberg and Knutsen (in press) found that more teens who had a prior history of being a bully attributed causes of bullying to the victim, and teens who had a prior history of being a victim, a bystander, or a bully/victim attributed the cause to the bully. In the students' conversations in Teräsahjo and Salmivalli (2003), the "deviance" was often associated with a repertoire of deserving (e.g., "she gets what's coming to her"), thereby constructing bullying and hostile attitudes against the victim as acceptable. Lahelma (2004) also found that students used this constructed "differentness" to justify bullying. Findings from Hara (2002) showed that bullies were more likely to blame the victims than were students who assumed other participation roles in bullying. In their study, Hymel, Rocke-Henderson, and Bonanno (2005) actually found that students who did not report engaging in bullying reported the lowest levels of moral disengagement, whereas those students who repeatedly bullied others reported the highest level of moral disengagement. Among the moral disengagement items, those that emerged as significant predictors of bullying were efforts to justify bullying as "okay" and efforts to blame the victims. These findings might be explained in terms of a self-serving bias among bullies.

Implications for Practitioners

In light of a social psychological perspective such as symbolic interactionism (cf. Blumer, 1969; Charon, 2007), bullying has to be understood as a joint action, and the meaning of bullying, its participants (victims, bullies, and bystanders), and causes are derived from or arise out of social interactions among students. These meanings are dealt with and modified through the interpretive process used by the students in dealing with the bullying they encounter or witness. Bullying prevention efforts and interventions should investigate and target teenagers' conceptions of the causes of bullying, since such mental representations are a source of interpretations, attitudes, and behavior in real situations (cf. Crick & Dodge, 1994). First, practitioners have to investigate and reflect on how teenagers think and reason about why bullying occurs. They have to build their instructions, explanations, conversations, and practices on teenagers' contemporary repertoire of knowledge, conceptions, and skills regarding bullying and other social and moral issues. "Moral growth comes about through the child's progressive construction of ways of understanding the world, and not just an accommodation to the positions and practices of adults and society" (Nucci, 2006, p. 663).

Second, some of the underlying moral assumptions in children's and teens' representations of bullying causes have to be challenged, which in turn show the urgency of relating moral and citizenship themes into bullying prevention and intervention. Thornberg (2010) gave some examples:

> The dominating social representation on bullying causes as a reaction to deviance among the children and its underlying logic of conformism and intolerance can, for example, be challenged by pointing out and inviting students into a deliberative discussion about the values of multiplicity, heterogeneity, social inclusion, caring community, and tolerance. The social representation on bullying as social positioning and its underlying logic of "social Darwinism," the social representation on bullying as social contamination and its underlying logic of "just do what others do," and the social representation on bullying as an amusing game and its underlying logic of sadism can all be challenged by inviting and promoting students to establish a moral atmosphere built on cooperation, participation, caring, and prosocial values. (p. 323)

Third, teenagers' gender has to be considered when designing and conducting bullying prevention and intervention practices among young people. As the preceding review indicates, boys more often explain bullying by blaming the victims as compared to girls (Gini, 2008; Hara, 2002; Thornberg & Knutsen, in press), who more often than boys blame the bullies (Frisén et al., 2008; Thornberg & Knutsen, in press). Such gender differences in explaining bullying and thus blaming the victim versus blaming the bully might at least in part contribute to better understanding why girls are more likely to show positive attitudes toward victims (e.g., Menesini et al., 1997; Rigby, 1996; Rigby & Slee, 1993) and are more likely to support or defend victims and less likely to reinforce bullies than boys (O'Connell, Pepler, & Craig, 1999; Salmivalli, Lagerspetz, Björkqvist, Östermalm, & Kaukiainen, 1996; Salmivalli & Voeten, 2004). Practitioners have to be aware of these gender differences and especially target boys' tendency to blame the victim. Simultaneously, they have to be aware that girls also blame the victim (e.g., Owens et al., 2000; Thornberg & Knutsen, in press).

Fourth, the preceding review indicates that bullies more often explain bullying by blaming the victims as compared to others, who more often than bullies blame the bullies (Hara, 2002; Hymel et al., 2005; Thornberg & Knutsen, in press). Bullying prevention and intervention programs have to deal with these differences. With reference to Bandura (2002) and Hoffman (2000), Thornberg and Knutsen (in press) argue, "blaming the victim as a self-serving bias among bullies helps them to minimize or diffuse their own role and responsibility as well as hindering their empathic arousal and moral concerns regarding the bullying situations, the victim's distress, and their own actions." In bullying prevention programs as well as when dealing with and educating identified bullies, practitioners have to address issues of: blaming the victim, justifying bullying by defining or labeling the victim as negatively deviant, empathy, and moral disengagement.

While the research on how children and teens explain bullying has been overlooked and is still low in numbers, a growing body of studies has recently emerged. Students' representations of and assumptions about bullying and people involved are critical components in the complex process of bullying. This review suggests that considering children's and teenagers' representations of bullying causes has the potential of yielding new insights into the ways in which we understand and address bullying.

References

Bandura, A. (2002). Selective moral disengagement in the exercise of moral agency. *Journal of Moral Education, 31,* 101–119.

Blumer, H. (1969). *Symbolic interactionism.* Berkeley: University of California Press.

Bosacki, S. L., Marini, Z. A., & Dane, A. V. (2006). Voices from the classroom: Pictorial and narrative representations of children's bullying experiences. *Journal of Moral Education, 35,* 231–245.

Buchanan, P., & Winzer, M. (2001). Bullying in schools: Children's voices. *International Journal of Special Education, 16,* 67–79.

Burns, S., Maycock, B., Cross, D., & Brown, G. (2008a). The power of peers: Why some students bully others to conform. *Qualitative Health Research, 18,* 1704–1716.

Burns, S., Maycock, B., Cross, D., & Brown, G. (2008b). "Woodpushers are gay": The role of provocation in bullying. *International Journal of Mental Health Promotion, 10,* 41–50.

Charon, J. M. (2007). *Symbolic interactionism: An introduction, an interpretation, an integration* (9th ed.). Upper Saddle River, NJ: Prentice Hall.

Cranham, J., & Carroll, A. (2003). Dynamics within the bully/victim paradigm: A qualitative analysis. *Educational Psychology in Practice, 19,* 113–132.

Crick, N. R., & Dodge, K. A. (1994). A review and reformulation of social information-processing mechanisms in children's social adjustment. *Psychological Bulletin, 115,* 74–101.

Cullingford, C., & Morrison, J. (1995). Bullying as a formative influence: The relationship between the experience of school and criminality. *British Educational Research Journal, 21,* 547–560.

Dodge, K. A., Coie, J. D., & Lynam, D. (2006). Aggression and antisocial behavior in youth. In N. Eisenberg, D. William, & R. M. Lerner (Eds.), *Handbook of child* psychology: Vol. 3. Social, emotional, and personality development (pp. 719–788). New York: Wiley.

Erling, A., & Hwang, C. P. (2004). Swedish 10-year-old children's perceptions and experiences of bullying. *Journal of School Violence, 3,* 33–43.

Frisén, A., Holmqvist, K., & Oscarsson, D. (2008). Thirteen-year-olds' perception of bullying: Definitions, reasons for victimization, and experience of adults' response. *Educational Studies, 34,* 105–117.

Frisén, A., Johnson, A., & Persson, C. (2007). Adolescents' perception of bullying: Who is the victim? Who is the bully? What can be done to stop bullying? *Adolescence, 42,* 649–761.

Gifford-Smith, M., & Rabiner, D. L. (2004). Social information processing and children's social competence: A review of the literature. In J. Kupersmidt & K. A. Dodge (Eds.), *Children's peer relations: From development to intervention to policy* (pp. 61–79). Washington, DC: American Psychological Association.

Gini, G. (2008). Italian elementary and middle school students' blaming the victim of bullying and perception of school moral atmosphere. *Elementary School Journal, 108,* 335–354.

Hamarus, P., & Kaikkonen, P. (2008). School bullying as a creator of pupil peer pressure. *Educational Research, 50,* 333–345.

Hara, H. (2002). Justifications for bullying among Japanese schoolchildren. *Asian Journal of Social Psychology, 5,* 197–204.

Hazler, R. J., & Hoover, J. H. (1993). What do kids say about bullying? *Education Digest, 58,* 16–20.

Hoffman, M. L. (2000). *Empathy and moral development: Implications for caring and justice.* Cambridge, UK: Cambridge University Press.

Hoover, J. H., Oliver, R., & Hazler, R. J. (1992). Bullying: Perceptions of adolescent victims in the Midwestern USA. *School Psychology International, 13,* 5–16.

Horowitz, J. A., Vessey, J. A., Carlson, K. L., Bradley, J. F., Montoya, C., McCullough, B., & David, J. (2004). Teasing and bullying experiences of middle school students. *Journal of the American Psychiatric Nurses Association, 10,* 165–172.

Hymel, S., Rocke-Henderson, N., & Bonanno, R. A. (2005). Moral disengagement: A framework for understanding bullying among adolescents. *Special Issue of Journal of Social Sciences, 8,* 1–11.

Lahelma, E. (2004). Tolerance and understanding? Students and teachers reflect on differences at school. *Educational Research and Evaluation 10,* 3–19.

Menesini, E., Esla, M., Smith, P. K., Genta, M. L., Giannetti, E., Fonzi, A., & Costabile, A. (1997). A cross-national comparison of children's attitudes toward bully/victim problems in school. *Aggressive Behavior, 29,* 1–13.

Nucci, L. (2006). Education for moral development. In M. Killen & J. Smetana (Eds.), *Handbook of moral development* (pp. 657–681). Mahwah, NJ: Lawrence Erlbaum Associates.

O'Connell, P., Pepler, D., & Craig, W. (1999). Peer involvement in bullying: Insights and challenges for intervention. *Journal of Adolescence, 22,* 437–452.

Owens, L., Shute, R., & Slee, P. (2000). "Guess what I just heard!": Indirect aggression among teenage girls in Australia. *Aggressive Behavior, 26,* 67–83.

Phillips, C. (2003). Who's who in the pecking order? Aggression and "normal violence" in the lives of girls and boys. *British Journal of Criminology, 43,* 710–728.

Rigby, K. (1996). *Bullying in schools and what we can do about it.* London: Jessica Kingsley.

Rigby, K., & Slee, P. T. (1993). Dimensions of interpersonal relation among Australian children and implications for psychological well-being. *Journal of Social Psychology, 133,* 33–42.

Salmivalli, C., Lagerspetz, K., Björkqvist, K., Östermalm, K., & Kaukiainen, A. (1996). Bullying as a group process: Participant roles and their relations to social status within the group. *Aggressive Behavior, 22,* 1–15.

Salmivalli, C., & Voeten, M. (2004). Connections between attitudes, group norms, and behavior in bullying situations. *International Journal of Behavioral Development, 28,* 246–258.

Swart, E., & Bredekamp, J. (2009). Non-physical bullying: Exploring the perspectives of Grade 5 girls. *South African Journal of Education, 29,* 405–425.

Teräsahjo, T., & Salmivalli, C. (2003). "She is not actually bullied": The discourse of harassment in student groups. *Aggressive Behavior, 29,* 134–154.

Thomson, P., & Gunter, H. (2008). Researching bullying with students: A lens on everyday life in an "innovative school." *International Journal of Inclusive Education, 12,* 185–200.

Thornberg, R. (2010). Schoolchildren's social representations on bullying causes. *Psychology in the Schools, 47,* 311–327.

Thornberg, R., & Knutsen, S. (in press). Teenagers' explanations of bullying. *Child and Youth Care Forum.*

Varjas, K., Meyers, J., Bellmoff, L., Lopp, E., Birckbichler, L., & Marshall, M. (2008). Missing voices: Fourth through eight grade urban students' perceptions of bullying. *Journal of School Violence, 7,* 97–118.

CHAPTER SEVEN

Desensitization to Media Violence

Kostas A. Fanti and Marios N. Avraamides

Introduction

Modern times are characterized by the increasing intrusion of technology and media in everyday life. People in Western societies, in particular, spend much of their time in front of television sets and computer monitors. Violent scenes are abundant in films and television programs, causing concern over the potential effects that media violence may exert on human personality and behavior. Furthermore, the increased capabilities of computers and the rise of game consoles in recent years has provided people, and especially youths, with the opportunity to interact with content that is in many cases of violent nature.

Studies on the effects of violent media are steadily increasing and show that both chronic and brief exposure to violence in films and video games leads to an increase of aggression (Anderson, 2004). Although skeptics argue that the relation between media violence and aggression is spurious, with constructs such as trait aggression held responsible for both aggressive behavior and preference for violent media (e.g., Freedman, 2002), recent studies using experimental methodologies with highly controlled designs have refuted such accounts and verified the presence of causal links. A recent meta-analytic review of studies on the effects of violent video games has shown that exposure to violent video games is causally linked to increases in aggressive behavior, aggressive cognition, aggressive affect, and cardiovascular arousal, as well as decreases in helping behavior (Anderson, 2004). The evidence for a causal link between media violence and aggression is so overwhelming that

Anderson (2004) claims that the "scientific debate over *whether* media violence has an effect is over" (p. 114).

Moving on from the debate on the effects of media violence, studies have concentrated on uncovering the mechanisms that underlie its effects. Repeated exposure to entertainment violence is believed to be a major contributor to aggressive and violent behavior in real life (Anderson & Bushman, 2002; Donnerstein & Smith, 1997; Huesmann, Moise, & Podolski, 1997), since media violence can (a) instigate imitation (Bandura, Ross, & Ross, 1963; Gould & Shaffer, 1986; Philips & Carstensen, 1986), (b) make real-world violence more acceptable (Gunter, 1994), (c) distort viewers' perceptions of real world crime and violence (Gerbner, Gross, Morgan, & Signorielli, 1994), (d) desensitize viewers to the suffering of victims of violence (Linz, Donnerstein, & Adams, 1989; Linz, Donnerstein, & Penrod, 1988; Malamuth & Check, 1981), and (e) increase the accessibility of violent constructs in memory (Berkowitz, 1984; Bushman, 1998).

The mechanism that will be explored in this chapter is *desensitization* to media violence. Wolpe (1982) defined desensitization as the diminished emotional responsiveness to a negative or aversive stimulus after repeated exposure to it. Carnagey, Anderson, and Bushman (2007) distinguished the effects of desensitization from the actual process by linking desensitization to physiological arousal. Thus, they defined desensitization as the "reduction in emotion-related physiological reactivity to real violence" (p. 490).

This chapter provides a short review of the literature on desensitization to media violence and its effects on behavior. Although it is not meant to be comprehensive, the chapter offers an overview of how desensitization has been investigated in the literature and what its behavioral consequences are.

Desensitization to Media Violence

Initial exposure to media violence typically produces aversive responses such as fear, increased heart rate, perspiration, discomfort, and disgust, although after prolonged and repeated exposure across a person's lifetime, the psychological impact of media violence reduces or habituates, and the observer becomes emotionally and cognitively desensitized to media violence across time (Carnegey et al., 2007; Cline, Croft, & Courrier, 1973; Funk, Bechtoldt-Baldacci, Pasold, & Baumgardner, 2004; Smith, & Donnerstein, 1998; Thomas, Horton, Lippincott, & Drabman, 1977). Desensitization may arise from different sources of screen-based media, including TV, movies, and video games. For example, Cline and colleagues (1973) and Thomas and colleagues (1977) found that individuals who experienced high levels of television violence in the past were more likely to be desensitized to violent film clips compared to viewers who watched only small amounts of television violence. Carnagey and colleagues (2007) found that children who were exposed to more video game violence in the past showed lower responsiveness to real world violence and were more likely to view violence as pleasurable in comparison to children who were not exposed to this form of media violence. Furthermore, Funk and colleagues (2004) provided evidence that children's exposure to movie or video game violence resulted in proviolence attitudes (cognitive desensitization) and lower empathy or sympathy for the victims of violence (emotional desensitization). Thus, it seems that chronic media violence exposure has lasting effects on viewers' attitudes toward violence and viewers' empathy toward the victims of violence through the process of desensitization. Although studies generally document desensitization to media violence by showing that people's reactive responses to violent media are diminished after chronic experience, desensitization can also be observed during short-term exposure to media violence (Fanti, Vanman, Henrich, & Avraamides, 2009).

According to Bandura, Ross, and Ross (1963) media violence may serve as an important source of imitative behavior, leading to media-mediated aggressive models. They further provided evidence that media violence has an immediate effect on an individual's behavior, providing initial evidence of the possibility that desensitization results from short-term exposure to media violence. In one study that we have carried out in our lab, participants viewed nine 2-minute video segments that included either violent acts or comedic episodes with their reactivity measured through a questionnaire administered after each video segment (Fanti et al., 2009). Results revealed the presence of a curvilinear relationship between time (i.e., number of scenes already watched) and levels of both enjoyment and sympathy for the victims of the violent acts. The violent segments initially produced aversive responses that tended to increase in intensity after watching the first few segments. However, for later scenes participants' levels of enjoyment started to increase and their sympathy levels to decrease dramatically. That is, even after watching 4–5 violent scenes, participants began to show evidence for desensitization to the violent content of the films. Importantly, although differences in the overall scores were found between people reporting involvement to real-life aggression acts and those who did not, desensitization was observed for both groups of participants.

The study of Fanti and colleagues (2009) investigated the process of desensitization at the cognitive level of information processing. That is, it assessed how people cognitively interpreted changes in neurophysiological states induced by the violent content. Other studies have examined desensitization at the neural level by relying on physiological measures.

Desensitization at the Physiological Level

Physiological desensitization refers to changes in the physiological state of the organisms that may be associated with chronic or brief exposures to violent content (e.g., decrease of arousal, changes in the activation of assemblies of neurons, etc.). In trying to understand the relationship between media violence and aggression, an arousal model between viewing media violence and aggressiveness was proposed by Watt and Krull (1977). This model suggests that the agent of arousal is the emotional reaction to violent content. Based on this model, research has provided evidence for the relation between physiological measures and arousal (high or low) by using electrodermal activity and heart rate (e.g., Bradley, Codispoti, Cuthbert, & Lang, 2001; Lang, Greenwald, Bradley, & Hamm, 1993; Vanman, Dawson, & Brennan, 1998). Electrodermal and heart rate activity reflect emotional responding to stimuli and are believed to be elicited by cognitive activity (Siddle, 1991). Both the electrodermal response and heart rate reactivity have been previously associated with violent scenes, suggesting that skin conductance and heart rate reactivity change with arousal during the viewing of violent scenes or pictures (Bradley et al., 2001; Kalamas & Gruber, 1998; Lang et al., 1993). For example, Kalamas and Gruber (1998) provided evidence that after viewing a violent television show and after hearing the sounds associated with violent media, individuals produced strong electrodermal responses. These findings indicate that viewers respond emotionally to violent stimuli. Bradley and colleagues (2001) also provided evidence of strong emotional arousal, as indicated by large skin conductance responses and cardiac deceleration recorded when participants viewed violent pictures. In addition to showing that watching violent pictures are associated with changes in skin conductance and heart rate, Lang and colleagues (1993) also provided evidence for viewers' emotional reactions to violent pictures with the use of facial electromyography. Thus, with the use of different physiological measures, researchers demonstrate an association between the viewers' emotional reactions and the experience of violence, either as violent pictures or as television violence.

Evidence that exposure to violence in video games also causes physiological desensitization is provided by the study of Carnagey and colleagues (2007). In this study, participants played either a violent or a nonviolent video game for 20 minutes and then watched 10-minutes video segments containing real life violence. Measures of heart rate and galvanic skin response (GRS) were taken before and after video game playing as well as during video viewing. Results showed that while heart rate increased from pregame to postgame, the increase was equal in the violent and nonviolent game conditions. However, whereas heart rate remained at the same level for the violent game condition during violent video viewing, it increased further in the nonviolent condition. Also, while GSR levels were equal for the two game conditions in pregame and postgame measurements, they decreased substantially during video viewing but only in the violent game condition. No such decrease was found in the nonviolent condition, where in fact a small nonsignificant increase was observed. The findings of Carnagey and colleagues (2007) suggest that playing a violent game for only 20 minutes is adequate to physiologically desensitize people to real life violence. Importantly, none of the effects they reported were mediated by trait aggressiveness. Thus, their results cannot be accounted for by individual differences in the susceptibility to media violence.

Bartholow, Bushman, and Sestir (2006) studied the link between violent game experience, desensitization, and aggression using electroencephalography (EEG). In this study, participants with varying levels of prior violent game experience were exposed to an oddball task in which violent or negative nonviolent pictures were occasionally presented within a series of neutral images. EEG signals were recorded throughout the picture-viewing task. Subsequently, participants carried out a version of the Competitive Reaction-Time (CRT) task (Taylor, 1967). In this task, participants are given the impression that they are competing with another participant in a task that entails fast reactions to auditory tones. In reality, however, whether a participant wins or not in a given trial was predetermined. Following winning trials, participants are given the opportunity to punish their opponent by delivering a loud noise to their ears. The intensity and the duration of the noise are used as a measure of aggression. Results from this experiment showed that a decrease in the amplitude of the P300 when viewing violent pictures was associated with greater violent game exposure. No changes in P300 were observed for negative or neutral pictures. As previous studies have shown that larger P300 amplitudes are elicited when a stimulus is evaluated as inconsistent with its context, Bartholow and colleagues (2006) suggested that the decrease of the P300 amplitude when viewing violent pictures is indicative of desensitization to violence. Furthermore, smaller P300 amplitudes for violent pictures were associated with higher aggression scores in the CRT task. Importantly, these findings remained significant even after controlling for individual differences in trait aggression. Overall, the findings of Bartholow and colleagues (2006) suggest that chronic exposure to violent games results in desensitization to violence, causing people to behave more aggressively.

Behavioral Correlates of Desensitization

Results from many studies suggest that one aspect of desensitization is the reduction of empathy (i.e., the sensitivity to the pain and suffering of others). A number of experiments conducted have demonstrated that helping behavior is reduced following exposure to media violence. For example, Bushman and Anderson (2009) had participants play a violent or a nonviolent video game in the lab for 20 minutes and then listen to the sounds of a staged fight supposedly taking place outside the lab. In the prerecorded fight, two people first argued, with one of the two persons subsequently injuring the other and leaving. Results from the experiment showed that although there was no difference in helping rates between participants exposed to the violent or nonviolent game, the former took longer to help, were less likely to report hearing the fight, and rated the fight as less serious than the latter. In a follow-up study conducted in the field, a woman confederate with a wrapped ankle dropped her crutches outside a movie theater before or after a violent or nonviolent movie show. Results revealed that the helping delay of the moviegoers was longer after having watched a violent movie than in the three other conditions.

The link between media violence exposure and helping behavior may reflect desensitization caused either in the short term or long term by violent content. Researchers have thus attempted to identify variables that may mediate the links between media violence exposure and its behavioral outcomes. For example, Bartholow, Sestir, and Davis (2005) examined whether the association between chronic exposure to game violence and aggression is mediated by variables such as empathy and hostile personality. Empathy refers to the reduced sensitivity to the pain and suffering of others (Funk et al., 2004). The first study, which relied on a self-report measure of aggressive behavior, showed that the strength of the relation between aggression and violent video game experience was reduced when either empathy or hostility levels were controlled for. The second study of Bartholow and colleagues (2005) used experimental methods to investigate whether this is also the case following brief exposure to video game violence. A number of participants from the first study were brought into the lab, where they played a violent or a nonviolent video game for 20 minutes and then they carried out the CRT task. As expected, participants who played the violent video game delivered noise blasts that were longer and louder. Furthermore, participants with greater previous experience with violent video games were more aggressive in the CRT task regardless of game condition. Unlike the first study, however, only hostility scores reduced substantially the magnitude of the association between

Desensitization to Media Violence

aggression and prior experience with violent video games. No such effect was found for empathy. Overall, the results of Bartholow and colleagues (2005) showed that chronic exposure to game violence leads to aggression, with hostility (and empathy to a lesser degree) partially accounting for this effect. Further analyses conducted in the second study suggest that chronic game violence functions to increase hostile perception biases, which in turn lead to aggression. These effects are compatible with the general hypothesis that chronic exposure to violent video games, and media violence in general, leads to desensitization to violence.

In an attempt to link exposure to media violence to behavioral consequences such as increased aggression, reduced helping behavior, etc., Anderson and Bushman (2001; also Bushman & Anderson, 2002) developed the General Aggression Model (GAM). The GAM provides a useful theoretical framework for understanding the role of desensitization in the route from media violence to aggressive behavior both for short-term and chronic exposure. According to this model, each exposure to media violence constitutes a learning trial in which aggression-related schemas and scripts in memory are activated. Even brief exposures to media violence impact a person's current internal state defined by cognitive, affective, and arousal variables. That is, each episode of media violence exposure serves to prime aggressive cognitions, to increase arousal, and to create an aggressive affective state. According to Anderson and Bushman (2001), the repeated activation of these structures leads to changes in five types of knowledge structures, namely, aggressive beliefs and attitudes, aggressive perceptual schemata, aggressive expectation schemata, aggressive behavior scripts, and aggression desensitization. Changes in these knowledge structures may induce an aggressive personality, which may in turn lead to changes in situational variables (e.g., the person seeks different types of social interactions and peer groups).

Support for the GAM has been provided by various studies showing that indeed brief exposure to media violence can alter the present internal state of the individual. For example, Anderson and Dill (2000) showed that playing a violent game made aggressive thoughts more accessible than playing a nonviolent game. In this study, participants played either a violent or a nonviolent game and then were asked to pronounce a list of words. Participants who played the violent game were faster at pronouncing the violent words than those who played the nonviolent game. Furthermore, Kirsh (1998) showed that game violence increases aggressive expectations. In this study, children played a violent or nonviolent game and then listened to stories describing a protagonist in various provocative situations. They were asked to identify themselves with the protagonist and respond to questions regarding their expectations for imminent actions. Children who played the violent game described more aggressive next actions than those who played the nonviolent game. Similarly, Bushman and Anderson (2002) showed that adult participants who played a violent game for 20 minutes and then responded to questions regarding the actions and the feelings of a story protagonist expected the protagonist to feel more angry and aggressive and react more aggressively to the situation.

Individual Differences

Although the literature provides a convincing account for the presence of a causal link between violent movies and aggression in both the laboratory and real life, it is of great importance to determine whether this link is mediated by personal characteristics. Thus, researchers also investigated the possibility that there are individual differences in the process of desensitization. Research on this topic reveals that trait aggressiveness is positively correlated with the desire to watch violent films, and media violence is found to elicit more aggression in high trait aggressive individuals than in low trait aggressive individuals (e.g., Bushman, 1995; O'Neal & Taylor, 1989). Furthermore, research has shown that participants with longer records of antisocial behavior exhibit more aggression after viewing violent films in lab-constructed situations (Hartmann, 1969). Berkowitz (1984) argued that in general violent movies can give the audience ideas that may then be translated into antisocial or overt behavior, and this behavior is likely to be in accordance with the viewers' interpretations of whether the witnessed action was appropriate, profitable, or morally justified. Therefore, Berkowitz argues for a bidirectional relationship in which the violent movies have an adverse effect on the viewer's behavior but in which the viewer brings his/her own interpretation of what he/she perceives.

Thus, it is possible that aggressive individuals enjoy the violence portrayed in the media more and are less concerned for the suffering of victims of violence. However, all individuals, regardless of personality, seem to get desensitized to media violence similarly (Bartolow, Bushman, & Sestir, 2006; Fanti et al., 2009). In the study by Fanti and colleagues (2009) aggressive behavior was related to the initial level of enjoyment of media violence, indicating that aggressive participants enjoyed the violent scenes more in comparison to the nonaggressive participants. In terms of sympathy, the more aggressive participants reported lower initial sympathy toward the victims of violence. Although the authors identified differences in the degree of enjoyment and sympathy toward the victim of violence, all individuals regardless of aggressive habits were desensitized to media violence in the same manner. This finding seems to rule out the hypothesis that aggressive individuals will exhibit a different desensitization-to-violence pattern because individuals with high trait aggression have permanently reduced inhibition to aggression and blunted evaluative categorization of violent stimuli (Bartholow et al., 2006).

Discussion and Future Directions

Despite the fact that most scientists agree that chronic exposure to media violence may have deleterious effects on personality and influence behavior, it is not yet fully established how these effects come about. The GAM of Anderson and Bushman (2001) offers a nice theoretical framework on which many studies have been carried out, yet the variables that are involved are so complex that further systematic research is needed before drawing definite conclusions about its validity. One avenue in which research on media violence could move is the examination of how various personality characteristics may make some people over others more prone to the effects of either brief or chronic exposure to media violence. Furthermore, as technology evolves so does the complexity of the media. Three-dimensional media is currently appearing in both TV and gaming, with the level of realism and interactivity of content continuously improving. Thus, new variables are constantly emerging, making the quest of understanding the impact of media violence more complex. For example, although many studies have shown that brief exposure to video game violence increases aggressive behavior, there is now evidence that wishful identification with the protagonists of violent video games further enhances the negative effects of media violence (Konijn, Nije Bijvank, & Bushman, 2007). Although realism and immersion did not directly influence the effects in this study, these variables were found to correlate with wishful identification. As violent content is getting increasingly more realistic and immersive in our days, so could the negative effects of media violence.

Moreover, desensitization may arise from different sources of screen-based media, including TV, movies, video games, and the Internet. Even though prior research suggested that viewers' get desensitized to TV, movie, and video game violence, it is not clear how Internet violence is related to desensitization or aggressive behavior. Moreover, current work provides evidence for a new form of violence, cyberbullying (i.e., sending threatening or harassing emails, instant messages, and chat room messages; Fanti, Demetriou, & Hawa, under review). This work suggests that individuals are not only exposed to violence through the Internet but also engage in these forms of violence, suggesting that Internet violence is interactive. Work currently performed in our lab provides strong support that exposure to Internet violence increases cyberbullying behaviors and cybervictimization; however, it remains unclear whether desensitization to Internet violence influences cyberbullying and cybervictimization or whether cyberbullies and cybervictims are more likely to be desensitized to media violence.

In conclusion, children, adolescents, and adults are exposed to high levels of violence, and evidence suggests that violence exposure can result in maladaptive behaviors and even abnormal brain functioning (Anderson et al., 2003; Bartholow et al., 2006; Mathews et al., 2005). Individuals may get so desensitized to violence that they may start believing that violence is normative. However, what is most frightening is not that viewers get desensitized to violence but that aggressive behaviors may result from such desensitization.

In closing, we should state that our belief is that the scientific literature clearly establishes the presence of deleterious effects from violence exposure and therefore it is about time that the entertainment industry took scientific findings into consideration. The media industry needs to be transformed from an industry responsible for desensitizing us to violence to an industry promoting and enhancing positive and prosocial behaviors. Our children should not live in a society that values the public viewing of violent content. Therefore, it may be prudent to consider creating a public policy against viewing such violent content to prevent long-term consequences.

Note

We thank Melina Nicole Kyranides and Christina Adamou for useful comments on a previous draft of this chapter. Support was provided by internal grant "Media Violence" from the University of Cyprus.

References

Anderson, C. A. (2004). An update on the effects of violent video games. *Journal of Adolescence, 27,* 113–122.

Anderson, C. A., Berkowitz, L., Donnerstein, E., Huesmann, L. R., Johnson, J., Linz, D., Malamuth, N., & Wartella, E. (2003). The influence of media violence on youth. *Psychological Science in the Public Interest, 4,* 81–110.

Anderson, C. A., & Bushman, B. J. (2001). Effects of violent video games on aggressive behavior, aggressive cognition, aggressive affect, physiological arousal,

and prosocial behavior: A meta-analytic review of the scientific literature. *Psychological Science, 12,* 353–359.
Anderson, C. A., & Bushman, B. J. (2002). The effects of media violence on society. *Science, 295,* 2377–2379.
Anderson, C. A., & Dill, K. E. (2000). Video games and aggressive thoughts, feelings, and behavior in the laboratory and in life. *Journal of Personality and Social Psychology, 78,* 772–790.
Bandura, A., Ross, D., & Ross, S. A. (1963). Imitation of film-mediated aggressive models. *Journal of Abnormal and Social Psychology, 66,* 3–11.
Bartholow, B. D., Bushman, B. J., & Sestir, M. A. (2006). Chronic violent video game exposure and desensitization to violence: Behavioral and event-related brain potential data. *Journal of Experimental Social Psychology, 42,* 532–539.
Bartholow, B. D., Sestir, M. A., & Davis, E. B. (2005). Correlates and consequences of exposure to video game violence: Hostile personality, empathy, and aggressive behavior. *Personality and Social Psychology Bulletin, 31,* 1573–1586.
Berkowitz, L. (1984). Some effects of thoughts on anti- and prosocial influences of media events: A cognitive-neoassociation analysis. *Psychological Bulletin, 95,* 410–427.
Bradley, M. M., Codispoti, M., Cuthbert, B. N., & Lang, B. J. (2001). Emotion and motivation: Defensive and appetitive reactions in picture processing. *Emotion, 1,* 276–298.
Bushman, B. J. (1995). Moderating role of trait aggressiveness in the effects of violent media on aggression. *Journal of Personality and Social Psychology, 69,* 950–960.
Bushman, B. J. (1998). Priming effects of media violence on the accessibility of aggressive constructs in memory. *Personality and Social Psychology Bulletin, 24,* 537–545.
Bushman, B. J., & Anderson, C. A. (2002). Violent video games and hostile expectations: A test of the General Aggression Model. *Personality and Social Psychology Bulletin, 28,* 1679–1686.
Bushman, B. J., & Anderson, C. A. (2009). Comfortably numb: Desensitizing effects of violent media on helping others. *Psychological Science, 20,* 273–277.
Carnagey, N. L., Anderson, C. A., & Bushman, B. J. (2007). The effect of video game violence on physiological desensitization to real-life violence. *Journal of Experimental Social Psychology, 43,* 489–496.
Cline, V. B., Croft, R. G., & Courrier, S. (1973). Desensitization of children to television violence. *Journal of Personality and Social Psychology, 27,* 360–365.
Donnerstein, E., & Smith, S. L. (1997). Impact of media violence on children, adolescents, and adults. In S. Kirschner, & D. A. Kirschner (Eds.), *Perspectives on psychology and the media* (pp. 29–68). Washington, DC: American Psychological Association.
Fanti, K. A., Demetriou, A., & Hawa, V. (under review). A longitudinal study of cyberbullying: Examining risk and protective factors.

Fanti, K. A., Vanman, E., Henrich, C. C., & Avraamides, M. N. (2009). Desensitization to media violence over a short period of time. *Aggressive Behavior, 35,* 179–187.

Freedman, J. L. (2002). *Media violence and its effects on aggression: Assessing the scientific evidence.* Toronto, Ontario, Canada: University of Toronto Press.

Funk, J. B., Bechtoldt-Baldacci, H., Pasold, T., & Baumgardner, J. (2004). Violence exposure in real-life, video games, television, movies, and the Internet: Is there desensitization? *Journal of Adolescence, 27,* 23–39.

Gerbner, G., Gross, L., Morgan, M., & Signorielli, N. (1994). Growing up with television: The cultivation perspective. In J. Bryant & D. Zillman (Eds.), *Media effects: Advances in theory and research* (pp. 17–41). Hillsdale, NJ: Lawrence Erlbaum Associates.

Gould, M. S., & Shaffer, D. (1986). The impact of suicide in television movies: Evidence of imitation. *New England Journal of Medicine, 315,* 690–694.

Gunter, B. (1994). The question of media violence. In J. Bryant & D. Zillman (Eds.), *Media effects: Advances in theory and research* (pp. 163–211). Hillsdale, NJ: Lawrence Erlbaum Associates.

Hartmann, D. P. (1969). Influence of symbolically modeled instrumental aggression and pain cues on aggressive behavior. *Journal of Personality and Social Psychology, 11,* 280–288.

Huesmann, L. R., Moise, J. F., & Podolski, C. L. (1997). The effects of media violence on the development of antisocial behavior. In D. M. Stoff, & J. Breiling (Eds.), *Handbook of antisocial behavior* (pp. 181–193). New York: Wiley.

Kalamas, A. D., & Gruber, M. L. (1998). Electrodermal responses to implied versus actual violence on television. *Journal of General Psychology, 125,* 31–37.

Kirsh, S. J. (1998). Seeing the world through Mortal Kombat–colored glasses: Violent video games and the development of a short-term hostile attribution bias. *Childhood, 5,* 177–184.

Konijn, E. A., Nije Bijvank, M., & Bushman, B. J. (2007). I wish I were a warrior: The role of wishful identification in the effects of violent video games on aggression in adolescent boys. *Developmental Psychology, 43,* 1038–1044.

Lang, P. J., Greenwald, M. K., Bradley, M. M., & Hamm, A. O. (1993). Looking at pictures: Affective, facial, visceral, and behavioral reactions. *Psychophysiology, 30,* 261–273.

Linz, D., Donnerstein, E., & Adams, S. M. (1989). Physiological desensitization and judgments about female victims of violence. *Human Communication Research, 15,* 509–522.

Linz, D., Donnerstein, E., & Penrod, S. (1988). Effects of long-term exposure to violent and sexually degrading depictions of women. *Journal of Personality and Social Psychology, 55,* 758–768.

Malamuth, N. M., & Check, J. V. P. (1981). The effects of mass media exposure on acceptance of violence against women: A field experiment. *Journal of Research in Personality, 14,* 436–446.

Mathews, V. P., Kronenberger, W. G., Wang, Y., Lurito, J. T., Lowe, M. J., & Dunn, D. W. (2005). Media violence exposure and frontal lobe activation measured by functional magnetic resonance imaging in aggressive and nonaggressive adolescents. *Journal of Computer Assisted Tomography, 29,* 287–292.

O'Neal, E. C., & Taylor, S. L. (1989). Status of the provoker, opportunity to retaliate, and interest in video violence. *Aggressive Behavior, 15,* 171–180.

Philips, D. P., & Carstensen, L. L. (1986). Clustering of teenage suicides after television news stories about suicide. *New England Journal of Medicine, 315,* 685–689.

Siddle, D. A. T. (1991). Orienting, habituation, and resource allocation: An associative analysis. *Psychophysiology, 28,* 245–259.

Smith, S. L., & Donnerstein, E. (1998). Harmful effects of exposure to media violence: Learning of aggression, emotional desensitization, and fear. In R. G. Geen & E. Donnerstein (Eds.), *Human aggression: Theories, research, and implications for social policy* (pp. 167–202). San Diego, CA: Academic Press.

Taylor, S. P., (1967). Aggressive behaviour and physiological arousal as a function of provocation and the tendency to inhibit aggression. *Journal of Personality, 35,* 297–310.

Thomas, M. H., Horton, R. W., Lippincott, E. C., & Drabman, R. S. (1977). Desensitization to portrayals of real life aggression as a function of television violence. *Journal of Personality and Social Psychology, 35,* 450–458.

Vanman, E. J., Dawson, M. E., & Brennan, P. A. (1998). Affective reactions in the blink of an eye: Individual differences in subjective experience and physiological responses to emotional stimuli. *Personality and Social Psychology Bulletin, 24,* 1007–1018.

Watt, J. H., & Krull, R. A. (1977). Examination of three models of television viewing and aggression. *Human Communication Research, 3,* 99–112.

Wolpe J. 1982. *The practice of behavior therapy* (3rd ed.). New York: Pergamon Press.

CHAPTER EIGHT

What We Do Matters: Making Shelter When Teachers Abuse Teens

Billie Wright Dziech

> Someone has to be responsible. Someone has to pick up the pieces. Someone has to make shelter.
>
> *May Sarton*

Sexual victimization of children and adolescents by their teachers captures public attention temporarily when a local or particularly horrific case occurs. If there is something unique about the perpetrator or the school, press coverage might last longer, as in the case of Robert "Pete" Peterson, a 65-year-old social studies teacher and camp director for Sidwell Friends Middle School in northwest Washington, D.C. Accused of inappropriate touching and sharing pornography with a male student, Peterson was fired after pleading guilty to one count of child sex abuse in 2010. The behaviors themselves were commonplace for perpetrators, but where the teacher worked was another matter, as well as a reminder that educator sexual abuse can occur anytime, anywhere. Sidwell Friends is the school that President and Mrs. Obama's daughters attend (Turque & Morse, 2010).

But even this case lost its impact once the media shifted focus to more salacious or gruesome spectacles, and the unsettling irony is that sexual abuse in elementary and secondary schools remains a complex and often misunderstood issue examined primarily through imperfect government data, obscure academic studies, and media accounts of high visibility cases. An attempt to reach a better understanding of the problem occurred in 2001 when the No Child Left Behind Act amended Section 5414 of the Elementary and Secondary Education Act of 1965 and mandated a study of sexual abuse in the nation's schools.

The result was Charol Shakeshaft's *Educator Sexual Misconduct: A Synthesis of Existing Literature* (2004), which discussed prevalence, offenders, targets, allegations, legal initiatives, the roles of unions, and prevention strategies. An Associated Press (AP) study of sexual misconduct in schools described the fate of the report succinctly: "[It] was largely ignored" (Irvine & Tanner, 2007). A flaw in Shakeshaft's review of the literature was that it conflated the term "sexual abuse" with the more inclusive and general phrase "sexual misconduct," and so an exact figure for abuse was not clear from her conclusion that 4.5 million of approximately 50 million public school students "are subject to sexual misconduct by an employee of a school sometime between kindergarten and 12th grade" (p. 18). Nevertheless, she later observed that "the physical sexual abuse of students in schools is likely more than 100 times the abuse by priests" (quoted in Dougherty, 2004).

But even the best surveys are finally only educated guesses. The most significant reason for this is that sex crimes have the lowest reporting rate of all criminal activities. Some targets never tell, and those who do often wait years to disclose. Then too principals and school boards and sometimes even parents resist reporting. Most of what we know about prevalence comes from law enforcement agencies, which cannot make accurate determinations because of underreporting and, equally significant, because not all cases that are investigated meet the rigorous standards necessary to qualify as abuse.

Differential definitions and data collection practices by legal agencies and the states also prohibit a coherent view of the national prevalence rate. Congress defines sexual abuse as a behavior by which one intentionally "causes another person to engage in a sexual act by threatening or placing that other person in fear . . . (or) engages in a sexual act with another person if that other person is—(A) incapable of appraising the nature of the conduct; or (B) physically incapable of declining participation in, or communicating unwillingness to engage in that sexual act" (18 U.S.C. § 2242).

But the states differ on factors related to that definition. Even though all states prohibit sex between adults and minors (those who are "incapable of appraising the nature of" sexual conduct and legally consenting to it), the term "minor" varies from state to state so that a minor is 16 in 30 states, 17 in 9 states, and 18 in 11 others. Generally used to describe the most dangerous offenders, even the term "predator" can differ from state to state. Then too data comparisons are confusing over time because some states compose crime statistics reports based on calendar years and others on their own fiscal years.

Studies have reported somewhat similar national prevalence rates or numerical estimates of victims. Shakeshaft (2004) extrapolated from her sources approximately a 6–10% prevalence rate for teacher sexual abuse. Based on a sample of 4,023 adolescents from 12 to 17 across all race and ethnic lines, Snyder (2000) reported a prevalence rate of 8.1%. Perhaps the most widely discussed report was the five-year study (2001–2005) by the AP, which found 2,570 cases "in which teachers were punished or removed from the classroom for sexual misconduct. The allegations ranged from fondling to rape" (Irvine & Tanner, 2007).

A possibly optimistic finding came from Finkelhor and Jones (2004), who relied on data from the National Abuse and Neglect Data System (NCANDS) to report a 40% decline in overall cases of child sexual abuse between 1992 and 2000. They cautioned that the decline could be the result of decades of aggressive response to the problem but also that the statistic could be inaccurate and that there might have been no real decline but simply changes in data collection. Although there are sharp differences of opinion about the validity and extent of the decrease, Finkelhor and Jones nevertheless maintained that at least some decline had occurred.

None of these studies focused exclusively on educator perpetrators, and so it is difficult to reconcile the reported decrease with the ever heightened outcry over unsafe schools. For the present, prevalence rates and theories about increases and decreases are at best speculative. Data from 1992–2000 and 2001–2010 might eventually prove similar or different. In the meantime, there are few research projects that document the problem at acceptable levels of reliability and validity because studies are so expensive and difficult to carry out. They must rely on questionable data because of underreporting; and when studies are done, they are likely to use small and dissimilar samples and methodologies. Equally problematic, of course, is the reluctance or refusal of school districts and teachers' unions to allow information about educator offenses in the public domain.

To understand the dynamics of sex abuse requires at least basic knowledge of its targets. Publications describing development of early adolescents (approximately 12 to 14 years of age) and those in the middle stage (approximately 15 to 18 years) are too numerous to count, but even a cursory examination of teens' characteristics reveals the immense psychological vulnerability that the poet Theodore Roethke recognized when he said, "So much of adolescence is an ill-defined dying, An intolerable waiting, A longing for another place and time, Another condition."

Adolescence is that agonizing period in which the struggle for identity and a sense of self-worth occurs. Tremendously egocentric, teenagers fluctuate wildly between overconfidence and self-deprecation as they strive to cope with relationships, gender roles, and their emerging sexuality. What psychologist David Elkind (1967) defined as the concept of personal fable often leads to their conviction that they are somehow unique and impervious to life's dangers and challenges. Great risk takers, they exhibit poor and even dangerous judgment at times. Many invite conflict and can be seriously aggressive and resistant to authority. Others who are conflict-avoidant enclose themselves within protective shells to shut out discordant emotions and relationships. Ironically, at this time when the young desperately need adult guidance and support, they are most likely to distance themselves from family as they seek peer approval, independence, and autonomy.

Popular books often capture everyday reality more directly than academic works, as Anthony Wolfe (2002) demonstrated when he described the fragility of adolescence in *Get Out of My Life, but First Could You Drive Me and Cheryl to the Mall*.

> The hallmark of adolescence . . . is a psychological change. . . . A new and powerful voice rises inside of children. They must obey this voice and in doing so, their lives change forever. . . .
>
> A new force within dictates that teenagers must now experience themselves as independent and able to exist on their own. No more can they feel close to or dependent on their parents. . . .
>
> This mandate eliminates the wonderful security of childhood. Day-to-day living takes on a quality of desperation. Life is no longer a game. . . . In this new world adolescents feel much more exposed and therefore more vulnerable than ever before. Things can get scary, even terrifying, and perhaps overwhelming. (pp. 14–15)

There are many explanations for the origins of this "new and powerful voice" that disrupts security, creates feelings of alienation, and contributes to events and behaviors that can become "scary." Most of the theories can be subsumed under familiar "nature-nurture" or "heredity-environment" terminology, and almost all possess some degree of credence. Biologists, for instance, have long stressed the importance of hormones in explaining teen behavior, and anthropologists emphasized the effects of culture on human development. Undoubtedly, adolescents are affected by these and any number of factors—parenting, early childhood experiences, education, nutrition, and peers—as well as biology and culture.

Even though the human brain has been of interest to civilizations as far back as the Egyptians, the expanding field of neuroscience has begun to shed the clearest light on the stage we call "adolescence." The complexity of brain studies makes it impossible here to explain in detail how the adolescent brain functions, yet a few basic points are worth noting. Prior to the development of magnetic resonance imaging (MRI) in the latter 20th century, scientists could study with accuracy only the brains of dead humans, a circumstance that for years led to the belief that the human brain was fully formed by age five. But with their capacity to examine detailed pictures of living brains, MRIs produced a shocking discovery: There is enormous plasticity and capacity for change occurring in the brain throughout adolescence, and this change is not completed until the third decade of life.

Probably the most important area of the brain that demands comment at this point is the prefrontal cortex, which is the center of most life skills—impulse control, empathy, organization, strategizing, prioritizing, decision making, behavior determination, insight, and sensitivity to feedback and repercussions of behavior (Weingberger, Elvevag, & Giedd, 2005). As an individual matures, connections are made within the prefrontal cortex that result from reinforcement of socially appropriate behaviors, but this is a very gradual process influenced by external factors such as parenting, education, and ethical training. Until the process is complete, the primitive part of the brain, the limbic system, exercises significant control so that during adolescence decisions and actions are frequently based on primitive instincts and desires.

Summarizing their discussion in "The Adolescent Brain: A Work in Progress," Weingberger and colleagues (2005) concluded:

> Research on the neurological development of teens confirms a long held, common sense view: teenagers are not the same as adults in a variety of key areas such as ability to make sound judgments when confronted by complex situations, the capacity to control impulses, and the ability to plan effectively. . . . Teens are full of promise, often energetic and caring, capable of making many contributions to their communities, and able to make remarkable spurts in intellectual development and learning. But neurologically, they are not adults. (p. 19)

Knowledgeable as the authors' remarks are, psychologist Michael J. Bradley's (2003) use of humor to portray adolescence is perhaps more compelling. In his award-winning popular book *Yes, Your Teen Is Crazy! Loving Your Kid without Losing Your Mind*, Bradley portrayed adolescence from both parents' and teens' perspectives. Having explained advancements in neuroscience that led to the realization that the brain is not completely developed in adolescence, he continued:

> The result is that the teen is trapped between the two worlds of childhood and adulthood. . . . Like a science fiction character he finds himself existing in two separate dimensions at the same time, with two completely different sets of rules, expectations, needs, and fears.
>
> Learning how to verbally approach adolescents today is the same rigorous baptism-by-fire known to rookie cops and new workers at mental hospitals. You can't just say what you think because many of the people you work with are mentally ill and cannot handle normal conversation. . . .
>
> Adolescence, at times, is a kind of mental illness. That raging child you love, who seems to be delighting in her torment of you, is often in just that kind of terrible pain. She is fighting for her soul, and she can't let anyone know, least of all her Uncle Louie, who loves to constantly tell her: "These are the best years of your life, kiddo. It's all downhill from here." (pp. 15–16)

The almost overwhelming challenge sexual abuse poses is that educator-offenders are far more likely than average citizens to understand the outrage and the pain of adolescence and to possess the trained verbal and emotional discipline necessary to capitalize on teens' feelings of entrapment "between the two worlds of childhood and adulthood." Perhaps the greatest mistake targets and their parents make is assuming not only that all educators are trustworthy and responsible but also that those who do not fit this ideal model are easily recognizable. Shakeshaft and Cohan (1994) reported that at the elementary school level, teachers who were sexually abusing children were often considered outstanding educators, just as Dziech and Weiner (1984) contended that a similar pattern occurred on the collegiate level. Parents at the Sidwell Friends school, for instance, were shocked to hear of the charges against Peterson. One said that her son "adored him" and another that he was "a wonderful teacher" (Birnbaum & Morse, 2010). Another difficulty is that perpetrators are often veteran educators whose offenses might not be detected for years.

Whatever their lengths of service and reputations, abusive educators are unlikely to wear labels declaring their identities. What distinguishes them from their peers is less their personal characteristics and teaching effectiveness than the process by which they approach teens during the most vulnerable developmental period of their lives. Sex is all around teenagers in contemporary society, but they know far less than they and many adults assume. "Trapped between the two worlds of childhood and adulthood"

(Bradley, 2003, p. 15), forced to obey "a new and powerful voice" (Wolfe, 2002, p. 14) that threatens to rob them of all security, adolescents are perfect targets for what is known as "grooming." It is a subtle process by which an offender slowly but surely establishes a connection with a young person in order to build a bond of trust so that feelings of insecurity, alienation, self-deprecation, and even sexual confusion will be alleviated and the teen will lower his or her inhibitions and become open to the possibility of a physical relationship.

This may have been the case with 16-year-old Jess Anderson, who left home in 2008 to live with 49-year-old Clive Richardson, a religious education teacher in the United Kingdom. The story attracted attention because three days after Richardson's third wife left with the younger of their two sons, he moved the teenager in, where she became stepmother to his 14-year-old son, Benjamin. Benjamin, who wanted to remain in his home, traveled to school on the same bus with Anderson and told his mother, "It's not right, Mummy, Jess goes to the same school as me" (Clarke, 2008b).

Richardson had a similar relationship with another 16-year-old student in 2006, and sources indicated the school was aware of rumors about his behavior with Anderson but did not act because it maintained it had no evidence. Subsequently, Richardson was granted a leave for depression, and his contract was not renewed. He and Anderson were able to remain in the house he and his wife rented because the wife worked and he declared he was incapacitated. Richardson and the girl announced they planned to marry when she was legally of age.

Meanwhile she e-mailed her family:

> I understand that what I am about to tell you will be upsetting and a shock. I was aware in early October that I was falling deeply in love with Clive. We first acknowledged feelings for each other in October 2007; he stopped being my teacher in April 2007, thus not breaking any rules. Like any couple we found we enjoyed one another's company and got along very well; he did not set out to seduce me or capture me or whatever else you or anyone else may think. I know you will be thinking that I have been brainwashed or "groomed" as the common phrase is these days, but I definitely have not had any one of these things done to me. (Clarke, 2008a)

Naomi Clarke, the reporter covering the story, noted that the girl wrote "she had taken advice from a solicitor, and reminded her mother—several times—that 'it is important you realise legally we have done nothing wrong'" (Clarke, 2008a).

The grooming procedure to which Anderson referred usually involves premeditated behavior that begins with the perpetrator's establishing a "special" relationship with the teen in order to gain trust and lower his or her inhibitions. It is a form of psychological manipulation in which the adult demonstrates singular interest in the young person and then tests his or her response through a gradual process that might involve creating opportunities for togetherness without others present, encouraging disclosure of personal information, providing the target with gifts or tokens of support, introducing discussion of inappropriate topics like sex, and normalizing physical contact by "accidental" and increasingly direct touching or hugging.

The grooming process has never been better depicted than in Pulitzer Prize–winning author Elizabeth Strout's 1998 novel, *Amy and Isabelle*. A single mother, Isabelle appears with her daughter in Shirley Falls when Amy is only an infant. Over time Isabelle builds a quiet and respectable but lonely life for herself and her child, who is 16 as the novel opens. No one, especially shy and insecure Amy, suspects the secret that is the key to Isabelle's extreme overprotectiveness. Years before when she was a teenager, Isabelle was seduced and became pregnant by her father's best friend, a married man with three children. "Thinking it is good to know she has a nice girl like Amy" (p. 134), Isabelle at the beginning of the novel has no reason to suspect that her naïve but beautiful daughter will change their lives forever when she succumbs to the sexual overtures of a teacher.

Thomas Robertson, the year-long replacement for an ailing math teacher, is the prototypic abuser from the moment he enters the classroom. He focuses almost immediately on Amy, telling her in front of her classmates, "You have a glorious head of hair. . . . But you hide behind it. We hardly ever get to see your face. . . . You're like a turtle, Amy. . . . So come on out, Amy Goodrow. Everyone's been asking about you" (p. 30). Unaccustomed to the attention, she hates him while his popularity increases with other students. After ignoring her for a few days, he compliments her on a dress she is wearing; and when she seems embarrassed, he sits down in the empty desk next to her and tells her softly, "A woman should learn to take a compliment gracefully" (p. 48).

To be called "a woman" by a popular teacher is, of course, a heady experience for a lonely teenager. The relationship unfolds gradually from that point until it finally spirals out of control. Robertson draws Amy toward him, then plays with her emotions by ignoring her. He impresses her with his knowledge and sensitivity. "It was like he was a mind reader" (p. 74), she thinks. They often stay after school to talk until finally he begins driving her home. Whereas before she had felt invisible in the alienation of adolescence, now she knows she is "not invisible to him. . . . No one, it seemed, had ever been this happy to see her" (pp. 92–93). Then Robertson gives her a copy of Yeats's poem "To a Young Girl." "Before she had been drawn to him as though he were a large, dark magnet pulling the nail of herself slowly across a vast room. But here she was, with a soft, imperceptible click; nowhere further to be drawn to. She had arrived, and now she loved him" (p. 93).

At the end of each ride home, Robertson covers new territory. He "accidentally" touches her knee, soon they are kissing lightly, and then he French kisses her. Amy wonders, "So did it mean he loved her? The kiss had not seemed loving. It had seemed, in a way, to have very little to do with her. But that was stupid, because you would only kiss someone that way if you liked them a great deal. Still, sitting [alone in her] quiet living room, she felt uneasy, almost sad" (p. 118). By the time spring approaches, they are parking in a secluded area every day, and she is doing whatever he asks. He tells her, "You're every man's dream. A horny girl. . . . I want you even hornier" (p. 142). Then one day as her mother's boss is driving home, he notices the empty car, leaves his own to discover whose it is, and finds instead Amy and the math teacher having sex in the woods.

When Isabelle is told of the incident, she confronts Robertson and tells him he must leave town. His response is that of a practiced offender: "Sure . . . I have no reason to stay" (p. 166), and Isabelle hears "in his remark the disposability of her daughter" (p. 167). She asks, "Have you any idea . . . how you have injured my child? . . . You have taken a very, very innocent girl and put you handprint on her forever" (p. 167). His answer is, "I'm afraid you've been a tad naïve about the nature of your passionate and unusually attractive daughter" (p. 167).

Against all evidence, Amy believes he will come back for her because "it was indescribably private what they had done. When people did that kind of thing . . . well, they loved each other incredibly. You had to be together after that" (p. 171). Isabelle's relationship with her sanctimonious boss is ruined by what he witnessed in the woods; to him, Amy is a "Nasty girl. Filthy thing" (p. 155). Amy and Isabelle suffer through a blistering, rainless summer of anger and estrangement. Refusing to believe her mother's contention that "that kind of man . . . says he cares for you because he wants what he wants" (p. 161), Amy wanders the streets compulsively in hopes that Robertson will return. Finally, she begins calling phone numbers of all the "Thomas Robertsons" in neighboring towns. After several disappointments, she reaches a woman who silently hands over the phone to a man whose voice is that of her teacher.

The phone picked up: "Hello?"

"Oh, Mr. Robertson. It's me. It's Amy Goodrow."

A pause. "I'm sorry," said Mr. Robertson in his lovely deep voice, "I'm afraid you have the wrong number."

"No, I don't. It's me, it's Amy. In Shirley Falls. You know."

"I'm afraid not," Mr. Robertson said slowly. "You have the wrong number. . . . I don't know who you are. And there is no need for you to call me here again" (p. 269).

Teacher-student relationships are doomed for all the reasons depicted in this conversation. Mr. Robertson is always "Mr. Robertson," never "Thomas," to Amy, even though he has explored the most intimate parts of her body. To her, he is first and foremost "a grownup [who will] know what to do" (p. 171) when her angry mother confronts him. Like a fairy tale princess waiting to be rescued, she believes he will eventually return for her. But because she is luckier than some of the real-life victims who never recover from educators' invasions into their lives, by the end of the summer she acquires "the half-formed knowledge that Mr. Robertson might be [in fact was] ultimately replaceable" (p. 304). He is replaceable because she never really knows him. Disparities of power and age, as well as his sexual desire that has "very little to do with her" (p. 118), make genuine knowing impossible.

For all its cruelty, Robertson's "I don't know who you are" (p. 269) is one of his few candid statements. He knows who he is and what he wants, he knows how to groom girls he targets because he understands adolescents, but he cannot finally know the individual Amy Goodrow since she does not and cannot at 16 know herself. These inabilities to penetrate beyond surface appearances are what make "consensual" relationships between teachers and students impossible—these and one final thought from Isabelle: "What we do matters" (p. 297).

Amy exhibits many characteristics emanating from the "sexual harassment syndrome" (see Paludi & Barickman, 1991). The most comprehensive analysis of effects on targets, the syndrome contains five categories: emotional reactions; physical reactions; changes in self-perception; social, interpersonal, and sexual effects; and career effects. Because offenders, targets, and behaviors vary so widely, the authors list several outcomes in each category. For example, Amy's reactions to her situation are complex and shifting, depending on what Robertson does or does not say and do and on her mother's behaviors.

From the beginning of the teacher's onslaught, Amy's emotions run the gamut through self-consciousness, confusion, insecurity, embarrassment, anxiety, frustration, fear, isolation, powerlessness, and betrayal. There are days in the beginning when her self-perception is heightened because of the relationship and others, especially once she is deserted, when she recognizes the hopelessness and powerlessness of her plight. Her preoccupation with Robertson causes her to become uncharacteristically distracted and disobedient at school. Once he is gone, she blames her mother and withdraws from her at the time both are in greatest need of each other.

Amy is, of course, a fictional character, but she is also emblematic of all adolescents who consent to sexual overtures from educators and end up "watching [themselves] out of control, reacting to things [they] know aren't real, yet somehow are real" (Bradley, 2003, p. 16). The loss they ultimately experience is irretrievable, as Robertson's first statement to Amy's class predicts: "You are young adults now. . . . There isn't anyone in this room . . . who needs to think of himself as a child again" (p. 26).

Fortunately, the majority of teens reject sexual advances by teachers. Unfortunately, few report educator misbehavior to appropriate authorities and even to their families or friends. Using data from Snyder's (2000) representative sample of 4,023 teenagers, research found that those who told someone, especially their mothers, within a month were less likely to experience major depressive episodes or to exhibit delinquent behaviors. Nevertheless, studies using representative samples estimated that approximately one in three targets never disclose sexual abuse and at least two in three never report it to social service or law enforcement agencies (Weingberger et al., 2005).

The reasoning for not doing so has been well documented during the decades that sexual harassment has attracted public attention. Even more than adult targets in the workplace, adolescents live in a world of "them versus us," and so they are reluctant and usually unlikely to report offenses. They recognize that offenders have far more power and status than they, and they know that perpetrators' relationships to others in power are often strong. Experience teaches teenagers that adults often assume they exaggerate or misperceive behaviors, and so targets doubt they will be believed. The media frenzy over teacher sexual abuse increases their anxiety about becoming known to others and embarrassing themselves and their families. They worry about losing friends and relationships, and most of all, they are concerned that they are somehow responsible for what has happened or that others will think they invited the educator's attention.

While these motivations doubtlessly affect nonreporting, another almost contradictory and perhaps original explanation might explain teens' silence. Those who believe themselves to be unique and special, heroes or heroines within their own personal fables, might well assume that they can manage on their own, that they do not need help from parents or school personnel. After all, the silence and protective covering that surrounds most educator sexual abuse is so profound that targets might reasonably assume their situations are singular. So they manage. They cope in the only ways they know, never recognizing the additional burden they might be inflicting on themselves. They avoid offenders, cut classes, stay away from school altogether, and sometimes even seek to change schools, all the while not realizing that their grades can be affected, that they are alienating themselves from peers and school activities, and that they are missing opportunities that will not come again. Nor do they consider that their silence endangers students yet to be targeted.

Although there is no data to prove this theory, it is worth noting that it, along with standard explanations for nonreporting, may explain the especially perilous responses of young males, who are far less likely to come forward when sexual offenses occur. The standard explanations for male students' silence are well-known and widely disseminated. Males are stereotyped as more sexual than females, and even with the escalation of hookup culture, a double standard still applies so that youthful sexual activity for boys remains far more acceptable than for girls and has become almost a rite of passage. Therefore, when a female teacher approaches a teenage boy, he might consider himself fortunate, or if he is uncomfortable, he might assume he is abnormal. Easily sexually aroused, adolescent males can also be manipulated into believing they "wanted" and even initiated sex. If an approach comes from a male educator, a heterosexual adolescent might fear he himself has recognizable homosexual characteristics.

Any of these scenarios could act as deterrents to reporting, but the personal fable motivation can also combine with upbringing and cultural stereotyping of males to discourage them from seeking help.

The asymmetrical, adversarial worldview (in which males are inculcated) takes perhaps its greatest toll in the realm of feelings. From childhood, boys learn that the route to center stage lies in winning, exhibiting physical prowess, telling jokes well, and eventually in making sexual conquests. There are few rewards, even today, for expressions of vulnerability or emotion; males discover very early that seeking help from others or admitting to self-limitations negates their quest for independence and status (Dziech & Hawkins, 1998, p. 90).

Ironically, the asymmetrical worldview that discourages male targets from admitting to victimization is often indirectly cited in attempted typologies of male perpetrators, who comprise the vast majority of sexual abusers. *Male Perpetrators of Child Maltreatment: Findings from NCANDS* (National Child Abuse and Neglect Data System, 2002) was based on a

2002 analysis of characteristics of 202,376 perpetrators in 18 states; two of their categories of victims were 12- to 15-year-olds and 16 years old and older. Out of all types of maltreatment, 26% of sex abuse cases were associated with males and only 2% with females. Findings by other researchers (e.g., Finkelhor, 1984) substantiate the gender disparity.

The motivations and characteristics of males who abuse are so diverse and complex that they may never be understood, but the challenge has not kept people from trying. In early research on male offenders, Groth and Birnbaum (1978) divided them into two categories: fixated and regressed. Fixated offenders focus exclusively on young children as opposed to those in the 12–18 age group and are thus not relevant in discussing adolescents.

Eventually, the FBI expanded on the NCANDS's typologies to describe categories of "situational offenders" and their characteristics.

> Regressed: Offenders have poor coping skills, target victims who are easily accessible, abuse children as a substitute for adult relationships;
>
> Morally Indiscriminate: Offenders do not prefer children over adults and tend to use children (or anyone accessible) for their own interests (sexual and otherwise);
>
> Sexually Indiscriminate: Offenders are mainly interested in sexual experimentation and abuse children out of boredom;
>
> Inadequate: Offenders are social misfits who are insecure, have low self-esteem, and see relationships with children as their only sexual outlet. (Terry and Tallon, 2004, p. 26)

Given widespread underreporting, heterogeneity of perpetrators, and the complexity of human beings, identification of causal factors for sexually abusive behavior can often appear speculative. One example is Bradford and Fedoroff's (2009) discussion of risk factors such as cognitive impairments from head injuries, maternal and paternal alcohol abuse, first birth order, and maternal advanced age at the time of the perpetrator's birth. In the aggregate, the research is both helpful and daunting because of the sheer number of theories, which may or may not prove valid and may or may not be applicable in school settings.

Noting that it is unlikely that any single theory can explain sexual abuse, they identified and classified those that have been proposed by various researchers. For example, Biological Theory asserts that physiological factors can lead to abnormal sexual behaviors, and Psychodynamic Theory maintains that sexual deviance is an expression of unresolved problems experienced during developmental stages. Behavioral Theory proposes that sexual deviance is a learned condition similar to the mechanisms by which conventional sexuality is learned, whereas Attachment Theory holds that humans have a propensity to develop strong emotional ties with others and that when they are deprived of these they act out because of stress and loneliness. Cognitive-Behavioral Theory focuses on offenders' tendency to diminish guilt and shame with justifications and excuses for their actions.

For decades most of the research on sex abusers concentrated on males. Then along came Mary Kay Letourneau. Although she conceived children with a student, Letourneau was not the first teacher to engage in outlandish behavior, but the twists and turns of her story would be extremely hard to duplicate. Vandiver and Kercher (2004) identified six categories of female offenders (heterosexual nurturers, noncriminal homosexuals, female sexual predators, young adult sexual exploiters, homosexual criminals, and aggressive homosexual women), but the teacher/lover category remains most characteristic of Letourneau. According to the researchers, women in this category frequently suffer from stressful relationships and can be extremely manipulative and controlling but nevertheless perceive their seduction of the young to be noncriminal because they convince themselves they are in genuinely romantic or mentoring situations. Letourneau clearly fits this type. She first met Vili Fualaau, a poor but artistically gifted child, when he was a student in her second-grade class. The mother of four was reportedly unhappily married by the time she became Fualaau's sixth-grade teacher and the affair began. She was 34, and he was 13. He later claimed they had sex 300 or 400 times. At some point, she became pregnant and accused her husband of abusing her when he discovered the relationship.

Either he or his cousin contacted authorities; Letourneau was arrested, pled guilty, and was convicted of child rape. During the trial, she was diagnosed as manic depressive and issued a tearful, almost hysterical apology in which she claimed to know that what she had done was legally and morally wrong. She was ordered to spend six months in jail and three years in treatment, on the condition that she avoid contact with Fualaau for the rest of her life. Less than a month after she was released from jail, she and the high school freshman were found having sex in her car, and she was sentenced to seven and a half years in prison, where she gave birth to her second child by the teenager. The boy's mother was awarded custody of his two little girls. While Letoureau was in prison, his family brought an unsuccessful lawsuit against the school district, charging it with emotional suffering and requesting costs for raising the children.

By the time of her 2004 release at age 42, Letourneau was well-known internationally; and even though the 21-year-old Fualaau had by then denied his previous affection for her, the two reunited after he won a court request to lift the no-contact order. They were married in a lavish wedding financed by the television show *Entertainment Tonight,* which also paid for exclusive access to their story. They are said to be living primarily off that money, and they have hosted "Hot for Teacher Night" promotions at a Seattle night club, where Fualaau has served as the disc jockey. In an Internet interview, he has acknowledged that he feels tensions with Letourneau's children from her previous marriage. His mother retains custody of their daughters. Letourneau has changed her name to Mary Kay Fualaau, and he prefers to be called D. J. Headline. D. J. Headline was arrested for extreme intoxication in late 2005.

The Letoureau case ignited an explosion of interest in sexually abusive educators, and the next to become a celebrity of sorts was a 23-year-old Florida reading teacher, Debra Lafave, who seduced a 14-year-old boy in 2004. When his mother notified authorities, Lafave admitted to having intercourse and oral sex with him at school, in her home, and in the back of her car while his cousin drove her and the student. Because the incidents occurred in two different counties, Lafave was arrested in both on separate sets of charges for lewd and lascivious behavior.

With his client facing a 30-year prison sentence, her attorney argued that her actions resulted from bipolar disease that caused radical mood swings and hypersexuality. While Lafave and her lawyer made the rounds of television stations, the boy reportedly suffered severe anxiety because of the media frenzy and fear his identity would become known. The final straw occurred when his mother discovered *Court TV* planned to cover the trial. She accepted a plea agreement. She later told reporter Rita Cosby (2006), "I couldn't imagine sitting there and looking at my son and then looking at him surrounded by the whole courtroom as well as looking at Lafave talking about things that shouldn't have happened to him. . . . It would come out and be written about again and again and again in all of the media. At what point would he have had a normal life in high school, much less be tagged with it the rest of his life?"

The agreement kept Lafave out of prison if she confessed to two counts of lewd and lascivious battery. Her sentence of only three years of house arrest and seven years of probation enraged both the public and the media. Charges were still standing in the second county, where the judge refused to accept a similar plea agreement because of the seriousness of the offenses; but without testimony from the victim, the case could not go forward, and Lafave was essentially free.

She continued media interviews, telling television's Matt Lauer (2006) that her "emotionally absent" father had affected her attitude toward men. In spite of the magazine photographs and her relationship with the boy, she claimed to be "the most modest person even today." Lafave conjectured that the basis for her actions was unresolved issues from having been traumatized as a 13-year-old when a teacher saw one of her boyfriends raping her in a closet and did nothing. She noted that a part of her desire to teach was that she "wanted to educate kids on issues like rape." Contrary to her penitent behavior during and immediately after the trial, she accused the 14-year-old of being the aggressor and said she thought he would experience guilt for "ratting her out."

This was too much for his mother, who had previously remained silent. She noted that "some of the prosecutors [she had] spoken with said [Lafave's story about being raped by an old boyfriend] was news to them, they hadn't heard that before." She listed additional untruths she believed Lafave had told and added, "She has never been remorseful. And that's been very clear from day one. . . . She was absolutely the aggressor from the very initial moment." When Cosby (2006) asked, "What do you think of Debra Lafave—you know, when you hear (her) comments, what kind of a person do you think Debra Lafave is, still to this day?" the mother replied, "She is calculated, she is manipulative, she is unremorseful and she is a sex offender."

Lafave's case did not seem unusual compared to the bizarre details of the Letourneau affair until reporters saw her. Once that happened, she gained the dubious distinction of holding second place only to Letourneau on the Internet site called "The 50 Most Infamous Female Teacher Sex Scandals." Attractive teacher offenders are not necessarily unique, but Lafave was pretty enough to have sought a modeling career before moving on to college, and so it took little time for the press to discover provocative images of the former teacher in *Makes and Models,* a motorcycle magazine. The photographs quickly flooded the Internet, and her attorney was accused of attempting to influence her sentence by arguing that to incarcerate her in "a Florida state women's penitentiary, to place an attractive young woman in that kind of hell hole, is like putting a piece of raw meat in with the lions" (Goldenberg, 2006).

The Letourneau saga was too strange to be taken seriously, but Lafave's slap-on-the-wrist sentence raised crucial and controversial issues. Critics argued that the defendant's appearance exerted undue influence on the court's decision to impose such a light sentence, and that belief continues to generate discussion. Probably it should not do so since a large body of research, anecdotal evidence, and common sense clearly establishes that physically attractive people enjoy privileges throughout life (Etcoff, 1999; Hatfield & Sprecher, 1986; Wolf, 1991). The courts are not exceptions (Efran, 1974; Jacobson, 1981; Kulka & Kessler, 1978; Mazzela &

Feingold, 1994); and while Lafave escaped jail time, she will probably never be able to convince most people that her appearance had no bearing on her punishment.

Far more controversial and inconclusive was the argument that gender bias in the legal system contributes to lighter sentences for females, especially in cases involving caretakers and educators. Research on female offenders is so recent and limited that the claim could be made either way. Compared to the volumes of studies on male offenders, far less exists about females, and attempts to develop typologies and scrutinize offender treatment demand greater analysis. Many contend that Lafave's case was an aberration, that female teachers do not routinely escape harsh sentences. They argue that lately female offenders receive greater public condemnation, as demonstrated by tabloid Web sites like "Jail BETA," "Bad Bad Teacher," or "The Big List," which chronicles the "sexpidemic" in the nation's schools.

Although research on female perpetrators is limited, there is credence in the argument that conviction and sentencing of males are justifiably affected by variables differentiating them and their crimes from females and their offenses. Research indisputably proves that males commit the most serious sexual offenses, tend to have more victims over time, are more likely to abuse children as well as adolescents, and more often use violence or threats. They are also different from female perpetrators in that they tend to deny offenses and are less likely to express remorse (Becker, Hall, & Stinson, 2002; Denov, 2001; Hislop, 2001, 2007).

Nevertheless, another assertion is that society's double standard affects judges and juries so that the sheer numbers of known male perpetrators becomes a sort of self-fulfilling prophecy leading to more findings of guilt and harsher sentences for male defendants (Becker et al., 2002; Denov, 2001). Proponents of this gender bias theory argue that people are likely to stereotype females as more passive and submissive than males, less capable of sexual arousal, less aggressive, less inclined to coerce or threaten, and more nurturing and caretaking. These assumptions, they say, lead to underreporting of female offenses, to significant differences in treatments of male and female defendants, and to overly sympathetic portrayals of female offenders as victims of childhood maltreatment, sexual victimization, and/or mental, stress, and relationship problems (Hislop, 2007).

Disputes over the legal system's treatment of male and female educators are doubtless worth considering, but they are far less urgent than discovering ways to protect the nation's schoolchildren from sexual abuse. In discussing sexual misconduct in general, the AP report (Irvine & Tanner, 2007) summarized this point.

There are three million public school teachers nationwide, most devoted to their work. Yet the number of abusive educators—nearly three for every school day—speaks to a much larger problem in a system that is stacked against victims. Most of the abuse never gets reported. Those cases reported end up with no action. Cases investigated sometimes can't be proven, and many abusers have several victims. And no one—not the schools, not the courts, not the state or federal governments—has found a surefire way to keep molesting teachers out of classrooms.

A classic example of the frequent revictimization of targets by school employees and districts, as well as the legal system, comes not from the United States but from Ontario, Canada, where Ken DeLuca, a veteran teacher who had served for years in different schools, was charged with 41 offenses involving 21 complainants, all but one of whom were former students ranging from ages 10 to 18. In 1999, Sydney L. Robins, a former judge of the Court of Appeals for Ontario, was appointed to review the handling of DeLuca's case that began in 1994 when DeLuca was sentenced to 40 months in prison for sexual misconduct with students in the Sault Ste. Marie School Board area. Robins's report was an attempt at damage control, an effort to provide information to an outraged community that had not been given details about unpublished criminal and civil proceedings in the teacher's case.

The abuse reported by DeLuca's survivors included kissing students, inserting his tongue into students' mouths, rubbing his body against the students, touching or rubbing students' breasts, having a student hold his penis while class was in session, lying on top of students and rubbing his body against theirs, touching students' genitals, rubbing his pelvis against students, biting a student's chest and vagina through her clothes, and intercourse.

Although complaints to teachers, administrators, and school board members continued over a period of 20 years, nothing was done, and DeLuca "easily moved from school to school, leaving behind emotionally wounded victims, with a fresh opportunity to victimize others" (Robins, 2000, Chapter 2).

Outrageous as they sound, the reabuses Robins identified in this case are not unusual. There are school systems across the United States where they happen every year. Some, but not all, states have made efforts to curtail educator abuse by requiring fingerprinting and background checks on new hires, but veteran teachers usually have no such obligations. Abusive teachers may move about from school to school and state to state with no records of bad behavior following them because it is easier to let them retire or resign than to terminate them and risk legal action. The AP report contended, "It's a dynamic so common it has its own nicknames—'passing the trash' or 'the mobile molester'" (Irvine & Tanner, 2007).

What We Do Matters 153

Out of inefficiency or deliberate intent, schools frequently fail to maintain records of complaints, fail to receive and investigate complaints appropriately, fail to provide support for complaining students, deny or minimize complaints, blame victims, and intimidate and even threaten complaining students. Robins determined that "the buck stopped" with the school board:

> Inadequacies in the Board's reaction to complaints against DeLuca may have represented some misguided notion by some officials of their powers and responsibilities. On the other hand, another inference is available on the evidence. . . . Board officials or employees may have . . . suspected DeLuca's abuse and refrained from making further inquiries out of loyalty for a colleague or concern for the reputation of their school system. . . . What cannot be disputed . . . is that the best interests of the complainants were not given paramount consideration (and) . . . little thought was given to the ongoing risk to other students. (Robins, 2000, Chapter 2)

In the United States, as in Ontario, adolescents, like children, pay an exorbitant price for parental, public, educator, union, and politician priorities. Some suffer because parents choose not to believe them. Other parents suspect the truth but are reluctant to act on their suspicions, fearing they will be disbelieved and that their children will be further damaged. They reason that other students will shun them and that the offender and his associates will find ways to punish them. To many, the wiser course seems to remain silent and ensure the adolescent avoids the offender or even, when possible, to move the teen to another school. As for the public, ignorance is too often bliss. To face the realities of what is happening in schools would entail anxiety and action, neither of which are pleasant or convenient prospects.

But parents and the public may not be the primary culprits in the educator sexual abuse crisis. Aside from offenders themselves, the greatest responsibility for making schools safe lies with teachers, their unions, administrators, and politicians. The AP reported:

> Legal loopholes, fear of lawsuits and inattention all have weakened the safeguards that are supposed to protect children in schools. The system fails hundreds of kids each year. . . .
> State efforts to strengthen laws against sex abuse by teachers have run into opposition from school boards and teachers unions. In Congress, a measure that would train investigators and create a national registry of offenders hasn't even gotten a hearing. Few leaders recognize—let alone attack—a national shame. [We] found efforts to stop individual offenders

but, overall, a deeply entrenched resistance toward recognizing and fighting abuse. It starts in school hallways, where fellow teachers look away or feel powerless to help. School administrators make behind-the-scenes deals to avoid lawsuits and other trouble. And in state capitals and Congress, lawmakers shy (away) from tough state punishments or any cohesive national policy for fear of disparaging a vital profession. (Irvine & Tanner, 2007)

Only a fool would dispute the fact that too many teachers "look away." Some choose not to see at all. Others recognize the signs and justify their silence out of fear they will be accused of rumor mongering and damaging the profession. When a teacher or administrator suspects a peer of sexual abuse, there are never acceptable reasons for silence and inaction. If educators console themselves by believing they are powerless or vulnerable in reporting suspicions, they need to remember what it feels like to be 15 years old, to be confused and afraid with no one to help. They need to recognize that the scars of sexual abuse don't end with adolescence but last a lifetime. Some school districts make serious attempts to combat the problem with courses that enable employees to recognize the signs of sex abuse and characteristics of abusers, but no amount of training can make a difference if individual educators lack the morality and professionalism to act on what they know or suspect.

Educators' unions and professional organizations also need to be realistic and honest about the problem. One union official quoted in the AP report called concerns about educator abuse "a witch hunt" (Irvine & Tanner, 2007). His statement represents the views of others in the profession, and while no one disputes teachers' apprehensions about false accusations, there is no reliable body of research to prove the validity of such concerns. Everson and Boat (1989) examined a large sampling of Child Protective Services cases and found doubt about children's and adolescents' veracity in only 4.7–7.6% of unsubstantiated cases. Oates and colleagues (2000) reported a 2.5% rate of false reporting, and Jones and McGraw (1987) found a rate of 1%. Significantly, these percentages apply to false reporting in all types of cases, and the majority occur in instances of parental separation or divorce.

Data from higher education replicates findings like these. A study by Robertson, Dyer, and Campbell (1988) reported false complaints to be approximately less than 1% of the annual total. They described this as a "maximum estimate" (p. 800), since some complaints that administrators listed as false might have been genuine given their definition.

Administrators and school boards are, in many cases, the greatest culprits when serious complaints occur; and as the Robins (2000) report indicated, they have numerous "tricks" at their disposal. They can pretend to take complaints seriously and then disregard them. They can fail to keep records or conveniently lose or misplace them. They can minimize abusive behavior. They can claim students lack sufficient evidence and intimidate and even threaten those who complain. And they usually have pat excuses for inappropriate handling of charges: They were trying to protect the accused or the student complainant or the school or all three. Sometimes the latter is true. Schools do find themselves in complicated positions when weighing the need to protect themselves against possible legal actions by complainants' parents or accused educators. But "possible" is the operative term here. Evidence from even the most abused is difficult to acquire, and perpetrators often confess and agree to leave quietly, so resolutions frequently occur without the public disclosure that school boards dread.

Fear of publicity and legal action are the forces that drive administrative and board reactions to sexual abuse. A quarter century of Supreme Court rulings on civil rights and sex discrimination have made them acutely aware of the large sums of money at risk if they are found responsible in abuse litigation. Public perception is that a young person has only to prove sexual abuse, and the school district will be held liable. Sometimes this is the case. Sometimes it is not. Regardless of proven facts in a case, school districts often fight to protect their finances and may or may not prevail.

One of the most publicized examples was reported by the AP (Irvine & Tanner, 2007). Troy Mansfield, a popular coach and teacher in Hamburg, Pennsylvania, began grooming Heather Kline when she was in his third-grade class. By the time she was 12, he was sending her e-mails, poems, and cards, hugging her, complimenting her on her appearance, and declaring his love for her. She lost her virginity to him in the seventh grade. When his arrest was announced, friends abandoned her and spread rumors, and even teachers criticized her. Kline suffered from depression and panic attacks and ran away from home at 16 without finishing school.

At last report in 2007, the 18-year-old was working as a grocery store cashier and hoping to get a GED. Mansfield's fainting and eventual plea of guilty when he heard some of his "love" letters to her being read in court might have provided closure (Oglesby, 2008). If so, it may be her only satisfaction because a federal judge dismissed her family's civil suit against Mansfield and Hamburg School District, finding that even though it "might have been negligent in failing to recognize a high risk of harm . . . there is no record evidence that prior to Mansfield's eventual arrest, [the administration] knew or should have known that Mansfield ever sexually abused Kline. The school's actions, therefore, do not amount to deliberate indifference to Kline's constitutional rights" (*Kline v. Mansfield,* Hamburg Area School District, Padasak).

Finally, there are the politicians. The AP report did find an increase in the numbers of teachers removed from classrooms during the period it surveyed, but the need for the states and federal government to coordinate reporting remains urgent. Shakeshaft's (2004) report has gathered dust for nearly a decade; research with all of its complexities and contradictions continues; the public notices sexual abuse by teachers infrequently in unusual cases; and in January 2009, Congressman Adam Putnam introduced H.R. 781, the Student Protection Act of 2009.

The Student Protection Act of 2009 requires that by fiscal year 2012, states have in effect laws and policies that require disciplining of any school, state, or local educational agency employee who, having reason to believe another employee has committed an act of sexual misconduct against a student, fails to report such act in the same manner the state requires the reporting of child abuse and neglect or, in the absence of such a requirement, as quickly as practicable. It requires each state to have a single, statewide commission for receiving and documenting such reports that: (a) establishes policies for investigating and reporting such allegations; and (b) has a toll-free number that can be used anonymously to report such allegations. It directs states to report to the Secretary of Education whenever an employee is terminated or punished on the basis of an act of sexual misconduct toward a student, including the reason such action was taken and the identification and last known address of such individual. It authorizes the secretary to penalize noncompliant states by reducing their funding under the Elementary and Secondary Education Act of 1965 by up to 5%. It directs the secretary to maintain a national database that contains, at a minimum, the details this act requires each state to report.

In 2009, H.R. 781 was referred to the House Committee on Education and Labor, where it awaits action. Meanwhile, "someone has to be responsible" (Sarton, 1994, p. 377) for safety in the nation's schools. "Someone has to care" (Sarton, 1994, p. 377) about the young. They must be taught to take responsibility for their actions and to seek support when they need help, but these are hard lessons, and the truth is that adolescents are not emotionally equipped or influential enough within school systems to control out-of-control sexual offenders. Families and friends usually bear the burden of making shelter and picking up the pieces when abuse occurs, yet too often these are preventable tasks, duties that belong ultimately to those in power.

References

Becker, J., Hall, S., & Stinson, J. (2002). Female sexual offenders: Clinical, legal, and policy issues. *Journal of Forensic Psychology Practice, 1*, 31–53.

Birnbaum, M., & Morse, D. (2010, January 22). Scope of teacher's alleged inappropriate contact probed. *Washington Post*. Retrieved on November 1, 2010, from www.washingtonpost.com/Education/District.

Bradford, J., & Fedoroff, J. (2009). The neurobiology of sexual behavior and the paraphilias. In F. Saleh, A. Grudzinskas, J. Bradford, & D. Brodsky (Eds.), *Sex offenders: Identification, risk assessment, treatment, and legal issues* (pp. 36–49). New York: Oxford University Press.

Bradley, M. (2003). *Yes, your teen is crazy! Loving your kid without losing your mind.* Gig Harbor, WA: Harbor Press.

Clarke, N. (2008a). The day I learned my 16-year-old daughter was having an affair with her RE teacher . . . from his wife. *Mail Online*. Retrieved on November 6, 2010, from www.dailymail.co.uk/.../The-day-I-learned-16-year-old-daughter-having-affair-RE-teacher-wife.

Clarke, N. (2008b). My husband the predator, by the wife of the 49-year-old RE teacher who's moved in with a 16-year-old deputy head girl. *Mail Online*. http://www.dailymail.co.uk/femail/article-513204/my-husband-predator-wife-49-year-old-R-E-teacher-whos-moved-16-year-old-deputy-head-girl.html.

Cosby, R. (2006). Victim's mom: LaFave interview "disturbing." MSNBC. Retrieved on November 5, 2010, from www.msnbc.msn.com/id/14840035/.

Denov, M. (2001). A culture of denial: Exploring professional perspectives on female sex offending. *Canadian Journal of Criminology, 43*(3), 303–329.

Dougherty, J. (2004, April 5). Sex abuse by teachers said worse than Catholic church. *Newsmax*. Retrieved on November 10, 2010, from archive.newsmax.com/archives/articles/2004/4/.../01552.shtml.

Dziech, B. W., & Hawkins, M. (1998). *Sexual harassment in higher education: Reflection and new perspectives.* New York: Garland Publishing.

Dziech, B. W., & Weiner, L. (1984). *The lecherous professor.* Boston: Beacon.

Efran, M. (1974). The effect of physical appearance on the judgment of guilt, interpersonal attraction, and severity of recommended punishment in a simulated jury task. *Journal of Research in Personality, 8*, 45–54.

Elkind, D. (1967). Egocentrism in adolescence. *Child Development, 38*, 1025–1034.

Etcoff, N. (1999). *Survival of the prettiest: The science of beauty.* New York: Anchor Books.

Everson, M., & Boat, B. (1989). False allegations of sexual abuse by children and adolescents. *Journal of the American Academy of Child and Adolescent Psychiatry, 28*, 230–235.

Finkelhor, D. (1984). *Child sexual abuse: New theory and research.* New York: Free Press.

Finkelhor, D., & Jones, L. (2004). Explanations for the decline in child sex abuse cases. *Juvenile Justice Bulletin,* pp. 1–11. Retrieved on November 5, 2010, from www.ncjrs.gov/pdffiles1/ojjdp/199298.pdf.

Goldenberg, S. (2006). Too pretty for prison. *The Guardian.* Retrieved on November 1, 2010, from www.guardian.co.uk/world/2006/mar/24/usa.gender.

Groth, A. N., & Birnbaum, H. J. (1978). Adult sexual orientation and attraction to underage persons. *Archives of Sexual Behavior, 7,* 175–181.

Hatfield, E., & Sprecher, S. (1986). *Mirror, mirror: The importance of looks in everyday life.* Albany, NY: SUNY Press.

Hislop, J. (2001). *Female sex offenders: What therapists, law enforcement and child protective services need to know.* Enumclaw, WA: Issues Press.

Hislop, J. (2007). Female sex offenders. Center for Sex Offender Management/Department of Justice. Retrieved on October 30, 2010, from www.csom.org/pubs/female_sex_offenders_brief.pdf.

Irvine, M., & Tanner, R. (2007). Sexual misconduct plagues U.S. schools. *Washington Post,* October 21–22. Available at http://www.washingtonpost.com/wp-syn/content/article/2007/10/21/AR2007102100144.html.

Jacobson, M. (1981). Effects of victim's and defendant's physical attractiveness on subjects' judgments in a rape case. *Sex Roles, 7,* 247–255.

Jones, D., & McGraw, J. (1987). Reliable and fictitious accounts of sexual abuse to children. *Journal of Interpersonal Violence, 2,* 27–45.

Kulka, R., & Kessler, J. (1978). Is justice really blind? The influence of litigant physical attractiveness on juridical judgment. *Journal of Applied Psychology, 8,* 366–381.

Lauer, M. (Interviewer). (2006). Debra Lafave: Crossing the line. *Dateline.* Retrieved on November 12, 2010, from www.msnbc.msn.com/id/14499056/.

Mazzella, R., & Feingold, A. (1994). The effects of physical attractiveness, race, socioeconomic status, and gender of defendants and victims on judgments of mock jurors: A meta-analysis. *Journal of Applied Social Psychology, 24,* 1315–1338.

National Child Abuse and Neglect Data System. (2002). *Male perpetrators of child maltreatment: Findings from NCANDS.* Retrieved on December 23, 2010, from http://aspe.hhs.gov/hsp/05/child-maltreat/report.pdf.

Oates, R., Jones, D., Denson, D., Sirotnak, A., Gary, N., Krugman, R. (2000). Erroneous concerns about child sexual abuse. *Child Abuse and Neglect, 24,* 149–157.

Oglesby, C. (2008). Cells, texting give predators secret path to kids. CNN. Retrieved on September 20, 2010, from articles.cnn.com/2008-01-11/justice/teachers...1_cell.../3?_....

Paludi, M., & Barickman, R. (1991). *Academic and workplace sexual harassment.* Albany, NY: SUNY Press.

Robertson, C., Dyer, E., & Campbell, D. (1988). Campus harassment: Sexual harassment policies and procedures at institutions of higher learning. *Signs: Journal of Women in Culture and Society, 13,* 792–812.

Robins, S. (2000). *The Robins Report: Protecting our students.* Retrieved on July 14, 2011, from http://www.theinquiry.ca/Robins.hide.php.

Sarton, M. (1994). *Kinds of love.* New York: Norton.

Shakeshaft, C. (2004). *Educator sexual misconduct: A synthesis of existing literature.* Washington, DC: U.S. Department of Education.

Shakeshaft, C., & Cohan, A. (1994). *In loco parentis: Sexual abuse of students in schools, what administrators should know.* Report to the U.S. Department of Education, Field Initiated Grants.

Snyder, H. (2000). *Sexual assault of young children as reported to law enforcement: Victims, incidence, and offender characteristics.* Washington, DC: National Center for Juvenile Justice.

Strout, E. (1998). *Amy and Isabelle: A novel.* New York: Vintage.

Terry, K., & Tallon, J. (2004). Child sexual abuse: A review of the literature. In John Jay College Research Team (Eds.), *The nature and scope of sexual abuse of minors by Catholic priests and deacons in the United States, 1950–2002.* Washington, DC: United States Conference of Catholic Bishops.

Turque, B., & Morse, D. (2010, January 21). Sidwell Friends fires teacher, Robert A. "Pete" Peterson, accused of sex abuse. *Washington Post.* Retrieved on September 10, 2010, from www.washingtonpost.com/Education/District.

Vandiver, D., & Kercher, G. (2004). Offender and victim characteristics of registered female sexual offenders in Texas: A proposed typology of female sexual offenders. *Sexual Abuse: A Journal of Research and Treatment, 16,* 121–137.

Weingberger, D., Elvevag, B., & Giedd, J. (2005). *The adolescent brain: A work in progress.* The National Campaign to Prevent Teen Pregnancy. Washington, DC. Retrieved on October 10, 2010, from www.thenationalcampaign.org/resources/pdf/BRAIN.pdf.

Wolf, N. (1991). *The beauty myth: How images of beauty are used against women.* New York: William Morrow.

Wolfe, A. (2002). *Get out of my life, but first could you drive me and Cheryl to the mall.* New York: Farrar, Straus & Giroux.

PART III

Community Responses to Teen Violence

CHAPTER NINE

Community Interventions: Providing Support for Adolescent Victims of Violence

Roseanne L. Flores

Today, although violence among teenagers has declined from its height in the late 1990s, it continues to be a public health problem (U.S. Department of Health and Human Services, 2001; Centers for Disease Control and Prevention, 2010a). According to the Centers for Disease Control (2010b), violence among youths can be defined as "harmful behavior that begins in adolescence and continues into early adulthood." It can take on many forms, from bullying to emotional and physical abuse to assault with or without a deadly weapon (Centers for Disease Control and Prevention, 2010a). Moreover, violence does not discriminate. It affects all adolescents across race, class, and gender.

Over the last decade, violence among teenagers has continued to become a public health problem because of an increase in the number of reported deaths, an increase in the use of medical facilities to take care of injuries caused by wounds from stabbings and shootings, as well an increase in health care costs within the community. These problems have escalated because of the risks that young people have been exposed to in their communities.

Recent research has shown that when youths are exposed to multiple risk factors at the individual, familial, or community level, they are in greater danger for becoming a perpetrator or victim of violence (Loeber, Farrington,

& Petechuk, 2003) as opposed to those exposed to fewer risks. Factors that have been associated with becoming victims of violence at the individual level are having a history of violence in the family or community, abusing alcohol or drugs, and having already been a victim of violence. At the familial level, it has been shown that adolescents who have parents who are not consistently involved, have a harsh parenting style, do not provide supervision, and engage in substance abuse are often in danger of experiencing violence in their lives. And finally, it has been demonstrated that association with gangs, delinquent peers, school failure, lack of involvement in positive outside activities, and living in high poverty and high crime neighborhoods all place youths at risk for becoming victims of violence. The following scenarios describe situations that are similar to the ones faced by many youths on a daily basis across the United States. If the obstacles faced by youths are not addressed by the communities in which they live, over time the youths will be unable to become healthy, competent, and self-confident adults. This lack of intervention will in turn only exacerbate the already existing public health dilemma within the United States for years to come. The challenge then is to provide supports and re sources for individuals, families, and communities that will not only help to buffer them against exposure to violence but also lead to the strengthening of their communities.

Experiences of Teenage Victims of Violence

Markus

Markus is a 14-year-old African American male in high school. He has taken on a part-time job after school to help pay for his clothing and music lessons. Markus wants to be a musician when he grows up and has been playing the violin since he was 7. Markus lives in a neighborhood where gang members rule the streets. He often tries to get home before dark, when the streets are somewhat crowded, because he is afraid that someone might rob him and take his violin. He was once openly made fun of by his peers but avoided the conflict because one of his neighbors passed by and walked him home. One day, however, the store owner asks Markus to stay later because another worker has not shown up for his shift. Markus is afraid he might lose his job if he says no, so he reluctantly stays. At 8:00 p.m., the other worker finally shows up and Markus leaves the store. As he walks home, he tries to walk down streets that are well lit and not desolate. However, in order for him to get home, he must walk through a deserted parking lot. He crosses the street and attempts to walk as quickly as he can, but he is not alone. He hears some rustling and begins to run. Three young boys jump out from behind a car and begin to chase him. They finally catch him and push him to the ground. They grab his violin and kick him in the stomach. Markus screams, "Give me back my violin." The boys kick him again and one pulls a gun. "If you don't shut your mouth, I'll kill you." Markus lays silent and the boys run away. He sobs not knowing what to do. At that point, an older man comes out of a building and says, "Come inside. I saw the whole thing. Don't you know you can't walk around here at night by yourself? You're lucky those boys didn't kill you. They killed my son last year for his coat!"

Katerina

Katerina is a 16-year-old girl of recent immigrants who goes to a private all-girls school. Katerina is not wealthy, but her parents have sacrificed to send her to this school because they were not happy with their local school and wanted their little girl to have the best. Since she was 13 years old, she has always wanted a leather jacket with a fur collar. All the girls in her local community have had this jacket since they were 14, but her mother felt that it was meant to be worn by an older girl and so did not buy it for her. However, Katerina's mother promises that when she turns 16 she will buy her the jacket, and true to her word, she gives Katerina the jacket on her 16th birthday. Katerina is thrilled and asks if she can wear the jacket to school. Although her mother is a little reluctant, she gives in because she wants to make her daughter happy. Katerina spends an enormous amount of time that morning getting ready for school because she wants to look extra special. In part, she wants to impress the girls in her school because they always have such nice clothes, some which are very expensive. As Katerina gets off the school bus, she hears the popular girls whispering. At first, she thinks they are admiring her new coat and she is quite pleased because now she thinks she has a good chance of fitting in with the crowd. However, as she gets closer, she realizes that they are not admiring her coat but mocking her! She hears one girl say, "Did you see that coat? I'm sure she must have gotten it at a secondhand shop. Look at that fur. It looks like a rat's tail." Katerina begins to cry and tries to pass by as quickly as she can. She takes off her coat and puts it in her locker and goes off to class. That afternoon, when she goes to her locker to gather her things, she finds that her jacket has been ripped and the fur collar has been cut into pieces. She finds a note tacked on her coat that says, "No one likes someone who pretends to be better than she is! Why don't you go back to your own neighborhood?" When Katerina arrives home that day, her mother asks about her day. Katerina tells her everything is fine, because she doesn't want her mother to worry, but deep down inside she worries about what she will face tomorrow. She decides she will tell her mother she is sick and not go to school in the morning.

David

David is a 15-year-old White male. Two years ago, David's parents divorced and David and his mother moved in with his grandparents to save money. David's mother felt her parents would provide David with a stable environment while she was at work. David's mother is a nurse and needs to work nights in order to support the family. Although David's grandparents are attentive, they are in their seventies and don't have as much energy as they did in the past. They worry because they often do not know where David goes after school. David's father is an engineer and has recently remarried. His wife is expecting a baby and so he has not been able to spend as much time with David as he once did. David has become very angry and has begun to isolate himself from his family. He feels he is all alone. Although he was once a very good student, his grades have begun to drop. One afternoon as he is returning from school, he meets a group of boys from his new school. "Hey dude, you're new aren't you?" David looks up and says, "Yes, I just moved here from New York." "Cool—I heard they have some good ganja in New York." David has never used drugs but wants to fit in, and so he says, "Yeah, me and my posse used to get some good stuff on the streets." The boys say, "You wanna try some of this?" David reaches over, says, "Why not?" and takes a puff. He spends the rest of the afternoon getting high. He has found a new set of friends! That night when David gets home his grandfather says, "David where have you been? Your grandmother and I have been worried sick. Don't you ever do this again!" David shoves his grandfather and knocks him to the floor, saying, "Shut up, old man, you can't tell me what do. You're not my father," and storms off. His grandparents begin to cry.

Each year, thousands of adolescents like Markus, Katerina, and David become victims of violence (Centers for Disease Control and Prevention, 2010a). Some, like Markus, will be physically assaulted; some, like Katerina, will be bullied; and some, like David, will become perpetrators of violence against others. Many will end up dead; others will end up in the juvenile justice system; and some will end up on the streets. So what can be done to help stop this spread of violence in families and communities? It has been suggested that although exposure to multiple risk factors can place adolescents in danger of becoming victims of violence, protective factors can help to offset the risks.

Protective Factors That Insulate Teens from Violence

Previous research has demonstrated that there are many things that can insulate adolescents from the negative effects of violence (Hilkene & Resnick, 2006; Thorton, Craft, Dahlberg, Lynch, & Baer, 2002). It has been suggested that parents' intolerance of delinquent behavior, a grounding in religious practices, doing well in school, parental attitudes and beliefs about doing well in school, open communication with parents, involvement in outside activities with one's family, positive community involvement, and the presence of a parent in the home can help to counteract some of the risks that youths are exposed to on a daily basis (Centers for Disease Control and Prevention, 2010b). According to Hilkene and Resnick (2006), protective factors can be innate, such as one's personality, or external, such as neighborhood poverty. Moreover, they can occur at the individual level, the family level, or the community level. In addition, it has been shown that protective factors have a tendency to co-occur within individuals and that they do not always express themselves uniformly across gender, race, and class. For example, whereas performing community service after school for 15 hours a week may be a protective factor for one group of teens, keeping them positively involved in the community, the same factor may pose a risk for another for another group, not giving them enough time to study so that they perform poorly in school.

In short, although there are a number of factors that can place youths at risk for becoming victims of violence, there are also many protective factors that can safeguard them against the deleterious consequences that exposure to violence in their homes and communities can have on their lives. Given what we know from the literature, one way of ensuring that young people are protected and insulated from the effects of violence is to work closely with communities, providing them with the best available research-based interventions that have been shown to work. By doing this, we will be able to produce physical and social environments where teens will thrive and become successful adults. Establishing community interventions can have positive effects on the lives of teenagers, their families, and the communities as a whole.

Community Interventions and Youth Violence

Previous research has shown that when adolescents are exposed to chronic poverty and violence, there is a tendency for them to express rage, distrust, and hopelessness (Greene, 1993). In order to counteract these emotions, which often lead to negative behaviors, it has been suggested that programmatic interventions be established to protect and provide adolescents with safe and supportive environments so that they can become successful adults. Several suggestions have been made to engage communities to partner with families and adolescents to create safe spaces. Because previous research has shown that there is a tendency for adolescents who lack exposure to positive role models to engage in delinquent behavior (Greene, 1993; Mendel, 2000), it has been proposed that houses of worship, after-school programs, and other youth services work closely with the juvenile justice system to intervene in the lives of these youths and their families to address some of the issues they are facing before they have to enter the system. Moreover, it has been suggested that adults in the community work as mentors to provide youths with positive role models. One such example is the One Hundred Black Men of America, Inc. (2010), whose primary goal is to mentor young people so that they can maximize their potential. The purpose of this organization and others like it is to help balance the negative stereotypes that teenagers are exposed to on a continuous basis. Another intervention that has been widely acclaimed over the last 15 years is the Strengthening Families model. This approach was originally developed to be used to lower the number of risk factors that were associated with the children of substance abusers; however, it has been used with families who do not engage in substance abuse (Kumpfer & Alavarado, 1998). The goals of this approach are: to be comprehensive, to focus on family (as opposed to focusing on only the child or only the parent), to provide long-term involvement instead of a short-term fix, to be culturally relevant, and to take a developmental approach when addressing the needs of the family (Kumpfer & Alavarado, 1998). Although this approach is not new, its potential has never been fully realized within the community. In support of this approach, recent research has demonstrated that working with families during the early years is a critical factor in preventing later forms of delinquent behavior (Loeber et al., 2003).

More recently, the American Psychological Association (2010), in an effort to prevent and protect children from violence, established a program called Adults and Children Together Against Violence (ACT). The purpose of this program is to work with families and communities to promote safe and healthy spaces that will help insolate children from violence. As part of the program, parents are provided information on child development in order to improve their parenting skills and reduce the possibility of abuse. This intervention provides a comprehensive approach in that it provides a network for children, families, and communities to work together to decrease children's exposure and experiences of violence.

With respect to developing safe physical spaces, it has been suggested that businesses and other community organizations work together to create clean and safe spaces where youths can feel free to play and socialize with their friends without being harassed. One such project that has been proposed is the creation of partnerships between the members of local communities to sponsor the cleanup of their local park. Here the community would gather at an appointed time to clean up and beautify their space. Such an opportunity would not only provide the neighborhood with a clean space but also serve as a model for young people of what can happen when adults in the community cooperate and work together.

And finally, because it has been shown that having a high grade-point average is a protective factor against violence, it is important to ensure that all youths are provided with opportunities to succeed academically. Those opportunities should not be the sole responsibility of the school, which is often underresourced, but should involve the use of other spaces, such libraries and youth centers, that can provide quiet places where teenagers can study. Many teens live in environments that are noisy and overcrowded and not conducive to studying, which is one reason why they might not do well academically, and so it is important that the community support them in their efforts to succeed academically. One outcome of such involvement would be youths who feel respected and valued as opposed to angry, isolated, and alone.

Furthermore, although academic success is critical to becoming productive adults, having appropriate social skills is also necessary in establishing relationships with one's peers. Again, communities should work together to provide after-school programs and youth centers that will allow teens to socialize in safe and organized spaces with adult supervision and role modeling so as to development the emotional intelligence they will need as they become young adults who are capable of solving conflicts without becoming violent.

In short, although youth violence has decreased over the last decade, it continues to be a public health problem that needs to be addressed before it becomes a crisis. Although we have many programs that currently support adolescent victims of violence, few are research based, and of those that are, many often work in isolation of other programs in the community. Moreover, many of these programs often serve the same families and end up duplicating services. Therefore, it is important going forward that programs in communities begin to pool their resources and develop partnerships that will best serve the needs of adolescents and their families. Taking this approach will not only strengthen families but also help to strengthen the community. And strong families living in strong communities will become the foundation for a strong country and not one at risk.

References

American Psychological Association. (2010) *Adults and Children Together Against Violence.* Retrieved on November 14, 2010, from http://actagainstviolence.apa.org/.

Centers for Disease Control and Prevention. (2010a). *Understanding youth violence: Fact sheet.* Atlanta, GA: Author.

Centers for Disease Control and Prevention. (2010b). *Youth violence: Facts at a glance.* Atlanta, GA: Author.

Federal Interagency Forum on Child and Family Statistics. (2010). *America's children in brief: Key national indicators of well-being.* Washington, DC: Author.

Greene, M. B. (1993). Chronic exposure to violence and poverty: Interventions that work for youth. *Crime and Delinquency, 39*(1) 106–124.

Hilkene, B., & Resnick, M. (2006). Healthy youth development: Science and strategies. *Journal of Public Health Management and Practice, 12,* S10–S16.

Kumpfer, K. L., & Alavarado, R. (1998). Effective family strengthening interventions. *Juvenile Justice Bulletin, 4,* 1–15.

Loeber, R., Farrington, D. P., Petechuk, D. (2003). Child delinquency: Early intervention and prevention. *Child Delinquency,* May, 1–18.

Mendel, R. A. (2000). *Less hype, more help: Reducing juvenile crime, what works—and what doesn't.* Washington, DC: American Youth Policy Forum.

One Hundred Black Men of America, Inc. (2010). Retrieved on November 16, 2010, from http://www.100blackmen.org/home.aspx.

Thorton, T. N., Craft, C. A., Dahlberg, L. L., Lynch, B. S., Baer, K. (2002). *Best practices of youth violence prevention: A sourcebook for community action* (Rev. ed.). Atlanta, GA: Centers for Disease Control and Prevention, National Center for Injury Prevention and Control.

U.S. Department of Health and Human Services. (2001). *Youth violence: A report of the surgeon general.* Washington, DC: Author.

CHAPTER TEN

Adolescents and Firearms

*Deanna L. Wilkinson, Ashley Hicks,
and Shelly Bloom*

Safety and human security are basic needs that promote the healthy development of children and adults alike. There are a number of factors that shape people's negative perceptions of personal safety including: direct victimization, vicarious victimization, mass media attention to violent victimization, moral panics that follow high-profile events, information networks, and individual personality traits. Urban youths residing in high-violence neighborhoods are particularly at heightened risk for violence-related outcomes. Perceptions of rising and high rates of violence on school property driven by the relatively rare but highly publicized multiple victim shootings in schools have resulted in an overemphasis on rare events, which takes resources away from efforts to prevent and reduce the more common types of violence that interrupt education efforts.

This chapter examines the trends and patterns in firearm violence and suicide, including data on youth access to guns and carrying and use behaviors. The chapter is organized in two major parts—part 1 consists of a review of the latest research on adolescent firearm violence, and part 2 focuses on the problem of adolescent firearm suicide. Finally, in light of the trends, patterns, and accumulation of knowledge about the risk and protective factors associated with adolescent firearm violence and suicide, we discuss recommendations for a comprehensive approach to reducing adolescent firearm violence.

Gun violence has been part of the collective psyche of Americans for the past several decades, with the impact being felt most severely among

African American urban youths. Homicide has been the leading cause of death for African Americans ages 15–24 since 1981 and is either the leading or second-leading cause of death for African Americans ages 25–34 from 1981–2005 (Centers for Disease Control and Prevention, 2009b). Whether in urban centers or, more recently, in the nation's rural heartlands, guns have been central to the character of youth violence for nearly 30 years (Wilkinson & Fagan, 2001; Zimring, 1999). Firearm suicide among youths is also a very significant public health problem that is bound up and associated with issues related to access and availability of firearms. Guns have played a significant role in shaping the developmental trajectories and behaviors of many inner-city youths, and through the extended reach of media reports, youths in suburban and rural areas have also grown up affected by images of and direct experiences with gun violence. Although violence has been a recurrent theme for decades in contributing to urban delinquency, youth gun violence became more prevalent and concentrated spatially and socially during the 1980s and 1990s (Cook & Laub, 1998; Fagan & Wilkinson, 1988a). Despite the declines in youth gun violence that occurred in the last decade, rates of gun death remain unacceptably high in the United States.

In this chapter, we review the lessons from nearly three decades of research on the adolescent firearms violence problem in the United States. First, we examine the trends and patterns in violence and gun-related attitudes and behaviors in the community and school contexts. To provide a comprehensive review, this includes studies drawn from nationally representative samples of youths, selected samples of urban youths, and target samples of criminal justice–involved youths. Second, we summarize several recent studies on the trends in youth violence specifically related to firearms violence and firearms suicide. Next, we address the issue of adolescent firearm use in suicide by examining the patterns, correlates, risk, and protective factors. Finally, in light of the trends and patterns in youth gun attitudes and behaviors, we discuss the need for comprehensive, community-based gun violence–reduction strategies. The intent of this chapter is to provide a general review of what we currently know about adolescents and guns by bringing together various research findings from social science and public health to provide an overall picture of youth gun violence–related behaviors across contexts.

The Epidemic of Adolescent Gun Violence

The epidemic of youth gun violence should be viewed in both historical and contemporary eras. Cook and Laub (1998) show that nearly all the volatility in adolescent gun homicide rates for the past 30 years was the result of rising and falling gun homicide rates among males ages 15–34 years old. There were three distinct epochs of gun violence, with peaks in 1972–1974, 1980, and 1993. The most recent peak was far higher than the previous peak, but its decline through 1994 was also more pronounced than either of the two earlier epidemics. Cook and Laub (2002) explain that "guns accounted for all of the youth homicide increase. . . . [T]he result is that the gun percentage in youth killings was almost as high in 1998 as in 1993, and much higher than in 1985" (p. 3). The widening gap between gun and nongun homicides was more pronounced for older adolescents. The growth rates for gun homicides by adolescents of all age categories were similar but rose more sharply for adolescents ages 18–24, compared with younger teens ages 13–17. Throughout this time, nongun homicides remained nearly constant for both age groups. Moreover, the rise in the percentage of adolescent homicides by guns was pronounced for most types of nonfamily victim-offender relationships: gang-related homicides, robberies and other felonies, brawls and disputes, and other known and unknown circumstances (Cook and Laub, 1998, Table 6, p. 56).

As shown in Figure 10.1, the trends in firearm homicide since 1981 were most alarming for African American youths. Over the 25-year period

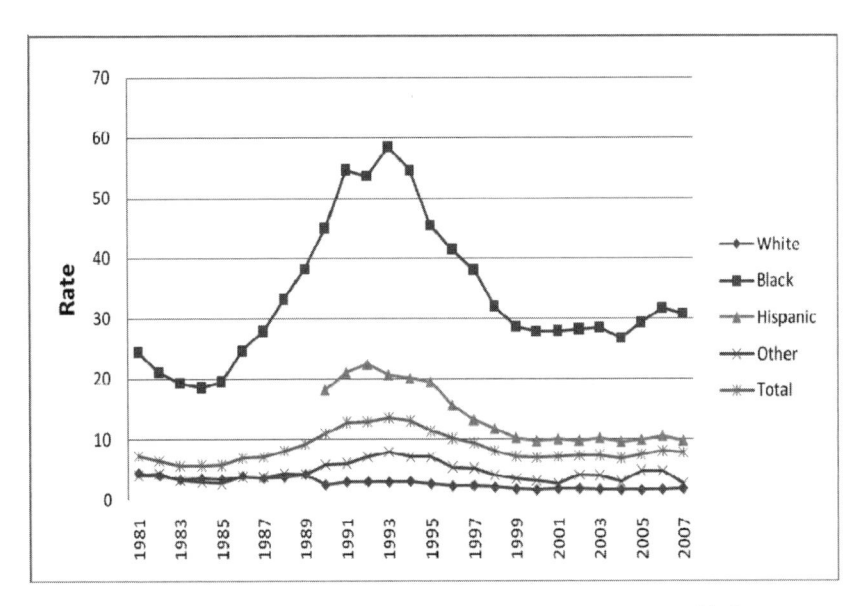

Figure 10.1 Trends in firearm homicide among 10- to 24-year-olds by race/ethnicity, 1981–2007.

Source: http://webappa.cdc.gov/sasweb/ncipc/mortratje9.html

of available data, Black youths aged 10–24 had a firearm homicide rate that peaked at 56.8 per 100,000 persons in 1993 and averaged 33.2 homicides over the series. In contrast, firearm homicide victimization rates peaked among White youths ages 10–24 at 5.95 per 100,000 in 1992 and with a 25-year average of 3.67 per 100,000 population. Ethnicity data became available beginning in 1990. Firearm homicide rates for Hispanic youths ages 10–24 peaked at 22.42 in 1992 and had a 15-year average of 15.38 per 100,000 population.

Elevated rates of shooting deaths among African American youths were a constant for nearly two decades with the rates exceeding the mean rate of 33.2 per 100,000 from 1988 to 1997. Analyses of the FBI Supplemental Homicide Reports suggests that adolescent gun homicides were a depressingly regular feature of the urban setting, with no temporal discontinuities within or across years (Cook & Laub, 1998). For more detailed information on the trends and patterns in juvenile gun homicide and violent crime, readers should consult Cook and Laub (1998), Cook and Ludwig (2004), Fagan and Wilkinson (1988a), Wilkinson and Fagan (1996), and Wilkinson and Fagan (2001).

Following the alarmingly high rates of gun violence in the early 1990s, many researchers began asking youths about their experiences with weapons and violence. The clearest indication from the available data is that there were unmeasured but obvious increases in access to handguns among urban youths that in some ways caught scholars, police, school officials, and policy makers by surprise. In general, the early survey-based studies revealed that urban male youths were involved in gun possession, gun carrying, and gun use at unprecedented rates, compared to earlier eras in American history. The picture that emerges from the survey data, which captures gun behaviors and nonlethal injury/perpetration of violence, parallels the trends in homicide data. Indeed, we see higher rates of reported fighting behaviors, weapon carrying, and victimization in the early 1990s with steady declines in subsequent years. Surveys conducted in urban schools or among high-risk samples tend to document the geographic, spatial, and demographic concentration of the problems. The most current data shows some recent declines in weapon carrying, victimization experiences, and violent behavior. Trends in improvements to school security and tightening disciplinary practices are also evident. It is impossible from existing data to make a causal link between increased security measures and reductions in violence-related risk factors. It is also difficult to determine what unexpected negative outcomes may come with zero-tolerance policies, school police officer presence, dress codes, surveillance technologies, and the like.

Beyond the Trend Data: What Survey Studies Tell Us about Youth Violence and Firearms

We have argued elsewhere that the most recent epidemic of juvenile gun violence led to adaptations in the everyday lives of inner-city adolescents, particularly African American and Latino youths (Fagan & Wilkinson, 1988a, 1988b, 1997; Wilkinson & Carr, 2008; Wilkinson & Fagan 1996, 2001). The most directly measured impact of the heightened firearm homicide rate was increased exposure to serious violence particularly in urban areas (Fagan, Wilkinson, & Davies, 2007). Increased exposure is thought to have resulted in increased fear of victimization, greater desire for self-protection, increased youth acquisition of firearms, and an increased perceived need to carry guns for personal safety. Relatively inexpensive handgun availability and diffusion to urban adolescents has also been linked to the increased rates of gun homicide and other gun violence. Estimates of gun carrying in school ranged from .1% to 15% (Harris, 1993) during the highest gun homicide peak years (1988–1997). Since 2000, the national surveillance surveys have either found school gun carrying rates below .1% or asked students about knowing someone who carried guns to schools in an effort to improve measurement accuracy. These rates of gun carrying are much higher among: (a) youths residing in inner-city neighborhoods, ranging from 6% of 11th graders in a Seattle study done by Callahan and Rivara (1992) to 25% in a Baltimore study completed by Webster, Gainer, and Champion (1993), and (b) youths already involved in the criminal justice system, ranging from 22% in a study of 856 juvenile arrestees from 11 U.S. cities published by Decker, Pennell, and Caldwell (1995) to 80.4% in a study of active violent youth offenders in New York completed by Wilkinson and Fagan (2001).

In this section, we summarize the results of existing national-level data sources for information on trends and patterns in violence among young people in the United States. For details about the methodology of these data sources, readers are directed to consult the original sources.

Violence-Related Risk Behaviors: Results of the National Youth Risk Behavior Survey, 1991–2009

In 1990, the Centers for Disease Control and Prevention initiated the National Youth Risk Behavior Surveillance System, known commonly as the Youth Risk Behavior Survey, to provide national-level estimates of the prevalence of risk-related behaviors among U.S. youths. The survey has been conducted biennially since then, providing information on trends and patterns of risk behaviors for the past 15 years (Centers for Disease

Control and Prevention, 1991; Eaton et al., 2006; Eaton et al., 2010; Grunbaum et al., 2002; Grunbaum et al., 2004; Kann et al., 1995; Kann et al., 1996; Kann et al., 1998; Kann et al., 2000). We summarize the key trend data related to weapons carrying and gun carrying during the 30 days prior to the survey and involvement and injury in a physical fight in the past 12 months. As shown in Figure 10.2, the percentage of students who reported being involved in a physical fight peaked at 42.5% in 1991 and declined consistently over time through 2009 to a low of 31.5%, and there was a slight increase in 2005 to 35.9%. Weapon-carrying behaviors followed the same pattern with a peak rate of 26.1% in 1991 followed by a steady decline to 17.1% in 2003; there was a minor uptick in 2005 of 18.5% followed by a decline to 18.0% in 2007 and to 17.5% in 2009. Gun-carrying data were available starting in 1993, with 7.9% of students reporting carrying a gun within the 30-day time period that year. Reported gun carrying declined to 4.9% in 1999 and rose to 5.9% in the 2009 survey. Reported injuries in physical fights started at 4.4% and changed little over time.

In addition, we examine the trends for students' weapon carrying on school property, avoidance and fear of unsafe school environments, victimization on school property, and involvement in physical fights

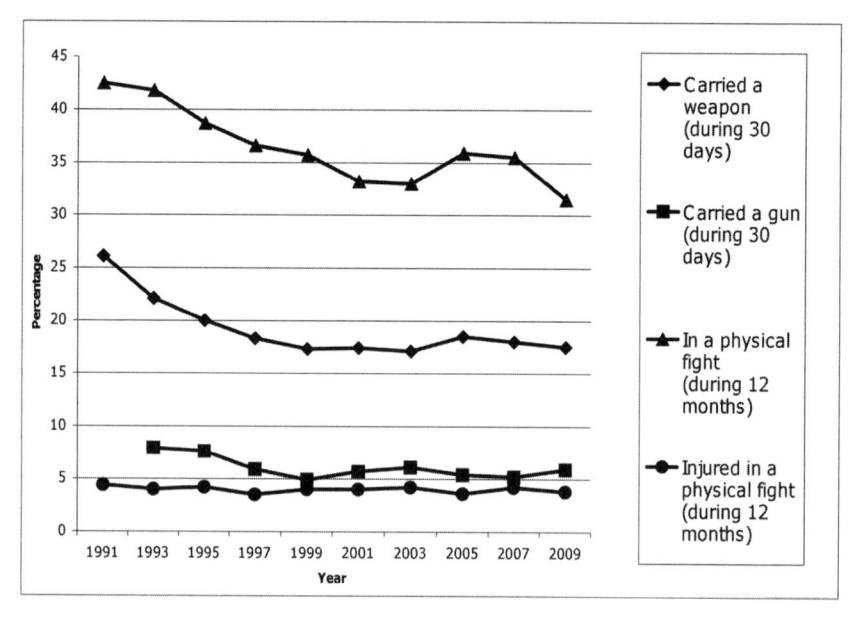

Figure 10.2 Weapon carrying and physical fights reported among students, 1991–2009.

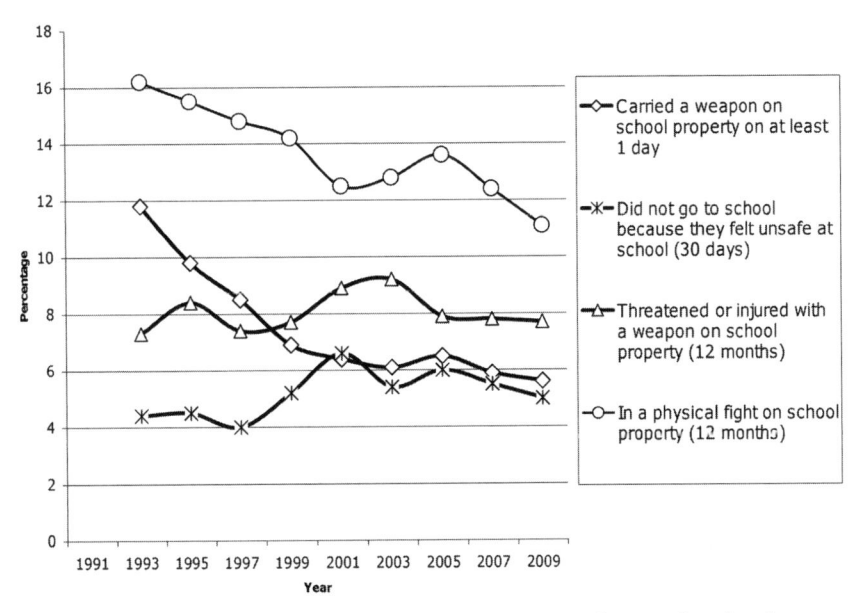

Figure 10.3 Youth Risk Behavior Survey: Trends in violence-related indicators on school property, 1991–2009.

Note: Data synthesized from Centers for Disease Control and Prevention, 1991; Eaton et al., 2006; Eaton et al., 2010; Grunbaum et al., 2002; Grunbaum et al., 2004; Kann et al., 1995; Kann et al., 1996; Kann et al., 1998; Kann et al., 2000.

on school property. As shown in Figure 10.3, the school-specific data followed a similar trend as the general violence data. Specifically, involvement in physical fighting peaked in 1993 with a rate of 16.2% of students reporting involvement in one or more fights in the 12-month period; the rate decreased steadily to 12.5% in 2001 and increased slightly to a rate of 13.6% in 2005, though it reached the record low in 2009 at 11.1%. Weapon carrying on school property was highest in 1993 (first year available) with 11.9% of students carrying a weapon one or more times in the 30 days preceding the survey. The rate drops to 6.1% in 2003 and increases slightly in 2005 to 6.5% but is at the record low of 5.6% in 2009. In 1993, 4.4% of students did not go to school out of fear and by 2005 approximately 6% of students had avoided school for safety concerns. Despite that earlier increase, only 5% of students surveyed avoided school because of safety concerns in 2009. The rate of being threatened or injured with a weapon on school property ranged from 7.3% in 1993 to 9.2% in 2003, but the changes were not statistically significant. These percentages have steadily decreased since 2003 to only 7.7% in 2009.

Overall Patterns in Gun Availability and Carrying

We located over 100 studies published since 1990 on patterns of gun availability, carrying, or use among school-age youths. These studies vary widely in terms of their samples, measurement, study period, methodology, and study purpose. We summarize some of the findings here. As mentioned above, youth access to guns is difficult to measure accurately. Braga and Kennedy (2001) found juveniles and youths obtained the majority of their guns through retail outlets and thefts. The gun trace on over 1,500 guns revealed that straw purchases accounted for 571 of the transactions. Using a mail survey of 731 10th- and 11th-grade boys, Sheley and Wright (1998) found that 50% felt that they could easily obtain a gun and 29% had carried a gun in the past year. Similarly, other research that used interview data from 615 Rochester males found that 22% of students acknowledged ever carrying a gun (Lizotte, Howard, Krohn, & Thornberry, 1996; Lizotte, Tesoriero, Thornberry, & Krohn, 1994). Callahan and Rivara (1992) surveyed 970 11th graders in Seattle and found that 34% had easy access to handguns and 6% admitted to carrying a gun to school, while the Slovak (2002) study of 171 rural students found 57% had access to a gun in the past year and 48% said they knew of someone else who had accessed a gun. Miller and Hemenway (2004) used phone calls to interview 5,801 California adolescents and found 33% had handled a gun. Using the same data, Vittes (2004) reported that less than 1% of respondents carried a handgun, 17.3% felt they could get one immediately, and 5.8% felt they could get one within 2 days. Using the 1995 National Survey of Adolescent Males, Cook and Ludwig (2004), however, found that 1 in 10 adolescents reported carrying a gun at least once a month; rural males reported the highest gun carrying prevalence at 14.7%. Cook and Ludwig (2004) attempted to disentangle the effects of gun availability at the county level with gun-carrying patterns among adolescent males in the National Survey of Adolescent Males. They found that gun carrying was significantly higher among males residing in gun ownership–prevalent counties. They concluded that:

> The nature of that causal influence is not identified by the statistical results, but it seems plausible that the mechanism is gun availability. Where guns are prevalent, adolescents will find it easier to borrow or steal or buy them from family members or other people. An alternative interpretation is that in counties where guns are more common, teens tend to be more experienced, knowledgeable or comfortable with guns. Both explanations grant a direct causal role to gun prevalence, whether it operates through availability (as in the first explanation) or learning (the second). In either case,

adolescent behavior is closely linked to gun prevalence among adults, and would be modified in response to a change in that context. (Cook and Ludwig, 2004, p. 49)

Gun Availability and Carrying in Disadvantaged Urban Neighborhoods

Focusing on availability of guns in highly disadvantaged neighborhoods, youths' reported access to available guns increases. Schubiner, Scott, and Tzelelpis (1993) conducted a study of 246 African American youths in an inner-city neighborhood and reported that 30% of the respondents could get a gun within one hour and another 30% reported easy access to a gun within one week, while Inciardi, Horowitz, and Pottieger (1993) surveyed 611 youths in Miami's inner-city neighborhoods and found that 48% of inner-city youths they interviewed carried a gun in the previous year. In addition, Schubiner and colleagues (1993) found that 42% of their inner-city sample had seen someone shot or knifed and 22% had seen someone killed through gun violence. Kahn, Kazimi, and Mulvihill (2001) interviewed students in both inner-city and non–inner-city high schools in New York and 57% of those surveyed reported that they, or someone close to them, had been injured by a gun; in a survey by Sheley, Wright, and Smith (1993) of 1,591 inner-city high school adolescents, 23% reported that it would be easy to get a gun, 80% reported that other students carried weapons to school, 20% had been threatened with a gun, and 12% had been shot at. Further, 80% of this sample reported that other students carried weapons to school. Using the Project on Human Development in Chicago Neighborhoods (PHDCN) data, which was not school based, Molnar, Miller, Azrael, and Buka (2004) found that lifetime estimations for concealed firearm carrying were at 4.9% for males and 1.1% for females. Approximately 3% of participants indicated they have carried a concealed firearm at one time or another. They found that youths are less likely to carry concealed weapons in neighborhoods with lower violence rates and higher perceived safety.

Other studies of inner-city adolescents find similarly high gun and other weapon prevalence rates. Sheley and Wright (1993) surveyed 758 male high school students and found that 45% of respondents reported being threatened with a gun or shot at en route to or from school. More recently Ding, Nelsen, and Lassonde (2002) sampled junior high school students in New York, where they found that males who had more experience with guns reported reacting more violently to frustration and participating in a greater number of violent acts than those with less gun experience.

Suburban and Rural Patterns of Gun Availability and Carrying

Rountree (2000) studied the rural-urban continuum in school-related weapons carrying by sampling students from three counties in Kentucky including an urban, suburban, and rural county. With a sample of over 18,000 6th- to 12th-grade students surveyed during the spring of 1996, the investigator drew a smaller random sample of just over 4,000. Rountree (2000) found that between 4% and 5% of students reported bringing a weapon to school. Urban students reported the lowest levels of weapon carrying at 4%. Most of the weapon carrying involved some type of weapon other than a firearm—less than 2% reported the weapon was a gun. Students from the urban county appeared to have fewer risks factors compared to the other counties, including self-ownership, peer carrying, and parental gun ownership. Wilcox and Clayton (2001) conducted a multilevel analysis to disentangle contextual effects on weapon possession in school using more than 6,000 students nested in 21 schools. At the school level, they found that weapon carrying varies widely by school; however, individual-level variables account for much of this variance. Controlling for the school-level variation, Wilcox and Clayton (2001) found that weapon carriers were male, older, non-White, and from lower SES households. In addition, victimization, problem behavior, gun ownership, and peer weapon carrying increased the likelihood of reported weapon carrying.

Carlson (2006) conducted a survey of 477 predominantly White youths, ages 11–19 in rural southwest Ohio during the 2000–2001 school year. Study youths experienced direct and vicarious gun violence victimization. Specifically, nearly 10% reported that they had a gun pointed at them at least sometime; 13% saw someone else have a gun pointed at them; about 7% had been shot or shot at; and 9% saw someone else shot or shot at. Carlson (2006) found that the majority of firearms that students obtained were from their homes, friends, or relatives. Males in the study reported higher levels of exposure to violence, and younger students reported more violence exposure than older students. School and neighborhood is where most exposure to violence reportedly took place; however, students were more likely to be beaten at home. Marsh and Evans (2007) examined the correlates of carrying a weapon to school among rural and urban youths recruited for school-based surveys in Arizona, California, Wyoming, and Nevada. The sample included 1,619 8th and 10th graders who completed the survey between 1998 and 2001. Marsh and Evans (2007) found that rural males were more likely to carry weapons than urban males. Overall, 17.4% of males reported carrying a weapon to school and 7.4% of females reported carrying a weapon to school in the past 30 days. Only about 1% of the sample reported carrying guns to school (no sex differences were found). Sixty-six percent of students reported concern about violence at school, while about 44% reported concerns about violence after school on the way home.

Reasons for Weapon Carrying

Rountree (2000) summarized the literature on the etiological factors of weapon carrying. She categorizes six main explanatory factors: sociodemographic patterns, fear and loathing, criminal lifestyle, proweapon socialization, social (dis)attachment, and contextual effects. In terms of sociodemographic patterns of weapon carrying, male gender, age (grades 9 and 10), and low SES are consistently found to be significantly associated with carrying behavior. In terms of fear as a motivator for weapon carrying, numerous studies find that students carry a weapon for protection from exposure to violence at school or in the neighborhood (Carlson, 2006; Kahn et al., 2001; Lizotte & Sheppard, 2001; Mateu-Gelabert, 2002; Webster et al., 1993). The convenience sample of inner-city junior high school students by Webster and colleagues (1993) revealed that 25% of males carried a gun for protection and 16% of these individuals carried a gun for protection on an everyday basis. In their study, the respondents stated they carried a gun for protection from both being threatened and being exposed to more violence and fighting where attitudes in their neighborhood seemed supportive of using a gun to shoot someone. Using the Rochester Youth Survey data, Lizotte and Sheppard (2001) found that 6% of the boys in their study owned a gun for protection during gang involvement, drug activity, and from general gun crime in their everyday lives. The LH Research survey found that 42% of the study feared that guns would shorten their lives (Harris, 1993). Involvement in criminal, delinquent, and other problem behavior is also considered an important factor in weapon carrying, especially gun carrying (Huff, 1998; Rountree, 2000; Sheley & Wright, 1995; Wilkinson & Fagan, 2001). Detachment from school is also thought to be a contributing factor to student weapon carrying. Jenkins (1997) conducted a study of school problem behavior and found that weak attachment to school explained a variety of delinquent acts at school, including weapon carrying.

Guns and the Peer Context

While the above studies have considered youths' access and attitudes toward guns, some researchers have also begun to investigate peers and gun use. As described above, Rountree (2000) summarized the prior literature on proweapon socialization. She found that particularly for adolescents, the proweapon socialization happens in the youth peer group with family socialization influencing sporting behaviors rather than weapon carrying in other contexts. Rountree notes that "perceptions of others' carrying guns to school significantly affect the likelihood of students' carrying weapons to school themselves" (2000, p. 297). Sheley and Wright (1998) reported that 14% of the study participants' peers carried a gun. Bjerregaard and Lizotte (1995) found that 33% of the respondents' peers carried a gun, and Sheley, McGee, and Wright (1992) found that 35% of respondents reported that their peers carried a gun outside the home. Finally, Williams, Mulhall, Ris, and DeVille (2002) reported 57% of participants stated that at least one of their friends carried a gun during the past year. For delinquent samples, we would expect higher reports of peer involvement in gun possession and carrying. The fact that nearly two-thirds of youth violence can be classified as co-offending situations increases the relevance of understanding the diffusion of guns within peer networks (Wilkinson, 2003).

These findings are especially important because research shows that adolescents increasingly turn to their peers for socialization and adaptation during their teenage years (Mateu-Gelabert, 2002; Wilkinson, McBryde, et al., 2009). Further, previous research has also found that respondents' having peers who carried a gun increased the chances that the respondent themselves carried a gun or were involved in violence (Lizotte et al., 1994, 1996; Luster & Oh, 2001; Zimmerman et al., 2004). Thus, peers have a major contributing factor in gun carrying and, we argue, in the construction of violent events involving gun use as well. Yet, while studies question respondents about their peers' access to guns, very few studies focus on respondents' perceptions of peers' actual use of guns or the influence peers have on respondents' use of guns.

In sum, across a wide range of sampling and measurement conditions, subgroups of adolescents consistently reported that guns are easily obtained, that they are frequently carried and readily used, that they are necessary for self-defense and survival, and that they influence the ways that teenagers view routine social interactions. Our review shows that youths residing in high contexts (i.e., a culture in which the youth has internalized meaning and information, and consequently little is stated explicitly in spoken or written messages) continue to have their developmental trajectories altered by exposure to firearm violence even after a nearly decade-long decline in youth gun violence.

Beyond the Trend Data: Findings from a Qualitative Study of Adolescents and Firearms

The New York City Youth Violence Study (NYCYVS) is perhaps the most detailed with regard to examining the experiences of youth perpetrators and victims of gun violence. The NYCYVS has shaped our understanding of the problem of youth violence by documenting how youth violence is heterogeneous; that is, there are multiple types with multiple explanations (Wilkinson, 2003; Wilkinson & Carr, 2008; Wilkinson & Fagan, 1996). Using ethnographic life history interviews with 416 16- to 24-year-old males from East New York, Brooklyn, and Mott Haven, Bronx, during the mid-1990s, the researchers were able to describe the social worlds of young African American and Latino males involved in violent behavior. The first publication from the study described recurrent themes in the situational contexts and scripts of gun violence among urban adolescents living in high crime areas (Wilkinson & Fagan, 1996). Fagan and Wilkinson (1988b) analyzed the functional aspects of violence for urban adolescents and described five goals important to adolescents that may result in violent acts: achieving and maintaining social status, acquisition of material goods, harnessing power, street justice and self-help, and defiance of authority. Fagan and Wilkinson concluded that "violence has become an important part of the discourse of social interactions, with both functional (status and identity), material, and symbolic meaning (power and control), as well as strategic importance in navigating everyday social dangers" (1988b, p. 88).

Further, Wilkinson (2001) described the adaptive role of violence in building a tough identity to avoid stigma and future victimization. She described a social hierarchy of violent identities that operate in dangerous neighborhoods and listed three ideal types of social identities that are related to violent performance: the crazy killer/wild identity, the holding-your-own identity, and the punk or herb identity. Wilkinson (2001) demonstrated that early victimization experiences shape youths' decisions to develop fighting skills, participate in violent encounters, align with tough (violent) peers, and acquire guns for self-protection. The presence and use of firearms, the involvement of younger adolescents in street-level drug sales, and the intensity of a violent normative code have effectively short-circuited established status hierarchies of the street. Her work has highlighted the importance of gun violence as a resource that adolescents use to cope with their dangerous social worlds. The process of finding a niche and forming a "safe" identity typically includes engaging in violent behavior. The link between victimization and perpetration of violence is becoming better understood.

The interplay between individual, group, cultural, situational, and macrostructural factors are critically important for understanding the experiences of urban adolescents who are at greatest risk for gun violence. The NYCYVS shows how ecological context shapes behavior. The dynamics of violence among minority male youths cannot be fully understood without exploring the contextual processes shaping the development of those dynamics, including violent youths' family situations, perceptions of their neighborhood environment, and experiences with mainstream institutions such as schools, community agencies, and employers. The composite that emerges from their experiences includes family dysfunction, repeated exposure to violence, institutional failure, limited achievement in school, and continued marginality as young adults (see Wilkinson, 2003). In the peer domain, the NYCYVS illuminates how peer social networks promote and facilitate youths' gun-related and other criminal behaviors (Fagan, Wilkinson, & Davies, 2007; Wilkinson, McBryde, et al., 2009). NYCYVS perceived a need to have guns for protection and they reported that most of their friends or associates also acquired, possessed, carried, and used guns for self-protection. Many of them also used guns in committing crime. In the community domain, the NYCYVS data shows how the breakdown in informal social control, resulting from fear, which drives adult withdrawal from youths, further fosters an environment in which violence can cycle (Wilkinson, 2007). Exposure to violence in the community negatively influences healthy adolescent development through negative modeling and curtailed opportunities for seeing alternatives to violent behavior (Wilkinson & Carr, 2008). Wilkinson and colleagues have documented the ways in which formal social control processes have limited efficacy to address the youth violence problem, resulting from serious mistrust of the police and the criminal justice system born partly from abuse, harassment, and cultural insensitivity (Wilkinson, Beaty, & Lurry, 2009).

Adolescents and Firearm Suicide

Prevalence

Adolescent suicide has become an issue of great concern within the United States. In 2007, suicide was the 11th leading cause of death in the United States and the 3rd leading cause in individuals ages 15–24. Over 4,000 youths (ages 15–24) died as result of suicide that year (Xu, Kochanek, Murphy, & Tejada-Vera, 2010). From 1999 to 2007, 38,988 youths ages 10–24 died as a result of suicide (5.03 rate) with over half of those suicides, 19,539, being committed with a firearm (3.53 rate).[1] Multiple studies show that firearms are the most common and most lethal method of suicide among adolescents (Lubell, Kegler, Crosby, & Karch, 2007; Miller, Hemenway, & Azrael, 2004; Romero & Wintemute, 2002; Shenassa, Catlin, & Bulka, 2003; Shields, Hunsaker, & Hunsaker, 2006; Webster, Vernick, Zeoli, & Manganello, 2004).

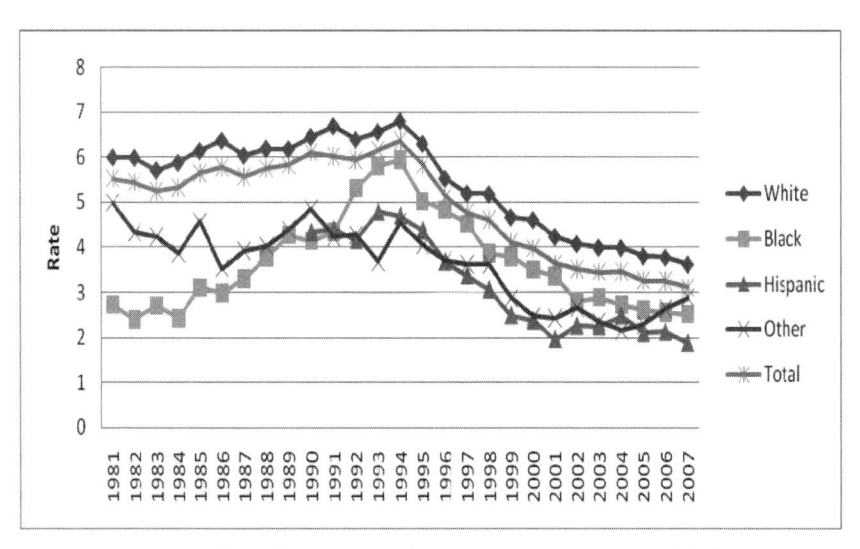

Figure 10.4 Trends in firearm suicide among 10- to 24-year-olds by race/ethnicity, 1981–2007.

Trends

Romero and Wintemute (2002) studied the epidemiology of suicide during the years 1980 to 1998 using data from the National Center for Health Statistics Mortality files. They found that during these two decades, rates of firearm suicide changed very little. Firearm suicide was the leading method of suicide within the nation and consistently exceeded the rate of firearm homicide. In 1998, youths ages 15–24 had an annual rate of 6.7 firearm suicides per 100,000 people, with suicide being the third-leading cause of death among adolescents. Lubell and colleagues (2007) analyzed suicide trends for adolescents during the years 1990–2004. This study found that from 1990 to 2003, the combined suicide rate for youths ages 10–24 declined 28.5%. However, from 2003–2004, the suicide rate for this same age group increased by 8%. Regarding firearm suicide, an increasing downward trend in the rate of firearm suicide for females was discovered (Lubell et al., 2007). An even more recent study by Bridge and colleagues (2010) noted that both the overall suicide rate and the firearm suicide rate for adolescents ages 10–24 has declined each year from 1992 to 2006 except for a sharp increase in 2004. Over this 14-year period, the overall suicide rate declined 23% and firearm suicide declined 45% from a rate of 5.93 in 1992 to 3.25 in 2006. These temporal patterns track the trend of a decline in youth firearm homicide as well. Nevertheless, firearm suicide still holds its position as the most common method of suicide among adolescents (Bridge et al., 2010; Lubell et al., 2007). Figure 10.4 shows the trends of firearm suicide in the U.S. from 1981 to 2007.

Who Is at Risk?

In terms of discussing risk factors for adolescent firearm suicide, there are three different types of factors that are most relevant. The first is fixed factors. Two examples of these include race/ethnicity and gender. Second is social or environmental factors, such as geographic location and availability of firearms. The third set is personal factors, such as depression, severe anger, and other mental health issues (Shain, 2007). This section briefly discusses some of the risk factors associated with adolescent firearm suicide.

Fixed Factors

Gender. Studies continue to show that adolescent males have higher rates of suicide, including firearm suicide, than their female counterparts (Bridge et al., 2010; Greydanus, Bacopoulou, & Tsalamanios, 2009; Romero & Wintemute, 2002). The World Health Organization (2009) found that from 1950 to 2005, males have consistently had higher suicide rates than females, and in 2005, males ages 15–24 had nearly five times the number of suicides than females. Studies report that 77–89% of all youth firearm suicides are committed by males, making males disproportionately the victims of this method of suicide (Azrael, Hemenway, Miller, Barber, & Shackner, 2004; Bridge et al., 2010; Centers for Disease Control and Prevention, 2009a; Joe & Kaplan, 2002; Shields et al., 2006; Wright, Wintemate, & Claire, 2008).

Race. Research has found that White adolescents (particularly White males) are more likely than adolescents who are Black or from other racial and ethnic groups to commit firearm suicide (Kubrin & Wadsworth, 2009; Romero & Wintemute, 2002); however, American Indian/Alaskan native males have the highest suicide rate (Shain, 2007). African American females have the lowest suicide rate, although their numbers are increasing in recent years (Shain, 2007). Although African American males still have lower rates of suicide than Caucasian males, the gap between them is narrowing. Joe and Kaplan (2002) found that between 1979 and 1997, the African American male firearm suicide rates increased by 133% and 24% for 15- to 19- and 20- to 24-year-olds, respectively. Other fixed risk factors include family history of suicide or suicide attempts, parental mental health problems, gay or bisexual orientation, a history of physical or sexual abuse, and a previous suicide attempt (Shain, 2007).

Social/Environmental Factors

Geographic location (rural v. urban). A very recent study (Nance, Carr, Kallan, Branas, & Wiebe, 2010) examined firearm mortality rates among youths ages 10–19 across U.S. counties using a rural-urban continuum. Results indicate that more rural counties experience higher rates of child and adolescent firearm homicide in the time period 1999–2006. Most rural counties had a firearm suicide rate that was 2.01 times higher than that of the most urban counties. Age comparisons within this study found that rates of suicide among 10- to 14-year-olds was similar to that of those 15–19; however, youths in both age groups who lived in the most rural counties had significantly higher rates of suicide than those who lived in the most urban counties (Nance et al., 2010).

Socioeconomic status (concentrated disadvantage). Kubrin and Wadsworth (2009) address the issue of concentrated disadvantage on young White and Black males. Using data from three sources (Mortality Multiple Causes of Death Records [MMCD], 1999–2001; Supplemental Homicide Reports; and 2000 Census), the authors used regression to examine the effects of structural characteristics (disadvantage) on young male suicide. Disadvantage was measured using the median family income, high school graduation, percentage of joblessness, and the percentage of female-headed households in the region. Findings indicate that cities with higher levels of joblessness and female-headed households and lower levels of income and high school graduation had higher levels of suicide for both young Black and White males. Further analysis showed that disadvantage was a statistically significant factor in both White and Black firearm suicides.

Firearm availability. A plethora of studies report that adolescent accessibility to firearms greatly increases the risk of adolescent suicide by firearms (Birckmayer & Hemenway, 2001; Grossman et al., 2005; Hardy, 2006; Joe & Kaplan, 2002; Webster et al., 2004). Birckmayer and Hemenway (2001) found that levels of firearm ownership are highly correlated with firearm suicides. Authors report that if this relationship is causal, then a 10% decrease in firearm ownership would result in an 8.2% decrease in firearm suicides. From 1981 to 2002, Miller and colleagues (2006) found that declines in household firearm prevalence were significantly associated with declines in firearm suicide. This association was most prominent with households with children (ages 0–19). For every 10% decline in the number of households with children and firearms, the rate of firearm suicide for children 0–19 declined by 8.3%. Shields and colleagues (2006) found that, specific to region, in a 10-year study of suicide cases for 11- to 24-year-olds in Kentucky (1993–2002), a gun was noted to be accessible (in the medical examiner's narrative) to the decedent in over half (61%) of firearm suicide cases. Similarly, Miller and colleagues (2004) found that in the northeast United States firearm prevalence was positively related to the rate of firearm suicide (and firearm suicide attempts) for all age groups including those age 15–24.

Additional socioenvironmental risk factors include impaired child-parent relationship, living outside of the home, the presence of a stressful life event, difficulties in school, social isolation, neither working nor in school, and an argument with a parent (Shain, 2007).

Personal Factors

Mental health problems. Shain (2007) states that mental health problems such as depression, severe anger, substance abuse, and bipolar disorder predispose and heighten an adolescent's risk of suicide; 90% of adolescent suicide victims meet the criteria for diagnosis of a psychiatric disorder (Shain, 2007). The National Youth Risk Behavior Surveillance System (YRBSS) found that in 2009, 26.1% of youths in grades 9 through 12 reported feeling sad or hopeless almost every day for at least two weeks. Additionally, the YRBSS reported that in 2009, 6.9% of high school age youths attempted suicide one or more times within the previous year (Centers for Disease Control and Prevention, 2010). See Figure 10.5 for the trends in high school youths attempted suicide over time.

Life experiences. Azrael and colleagues (2004) suggest that youths' life experiences greatly affect whether they use a firearm. These researchers investigated how the demographic, behavioral, and experiential characteristics relate to whether youths use a firearm to commit suicide. The results

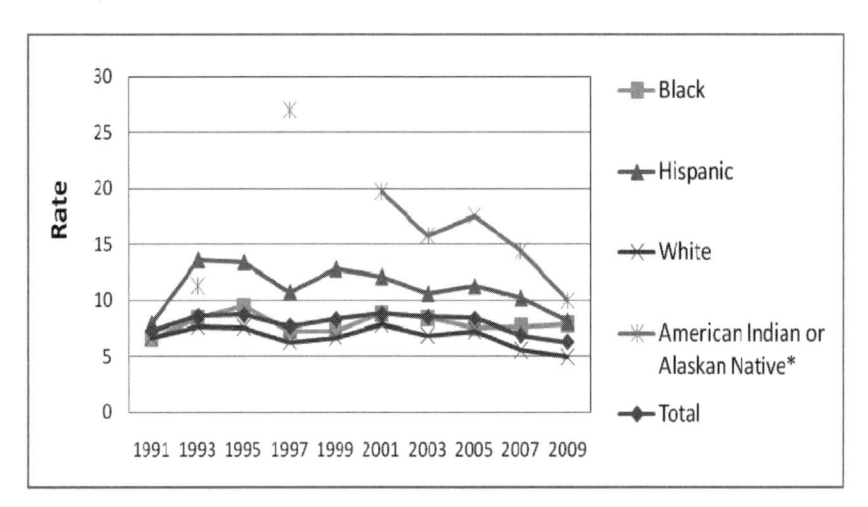

Figure 10.5 Attempted suicide one or more times in the past 12 months (years 1991–2009) by race.

Source: Centers for Disease Control and Prevention, 2010.

from this study suggest that, specifically, youths who have not experienced a life crisis or had previously expressed suicidal thoughts were more likely to use a firearm for suicide. The research thus implies that because these youths do not necessarily have the skills to resolve their life crises, they impulsively decide to use a gun. The study by Azrael and colleagues (2004) may suggest that with primary prevention tactics, youths can learn skills to resolve a conflict so that they do not make rash decisions in the heat of the moment.

Prevention

As discussed in the previous section, a wide variety of factors are important when understanding an adolescent's risk for suicide. One factor that has received much attention in the arena of adolescent suicide prevention is the availability of firearms. Research suggests that as rates of gun availability increase in particular regions, so do youth firearm suicide rates (Kubrin & Wadsworth, 2009; Miller et al., 2006). In their case control study, Grossman and colleagues (2005) found that case firearms (those used in an incident where a youth under age 20 accessed a gun and shot him- or herself intentionally or unintentionally) were less likely to be stored locked, unloaded, separate from ammunition, or with locked ammunition than control firearms. These four safe storage procedures were said to have a protective affect on suicide attempts among adolescents and children, yet case firearms (those that youths had used to cause injury) were less likely to be stored safely. Webster and colleagues (2004) examined the effects of federal and state laws mandating a minimum age for the purchase and/or possession of a handgun and state Child Access Prevention (CAP) laws requiring safe storage of a firearm on the firearm suicide rates of youths age 14–20 from 1976 to 2001. They found that minimum purchase/possession laws did not significantly affect the suicide rates of youths in this age group. However, they did find that CAP laws did result in a modest decrease in the rate of firearm suicide for youths ages 14–17. In addition, Wright and colleagues (2008) found that the majority of guns used for suicide by adolescents in California during 1997–1999 were owned by someone within the adolescent's household. Kubrin and Wadsworth (2009) also found that for young Black males, the accessibility of firearms within their community diminished the significance of disadvantage's effect on firearm suicide rates; this suggests that the presence of firearms apart from socioeconomic disadvantage is what heightens the risk for young Black male suicide. All of these findings emphasize the need for the safe storage of and limiting youths' access to firearms as important mechanisms to reducing the prevalence of adolescent firearm suicide.

Scholars have offered a variety of prevention approaches that warrant attention. Bridge and colleagues (2010) argues that the identification of modifiable risk factors (social, psychiatric, psychological, and circumstantial) would allow for the development of targeted public health interventions that holistically address adolescent suicide. Similarly, Shain (2007) acknowledges adolescent suicide as a public health issue and argues that identification of risk factors by pediatricians would help for the treatment and prevention of adolescent suicide. This argument stresses that the interventions must be targeted to the particular adolescent. Hardy (2006) addresses the multiple facets of adolescent firearm suicide prevention by acknowledging both the legislative reform put forth by the CAP laws and community-based, parent, and child education programming. Despite the apparent promise of educational programs, efficacy studies are needed to advance our understanding of how such programs lead to behavioral change. Birckmayer and Hemenway (2001) noted that many prevention programs targeted to youth suicide are too narrow; many youth suicide victims are "healthy," thus programs that address mental illness, suicide ideation, etc., may not address the needs of all youths. Instead, prevention programs should be more holistic.

Conclusions

Adolescence is a period of development in which attitudes and behaviors are shaped and molded through social interactions with others. Youths' opinions about and behaviors related to firearms and firearm violence are greatly shaped by the community context of development. Despite the widely publicized suburban and rural school shootings during the past two decades, gun violence is spatially concentrated in distressed urban areas. Researchers have consistently shown that youths who grow up in disadvantaged neighborhoods with high concentrations of poverty, single female–headed households, residential mobility, low collective efficacy, and high crime rates are more likely than advantaged youths to experience a wide range of negative outcomes. These include depression, victimization, involvement in delinquency, associating with delinquent peers, gang involvement, school failure and dropout, teen parenthood, suicide, gun carrying, violent offending, and other serious problems (Gorman-Smith, Henry, & Tolan, 2004; Sampson, Morenoff, & Earls, 1999; Wilkinson & Carr, 2008). In the aggregate, there is less youth firearm violence today then there was at the height of the youth gun violence epidemic, yet the rates remain unacceptably high for subpopulations of youths who live in dangerous environments.

Firearms impact the lives of adolescence differentially. Urban minority youths living in poverty are particularly vulnerable to the negative consequences of exposure to community violence, direct victimizations, and learning violence scripts from their peers. Efforts to respond to and contain the youth gun violence epidemic of the early 1990s can be largely characterized as embracing the "nothing works" myth and focusing resources on selective incapacitation and punishment rather than on prevention and rehabilitation. Violence is now recognized as a public health problem that is preventable, yet few resources are allocated toward effective prevention through comprehensive strategies that recognize the complex interaction between individual, group, situational, and structural determinants.

Violence is also recognized as a problem that needs to be addressed across multiple contexts and systems, such as education, health, human services, criminal and juvenile justice, and grassroots organizations. Collaborative partnerships built on trust and mutual respect between community stakeholders and researchers have proven to be advantageous in the planning, implementation, and evaluation of comprehensive community health promotion and crime prevention initiatives (Skogan, Hartnett, Bump, & Dubois, 2005). Comprehensive community-based prevention efforts to address youth gun violence must also include efforts to address other comorbid problem behaviors, including suicide. Reducing youth access to firearms would certainly be a positive step in reducing firearm violence and suicide among adolescents. Recent research has identified numerous prevention and intervention strategies that are effective (Kennedy, 2009; Papachristos, Meares, & Fagan, 2007; Ransford et al., 2010; Skogan et al., 2005; Webster, Vernick, & Mendel, 2009).

Note

We acknowledge the financial support from the Ohio State University College of Education and Human Ecology and the OSU Office of Outreach and Engagement that made this work possible. The opinions are solely those of the authors.

1. Retrieved on October 8, 2010, from WISQARS Injury Mortality Reports, 1999–2007, http://webappa.cdc.gov/sasweb/ncipc/mortrate10_sy.html.

References

Azrael, D., Hemenway, D., Miller, M., Barber, C., & Schackner, R. (2004). Youth suicide: Insights from 5 years of Arizona Child Fatality Review Team data. *Suicide and Life-Threatening Behavior, 34,* 36–43.

Birckmayer, J., & Hemenway, D. (2001). Suicide and firearm prevalence: Are youth disproportionately affected? *Suicide and Life-Threatening Behavior, 31,* 303–310.

Bjerregaard, B., & Lizotte, A. (1995). Gun ownership and gang membership. *Journal of Criminal Law and Criminology, 86,* 37–58.

Braga, A., and Kennedy, D. (2001). The illicit acquisition of firearms by youth and juveniles. *Journal of Criminal Justice, 29,* 379–388.

Bridge, J., Greenhouse, J., Sheftall, A., Fabio, A., Campo, J., & Kelleher, K. (2010). Changes in suicide rates by hanging and/or suffocation and firearms among young persons aged 10–24 years in the United States: 1992–2006. *Journal of Adolescent Health, 46,* 503–505.

Callahan, C., & Rivara, F. (1992). Urban high school youth and handguns. *Journal of the American Medical Association, 267,* 3039–3042.

Carlson, K. (2006). Poverty and youth violence exposure: Experiences in rural communities. *Children and Schools, 28,* 87–96.

Centers for Disease Control and Prevention. (1991). Health objectives for the nation weapon-carrying among high school students—United States 1990. *Mortality and Morbidity Weekly Report, 40,* 681–684.

Centers for Disease Control and Prevention. (2009a). Suicide Prevention. Retrieved on October 2, 2010, from http://www.cdc.gov/violenceprevention/pub/youth_suicide.html.

Centers for Disease Control and Prevention. (2009b). *WISQARS Injury Mortality Reports, 1981–1998 [Data File].* Conducted by the National Center for Injury Prevention and Control. Atlanta, GA: Author. Retrieved on October 5, 2010, from http://webapp.cdc.gov/sasweb/ncipc/mortrate9.html.

Centers for Disease Control and Prevention. (2010). *WISQARS Injury Mortality Reports, 1999–2007 [Data File].* Atlanta, GA: Author. Retrieved on October 5, 2010, from http://webapp.cdc.gov/sasweb/ncipc/mortrate10_sy.html.

Cook, P., & Laub, J. (1998). The unprecedented epidemic in youth violence. In M. Tonry & M. Moore (Eds.), *Crime and justice: Annual review of research* (Vol. 24, pp. 27–64). Chicago: University of Chicago Press.

Cook, P., & Laub, J. (2002). Recent trends in youth violence in the United States. *Crime and Justice, 29,* 1–37.

Cook, P., & Ludwig, J. (2004). Does gun prevalence affect teen gun carrying after all? *Criminology, 42,* 27–54.

Decker, S., Pennell, S., & Caldwell, A. (1995). *Arrestees and guns: Monitoring the illegal firearms market.* Washington, DC: U.S. Department of Justice, National Institute of Justice.

Ding, C., Nelsen, E., & Lassonde, C. (2002). Correlates of gun involvement and aggressiveness among adolescents. *Youth and Society, 34,* 195–213.

Eaton, D., Kann, L., Kinchen, S., Ross, J., Hawkins, J., Harris, W., Lowry, R., et al. (2006). Youth risk behavior surveillance—United States, 2005. *Morbidity and Mortality Weekly Report, 55*(SS-5), 1–108.

Eaton, D., Kann, L., Kinchen, S., Shanklin, S., Ross, J., Hawkins, J., Harris, W., et al. (2010). Youth risk behavior surveillance—United States, 2009. *Morbidity and Mortality Weekly Report, 59*(SS-5), 1–148.

Fagan, J., & Wilkinson, D. (1988a). Guns, youth violence, and social identity in inner cities. In M. Tonry & M. Moore (Eds.), *Crime and justice: A review of research* (Vol. 24, pp. 105–187). Chicago: University of Chicago Press.

Fagan, J., & Wilkinson, D. (1988b). The social contexts and functions of adolescent violence. In D. Elliott, B. Hamburg, & K. Williams (Eds.), *Violence in American schools* (pp. 55–93). New York: Cambridge University Press.

Fagan, J., & Wilkinson, D. (1997). Firearms and youth violence. In D. Stoff, J. Belinger, & J. Maser (Eds.), *Handbook of antisocial behavior* (pp. 551–567). New York: Wiley.

Fagan, J., Wilkinson, D., & Davies, G. (2007). Social contagion of violence. In D. Flannery, A. Vazsonyi, & I. Waldman (Eds.), *The Cambridge handbook of violent behavior and aggression* (pp. 668–723). New York: Cambridge University Press.

Gorman-Smith, D., Henry, D., & Tolan, P. (2004). Exposure to community violence and violence perpetration: The protective effects of family functioning. *Journal of Clinical Child and Adolescent Psychology, 33,* 439–449.

Greydanus, D., Bacopoulou, F., & Tsalamanios, E. (2009). Suicide in adolescents: A worldwide preventable tragedy. *Keio Journal of Medicine, 58,* 95–102.

Grossman, D., Mueller, B., Riedy, C., Dowd, M., Villaveces, A., Prodzinski, J., Nakagawara, J., et al. (2005). Gun storage practices and risk of youth suicide and unintentional firearm injuries. *JAMA: Journal of the American Medical Association, 293,* 707–714.

Grunbaum, J., Kann, L., Kinchen, S., Ross, J., Hawkins, J., Lowry, R., Harris, W., et al. (2004). Youth risk behavior surveillance: United States, 2003. *Morbidity and Mortality Weekly Report, 53,* 1–100.

Grunbaum, J., Kann, L., Kinchen, S., Williams, B., Ross, J., Lowry, R., & Kolbe, L. (2002). Youth risk behavior surveillance: United States, 2001. *Morbidity and Mortality Weekly Report, 51,* 1–68.

Hardy, M. (2006). Keeping children safe around guns: Pitfalls and promises. *Aggression and Violent Behavior, 11,* 352–366.

Harris, L. (1993). *A survey of experiences, perceptions, and apprehensions about guns among young people in America.* Cambridge, MA: Harvard University.

Huff, C. (1998). *Comparing the criminal behavior of youth gangs and at-risk youths, research in brief.* Washington, DC: National Institute of Justice.

Inciardi, J., Horowitz, R., & Pottieger, A. (1993). *Street kids, street drugs, street crime.* Belmont, CA: Wadsworth Publishing Co.

Jenkins, P. (1997). School delinquency and the school social bond. *Journal of Research in Crime and Delinquency, 34,* 337–367.

Joe, S., & Kaplan, M. (2002). Firearm-related suicide among young African-American males. *Psychiatric Services, 53,* 332–334.

Kahn, D., Kazimi, M., & Mulvihill, M. (2001). Attitudes of New York City high school students regarding firearm violence. *Pediatrics, 107,* 1125.

Kann, L., Kinchen, S., Williams, B., Ross, J., Lowry, R., Grunbaum, J., & Kolbe, L. (2000). Youth risk behavior surveillance: United States, 1999. *Morbidity and Mortality Weekly Report, 49,* 1–96.

Kann, L., Kinchen, S., Williams, B., Ross, J., Lowry, R., Hill, C., Grunbaum, J., et al. (1998). Youth risk behavior surveillance: United States, 1997. *Morbidity and Mortality Weekly Report, 47,* 1–63.

Kann, L., Warren, C., Harris, W., Collins, J., Douglas, K., Collins, M., Williams, B., et al. (1995). Youth risk behavior surveillance: United States, 1993. *Morbidity and Mortality Weekly Report, 44,* 1–56.

Kann, L., Warren, C., Harris, W., Collins, J., Williams, B., Ross, J., & Kolbe, L., et al. (1996). Youth risk behavior surveillance: United States, 1995. *Morbidity and Mortality Weekly Report, 45,* 1–63.

Kennedy, D. (2009). *Deterrence and crime prevention: Reconsidering the prospect of sanction.* New York: Routledge.

Kubrin, C., & Wadsworth, T. (2009). Explaining suicide among Blacks and Whites: How socioeconomic factors and gun availability affect race-specific suicide rates. *Social Science Quarterly, 90,* 1203–1227.

Lizotte, A., Howard, G., Krohn, M., & Thornberry, T. (1996). Patterns of illegal gun carrying among young urban males. *Valparaiso University Law Review 31,* 375–393.

Lizotte, A., & Sheppard, D. (2001). *Gun use by male juveniles: Research and prevention* (Juvenile Justice Bulletin NCJ 188992). Washington, DC: U.S. Department of Justice, Office of Justice Programs, Office of Juvenile Justice and Delinquency Prevention.

Lizotte, A., Tesoriero, J., Thornberry, T., & Krohn, M. (1994). Patterns of adolescent firearms ownership and use. *Justice Quarterly, 11,* 51–73.

Lubell, K. M., Kegler, S., Crosby, A., & Karch, D. (2007). Suicide trends among youths and young adults aged 10–24 years—United States, 1990–2004. *Morbidity and Mortality Weekly Report, 56,* 905–908.

Luster, T., & Oh, S. (2001). Correlates of male adolescents carrying handguns among their peers. *Journal of Marriage and Family, 63,* 714–726.

Marsh, S., & Evans, W. (2007). Carrying a weapon to school: The influence of youth assets at home and school. *Journal of School Violence, 6,* 131–147.

Mateu-Gelabert, P. (2002). *Dreams, gangs, and guns: The interplay between adolescent violence and immigration in a New York City neighborhood.* New York: Vera Institute of Justice, National Development Research Institute.

Miller, M., Azrael, D., Hepburn, L., Hemenway, D., & Lippmann, S. (2006). The association between changes in household firearm ownership and rates of suicide in the United States, 1981–2002. *Injury Prevention, 12,* 178–182.

Miller, M., & Hemenway, D. (2004). Unsupervised firearm handling by California adolescents. *Injury Prevention, 10,* 163–168.

Miller, M., Hemenway, D., & Azrael, D. (2004). Firearms and suicide in the northeast. *Journal of Trauma, Injury, Infection, and Critical Care, 57,* 626–632.

Molnar, B., Miller, M., Azrael, D., & Buka, S. (2004). Neighborhood predictors of concealed firearm carrying among children and adolescents: Results from the Project on Human Development in Chicago Neighborhoods. *Archives of Pediatrics and Adolescent Medicine, 158,* 657–664.

Nance, M., Carr, B., Kallan, M., Branas, C., & Wiebe, D. (2010). Variation in pediatric and adolescent firearm mortality rates in rural and urban U.S. counties. *Pediatrics, 25,* 1112–1118.

Papachristos, A., Meares, T., & Fagan, J. (2007). Attention felons: Evaluating Project Safe Neighborhood in Chicago. *Journal of Empirical Legal Studies, 4,* 223–272.

Ransford, C., Kane, C., Metzger, T., Quintana, E., & Slutkin, G. (2010). An examination of the role of CeaseFire, the Chicago Police, Project Safe Neighborhoods, and displacement in the reduction in homicide in Chicago in 2004. In R. Chaskin (Ed.), *Youth gangs and community intervention: Research, practice, and evidence* (pp. 76–108). New York: Columbia University Press.

Romero, M., & Wintemute, G. (2002). The epidemiology of firearm suicide in the United States. *Journal of Urban Health: Bulletin of the New York Academy of Medicine, 79,* 39–48.

Rountree, P. (2000). Weapons at school: Are the predictors generalizable across context? *Sociological Spectrum, 20,* 291–324.

Sampson, R., Morenoff, J., & Earls, F. (1999). Beyond social capital: Spatial dynamics of collective efficacy for children. *American Sociological Review, 64,* 633–660.

Schubiner, H., Scott, R., & Tzelepis, A. (1993). Exposure to violence among inner-city youth. *Journal of Adolescent Health, 14,* 214–219.

Shain, B. (2007). Suicide and suicide attempts in adolescents. *Pediatrics, 120,* 669–676.

Sheley, J., McGee, Z., & Wright, J. (1992). Gun violence in and around inner-city schools. *American Journal of Diseases of Children, 146,* 677–682.

Sheley, F., & Wright, J. (1993) *Gun acquisition and possession in selected juvenile samples.* Washington, DC: U.S. Department of Justice, National Institute of Justice, Office of Juvenile Justice and Delinquency Prevention.

Sheley, J., & Wright, J. (1995). *In the line of fire: Youth, guns, and violence in urban America.* New York: Aldine de Gruyter.

Sheley, J., & Wright, J. (1998). *High school youths, weapons, and violence: A national survey.* Washington, DC: Department of Justice, National Institute of Justice.

Sheley, J., Wright, J., & Smith, M. (1993). *Firearms, violence and inner-city youth: A report of research findings.* Washington, DC: U.S. Department of Justice, National Institute of Justice.

Shenassa, E. D., Catlin, S., & Bulka, S. (2003). Lethality of firearms relative to other suicide methods: A population based study. *Journal of Epidemiology and Community Health, 57,* 120–124.

Shields, L., Hunsaker, D., & Hunsaker, J. (2006). Adolescent and young adult suicide: A 10-year retrospective review of Kentucky medical examiner cases. *Journal of Forensic Sciences, 51,* 874–879.

Skogan, W., Hartnett, S., Bump, N., & Dubois, J. (2005). *Evaluation of ceasefire-Chicago* (Grant Number 2005-MU-MU-003. National Institute of Justice). Evanston, IL: Northwestern University.

Slovak, K. (2002). Gun violence and children: Factors related to exposure and trauma. *Health and Social Work, 27,* 104–112.

United States Department of Justice, Bureau of Justice Statistics. (1995). National Crime Victimization Survey: School Crime Supplement. doi:10.3886/ICPSR06739

Vittes, K. (2004, November). *Risk-taking behavior among adolescents who say they can get a handgun: Comparison with those who say they cannot and those who have a handgun.* Poster session presented at the 132nd annual meeting of the American Public Health Association, Washington, DC.

Webster, D. W., Gainer, P., & Champion, H. (1993). Weapon carrying among inner-city junior high school students: Defensive behavior vs. aggressive delinquency. *American Journal of Public Health, 83,* 1604–1608.

Webster, D. W., Vernick, J., & Mendel, J. (2009). *Interim evaluation of Baltimore's Safe Streets Program.* Baltimore, MD: Johns Hopkins, Bloomberg School of Public Health, Center for the Prevention of Youth Violence.

Webster, D., Vernick, J., Zeoli, A., & Manganello, J. (2004). Association between youth-focused firearm laws and youth suicides. *JAMA: Journal of the American Medical Association, 292,* 594–601.

Wilcox, P., & Clayton, R. (2001). A multilevel analysis of school-based weapon possession. *Justice Quarterly, 18,* 509–541.

Wilkinson, D. (2001). Violent events and social identity: Specifying the relationship between respect and masculinity in inner city youth violence. In D. Kinney (Ed.), *Sociological studies of children and youth* (Vol. 8, pp. 231–265). Stamford, CT: Elsevier Science.

Wilkinson, D. (2003). *Guns, violence, and identity among African-American and Latino youth.* New York: LFB Scholarly Publishing LLC.

Wilkinson, D. (2007). Local social ties and willingness to intervene: Textured views among violent urban youth of neighborhood social control dynamics and situations. *Justice Quarterly, 24,* 185–220.

Wilkinson, D., Beaty, C., & Lurry, R. (2009). Youth violence-crime or self-help? Marginalized urban males' perspectives on the limited efficacy of criminal justice system to stop youth violence. *Annals of the American Academy of Political and Social Science, 623,* 25–38.

Wilkinson, D., & Carr, P. (2008). Violent youths' responses to high levels of exposure to community violence: What violent events reveal about youth violence. *Journal of Community Psychology, 36,* 1026–1051.

Wilkinson, D., & Fagan, J. (1996). The role of firearms in violence 'scripts': The dynamics of gun events among adolescent males. *Law and Contemporary Problems, 59,* 55–90.

Wilkinson, D., & Fagan, J. (2001). What we know about gun use among adolescents. *Clinical Child and Family Psychology Review, 4,* 109–132.

Wilkinson, D., McBryde, M., Williams, B., Bloom, S., & Bell, K. (2009). Peers and gun use among urban adolescent males: An examination of social embeddedness. *Journal of Contemporary Criminal Justice, 25,* 20–44.

Williams, S., Mulhall, P., Ris, J., & DeVille, J. (2002). Adolescents carrying handguns and taking them to school: Psychosocial correlates among public school students in Illinois. *Journal of Adolescence, 25,* 551–567.

World Health Organization (2009). Suicide rates (per 100,000) by gender, USA, 1950–2005. Retrieved on October 10, 2010, from http://www.who.int/mental_health/media/unitstates.pdf.

Wright, M., Wintemute, G., & Claire, B. (2008). Gun suicide by young people in California: Descriptive epidemiology and gun ownership. *Journal of Adolescent Health, 43,* 619–622.

Xu, J., Kochanek, K., Murphy, S., & Tejada-Vera, B. (2010). Deaths: Final data for 2007. *National Vital Statistics Reports, 58*(19). Hyattsville, MD: National Center for Health Statistics.

Zimmerman, M., Morrel-Samuels, S., Wong, N., Tarver, D. Rabiah, D., & White, S. (2004). Guns, gangs, and gossip. *Journal of Early Adolescence, 24,* 385–411.

Zimring, F. (1999). *American youth violence.* New York: Oxford.

CHAPTER ELEVEN

Delinquency and Violent Behavior in Girls: Prominent Risks and Promising Interventions

Ann Booker Loper, Emily B. Nichols, and Caitlin M. Novero

A time-honored nursery rhyme tells us that girls should be made of "sugar and spice and all things nice." It is unsurprising that we are curious and often shocked by girls who violate this dictum and instead act in ways that are delinquent, violent, or otherwise "not nice." The easy stereotypes for this group of girls have familiar but very different slants: These girls must be morally deficient, perhaps sexually promiscuous. Or, these girls must be overly masculine and emulating boy behavior. Emerging data reveal that neither of these easy generalizations encompasses what is happening with delinquent girls today. To better understand these young women, we need to ask: What are the trends in female delinquent offending? What are the stressors and risk factors that characterize the girls who offend? What can be done to intervene in the lives of these girls at risk?

Current Trends in Female Juvenile Offending

As is the case with adult offenders, most juvenile offenders—both violent and nonviolent—are male. The Federal Bureau of Investigation (FBI) tracks arrests each year and delineates patterns by gender and other demographic indices. In a summary of arrests during 2008 (FBI, 2009), boys accounted for 70% of juvenile arrests, 93% of the arrests for homicide, 83% of violent offenses in general, and 64% of major property offenses. This discrepancy is consistent with patterns found in adult offenders. The typical juvenile delinquent is not a girl, and patterns of offending by girls are different from those of boys.

However, girls are becoming a greater portion of the growing juvenile delinquency population. Although some recent arrest trends suggest a slowdown, there has been a sharp increase in the number of U.S. youths involved in criminal activity during the last 20 years. In general, where indices of criminal offending have increased, the incline has been sharper for girls, and where rates have decreased, the decline has been less for girls. The net result is that there is a greater proportion of girls involved in the justice system today than 20 years ago. For example, in contrast to an approximate 19% decrease in arrests of boys during years 1999–2000, rates of arrests of girls decreased by approximately 8% (FBI, 2009). The proportionate shift is likewise evident in juvenile court records. For example, between 1985 and 2007, the number of delinquency cases brought to juvenile courts involving girls approximately doubled, in contrast to a 30% increase among boys (Puzzanchera, Adams, & Sickmund, 2010). While girls represented approximately 19% of juvenile court cases in 1985, they accounted for nearly 28% of such cases in 2005 (Puzzanchera & Kang, 2008). In particular there has been a notable incline between 1985 and the late 1990s (see Figure 11.1).

The rise in the number of young female offenders raises the inevitable question: Are girls getting more violent today? The answer, it seems, is that it depends on how you measure it. Recent arrest data show that during the past 10 years, major violent offending by girls has declined 10% (FBI, 2009). The proportion of violent offenses in comparison to the total number of arrests of girls has remained stable: In 1999, approximately 2.7% of female arrests were for major violent offenses, in comparison to 2.6% in 2008. However, there has been a remarkable 12% increase (in contrast to an approximately 6% decline among boys) in the number of arrests for "simple" assaults and an 18% increase (in contrast to a 5% decline among boys) in minor "disorderly conduct" arrests. The increases in violent offending seem to be within the realm of lesser violent acts, suggesting that in many cases the female juvenile arrestee is not engaging in "hard crime" but is increasingly arrested for fractious and aggressive interpersonal interchanges.

Rather than focusing on whether girls are becoming more violent, a better question may be to try to understand what violent behavior by girls

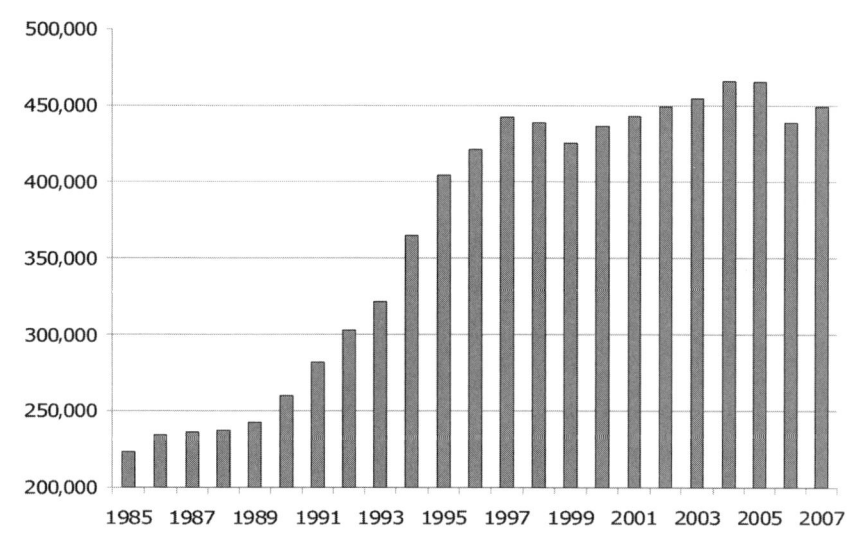

Figure 11.1 Female delinquency cases handled by juvenile courts in the United States, 1985–2007.

Source: Puzzanchera, C., and Kang, W. (2010). "Easy Access to Juvenile Court Statistics: 1985–2007." http://ojjdp.ncjrs.gov/ojstatbb/ezajcs/

looks like. Homicide stands as arguably the most violent offense. National records of homicides are available from the FBI Supplementary Homicide Report, which gives details regarding each homicide incident. Several investigations converge on the conclusion that homicides committed by girls have a strong relational context that differs substantially from that of boys. Loper and Cornell (1996) examined FBI homicide records and found that proportionately more homicides committed by girls reflected types of domestic distress. Girls were proportionately more likely than boys to target members of their own family. They were less likely than boys to commit homicide in conjunction with another criminal activity (e.g., robbery). The girls were much less likely than boys to use firearms and instead often seemed to use a weapon of convenience, such as a nearby knife. Most strikingly, nearly one-fourth of the homicides by girls involved the death of a child under three years old, seeming to reflect the stress of teenage parenthood. Other studies have likewise documented contextual differences between the homicides of boys and girls that highlight domestic issues (Roe-Sepowitz, 2009; Snyder, Sickmund, & Poe-Yamagata, 1996).

Consistent with the importance of the domestic context for girls' offending, delinquent girls may frequently find themselves facing domestic violence charges. Herrera and McCloskey (2001) examined the arrest records and context for violent offending committed by 42 boys and 33 girls living in a midsize U.S. city. They found that although boys and girls had a similar percentage of domestic violence arrests, the contexts differed. While such charges were usually accompanied by a variety of other violent offenses committed outside of the home for boys, domestic charges accounted for nearly all (89%) of the violent offending among the girls. Domestic difficulties among girls are likewise reflected in recent national arrest data, which indicate that approximately 10% of the arrests of girls in 2008 were for running away from home (FBI, 2009). A thorough understanding of juvenile delinquency and violence among girls involves understanding the role of interpersonal relationships with family and intimates and the pathways by which disruptions in such relationships can lead to delinquent and violent behaviors.

Roots of the Trouble: Risk Factors for Juvenile Female Offending and Violent Behavior

Several scholars have argued that the development of healthy interpersonal relationships with family, peers, and intimates is essential in the lives of developing girls (Brown & Gilligan, 1992; Chesney-Lind, 1997). Consistent with this theme, girls who engage in criminal or violent behavior collectively represent a group with remarkable interpersonal and relational stressors. Problematic family relationships, a history of abuse and victimization, and mental illness appear to be prominent among female offenders and are more salient predictors of delinquent and violent behavior in girls. High levels of substance abuse and involvement with asocial groups further complicate troubled histories and can lead to problematic behaviors.

Sexual and Physical Victimization

As is the case among adult criminal offenders, girl delinquents frequently evidence a history of physical and sexual victimization, typically at higher levels than delinquent boys. For example, Belknap and Holsinger (2006) reported differences in self-reported abuse histories among 163 girls and 281 boys who were housed in Ohio youth correctional institutions and found proportionately more girls reported verbal, physical, and sexual abuse than did the boys. The differences were particularly striking in terms of sexual abuse. Approximately 59% of the girls in contrast to 19% of the boys reported having unwanted sexual contact. Moreover, among boys and girls who experienced such adverse events, girls were more likely to have endured multiple occasions of abuse. These results are consistent with numerous other studies that concur on the conclusion that delinquent girls experience levels of abuse that are beyond that of delinquent boys and that a history of abuse is linked to delinquent behavior in girls (Daigle, Cullen, & Wright, 2007).

Not surprisingly, a history of abuse is associated with an increased likelihood for emotional disregulation and turmoil that can lead to numerous behavioral problems, including aggressive and violent behavior. Odgers and colleagues (2007) sought to understand variations among the female delinquency population and how subtypes of girl delinquents may experience different stressors and risks. Using latent class analysis, they observed that the girls who were serving sentences in state juvenile correctional facilities could be classified into three distinct groups: girls with a high propensity for committing violent and delinquent actions, those likely to engage only in delinquent actions, and those with a lesser likelihood of committing either type of offenses. They then examined differences between these classification types in terms of the girls' histories of abuse and mental illness. The results showed clear differences between groups with higher levels of problems among the violent delinquent group. When compared to the delinquency only class, those who had a high propensity for violent and delinquent offending were 7.5 times more likely to have experienced sexual abuse. These striking results imply that sexual abuse may serve as a tipping point between a nonviolent and violent female offender.

Troubled Family Life

The high levels of physical and sexual abuse among delinquent girls reflect, in part, dysfunctional and troubled family contexts. Among juvenile offenders who have a history of abuse, the majority are abused by a caregiver (Synder & Sickmund, 2006). In an examination into the lives of 444 incarcerated youths, Belknap and Holsinger (2006) found that 74.8% and 22.7% of incarcerated girls were victims of physical and sexual assault, respectively, by family members. As a result of the abuse, some girls attempt to escape by running away. The National Center of Juvenile Justice (Synder & Sickmund, 2006) reports that almost a quarter of youths charged with running away from home indicate doing so to avoid physical or sexual abuse at home. This fact is of particular salience as females make up the majority (61%) of youths who run away from home (Synder & Sickmund, 2006). Consistent with this notion of a linkage between abuse and running away, Belknap and Holsinger (2006) observed that 14% of their sample of delinquent girls stated that they would rather remain in prison than return home, leading the authors to speculate that, in some cases, girls might commit offenses to escape traumatic home environments.

Exposure to violence within the home setting appears to be a particularly prominent risk for delinquency in girls. Herrera and McCloskey (2001) examined the impact of family violence on boys and girls by examining the impact of witnessing or experiencing home abuse. Two types of cohorts of mothers, those with and without a history of domestic abuse, were interviewed and given self-report measures concerning home levels of child abuse, marital violence, and other demographic features. One child of each of the mothers was queried regarding abuse experiences within the family. Herrera and McCloskey then examined the juvenile court records for the children of these mothers five years after the interviews in order to assess the impact of the previous home environments, as described in interviews, on juvenile offending. Results underscored the importance of early exposure to family violence. For both boys and girls, witnessing marital violence increased the likelihood of violent offending. But for girls, the experience of being abused also predicted future violent offending. Moreover, as previously noted, most of the violent offending by these girls was within the context of domestic violence directed toward family members. The study provides a picture of violent offending among girls that is both predicted and manifested by violence within the home and family.

The mother-daughter relationship may be of particular importance in understanding female delinquency and violence. In a study of exposure to parental violence, Moretti, Obsuth, Odgers, and Reebye (2006) found that girls who observed their mothers acting aggressively toward intimate partners were themselves more aggressive in relationships with friends and romantic partners. Along similar lines, Lahey and colleagues (2006) found evidence that self-reported maternal delinquency, defined broadly to include violence perpetration, intentional property damage, and dealing drugs, was associated with heightened conduct problems among their daughters.

Giordano and Mohler Rockwell (2001) suggest that mothers of delinquent girls, as well as other women who are involved in their upbringing, may socialize their daughters to stand-up for themselves through violence. The authors interviewed 109 women who were previously incarcerated as juveniles and asked them to reflect on factors that contributed to the development of delinquent behavior and criminality. Several of the women highlighted the impact of their mother's own criminality and drug use and the lessons learned from female family members who explicitly taught the importance of violence as a problem solution: "I was not a fighter. . . . I got chased home from school . . . and finally my grandmother told me that she wasn't going to let me in the house until I learned to fight my way out of it" (Giordano & Mohler Rockwell, 2001, p. 15). In concert, studies by Moretti and colleagues (2006), Lahey and colleagues (2006), and Giordano and Mohler Rockwell (2001) converge on the notion that girls can learn to use violence both indirectly, by witnessing their mothers' experiences as a violence victim or perpetrator, or directly, through mothers or mother figures teaching them to use violence as a defense. In consideration of the high rates of physical and sexual abuse among female criminals in general, it is likely that criminal mothers share similar victimization histories as their juvenile daughters. It is not surprising that these women, with extensive histories of being the victim, feel their lessons are warranted and perhaps vital to the survival of their daughters.

Historically, girls have often been seen as needing more protection and monitoring than boys. Consistent with this notion, studies have suggested that careful parental monitoring of a girl's social and academic activities reduces the likelihood of female delinquency (Wong, Slotboom, & Bijleveld, 2010). In a recent study of differences in predictors of assaultive behavior between boys and girls (Park, Morash, & Stevens, 2010), a lack of parental monitoring emerged as a risk factor for girls but not for boys. The authors reviewed the self-reports of over 2,500 youths surveyed as part of the National Longitudinal Survey of Youth. They specifically examined the information about delinquency risk factors present when the youths were 12–13 years old and then followed up with information regarding assaultive behavior accounts when the youths were in late adolescence. They found that for both girls and boys, early evidence of hopelessness, school dropouts, and gang association predicted future assaultive behavior. However, two unique predictors of later assaultive behavior in girls reflected home variables. For girls, but not boys, poor parental monitoring and running away before 13 years old were solid predictors of future trouble.

Mental Illness and Emotional Distress

Compared to both delinquent males and the general population, females have higher levels of mental health problems. Both women and girl offenders exhibit high rates of conduct disorder, depression, anxiety, ADHD, and PTSD and typically suffer from more than one such disorder (Blackburn, Mullings, Marquart, & Trulson, 2007; Cauffman, Feldman, Waterman, & Steiner, 1998; Cauffman, Lexcen, Goldweber, Shulman, & Grisso, 2007; Dixon, Howie, & Starling, 2004; James & Glaze, 2006; Lederman, Dakof, Larrea, & Li, 2004; McCabe, Lansing, Garland, & Hough, 2002; Teplin, Abram, McClelland, Dulcan, & Mericle, 2002).

Fazel, Doll, and Langstrom (2008) statistically summarized multiple separate studies of mental illness among incarcerated adolescents and observed that girls had high rates of major depression (29.2%), ADHD (18.5%), and conduct disorder (52.8%). Consistent with the high rates of depression, higher rates of self-harm and attempted suicide are found among delinquent girls. In an investigation of mental illness among a sample of 100 females in juvenile detention, Dixon and colleagues (2004) found that over half (57%) had attempted suicide on multiple occasions. Finally, in line with the previously summarized high levels of physical and sexual abuse, delinquent girls more frequently suffer from symptoms of post-traumatic stress disorder in comparison to delinquent boys and community populations (Abram et al., 2004; Ariga et al., 2008; Cauffman et al., 1998).

The high level of mental distress and poor emotional regulation observed among delinquent girls is an importance consideration when viewing violent behavior among female adolescents. Hamerlynck, Doreleijers, Vermeiren, Jansen, and Cohen-Kettenis (2008) gathered information regarding mental pathology correlates of aggressive behavior among a sample of detained adolescent girls. Girls were classified as having no, mild, or high levels of aggression based on frequency of self-report of violent theft, weapon usage, physical violence, sexual assault, or animal cruelty during the previous year. The groups were then compared to each other in terms of clinical diagnoses for various mental conditions, as well as in terms of parent-reported conduct problems. Consistent with other studies of mental illness, there were high levels of emotional and behavioral distress in the sample as a whole. However, levels of pathology varied in line with the levels of aggression. Not surprisingly, the high aggressive group was more likely to receive diagnoses for disruptive behavior disorders. However, high aggressive girls also collectively showed higher levels of suicidality and post-traumatic stress symptoms than did the lower aggression groups. Girls in the high aggressive group fell within the clinically significant range for post-traumatic symptoms at approximately three times the rates for those in the nonaggressive group (39.5% versus 12.9%). Girls in the high aggressive group more frequently reported at least one symptom on a measure of suicidality than did those in the nonaggressive group (59.1% versus 36.4%). Other studies have uncovered a similar linkage between depression and aggressive behavior in delinquent girls (Blackburn et al., 2007; Donnellan, Trzesniewski, Robins, Moffitt, & Caspi, 2005).

The high levels of family disruption as well as high levels of trauma and abuse may be prominent factors that contribute to mental illness among female delinquents. Ariga and colleagues (2008) found that 54.7%

of female delinquent detainees who met criteria for PTSD reported past trauma sexual abuse, while 45.3% reported being a victim of violence, and 32.8% reported childhood maltreatment. Similarly, Blackburn and colleagues (2007) found sexual maltreatment to be significantly related to levels of depression. There is also evidence of a higher rate of familial mental health among females compared to males, potentially adding to the milieu of mental health problems through biological and environmental influences (Belknap & Holsinger, 2006; Moffitt & Caspi, 2001). Individual factors such as impulsivity, emotion regulation, and personality play a part in the development of violent behavior. However, it is likely that a portion of these young women are externalizing feelings associated with traumatic personal histories of victimization and tough family environments.

Substance Abuse

One plausible mechanism for linking prior victimization, difficult family circumstances, and high mental illness with violent behavior in delinquent girls is substance abuse. Arguably, the escape provided by drugs serves to assuage feelings of pain associated with troubled histories while leading girls to greater criminal involvement.

There is strong evidence that substance usage by female delinquents is linked to aggressive and violent behavior. A recent national probability survey of 33,091 female adolescents (SAMHSA, 2009) queried girls about their engagements in individual fights, groups fights, or intentional attacks on others, as well as their use of alcohol and illicit drugs during the previous year. Results, depicted in Figure 11.2, indicated that fighting and substance use were related: Girls who engaged in violent delinquent behaviors were significantly more likely to report binge drinking (15.1% vs. 6.9%), marijuana use (11.4% vs. 4.1%), and use of other illicit drugs (9.2% vs. 3.2%) than were girls who reported no violent activity. Moreover, a greater variety of violent behaviors was associated with increased likelihood of substance usage. Over one-fourth of the girls who reported three or more types of violent behaviors engaged in binge drinking, in contrast to approximately 6% of the girls who did not engage in violent actions.

Similar trends are found in incarcerated female juvenile populations. Hamerlynck and colleagues (2008) interviewed 216 Dutch incarcerated adolescent females regarding aggressive activities (e.g., cruelty to animals, fighting) and evaluated the girls for mental health disorders including substance abuse and dependence. Similar to the SAMHSA (2009) findings, the mildly and severely aggressive girls also had higher rates of drug and alcohol abuse and dependence than those reporting no aggressive activity.

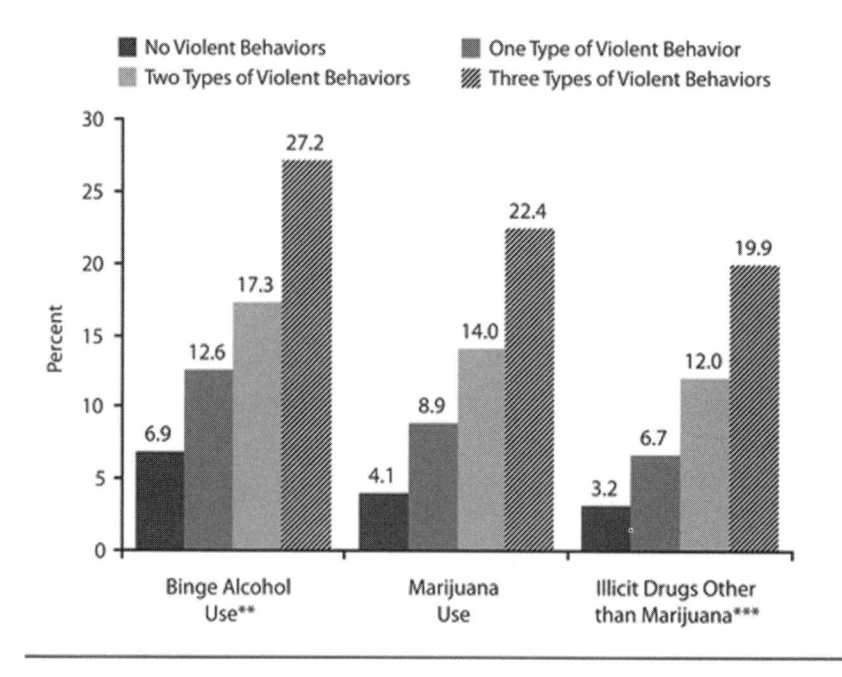

Figure 11.2 Past month substance use among females ages 12 to 17, by number of types of violent behaviors,* 2006 to 2008.

* Violent behavior is defined as getting into a serious fight at school or work, participating in a group-against-group fight, or attacking others with the intent to seriously hurt them.

** Binge alcohol use is defined as drinking five or more drinks on the same occasion (i.e., at the same time or within a couple of hours of each other) on at least 1 day in the past 30 days.

*** Includes cocaine (including crack), inhalants, hallucinogens, heroin, or prescription-type drugs used nonmedically.

Source: 2006 to 2008 National Surveys on Drug Use and Health (SAMHSA, 2009).

These results echo those reported by the study by Dixon and colleagues (2004) of female juvenile offenders, of whom over 70% were detained for violent crimes. Nearly all of the girls in the sample of offenders (85%) met criteria for a current substance abuse disorder.

Given this evidence of concomitant high levels of substance usage and delinquency in girls, the question arises whether girls' all-too-frequent poor family functioning and mental health problems lead to substance abuse. Gavazzi, Lim, Yarcheck, Bostic, & Scheer (2008) investigated the relationship between mental health, family functioning, and substance usage in a survey of 2,646 court-involved youths (1,009 females) using an online data collection instrument. Mental health was measured using self-reports of internalizing (e.g., Do you ever feel sad, moody, or depressed?) and externalizing items (e.g., Do you ever have difficulty controlling your anger?). Other self-report items queried usage of substances as well as impressions of family conflict. The study specifically sought to untangle the relationship among risk variables for substance usage: For delinquent youths, does family disruption lead to mental illness that, in turn, leads to substance problems, or does family disruption simultaneously lead to both substance problems and mental distress? The authors found support for the latter notion. For both boys and girls, disrupted family processes were associated with higher levels of both mental health problems and substance disorders.

In a similar study, Lennings, Kenny, Howard, Arcuri, and Mackdacy (2007) summarized data from seven studies of female Australian juvenile delinquent populations and sought to determine likely causal directions between family dysfunction, mental illness, and substance abuse. In contrast to the Gavazzi and colleagues (2008) study, they found that while severity of mental illness predicted levels of substance abuse, impaired family functioning was related to substance abuse indirectly through the mediating influence of associated poor mental health. The different findings in these two studies underscore the difficulty of untangling the direction of effects among the many adversities experienced by delinquent girls. Nonetheless, both studies converge on the conclusion that family dysfunction and poor mental health relate, either directly or indirectly, to elevated levels of substance usage.

The role of previous victimization is plausibly another factor that may connect substance abuse and offending among delinquent girls. Neff and Waite (2007) examined risk factors, including victimization by a family member or an outsider, for substance abuse in a population of 5,000 incarcerated juveniles (11% females) who were admitted to the Virginia Department of Juvenile Justice between 1997 and 2003. Both boys and girls reported high levels of drug use, but females reported significantly more frequent usage of alcohol, cocaine, crack, stimulants, and hallucinogen. Females also reported starting to use alcohol and marijuana, as well as harder drugs such as crack and cocaine, at an earlier age than did the boys. Neff and Waite examined various predictors of substance abuse to determine whether there were gender differences in patterns of predicting abuse from risk factors. Generally, they found similar profiles between the boys and girls in terms of the ways in which risk factors were associated with varying types of substance abuse. However, previous victimization served as a significant predictor of early drug use in female, but not male, offenders, implying that girls who experience victimization may be particularly vulnerable to early experiences of substance problems. These results are consistent with the hypothesis that victimized girls may early on seek relief through mind- and mood-altering substances.

Promising Intervention for Violent and Aggressive Girls

Delinquent girls who engage in aggressive or violent behavior are a relatively small portion of the larger body of youths involved in delinquent activity. However, the adversities and challenges associated with this group are substantial. Gender-specific intervention has been highlighted by a number of scholars (Chesney-Lind, 1997; Covington & Bloom, 2006; Sorbello, Eccleston, Ward, & Jones, 2002) who argue against an assumption that effective treatment and prevention programs designed for boys automatically transfer to girls. Intervention with girls, therefore, requires attention to the contexts, communication patterns, and risk factors that are prevalent among delinquent and violent girls. Accordingly, gender-sensitive programs use a treatment lens that includes skills and support for dealing with victimization, poor family functioning, emotional distress, and substance usage, among other risk factors. We highlight two programs that address such features and have undergone scientific inquiry regarding effectiveness. The first program is a preventive intervention designed to be conducted in a community setting with young at-risk girls, while the second addresses needs of older girls after they have become seriously involved in criminal activity.

SNAP-Girls Connection

The SNAP-Girls Connection program (SNAP-GC; Pepler et al., 2010), formerly the Earlscourt Girls Connection (Pepler, Walsh, & Levene, 2004; Walsh, Pepler, & Levene, 2002) is a community-based program designed to treat aggressive and antisocial young girls under the age of 12. The program is structured to aid at-risk youths and families to "Stop Now and Plan." The program draws from an earlier cognitive-behavioral program that was found to be effective for boys (Augimeri, Farrington, Koegl, & Day, 2007), and places emphasis on the role of individual, familial, and community risk factors in shaping a girl's development. The SNAP-GC program evolved based on clinical observations that the program as designed for boys was not sufficiently meeting the needs of young at-risk girls. Therefore, as a gender-sensitive adaptation of the program, SNAP-GC focused on enhancing health, family, and peer relationships (Pepler et al., 2010).

The SNAP-GC program is composed of three components intended for girls ages 6–12. The first component is a 12-session after-school group, during which the girls are taught cognitive behavioral strategies, for managing impulsivity and anger, and social problem-solving skills. The second component is a concurrent 12-session parenting group to provide personal support, strategies for anger management, and skills in dealing with problem behaviors of their daughters. During the final component, entitled GGUH (Girls Growing Up Healthy), the mothers and daughters join in an 8-week group (Pepler et al., 2004). The GGUH group begins once the mothers and daughters complete their separate programs. Thereby, the groups become a place where the pairs can practice the previously learned skills and develop stronger relationships.

The SNAP-GC activities are based on cognitive-behavioral theory and designed to help the girls develop accurate interpretations of and appropriate responses to social interactions (Walsh et al., 2002). During the girls' group component, the participants are taught strategies such as finding another person to interact with or asking for help. Girls are also taught to use specific positive self-statements when they find themselves in the face of a stressor, or a "trigger." Levene, Walsh, Augimeri, and Pepler (2004) reported that the most common type of trigger among this population tends to concern the girls' appearance (e.g., being called ugly). In a specific session designed to deal with these triggers, the girls are taught to recognize the thoughts and feelings that precede aggression through the use of a cartoon depicting a group of girls whispering with empty thought bubbles above their heads. The girls are directed to imagine themselves being left out of the group, which the authors report stirs up and reveals the negative distortions that lead to the girls' aggressive behavior. Similarly, as a way to capture the pattern of the girls' distortions or triggers and responses to them, the girls are asked to keep a record of any problems (i.e., aggressive interactions) they encounter in a "Hassle Log." Within the group, the girls take turns reviewing problems from the Hassel Log that arose since the previous session. The group brainstorms ideas for solving each individual girl's problems. Each girl decides which idea would work best and then practices the new solution through a role-play with another girl.

An early evaluation of the first four years of the program concluded that the intervention was effective in reducing problem behaviors while promoting prosocial behaviors (Walsh et al., 2002; Pepler et al., 2004). The characteristics of girls in the study resonate with many of the previously described adversities among typical female juvenile offenders. A substantial portion of mothers reported that their daughters had clinically significant mental health problems. Specifically, almost half (42%)

of parents reported their daughters to be in the clinical range for depression and anxiety problems. A majority of parents (59%) also reported that their daughters had clinically significant social problems. Several parents also reported their children experienced significant environmental adversities: 7% of girls had stayed overnight in foster care or group home and 16% of parents had been charged or arrested for a crime (Pepler et al., 2004). Finally, some parents reported that their daughters were victims of physical (10%) and sexual abuse (8%) (Walsh et al., 2002). Though these percentages of victimization are lower than what would be expected given the high proportions of these issues observed in studies with similar populations, it is possible that parents underreported such incidents or were not aware of them at the time of questioning. This combination of risk factors in a sample of young girls under 12 years old makes them likely candidates for future problems and a good target for intervention.

Data was collected through parent reports of their daughters' behavior at three time points: prior to the intervention ($n = 98$), at 6 months ($n = 72$), and 12 months ($n = 58$). Results indicated significant decreases in parent-reported cruelty, bullying, and physical attacks on people, with a moderate effect ($d = .42$)[1] evident at 6 months on an overall externalizing behavior score. A reduction of symptoms of conduct disorder and oppositional defiant disorder was reported at both follow-up time points. The girls' social relationships also were enhanced. Peer and adult relations were strengthened over time with large effects apparent at 6 months ($d = .72$) and moderate effects at 12 months ($d = .51$). In a secondary report of the data, Pepler and colleagues (2004) presented information showing that the girls demonstrated less angry and resentful behavior, temper tantrums, and crankiness at follow-up assessments.

These encouraging results were followed by a study of the first two components of SNAP-GC, the girls' group and the parents' group. Pepler and colleagues (2010) built on the previous research by adding a wait-list control group and measures from the participating girls and their teachers. The sample was comprised of 80 girls (ages 5–11) who were referred due to problematic behaviors and admitted into the program during an 18-month period. Participants were randomly assigned to treatment ($n = 45$) and wait-list ($n = 35$) groups after the sample had been stratified to ensure similar age and severity of behavior. Behavior change was assessed through both parent and teacher reports at three time points. A well-standardized parent report of child behavior (Child Behavior Check List; Achenbach & Rescorla, 2001) assessed changes in internalizing symptoms (e.g., anxiety, depression, physical complaints), externalizing symptoms (e.g., rule breaking, aggression, inattention), and social problems, as well as the girls' likely diagnosis of either conduct disorder or attention deficit hyperactivity disorder. An alternate version of the measure that is designed for teacher report (Achenbach, 1991) assessed similar constructs within the school context. Additionally, the authors collected information regarding the changes in parenting effectiveness, as assessed by both the parent and participating girl.

Parent reports indicated that after treatment the girls demonstrated lower levels of internalizing symptoms, externalizing behavior, social problems, and clinical diagnoses compared to the wait-list group, while controlling for levels observed at the initial assessment. These differences were maintained six months after treatment. However, teachers did not report observing significant differences between groups. The authors suggested that teachers may not be as sensitive to behavior change as parents and that their perceptions of aggressive girls may take more time to change. Further, girls may have a harder time generalizing their behavior change from the clinical and family setting to the school setting.

Changes in parenting skills were assessed by the parent report of their own effectiveness coupled with the daughter report of the parents' nurturance, monitoring, and rejection. Most parents in the intervention perceived that they became more effective over the course of the intervention; however, these perceived improvements, with one exception, did not substantially differ from perceived changes of the parents in the waiting list. A clearer pattern of difference emerged with the report from the girls themselves. In comparison to wait-list participants, the girls who received the SNAP-GC intervention were less likely to rate their mothers as being angry, yelling, or threatening physical violence. Although the authors did not evaluate the mediating effects of these changes in parenting skills, it is plausible that they served to support the observed positive behavioral changes.

Multidimensional Treatment Foster Care

SNAP-GC is geared toward prevention of delinquency in girls by early intervention. However, for girls who continue on a path of delinquency and become involved in the juvenile justice system, more intensive intervention is needed. A recent exemplary intervention for justice-involved youths is the Multidimensional Treatment Foster Care (MTFC) program (Chamberlain & Reid, 1998; Eddy & Chamberlain, 2000). Although the intervention was originally validated with boys, a recent gender-specific adaptation of the program has been shown to be highly effective with seriously delinquent girls (Chamberlain, 2003; Chamberlain, Leve, &

DeGarmo, 2007; Leve, Chamberlain, & Reid, 2005; Leve, Fisher, & Chamberlain, 2009). The adaptation retains elements of the original version for boys but adds a gender-sensitive focus on the impact of abuse and trauma, poor emotional regulation, and social aggression.

The program is geared to court-referred girls who temporarily live in the home of a trained foster parent as an alternative to residential intervention that would remove her from home and community. MTFC specifically addresses delinquent girls' history of abuse and poorly functioning families by intervening with the family while the girls receive individual therapy in their foster home. MTFC aims to create "supports and opportunities for children and adolescents so they can have a successful community living experience" (Chamberlain, 2003, p. 303) and to work with the girls' families to improve the parenting and home environment once they leave MTFC. The intervention consists of an average six-month stay in a certified and supervised therapeutic foster home. Case supervisors have daily phone conferences with foster parents to check on the girls' progress and the foster parents' stress level. Supervisors also monitor the girls' school attendance, performance, and homework completion. Foster parents implement a behavioral program to reinforce the girls' strengths and to set clear boundaries and consequences for problem behavior, such as aggression. Foster parents also attend a weekly foster parent training, supervision, and general support group. In order to assure continuity after girls leave their foster home, biological parents or previous guardians participate in family therapy with their daughters.

In a presentation of the benefits of MTFC, Saldana and Buchanan (2010) described the case of a young girl, Olivia, who initially asserted that she was interested only in smoking marijuana and that she enjoyed the risk of hiding her use from her caregivers. After six months of therapy, however, Olivia realized that she wasn't able to meet her goals because of her drug use. She wanted to change her identity from being a "pothead" to an aspiring architect. Having made such a decision, Olivia needed real skills for implementing change. Accordingly, she and her therapist videotaped role plays of risky drug scenarios and practiced how to problem solve in those situations. Her skills coach helped Olivia to come up with replacement behaviors as alternatives to smoking pot and to increase involvement in prosocial activities. As her skills coach was working with Olivia to realistically plan for her future as an architect, the family therapist worked with Olivia's parents on how to reinforce prosocial activities, increase Olivia's supervision, and set consequences for using drugs.

Between 1997 and 2002, the Oregon juvenile court system teamed with researchers from the Oregon Social Learning Center to implement a randomized controlled trial to test the effectiveness of MTFC in female juvenile populations (Leve et al., 2005). Judges referred 103 girls, ages 15–19, to out-of-home care. These girls were then randomly assigned to either MTFC ($n = 37$) or a community-based group home program ($n = 44$). The community group home intervention received by the control group was the typical services offered for girls referred by presiding judges for out-of-home care. The referred girls had substantial justice involvement, with a lifetime average of nearly 12 criminal referrals; nearly three-fourths of the girls had at least one prior felony. Based on data collected in an earlier study that included a large portion of the Leve and colleagues (2005) sample (Chamberlain, 2003), several risk factors among the girls resonate with risks previously described in this chapter. Nearly three-fourths of the girls had at least one parent convicted of a crime, and approximately 66% and 72%, respectively, had records of documented physical or sexual abuse. Consistent with this picture of likely problematic family functioning, over 90% of the girls had previously run away from home at least once. Over 80% were characterized as heavy drug or alcohol users. Notably, for each of these risk factors, girls evidenced higher levels of adversity than did the justice-referred boys.

Twelve months after program entry, the girls placed in MTFC had significantly lower caregiver reports of delinquent acts and problem behavior than did those who were placed in the usual alternative home care (Leve et al., 2005). Of central importance to this population, intervention girls spent fewer days in a locked setting than did those from the control condition (22 versus 56 days) and had fewer parent-reported delinquent behaviors. While there was a trend for criminal referrals to decline over the period, differences were not significant. Differences were not apparent regarding the girls' self-reported delinquent acts.

In a subsequent follow-up of the girls in the Leve and colleagues (2005) study, Chamberlain and colleagues (2007) found that effects were well maintained two years after intervention. The follow-up study used a statistical modeling analysis that enabled detection of changes for individual trajectories over the course of the two-year period. Results indicated that girls in the MTFC program had greater reductions in delinquency over the two-year period, as indicated by fewer days in locked settings, fewer criminal referrals, and the self-reports of delinquent activities ($d = .65$) The authors were also able to model the differences in the rates of change in delinquency for both groups. Results indicated that while both groups over time showed a decline in delinquent activities, the rate of the reduction for the girls in the MTFC intervention was significantly sharper. Thus, the treated girls showed both a greater amount of change in delinquency as well as a faster pace of improvement.

Conclusion

A closer look at girls involved in justice systems reveals that as a group, they experience numerous adversities and roadblocks on the way to adulthood. The frequently fractured family relationships mean that these girls may not receive sufficient warmth and affection or thoughtful parental supervision. Indeed, in many cases, the girls may experience victimization from trusted family members or friends that leads to disenfranchisement and a mistrust of relationships. Numerous mental health problems are common. These adversities work in tandem, either as a cause or correlate of delinquency, and many such girls seek the escape and comfort provided by unhealthy substance usage, which compounds the existing problems.

However, the growing body of strong scholarship regarding delinquent girls is promising and offers a roadmap for innovative and effective treatments. Like the two programs described in this chapter, such treatment specifically attends to possible historical victimization, recognizes and treats difficulties with interpersonal relationships, provides opportunities to form healthy family relationships, and enables skills for desisting from excessive alcohol and drug usage. While such treatment does not, and maybe should not, lead to young women becoming "sugar and spice," it can lead to a life for girls, their family, and the community that holds promise for "all things nice."

Note

1. The symbol d represents the standardized mean difference between two measures.

References

Abram, K. A., Teplin, L. A., Charles, D. R., Longworth, S. L., McClelland, G. M., & Dulcan, M. K. (2004). Posttraumatic stress disorder and trauma in youth in juvenile detention. *Archives of General Psychiatry, 61,* 403–410.

Achenbach, T. M. (1991). *Manual of the teacher's report form and 1991 profile.* Burlington: University of Vermont, Department of Psychiatry.

Achenbach, T. M., & Rescorla, L. A. (2001). *Manual for the ASEBA school age forms and profile.* Burlington: University of Vermont.

Ariga, M., Uehara, T., Takeuchi, K., Ishige, Y., Nakano, R., & Mikuni, M. (2008). Trauma exposure and posttraumatic stress disorder in delinquent female adolescents. *Journal of Child Psychology and Psychiatry, 49,* 79–87.

Augimeri, L. K., Farrington, D. P., Koegl, C. J., & Day, D. M. (2007). The under 12 outreach project: Effects of a community-based program for children with conduct problems. *Journal of Child and Family Studies, 16,* 799–807.

Belknap, J., & Holsinger, K. (2006). The gendered nature of risk factors for delinquency. *Feminist Criminology, 1,* 48–71.

Blackburn, A. G., Mullings, J. L., Marquart, J. W., & Trulson, C. R. (2007). The next generation of prisoners: Toward an understanding of violent institutionalized delinquents. *Youth Violence and Juvenile Justice, 5,* 35–56.

Brown, L. M., & Gilligan, C. (1992). *Meeting at the crossroads: Women's psychology and girls' development.* Cambridge, MA: Harvard University Press.

Cauffman, E., Feldman, S. S., Waterman, J., & Steiner, H. (1998). Posttraumatic stress disorder among female juvenile offenders. *Journal of the American Academy of Child and Adolescent Psychiatry, 37,* 1209–1216.

Cauffman, E., Lexcen, F. J., Goldweber, A., Shulman, E. P., & Grisso, T. (2007). Gender differences in mental health symptoms among delinquent and community youth. *Youth Violence and Juvenile Justice, 5,* 287–307.

Chamberlain, P. (2003). The Oregon multidimensional treatment foster care model: Features, outcomes, and progress in dissemination. *Cognitive and Behavioral Practice, 10,* 303–312.

Chamberlain, P., Leve, L. D., & DeGarmo, D. S. (2007). Multidimensional treatment foster care for girls in the juvenile justice system: Two-year follow-up of a randomized clinical trial. *Journal of Consulting and Clinical Psychology, 75,* 187–193.

Chamberlain, P., & Reid, J. (1998). Comparison of two community alternatives to incarceration for chronic juvenile offenders. *Journal of Consulting and Clinical Psychology, 66,* 624–633.

Chesney-Lind, M. (1997). *The female offender: Girls, women, and crime.* Thousand Oaks, CA: Sage.

Cohen, J. (1988). *Statistical power analysis for the behavioral sciences* (2nd ed.). New York: Lawrence Erlbaum Associates.

Covington, S., & Bloom, B. (2006). Gender responsive treatment and services in correctional settings. *Women and Therapy, 29,* 9–33.

Daigle, L. E., Cullen, F. T., & Wright, J. P. (2007). Gender differences in the predictors of juvenile delinquency: Assessing the generality-specificity debate. *Journal of Youth Violence and Juvenile Justice, 5,* 254–286.

Dixon, A., Howie, P., & Starling, J. (2004). Psychopathology in female juvenile offenders. *Journal of Child Psychology and Psychiatry 45,* 1150–1158.

Donnellan, M. B., Trzesniewski, K. H., Robins, R. W., Moffitt, T. E., & Caspi, A. (2005). Low self-esteem is related to aggression, antisocial behavior, and delinquency. *Psychological Science, 16,* 328–335.

Eddy, J. M., & Chamberlain, P. (2000). Family management and deviant peer association as mediators: Impact of treatment condition on youth antisocial behaviors. *Journal of Consulting and Clinical Psychology, 68,* 857–863.

Fazel, S., Doll, H., & Langstrom, N. (2008). Mental disorders among adolescents in juvenile detention and correctional facilities: A systematic review and metaregression analysis of 25 surveys. *Journal of the American Academy of Adolescent Child Psychiatry, 47,* 1010–1019.

Federal Bureau of Investigation (FBI). (2009). Ten-year arrest trends by sex, 1999–2008. *Crime in the United States 2008*. Retrieved on October 25, 2010, from http://www2.fbi.gov/ucr/cius2008/index.html.

Gavazzi, S., Lim, J., Yarcheck, C., Bostic, J., & Scheer, S. (2008). The impact of gender and family processes on mental health and substance use issues in a sample of court-involved female and male adolescents. *Journal of Youth and Adolescence, 37*, 1071–1084.

Giordano, P. C., & Mohler Rockwell, S. (2001). Differential association theory and female crime. In S. S. Simpson (Ed.), *Of crime and criminality: The use of theory in everyday life* (pp. 3–24). Thousand Oaks, CA: Pine Forge.

Hamerlynck, S. M. J. J., Doreleijers, T. A. H., Vermeiren, R., Jansen, L. M. C., & Cohen-Kettenis, P. T. (2008). Agression and psychopathology in detained females. *Psychiatry Research, 159*, 77–85.

Herrera, V. M., & McCloskey, L. A. (2001). Gender differences in the risk for delinquency among youth exposed to family violence. *Child Abuse and Neglect, 25*, 1037–1051.

James, D. J., & Glaze, L. E. (2006) *Mental health problems of prison and jail inmates*. Washington, DC: U.S. Department of Justice, Bureau of Justice Statistics.

Lahey, B. B., Van Hulle, C. A., Waldman, I. D., Rodgers, J. L., D'Onofrio, B. M., Pedlow, S., Rathouz, P., & Keenan, K. (2006). Testing descriptive hypotheses regarding sex differences in the development of conduct problems and delinquency. *Journal of Abnormal Child Psychology, 34*, 737–755.

Lederman, C. S., Dakof, G. A., Larrea, M. A., & Li, H. (2004). Characteristics of adolescent females in juvenile detention. *International Journal of Law and Psychiatry, 27*, 321–337.

Lennings, C. L., Kenny, D. T., Howard, J., Arcuri, A., & Mackdacy, L. (2007). The relationship between substance abuse and delinquency in female adolescents in Australia. *Psychiatry, Psychology, and Law, 14*, 100–110.

Leve, L. D., Chamberlain, P., & Reid, J. B. (2005). Intervention outcomes for girls referred from juvenile justice: Effects on delinquency. *Journal of Consulting and Clinical Psychology, 73*, 1181–1185.

Leve, L. D., Fisher, P. A., & Chamberlain, P. (2009). Multidimensional treatment foster care as a preventive intervention to promote resiliency among youth in the child welfare system. *Journal of Personality, 77*, 1869–1902.

Levene, K. S., Walsh, M. M., Augimeri, L. A., & Pepler, D. J. (2004). Linking identification and treatment of early risk factors for female delinquency. In M. M. Moretti, C. L. Odgers, & M. A. Jackson (Eds.), *Girls and aggression: Contributing factors and intervention principles* (pp. 147–163). New York: Kluwer Academic/Plenum.

Loper, A., & Cornell, D. (1996) Homicide by juvenile girls. *Journal of Child and Family Studies, 5*, 323–336.

McCabe, K. M., Lansing, A. E., Garland, A., & Hough R. (2002). Gender differences in psychopathology, functional impairment, and familial risk factors among adjudicated delinquents. *Journal of the American Academy of Child and Adolescent Psychiatry, 41*, 860–867.

Moffitt, T. E., & Caspi, A. (2001). Childhood predictors differentiate life-course persistent and adolescence-limited antisocial pathways among males and females. *Development and Psychopathology, 13,* 355–375.

Moretti, M. M., Obsuth, I., Odgers, C. L., & Reebye, P. (2006). Exposure to maternal vs. paternal violence, PTSD, and agression in adolescent girls and boys. *Agressive Behavior, 32,* 385–395.

Neff, J., & Waite, D. (2007). Male versus female substance abuse patterns among incarcerated juvenile offenders: Comparing strain and social learning variables. *Justice Quarterly, 24,* 106–132.

Odgers, C. L., Moretti, M. M., Burnette, M. L., Chauhan, P., Waite, D., & Reppucci, N. D. (2007). A latent variable modeling approach to identifying subtypes of serious and violent female juvenile offenders. *Agressive Behavior, 33,* 1–14.

Park, S., Morash, M., & Stevens, T. (2010). Gender differences in predictors of assaultive behavior in late adolescence. *Youth Violence and Juvenile Justice, 8,* 314–331.

Pepler, D. J., Walsh, M. M., and Levene, K. S. (2004). Intervention for aggressive girls: Tailoring and measuring the fit. In M. M. Moretti, C. L. Odgers, & M. A. Jackson (Eds.), *Girls and aggression: Contributing factors and intervention principles* (pp. 131–145). New York: Kluwer Academic/Plenum.

Pepler, D. J., Walsh, M., Yuile, A., Levene, K., Jiang, D., Vaughan, A., & Webber, J. (2010). Bridging the gender gap: Interventions with aggressive girls and their parents. *Prevention Science, 11,* 229–238.

Puzzanchera, C., Adams, B., & Sickmund, M. (2010). *Juvenile court statistics 2006–2007.* Pittsburgh, PA: National Center for Juvenile Justice. Retrieved on October 15, 2010, from http://www.ncjjservehttp.org/ncjjwebsite/pdf/jcsreports/jcs2007.pdf.

Puzzanchera, C., & Kang, W. (2008). *Juvenile Court Statistics Databook.* Pittsburgh, PA: National Center for Juvenile Justice. Retrieved on October 15, 2010, from http://ojjdp.ncjrs.gov/ojstatbb/jcsdb/asp/demo.asp.

Roe-Sepowitz, D. E. (2009). Comparing male and female juveniles charged with homicide: Child maltreatment, substance abuse, and crime details. *Journal of Interpersonal Violence, 24,* 601–617.

Saldana, L., & Buchanan, R. (2010, April). *Multidimensional treatment foster care: What's new in MTFC?* Symposium conducted in Boulder, CO.

Snyder, H. N., & Sickmund, M. (2006). *Juvenile offenders and victims: 2006 National Report.* Washington, DC: U.S. Department of Justice, Office of Justice Programs, Office of Juvenile Justice and Delinquency Prevention. Retrieved on October 15, 2010, from http://www.ojjdp.gov/ojstatbb/nr2006/.

Snyder H. N., Sickmund, M., & Poe-Yamagata, E. (1996). *Juvenile offenders and victims: 1996 update on violence.* Pittsburg, PA: National Center for Juvenile Justice. Retrieved on October 15, 2010, from http://www.ncjrs.gov/pdffiles/90995.pdf.

Sorbello, L., Eccleston, L., Ward, T., & Jones, R. (2002). Treatment needs of female offenders: A review. *Australian Psychologist, 37,* 198–205.

Substance Abuse and Mental Health Services Administration (SAMHSA). (2009). *The NSDUH report: Violent behaviors among adolescent females.* Rockville, MD: Office of Applied Studies. Retrieved on October 25, 2010, from http://www.oas.samhsa.gov/2k9/171/171FemaleViolence.htm.

Teplin, L. A., Abram, K. M., McClelland, G. M., Dulcan, M. K., & Mericle, A. A. (2002). Psychiatric disorders in youth in juvenile detention. *Archives of General Psychiatry, 59,* 1133–1143.

Walsh, M. M., Pepler, D. J., and Levene, K. S. (2002). A model intervention for girls with disruptive behavior problems: The Earlscourt Girls Connection. *Canadian Journal of Counseling, 36,* 297–311.

Wong, T. M. L., Slotboom, A., Bijleveld, C. J. H. (2010). Risk factors for delinquency in adolescent and young adult females: A European review. *European Journal of Criminology, 7,* 266–284.

CHAPTER TWELVE

Broadening the Frame of Violence Prevention through the Promotion of Youth Community Engagement

Jessica J. Collura, Brian D. Christens, and Shepherd Zeldin

Youth violence surged to unprecedented levels during the late 1980s and early 1990s. Since the mid-1990s, there have been promising signs that it is declining, with national arrest records, victimization data, and hospital emergency room records all showing downward trends (U.S. Department of Health and Human Services, 2001). Despite this, youth violence remains a pressing issue in the United States. As of 2007, homicide was still the second-leading cause of death for young people between the ages of 10 and 24 and the leading cause of death among African American youths (Centers for Disease Control and Prevention, 2010). Youths ages 15–24 are still at the greatest risk of being both a victim and perpetrator of homicide. In addition, 19.9% of all high school students have reported being bullied on school property in the past 12 months (Centers for Disease Control and Prevention, 2010).

In this chapter, we argue that the policy and programmatic responses aimed at youth violence reduction should be broadened to include a focus on youth agency and transactional interventions. We begin by examining common misperceptions about youths and youth violence that often underlie inadequate responses. Next, we provide a conceptual rubric for thinking about youth violence reduction strategies. This rubric has two primary dimensions: (a) orientations to youth violence prevention and (b) ecological levels of intervention. Orientations to youth violence prevention can be conceptualized as a spectrum from control to prevention to agency approaches. The second dimension, ecological levels of intervention, can be understood according to the following categories: individual-level interventions, environment or setting-level interventions, and transactional interventions. We conclude with examples of program models that illustrate our central argument: Youth violence reduction strategies need to be broadened to include more transactional and agency-oriented approaches. The common factor between these approaches is youth community engagement.

Misconceptions of Youth and Violence

There are several prevalent misconceptions about young people and violence. These fallacious beliefs not only distance youths from opportunities to engage meaningfully in their communities but also lead to misguided policies and programs. Public misunderstandings of youths and violence often fuel punitive responses to crime. An example of this is the implementation of policies that permit young people to be tried and prosecuted as adults, in spite of substantial evidence demonstrating that youths prosecuted in adult courts have higher recidivism rates than those prosecuted in juvenile courts (Bishop, 2006; Soler, 2001). Acknowledging the discrepancies between public beliefs and the evidence on youths and violence is key to creating appropriate interventions designed to reduce youth violence.

The general public perceives adolescence as a tumultuous and dangerous developmental stage. This notion originated in G. Stanley Hall's seminal work, which characterized adolescence as a period of "storm and stress" (Lerner, Dowling, & Anderson, 2003). Although this view is largely unsupported by contemporary research, negative stereotypes about adolescents continue to permeate American society. To illustrate, one recent study found that only 16% of a nationwide sample of adults believed that young people under the age of 30 share most of their moral or ethical values (Bostrom, 2000).

There are also widespread beliefs that youths are uninterested in and incapable of contributing to their communities. Scales and colleagues (2001) found that when adults assess the importance of 19 possible actions that can be taken on behalf of youths, 2 of the least frequent responses were to "seek young people's opinions when making decisions that affect them" and to "give young people lots of opportunities to make their communities better places." Even in youth-serving organizations, adults are ambivalent about young people's abilities to participate in decision making and action (Costello, Toles, Spielberger, & Wynn, 2000).

These public assumptions are not supported by research. For example, almost two-thirds of a national sample of youths reported that it is very important to give back to their communities (Peter Hart Research Associates, 1998). Further, youths have the competency to contribute. Many young people have a high level of decision-making competence by the age of 15 and are capable of contributing (Zeldin, 2004). This growing body of research suggests that youths are meaningfully contributing to their communities (Christens & Zeldin, in press), from participating on boards with elected officials (Zeldin, Petrokubi, & MacNeil, 2007) to organizing efforts for community change (Christens & Dolan, in press; Kirshner, 2009).

In addition to the misconceptions about youths, research also suggests that adults tend to overestimate or exaggerate the rate of youth violence (Gilliam & Bales, 2001). For example, many parents view America's schools as dangerous and unsafe, but these fears are inconsistent with the facts regarding school violence. Youths are actually safer in schools compared to most other settings where they spend time (Cornell, 2006; Goldstein & Conoley, 2004), and recent statistics demonstrate that school violence has actually been on the decline (Centers for Disease Control and Prevention, 2010).

Studies indicate that the public also often equates youth crime with race, perceiving young African American and Hispanic men as being less law abiding and more apt to commit violent crimes (Gilliam, 1998; Males, 1999). However, when considered in isolation from other demographics, racial and ethnic characteristics are not indicative of an adolescent's propensity for engaging in violence (U.S. Department of Health and Human Services, 2001). Another common misconception is that violence is a premeditated act directed toward innocent bystanders, when in fact research has long demonstrated the opposite is true; the majority of violent crimes occur between friends and acquaintances or within families (Basile, Chen, Black, & Saltzman, 2007; Hepburn, 1973; Prothrow-Stith, 1987).

Orientations to Youth Violence Reduction

Orientations that underlie public responses to youth violence reduction can be thought of as a spectrum from control to prevention to agency (Figure 12.1). The first orientation is control, the belief that the public should reduce youth violence through measures such as surveillance,

Orientations to Youth Violence Reduction

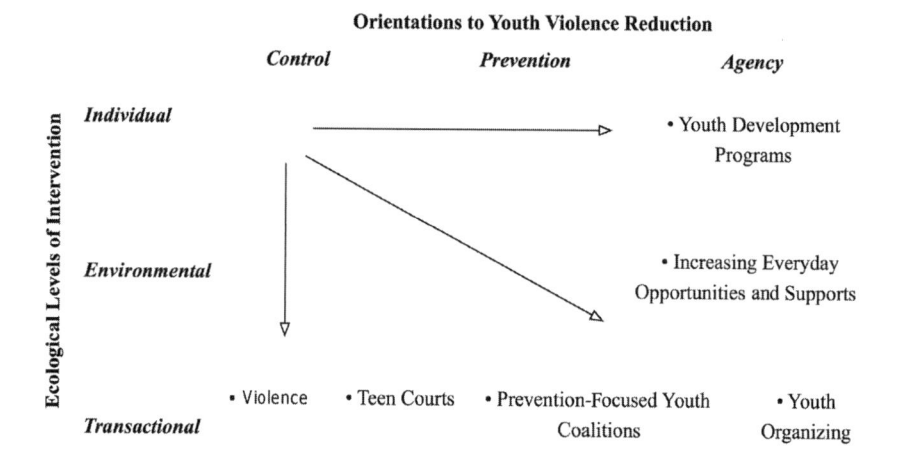

```
                    Control        Prevention              Agency

  Individual        ─────────────────────────────▶   • Youth Development
                             ╲                          Programs
                              ╲
                               ╲
  Environmental        │        ╲                   • Increasing Everyday
                       │         ╲                    Opportunities and Supports
                       │          ╲
                       ▼           ▽
                    • Violence  • Teen Courts  • Prevention-Focused Youth     • Youth
  Transactional                                   Coalitions                   Organizing
```

(Left axis: Ecological Levels of Intervention)

Figure 12.1 Broadening the frame: Moving from individual-level and controlling strategies to transactional and agency-oriented strategies for reducing youth violence.

detainment, and punishment. The underlying assumption is that by controlling young people, society can reduce their participation in undesirable activities. A second orientation to youth violence is prevention, which focuses on implementing interventions before significant problems occur. Prevention strategies range from public education campaigns to targeted, intensive therapy for youths who repeatedly engage in delinquent behavior. The third orientation, and we argue the most frequently overlooked, is that of youth agency. Youth agency recognizes that all youths are capable of contributing to their environments in positive ways and, therefore, emphasizes approaches that promote community engagement.

Control. The United States relies primarily on the juvenile justice system—including police and courts—to control young people through both the threat and enactment of punishment. This system attempts to deter youths from participating in illegal activities through the use of punitive measures, including surveillance and incarceration. Given the prevalent view of youth as a developmental period of storm and stress and youth violence as an inevitable societal problem, it is not surprising that the dominant policy response has been the adoption of such punitive measures.

It is significant to note that the juvenile justice system attempts to implement evidence-based initiatives, such as community-based alternatives to secure confinements. However, these practices are not consistently evident because the justice system is responsible for administering the harsh crime policies adopted in legislatures (Zeldin, 2004). Indeed, in the past 30 years, state legislatures have instituted multiple reforms that seek to punish and control young offenders (Bishop, 2006). Examples of such reforms include: the expansion of courts' sentencing authority in order to permit certain sentences to extend into the adult years, the amendment of juvenile codes to endorse the goals of punishment and protection of public safety, and the removal of confidential protections of juvenile court records (Bishop, 2006; Soler, 2001).

Equally concerning is the fact that the juvenile justice system seems to have adopted the public's belief that the primary perpetrators of youth violence are African American and Hispanic men (Gilliam & Bales, 2001). Although there is no racial difference in young people's self-reported rates of violent behavior, the arrest rates by race differ greatly (U.S. Department of Health and Human Services, 2001). This lack of consistency and fairness toward youths of color is a contributing factor to repeated mistreatment in the system.

Prevent. Public health professionals, along with social workers and community development professionals, have long advocated for, and advanced, prevention strategies as a means to reduce youth violence. Prevention strategies are classified into three categories: primary, secondary, and tertiary (Turnock, 2001). Primary prevention seeks to identify the risk factors associated with violence and to educate the general population on practical solutions. An example of primary prevention to reduce youth violence is a public information campaign that raises awareness about the dangers associated with keeping firearms in the home. Secondary prevention focuses on individuals who are at risk or are beginning to engage in delinquent behavior. Programs for secondary prevention of delinquent behavior often seek to inoculate youths against social problems through training sessions in decision making, impulse control, and anger management (Botvin, Griffin, & Nichols, 2006). Finally, tertiary prevention targets individuals who are engaged in a cycle of violent or delinquent behavior. Strategies for the reduction of youth violence range from intensive individual and family counseling to enrollment in special schools.

While prevention orientations are commendable for being proactive rather than reactive, there are still limitations. Namely, this approach primarily focuses on deterring young people from risky and delinquent behavior rather than seeking to meet the fundamental developmental needs of all young people. By focusing solely on preventing problems, the prevention approach unintentionally reinforces inaccurate societal perceptions of adolescents. This conception of youths as potential victims and problems has been recently countered by accounts of youths as assets.

Agency. The agency orientation to violence reduction is based on the principles of positive youth development (PYD). PYD is both a theory and practice that emphasizes "the growing capacity of a young person to understand and act on the environment" (Hamilton & Hamilton, 2004, p. 3). A key tenet of PYD is that youths are resources to be nurtured, not problems to be solved (Damon, 2004). This more holistic approach focuses on not just preventing problems but also building on youth strengths.

A central component of PYD theory and practice is youth agency, the recognition that youths are actors in their own development and are significant resources for creating the contexts and communities that promote positive development (Benson, Scales, Hamilton, & Sesma, 2006). An agency orientation, as theorized in PYD, emphasizes the need to engage youths in their communities. There are a range of opportunities through which youths can participate in community decision making and action. Examples include engaging young people on the boards of youth-serving agencies, on youth councils that advise elected officials, on community coalitions, or in community-organizing efforts. Agency-oriented approaches integrate young people into the "adult world" and give them a voice in the matters and policies that impact their lives. In short, youth agency recognizes that young people can and should inform the settings that in turn impact their development.

Unfortunately, youth agency is not supported by dominant policies or institutional practices in the United States. This is especially true of initiatives aimed at reducing youth violence. As Peterson, Dolan, and Hanft (2010) note, the participation "of students in the identification and implementation of violence prevention programs is almost completely ignored in the literature of violence prevention" (p. 236). Although some public agencies are beginning to create incentives for youth engagement in community decision making, there still remains little institutionalized support at the national or state level (Forum for Youth Investment, 2002).

Ecology of Interventions for Reducing Youth Violence

As with the orientations presented in the previous section, the concept of ecology provides a conceptual framework for making distinctions between different approaches to youth violence reduction. For the purposes of this analysis, we draw on Bronfenbrenner's (1977) conception of the human ecological environment as "a nested arrangement of structures each contained within the next" (p. 514). In a human ecological perspective, individuals are viewed in the context of their environments, similar to biology's understanding of organisms as components of their ecosystems. We conceptually identify three categories of intervention for youth violence reduction that are focused on different components of an ecological system: (a) interventions that emphasize the choices, propensities, responsibilities, and capabilities of individuals; (b) interventions that emphasize the role of settings and environmental factors in constraining or facilitating the occurrence of crime; and (c) interventions that emphasize activities or processes that simultaneously alter individuals and their ecological environments. Inherent in each type of intervention approach is an understanding of the etiology of youth violence. That is, by choosing an intervention approach, one makes a tacit statement about one's own attributions of responsibility for the occurrence of violence.

Individual-level interventions. Individual-level interventions emphasize the choices, propensities, responsibilities, and capabilities of individuals. Individual-level strategies are diverse. Some are control focused, others are focused on prevention, and still others focus on youth agency (see Figure 12.1). At the control end of the spectrum are policies and programs that seek to reduce violence by creating disincentives for individuals to engage in violent behaviors. Most of the functions of systems of juvenile justice can be characterized as individual-level, control-oriented interventions. In these interventions, individuals who commit violent acts are held responsible and punished according to the severity of the crime. The threat that this individual poses to society is temporarily removed while the individual is incarcerated. Alongside the punitive functions of this system, some attempts are made during and after incarceration to rehabilitate the individual and to create a system of stronger disincentives for relapses of violent behavior. Although this system represents the mainstream of intervention for reducing youth violence, there is little evidence to support its effectiveness (Pratt, 2008).

In the middle of the spectrum lie individual-level approaches to prevention that seek to reduce the susceptibility of individuals to engage in violence and other problem behaviors. This often takes the form of school-based programs that seek to inform young people of the risks and consequences of engaging in these behaviors, train young people in alternative strategies, or develop a set of competencies that are believed to make individuals less susceptible to engaging in drug abuse, gang membership, or violence. A fundamental premise of such programs is that individuals can be inoculated from such susceptibilities. For example, under Attorney General Alberto Gonzales, the Department of Justice began implementing a Gang Resistance Education and Training (GREAT) program. GREAT's objective is "an immunization against delinquency, violence, and gang membership" (Department of Justice, 2010). Claims are often made that these programmatic forms of intervention represent "evidence-based" effective practice. However, the evaluations that lead to these claims are frequently plagued by faulty evaluation practices (Gorman, Conde, & Huber, 2007) and conflicts of interest in which the creators of the program are also conducting the evaluation (Gorman & Conde, 2007).

At the agency end of the spectrum are youth development programs that seek to build developmental assets of young people (top right in Figure 12.1). These programs do not focus on deficits or risks of problem behaviors like violence. Instead, they focus on building what Lerner and colleagues (2005) call the five C's of positive youth development: competence, confidence, connection, character, and caring. In a review of youth development programs, Roth and Brooks-Gunn (2003) identify the goals and practices of youth-serving organizations and development programs. These include preventing problem behaviors but also include providing a supportive and empowering environment, family and community connections, and expectations for positive behavior. Hence, the goals of youth development programs extend well beyond avoiding violence into concepts like "thriving" and—at an aggregate level—development of a civil society (Lerner, Dowling, & Anderson, 2003). The notion, substantiated by an emerging body of research is that the promotion of positive youth development outcomes decreases the likelihood of problem behaviors (Benson, Scales, Hamilton, & Sesma, 2006).

Environment or setting-level interventions. Environment or setting-level interventions begin with the idea that while individuals may have propensities toward certain types of behaviors, some features of environments are conducive to these behaviors while other features of environments are inhibitive or preventive. This perspective draws on Lewin's (1935) dynamic theory of personality, which posits that behavior can best be understood as a function of a person's characteristics and their environment ($B = f[P, E]$). Yet the modern Western proclivity to attribute responsibility to individuals can stand in the way of implementing interventions that are focused on changing settings and environments rather than changing individuals. This individualist bias is evidenced in much social theory and practice. For example, consider the crime displacement perspective on violence, which argues that if opportunities to commit crime are reduced in one location, perpetrators will simply go elsewhere in search of opportunities to commit crime. The assumption inherent in this view is that criminality is a personal characteristic rather than an interactive function of persons and environments. In reality, there is very little evidence that crime displacement occurs (Weisburd et al., 2006), but the persistence of public belief in crime displacement illustrates the difficulty in overcoming individualist bias and moving beyond individual-level interventions to those that focus on other ecological levels.

Like individual-level interventions, environmental and setting-level interventions are diverse. They range from interventions that are control oriented to those that are focused on prevention and agency. At the control end of the spectrum lie environmental interventions that block criminal opportunities or otherwise discourage or complicate the occurrence of crime. Examples include fences, gated communities, alarm systems, or surveillance. In the middle of the spectrum are interventions that seek to prevent violence through environmental interventions that are not punitive or threatening. Examples include prevention through urban designs that increase urban and suburban residential density (Christens & Speer, 2005), defensible space, or decrease environmental incivilities (Perkins, Wandersman, Rich, & Taylor, 1993). Other examples include efforts to reduce or mitigate the social conditions that give rise to violence, including policies that ensure human rights, environmental justice, and citizen security (Moser & McIlwaine, 2006) or address oppression with a focus on community well-being (Prilleltensky, 2008).

At the agency end of the spectrum are interventions that increase everyday opportunities and supports (middle right of Figure 12.1) to create the preconditions for peaceful settings and environments. This strategy is consistent with many of the goals of PYD. In particular, Benson, Scales, Hamilton, and Sesma (2006) highlight opportunities for skill building and belonging and supportive relationships that promote autonomy and positive social norms. In addition, increasing everyday opportunities and supports can include the creation of new recreational and extracurricular activities, new educational and employment opportunities, and new settings—such as new after-school programs or new community centers—which can function as venues for the facilitation of youth development.

Transactional interventions. We turn now to a third category of interventions, transactional interventions: those that emphasize activities or processes that simultaneously alter individuals and their ecological environments. The term "transaction" is drawn from Dewey and Bentley (1946), who distinguish transaction from self-action and interaction as ways of understanding the world. Transaction is distinguished from both self-action and interaction by a refusal to view individual entities or their interactions as detachable. A transactional view seeks to understand whole processes or actions with an understanding that there are no independent intrinsic qualities that these entities possess. Altman and Rogoff (1987) draw on Dewey and Bentley and others to set forth four worldviews in psychology:

trait, interactional, organismic, and transactional. For Altman and Rogoff, the transactional worldview involves "the study of the changing relations among psychological and environmental aspects of holistic unities" (p. 9). Hence, transactional strategies for youth violence reduction seek to alter the relations between youths and their settings and environments. In other words, unlike strategies that intervene only on individuals or their environments, transactional interventions focus on the relationships between youths and their environments.

In practice, transactional interventions are much less common than those focused on individuals or environments and settings. For example, writing about educational intervention, Dokecki, Scanlan, and Strain (1972) describe a pendulum effect, in which the dominance of individualistic interventions leads to calls for more social systemic interventions and vice versa. The authors suggest that "exclusive positions, either social system or individual oriented, may end up looking similar, structurally at least, and perhaps are similarly incomplete and unable to handle complex social problems" (p. 183). We assert that strategies for youth violence reduction that are focused on community engagement represent promising models of transactional interventions.

Agency-Oriented and Transactional Interventions to Reduce Youth Violence

Our central argument in this chapter is that the frame for interventions to reduce youth violence should be broadened to include more transactional approaches as well as more approaches that emphasize youth agency. Figure 12.1 depicts this argument. The majority of interventions are currently individual oriented and focused on control. While these approaches may be appropriate in some cases, they are not always optimal solutions. By combating public misconceptions on youth violence and understanding youth development in an ecological context, the frame can be broadened to include more interventions that focus on youth agency and ecological transactions. In order to make these approaches tangible, we put forward three specific models for reducing youth violence that employ a transactional and agency-oriented approach: teen courts, youth coalitions, and youth organizing. The common denominator of these models is youth community engagement.

Teen courts. Teen courts, also known as youth courts or peer juries, are an alternative for young people who have committed minor offenses, such as vandalism, stealing, or the possession of drugs. Rather than going to juvenile court and risking formal prosecution, young offenders can opt to attend teen court and avoid having a legal record (Butts, Buck, &

Coggeshall, 2002). The approach is based on the premise that a young person is less likely to reoffend if he or she is held accountable for the crime and also provided with an opportunity to positively reengage with the community (Forgays & DeMilio, 2005).

Teen courts function similarly to juvenile courts except the young offender is tried and sentenced by peers rather than adults. Youth volunteers—many of whom are former offenders returning to participate in other cases—serve as jurors, attorneys, judges, and court clerks. The youth volunteers are ultimately responsible for developing a sentence that reflects restorative justice principles, meaning the sentence must focus on building responsibility and reengagement in the young offender (Bazemore, 2001). Sentences often include serving on a teen court jury, engaging in community service, writing an apology letter to their parent(s) and the victim of their offense, or writing an essay about the effects of crime on the community (Butts et al., 2002). Sentencing allows youths to serve in a responsible role, empowering the young person to engage in prosocial behavior (Peterson-Badali, Ruck, & Koegl, 2001). In this model, youths become agents of restorative justice, not simply recipients.

Teen courts are rapidly expanding in the United States, growing from 78 programs in 1994 to 1,050 in 2005 (Pearson & Jurich, 2005). Given their prevalence, greater attention is now given to measuring and evaluating their effectiveness. The results are promising. For example, Harrison, Maupin, and Mays (2001) found that teen court first-time offenders had recidivism rates of 30% or less. Similarly, Butts and colleagues (2002) report that the youth court offenders had a lower recidivism rate than offenders processed through traditional juvenile courts in three surveyed states.

By altering the environments in which young offenders are prosecuted and tried, and by allowing youths to exercise some degree of agency in these settings, teen courts represent a transactional model that incorporates youth agency. Because teen courts operate within the juvenile justice system, however, the overarching orientation is still control.

Youth coalitions. Youth coalitions bring together diverse community stakeholders—including young people, parents, educators, nonprofit managers, business leaders, and public officials—to address a youth issue of mutual concern (Collura, Graff, & Zeldin, 2009). Youth coalitions may address a variety of youth-related concerns and serve as a valuable resource for the community. For example, the communitywide coalition in Oazakee County, Wisconsin, composed of youths and adults, works primarily on improving young people's relationships with local law enforcement. However, the coalition also provides input to the park and recreation board, business improvement district, and the chamber of commerce.

Engaging youths in coalitions is a promising approach for both community change and healthy youth development. Because coalitions engage a diversity of institutions and citizens and encourage cross-sector networking and resource sharing, they have the potential to make community change (Chavis, 2001). Youth coalitions, in particular, provide an effective forum for youth engagement and voice. When young people help define community problems and solutions and participate in settings where they wield influence, they develop a greater sense of community (Evans, 2007). Coalitions also have the potential to build strong relationships between youths and adults. Such relationships serve an important protective and developmental function: They can help prevent youths from engaging in problem behaviors while concurrently helping to promote knowledge, competency, and initiative among youths (Zeldin, Larson, Camino, & O'Connor, 2005). In addition, there is growing evidence that social connectedness is inversely associated with rates of crime at the community level (Kawachi, Kennedy, & Wilkinson, 1999). Youth coalitions engage young people and alter the environments in which policy decisions are made. Hence, this transactional model incorporates youth agency.

Youth organizing. Youth organizing "trains young people in community organizing and advocacy, and assists them in employing these skills to alter power relations and create meaningful institutional change in their communities" (Funders Collaborative of Youth Organizing, 2009). This practice is based on the belief that effective youth development and concrete social change occur in tandem. Youth organizing gained considerable momentum during the 1990s, with increasing evidence that it was an effective way for young people to develop leadership skills, effect concrete community change, and become politically engaged (Delgado & Staples, 2008). Perhaps because of its explicit emphasis on empowerment and social justice, youth organizing has been more effective than other youth development programs at engaging diverse youths, particularly youths of color (Yee, 2008).

Many youths engage in organizing because the issues have personal meaning to them. For example, young women who lived in poverty and had been involved with the juvenile justice system organized and established the Center for Young Women's Development in San Francisco. The center's programs are designed to help disenfranchised young women become employed citizens working to improve their communities. Toward that end, the organization is run completely by low-income women who have progressed through the center's programs (Camino & Zeldin, 2002).

There is a growing body of evidence for supporting youth organizing as an empowering approach to youth engagement and violence prevention (Christens & Dolan, in press; Peterson et al., 2010). Youth organizing efforts have lobbied against punitive California legislation that would lead to increased youth incarceration (Gambone et al., 2006), led successful campaigns to increase affordable childcare access for high school–aged mothers (Ginwright, 2003), and expanded after-school programs with the aim of reducing youth violence (Peterson et al., 2010). Researchers are also documenting the positive impacts of youth organizing on both the young participants and their communities. Zeldin, Petrokubi, and Camino (2008) demonstrate that young people involved in organizing develop a sense of belonging and collective efficacy, an increase in sociopolitical awareness and civic competence, and an increase in community connections. Christens and Dolan (in press) describe a youth organizing effort in which young people work to reduce violence and crime through advocacy for policies that support youth development. In the process, they develop leadership skills, such as confidence in public speaking, research expertise, and a greater understanding of social and political issues. Hence, youth organizing is a particularly promising model, representing both a transactional and an agency-oriented approach to reducing youth violence.

Broadening the Frame

In this chapter, we provided a conceptual rubric for understanding approaches to youth violence reduction. The two dimensions of this rubric are orientations and ecological levels of intervention. Based on these two dimensions, we assert that policy and program responses aimed at youth violence reduction should be broadened to include more strategies that focus on youth agency and transactional interventions (see Figure 12.1). The commonality of these interventions is that they engage youths in their communities. Youth development programs and setting-level interventions focus on building youth agency through the development of supportive relationships with peers and adults. Youth coalitions and youth organizing engage youths in community-level decision making. Even teen courts, which employ a more traditional control orientation to juvenile justice, create a setting where youths can exercise agency.

To be clear, we are not arguing for an exclusive focus on these models of interventions. Indeed, control-oriented and individual-level approaches are necessary in some cases. We are, however, arguing that there is an imbalance in intervention approaches that favors individual-level interventions over environmental and transactional interventions and favors control-oriented approaches over preventive and agency-oriented approaches. This imbalance is reflective of prevalent misconceptions of youth violence. To broaden the frame and rectify the imbalance, community engagement approaches to youth violence prevention must be rigorously evaluated, and findings must be translated into practice. Finally, the broader public and key decision makers (e.g., police, judges, prosecutors, legislators, etc.) must become more involved in combating misconceptions of youth violence and helping to broaden the frame.

Note

The authors wish to thank Kyle Miller and John Sands for helpful comments on a draft of this chapter.

References

Altman, I., & Rogoff, B. (1987). World views in psychology: Trait, interactional, organismic, and tranactional perspectives. In D. Stokols & I. Altman (Eds.), *Handbook of environmental psychology* (pp. 7–40). New York: Wiley.

Basile, K. C., Chen, J., Black, M. C., & Saltzman, L. E. (2007). Prevalence and characteristics of sexual violence victimization among U.S. adults, 2001–2003. *Violence and Victims, 22,* 437–448.

Bazemore, G. (2001). Young people, trouble, and crime: Restorative justice as a normative theory of informal social control and social support. *Youth and Society, 33,* 199–226.

Benson, P. L., Scales, P. C., Hamilton, S. F., & Sesma, A. (2006). Positive youth development: Theory, research, and applications. In W. Damon & R. M. Lerner (Eds.), *Handbook of child psychology: Vol. 1. Theoretical models of human development* (6th ed., pp. 894–941). Hoboken, NJ: Wiley.

Bishop, D. M. (2006). Public opinion and juvenile justice policy: Myths and misconceptions. *Criminology and Public Policy, 5,* 653–664.

Bostrom, M. (2000). Teenhood: Understanding attitudes toward those transitioning from childhood to adulthood. In S. Bales (Ed.), *Reframing youth issues* (Working Papers). Washington, DC: FrameWorks Institute and Center for Communications and Community, UCLA.

Botvin, G., Griffin, K., & Nichols, T. (2006). Preventing youth violence and delinquency through a universal school-based prevention approach. *Prevention Science, 7,* 403–408. doi:10.1007/s11121-006-0057-y

Bronfenbrenner, U. (1977). Toward an experimental ecology of human development. *American Psychologist, 32,* 513–531. doi:10.1037/0003-066X.32.7.513

Butts, J., Buck, J., & Coggeshall, M. (2002). *The impact of teen court on young offenders.* Washington, DC: Urban Institute.

Camino, L., & Zeldin, S. (2002). From periphery to center: Pathways for youth civic engagement in the day-to-day life of communities. *Applied Developmental Science, 6,* 213–220.

Centers for Disease Control and Prevention. (2010). *Youth violence: Facts at a glance.* Retrieved on September 12, 2010, from www.cdc.gov/ViolencePrevention/pdf/yv-datasheet-a.pdf.

Chavis, D. M. (2001). The paradoxes and promise of community coalitions. *American Journal of Community Psychology, 29,* 302–320.

Christens, B. D., & Dolan, T. (in press). Interweaving youth development, community development, and social change through youth organizing. *Youth and Society.*

Christens, B. D., & Speer, P. W. (2005). Predicting violent crime using urban and suburban densities. *Behavior and Social Issues, 14,* 113–127.

Christens, B. D., & Zeldin, S. (in press). Community engagement. In R. J. R. Levesque (Ed.), *Encyclopedia of adolescence.* New York: Springer.

Collura, J., Graff, A., Zeldin, S. (2009). *Youth voice at the local level.* Madison, WI: UW-Extension 4-H Youth Development. Retrieved from http://www.uwex.edu/ces/4h/yig/2009YPCLConferenceInformation.cfm.

Cornell, D. G. (2006). *School violence: Fears versus facts.* Mahwah, NJ: Lawrence Erlbaum Associates.

Costello, J., Toles, M., Spielberger, J., & Wynn, J. (2000). History, ideology, and structure shape the organizations that shape youth. In Public/Private Ventures (Ed.), *Youth development: Issues, challenges, and directions* (pp. 185–231). Philadelphia: Public/Private Ventures.

Damon, W. (2004). What is Positive Youth Development? *Annals of the American Academy of Political and Social Sciences, 591,* 13–24.

Delgado, M., & Staples, L. (2008). *Youth-lead community organizing: Theory and action.* New York: Oxford University Press.

Department of Justice, Office of Justice Programs. (2010). Programs: The gang resistance education and training (GREAT) program. Available: http://www.ojp.usdoj.gov/BJA/grant/great.html.

Dewey, J., & Bentley, A. F. (1946). Interaction and transaction. *Journal of Philosophy, 43,* 505–517.

Dokecki, P. R., Scanlan, P., & Strain, B. (1972). In search of a transactional model for educational intervention: Reactions to Farber and Lewis. *Peabody Journal of Education, 49,* 182–187. doi:10.2307/1492054

Evans, S. (2007). Youth sense of community: Voice and power in community contexts. *Journal of Community Psychology, 35,* 693–709. doi:10.1002/jcop.20173

Forgays, D. K., & DeMilio, L. (2005). Is teen court effective for repeat offenders? A test of the restorative justice approach. *International Journal of Offender Therapy and Comparative Criminology, 49,* 107. doi:10.1177/0306624X04269411

Forum for Youth Investment. (2002). *State youth policy: Helping all youth to grow up fully prepared and fully engaged.* Takoma Park, MD: Author.

Funders Collaborative of Youth Organizing. (2009). What is youth organizing? Retrieved on February 10, 2010, from http://fcyo.org/whatisyouthorganzing.

Gambone, M. A., Yu, H. C., Lewis-Charp, H., Sipe, C. L., & Lacoe, J. (2006). Youth organizing, identity support, and youth development agencies as avenues for involvement. *Journal of Community Practice, 14,* 235–253.

Gilliam, F. (1998). *Youth crime and the superpredator news frame: The impacts of television on attitudes about crime and race.* Washington, DC: The National Funding Collaborative on Violence Prevention.

Gilliam, F., & Bales, S. (2001). Strategic frame analysis: Reframing America's youth. *Social Policy Report, 15,* 3–15.

Ginwright, S. (2003). Youth organizing: Expanding possibilities for youth development. *Occasional Paper Series on Youth Organizing.* Retrieved on November 8, 2010, from http:www.fcyo.org and available from Jewish Fund for Justice, 260 Fifth Avenue, Suite 701, New York, NY 10001.

Goldstein, A. P., & Conoley, J. C. (2004). *School violence intervention: A practical handbook.* New York: Guilford.

Gorman, D. M., & Conde, E. (2007). Conflict of interest in the evaluation and dissemination of "model" school-based drug- and violence-prevention programs. *Evaluation and Program Planning, 30,* 422–429. doi:10.1016/j.evalprogplan.2007.06.004

Gorman, D. M., Conde, E., & Huber, J. C. (2007). The creation of evidence in "evidence-based" drug prevention: A critique of the Strengthening Families program plus Life Skills Training evaluation. *Drug and Alcohol Review, 26,* 585–593. doi:10.1080/09595230701613544

Hamilton, S. F., & Hamilton, M. A. (2004). *The youth development handbook: Coming of age in American communities.* Thousand Oaks, CA: Sage.

Harrison, P., Maupin, J. R., & Mays, G. L. (2001). Teen court: An examination of the processes and outcomes. *Crime and Delinquency, 47,* 243–264.

Hepburn, J. R. (1973). Violent behavior in interpersonal relationships. *Sociological Quarterly, 14,* 419–429.

Kawachi, I., Kennedy, B. P., & Wilkinson, R. G. (1999). Crime: Social disorganization and relative deprivation. *Social Science Medicine, 48,* 719–31.

Kirshner, B. (2009). Power in numbers: Youth organizing as a context for exploring civic identity. *Journal of Research on Adolescence, 19,* 414–440. doi:10.1111/j.1532-7795.2009.00601.x

Lerner, R. M., Dowling, E. M., & Anderson, P. M. (2003). Positive youth development: Thriving as the basis of personhood and civil society. *Applied Developmental Science, 7,* 172–180. doi:10.1207/S1532480XADS0703_8

Lerner, R. M., Lerner, J. V., Almerigi, J. B., Theokas, C., Phelps, E., Gestsdottir, S., et al. (2005). Positive youth development, participation in community youth development programs, and community contributions of fifth-grade adolescents: Findings from the first wave of the 4-H study of positive youth development. *Journal of Early Adolescence, 25,* 17–71. doi:10.1177/0272431604272461

Lewin, K. (1935). *A dynamic theory of personality.* New York: McGraw-Hill.

Males, M. (1999). *Framing youth: Ten myths about the next generation.* Monroe, ME: Common Courage Press.

Moser, C. O. N., & McIlwaine, C. (2006). Latin American urban violence as a development concern: Toward a framework for violence reduction. *World Development, 34,* 89–112. doi:10.1016/j.worlddev.2005.07.012

Pearson, S., & Jurich, S. (2005). *Youth court: A community solution for embracing at-risk youth.* Washington, DC: American Youth Policy Forum.

Perkins, D. D., Wandersman, A., Rich, R. C., & Taylor, R. B. (1993). The physical environment of street crime: Defensible space, territoriality, and incivilities. *Journal of Environmental Psychology, 13,* 29–49. doi:10.1016/S0272-4944(05)80213-0

Peter Hart Research Associates. (1998). *New leadership for a new century.* Washington, DC: Author.

Peterson, T. H., Dolan, T., & Hanft, S. (2010). Partnering with youth organizers to prevent violence: An analysis of relationships, power, and change. *Progress in Comunity Health Partnerships: Research, Education, and Action, 4,* 235–242.

Peterson-Badali, M., Ruck, M. D., & Koegl, C. J. (2001). Youth court dispositions: Perceptions of Canadian juvenile offenders. *International Journal of Offender Therapy and Comparative Criminology, 45,* 593–605.

Pratt, T. C. (2008). *Addicted to incarceration: Corrections policy and the politics of misinformation in the United States.* Thousand Oaks, CA: Sage.

Prilleltensky, I. (2008). The role of power in wellness, oppression, and liberation: The promise of psychopolitical validity. *Journal of Community Psychology, 36,* 116–136. doi:10.1002/jcop.20225

Prothrow-Stith, D. (1987). *Violence prevention curriculum.* Newton, MA: Educational Development Center.

Roth, J. L., & Brooks-Gunn, J. (2003). What exactly is a youth development program? Answers from research and practice. *Applied Developmental Science, 7,* 94–111. doi:10.1207/S1532480XADS0702_6

Scales, P., Benson, P., Roehlkepartain, E., Hintz, N., Sullivan, T., & Mannis, M. (2001). The role of neighborhood and community in building developmental assets for children and youth: A national study of social norms among American adults. *Journal of Community Psychology, 29,* 703–727.

Soler, M. (2001). *Public opinion on youth, crime, and race: A guide for advocates.* Washington, DC: Building Blocks for Youth.

Turnock, B. J. (2001). *Public health: What it is and how it works* (2nd ed.). Gaithersburg, MD: Aspen Publishers, Inc.

U.S. Department of Health and Human Services. (2001). *Youth violence: A report of the surgeon general.* Rockville, MD: U.S. Department of Health and Human Services, Office of the Surgeon General. Retrieved from http://www.surgeongeneral.gov/library/youthviolence/default.htm.

Weisburd, D., Wyckoff, L. A., Ready, J., Eck, J. E., Hinkle, J. C., & Gajewski, F. (2006). Does crime just move around the corner? A controlled study of spatial displacement and diffusion of crime control benefits. *Criminology, 44,* 549–592. doi:10.1111/j.1745-9125.2006.00057.x

Yee, S. M. (2008). Developing the field of youth organizing and advocacy: What foundations can do. *New Directions for Youth Development, 117*(Winter), 109–124.

Zeldin, S. (2004). Preventing youth violence through the promotion of community engagement and membership. *Journal of Community Psychology, 32,* 623–641. doi:10.1002/jcop.20023

Zeldin, S., Larson, R., Camino, L., & O'Connor, C. (2005). Intergenerational relationships and partnerships in community programs: Purpose, practice, and directions for research. *Journal of Community Psychology, 33,* 1–10.

Zeldin, S., Petrokubi, J., Camino, L. (2008). *Youth-adult partnerships in public action: Principles, organizational culture, and outcomes.* Washington, DC: The Forum for Youth Investment.

Zeldin, S., Petrokubi, J., & MacNeil, C. (2007). *Youth-adult partnerships in community decision-making: What does it take to engage adults in the practice?* Chevy Chase, MD: National 4-H Council.

CHAPTER THIRTEEN

Abusive Adolescent Boys in Adulthood

William E. Schweinle

Abuse is a very broad topic with a number of differing scientific, legal, and lay definitions (Bratton, Roseman, & Schweinle, in press). Abuse can occur within families, between peers, between partners, etc. However, this chapter focuses on a relatively narrow area of abuse: What happens to abusive adolescent males when they become adults and what might be done to stop potentially abusive adolescent boys from becoming adult partner abusers? I focus on young men because, while adolescent girls and adult women may strike their male partners as often as their male partners strike their female partners (Centers for Disease Control and Prevention, 2009), women generally do not hit as hard as men and are not as likely to cause serious injury to their partners (Campbell, 2004; Morse, 1995; Schaefer & Caetano, 1998).

It is important to focus on adolescent boys because as they become adult men, generally from age 15 to age 25, the likelihood that they will be involved in a close relationship increases. The likelihood that a male will abuse his partner also rapidly increases during this time (O'Leary, 2000). This may be a good time to intervene in ways that may prevent partner-abusive behaviors during adulthood.

In order to make this assertion, it is important to ascertain whether abusive or potentially abusive adolescent males become abusive adult males and if intervention programs actually work. If this is the case, then it is important to demonstrate whether adolescence, the time when young men are beginning to explore close relationships, might be a better developmental stage than adulthood for interventions designed to reduce adult abusiveness. This chapter reviews the relevant literature and recommends that intervention with potentially partner-abusive males be made during their adolescence, when it might be more effective than intervention during a partner-abuser's adulthood.

Young Aggressors Become Adult Abusers

There is some scientific evidence supporting the conclusion that aggressive boys develop into abusive men. For instance, Herrenkohl, Huang, Tajima, and Whitney (2003) found that 15- to 18-year-olds who were violent toward peers were more likely to be violent toward their intimate partners in adult life. Further, Foshee, Benefield, Ennett, Bauman, and Suchindran (2004) found that physical fighting with adolescent peers predicts partner abuse during adulthood. These results suggest two things. First, adolescents who are violent toward others have a greater tendency to be violent toward their romantic partners when they become adults. Second, because of this relationship between adolescent violence and adult partner violence, it is possible to predict with some reliability which adolescent males are likely later to abuse their adult partners.

Longitudinal prospective studies further support the argument that abusive teens are more likely than nonabusive teens to become partner-abusive adults. For instance, Woodward, Fergusson, and Horwood (2002) followed a cohort of New Zealand youths from birth through their 21st year. The youths who behaved in an antisocial manner early in life were significantly more likely to abuse their partners later in life. Further, Magdol, Moffitt, Caspi, and Silva (1998) found among a sample of 992 New Zealanders, who were tracked from birth to 21 years of age, that aggressive delinquency at age 15 was significantly predictive of partner abuse at age 21. Finally, O'Donnell and colleagues (2006) found similar results among an American sample when they surveyed 977 8th graders and then resurveyed the group again around their 19th birthdays. Similarly, Ehrensaft and colleagues (2003) followed 543 children from 1975 to 1999. The children and their mothers were interviewed several times over this time span. The teens who had been abused as children, who had witnessed violence between parents, and who exhibited the most conduct-disordered behaviors while growing up were the most likely to cause injury to their partners as adults. Taken together, these results offer strong evidence that physically aggressive teens tend to become partner-abusive adults.

If we are to conclude that interventions work for teens, then we must determine whether intervention works at all. If so, then investing intervention effort on at-risk adolescents might not be the best strategy for several reasons. First, while violent adolescents are more likely to become partner-violent adults, not all will. Therefore, one would have to intervene with a larger number of adolescents in order to, hopefully, intervene with the ones who will become abusive adults. If, however, intervention efforts are focused specifically on the men who have demonstrated abusive behavior, then the intervention would need to be brought to a smaller number of people, which could concentrate and/or better focus the available intervention resources.

Abusive Men Are Likely to Continue to Be Violent

In general, several investigators have studied the likelihood that an abusive male will stop abusing on his own or through an abuser treatment program. For instance, Feld and Straus (1990) sent questionnaires to 8,145 families over a two-year period as part of their very influential and ongoing National Family Violence Survey (Straus & Gelles, 1990). This longitudinal research was designed specifically to look for changes in abusive behavior over time. Feld and Straus found that about two-thirds of men who had been physically abusive at least three times in the year before completing the first questionnaire were still abusive a year later. If we generalize these findings to the population of men at large, then the probability that an abusive man will stop abusing his wife is substantially less than a coin flip. In other words, it is reasonable to expect that a man who has been abusive will continue to be abusive. Unfortunately, Feld and Straus (1990) did not measure other forms of abuse in their sample, e.g., psychological or financial abuse. Thus, the third of the men in the sample who were no longer physically abusive may have stopped physical abuse and switched to or continued psychological or other forms of abuse.

O'Leary and colleagues (1989) conducted a similar longitudinal study of 272 newly married couples. Similar to the Feld and Straus (1990) findings, almost two-thirds (65%) of the men in the sample who were physically violent before marriage also physically abused their wives in the two and a half years following the first interview. Again, no data were collected about the men's psychological and other nonphysical forms of abuse. However, the results were clear: Only about one in three physically abusive men stop physically abusing their wives.

In a similar longitudinal design, Quigley and Leonard (1996) followed 188 newly married couples in which the husband had been physically abusive of his fiancée in the previous year. The engaged partners completed their questionnaires separately and submitted them separately by mail. The couples were also paid separately for completing and returning the questionnaires. This process was repeated one year into the couples' marriages and again at three years into their marriages. While the most violent men were the least likely to stop being violent, the minimally violent men in this sample still had a two out of three chance of continuing their violence in the second and third years of the marriage. While it is possible that an abusive husband will stop being violent, the chance that he will is very low.

The studies mentioned above did not investigate forms of abuse other than physical. Aldarondo (1996), however, in his three-year study of 772 married couples, extended previous work by looking into the husbands' emotional abuse of their wives. Interestingly, all of the husbands who were physically violent in the first year of the study continued to be emotionally abusive in the second and third years. So, even if the man stopped physically assaulting his wife, he continued to abuse her emotionally during the second and third years of their marriage. This finding answers questions left by other studies in that it suggests that abusive men who stop physically abusing their wives are likely to keep abusing them emotionally.

Jacobson and Gottman (1998) further extended this line of research by looking into men's systematic use of intimidation (e.g., physical, emotional, etc.) to control their female partners. This study involved a sample of 140 married couples over two years. This is a much deeper look at couples with an abusive husband because it included the spouses' physiological (i.e., polygraph-type) reactions as well as videotape analysis of the spouses' facial expressions and other interaction behaviors while the husband and wife discussed a problematic marital issue. In summary, while 54% of the men in the sample reduced their physical violence during the two-year course of the study, only 7% of the men completely stopped being physically violent over the two-year time frame. Jacobson and Gottman argue that the reduction in physical violence by some of the men may have been replaced by emotional abuse, because once the man had established dominance and control, he could use less extreme abuse methods (e.g., emotional or financial abuse) that were not likely to result in incarceration.

Interestingly, Jacobson and Gottman (1998) found that among the men who stopped being violent or became less physically violent, nothing the women did appeared to explain why the men stopped their abusive behavior. It therefore stands to reason that only characteristics of the abusers themselves predict whether the violence will decrease or ultimately stop.

So, are violent men likely to continue to be violent? The answer is yes; an abusive adult male will probably continue to be abusive over the course of and across his relationship(s). Findings across several studies support the old adage among psychologists: The best predictor of future behavior is past behavior. It also appears that if an abusive adult male reduces or ceases his physical violence, then the often-accompanying emotional abuse will continue or take the place of physical assault in the man's pursuit of control and domination in his marriage.

Adult Abuser Treatment Programs

Several batterer programs have been created and are used in state and military criminal justice settings. The following discussion is based on the work of Babcock, Green, and Robie (2004); Gondolf (2002); and Roberts (2002). Both Gondolf and Roberts described several of the various batterer treatment programs that have been developed. Babcock and colleagues conducted a meta-analysis of the effectiveness of these programs in halting men's abusive behavior. It is important to point out that batterer intervention programs, whether voluntary or court mandated, are essentially after-the-fact attempts to reduce wife abuse. In other words, these programs are for men who have already demonstrated their abusive nature.

The Duluth model (Paymar, 1993; Pence & Paymar, 1993) is perhaps the most widely used batterer intervention program (BIP) in the United States. The Duluth model is built on the idea that abusive men abuse their partners to achieve and maintain power and control in the relationship. The "Power and Control Wheel" developed by Pence and Paymar (1993) diagrams the central theory of the Duluth model, which focuses on stopping the abuse immediately and on changing men's attitudes that abusive behavior is OK. (Note that there is a positive relationship between attitudes that are permissive of abuse and actual abuse; Schwartz, O'Leary, & Kendziora, 1997.) Duluth model practitioners combine parts of several different approaches to try to change abusive men's attitudes toward women and abusive behavior.

Another BIP approach is based in psychodynamic theory (Browne & Saunders, 1997; Dutton, 1998; Stosney, 1995). Psychodynamic treatment focuses on the personality of the abuser and holds that men's abusive behavior is the product of the men's life experiences from birth to present. Psychodynamic abuser therapy includes offering abusive men positive support and the camaraderie of other men through group sessions. Because there is an important association between insecure attachment and abuse (see Dutton, 1998, for an overview), these sessions are designed to help the abuser become better able to attach or emotionally bond to his partner and, as a result, have relationships with less fear and no abuse.

There are other approaches, including anger management and couples counseling (Geffner & Mantooth, 2000). One problem with anger management is the possible inference that the abuser is somehow provoked by the victim. This is simply not the case (cf. Schweinle & Ickes, 2007; Schweinle, Ickes, & Bernstein, 2002; Schweinle, Ickes, Rollings, & Jacquot, 2010). By treating partner abuse as a relationship problem, couples therapy also implies that the victim is perhaps in part to blame for the abusive behavior and that both partners, the abuser and the victim, need to work together to stop the abuse. Again, this is a false assumption because recent findings have demonstrated that abusiveness is a characteristic of the abuser not the victim. Worse still, couples therapy places the woman in close contact with her abuser to discuss potentially explosive relationship issues. This is inherently risky.

Babcock and colleagues (2004) conducted a thorough meta-analysis of 22 scientific articles on batterer treatment program effectiveness. The treatment programs reviewed included the Duluth model, cognitive behavior therapy, anger management, probation, and other abuser treatment modalities. The experimental methods included quasi- and true-experimental designs. Unfortunately, Babcock and colleagues found that the recidivism rates for the abusers who were treated were very similar to the recidivism rates for men who were not treated at all. Further, the differences between treatment types (e.g., Duluth model vs. cognitive behavior therapy) were not significant. Finally, they summarize that the likelihood that a treated batterer will reabuse is about 40%, whereas for a nontreated batterer it is about 35%. In summary, they found that abuser treatment programs are not very effective in stopping abuse.

Jackson, Feder, Forde, Davis, Maxwell, and Taylor conducted a similar but smaller review of two BIP for the National Institute for Justice (2003). These studies compared Duluth model treatment and cognitive-behavioral therapy to probation alone. One program was in Broward County, Florida; the other was in Brooklyn, New York. The findings were startling. Generally speaking, neither of the batterer intervention programs was much more effective than probation alone. In fact, in Broward County, the men who were assigned to the BIP were slightly *more* likely to abuse their partners again than the men who were given only probation.

Batterer intervention programs are built on reasonable psychological theory and follow rational assumptions that seem to explain why men abuse and what can be done to stop the abuse. Unfortunately, however, the only reasonable conclusion that can be drawn from the research reviewed here is that we are unlikely to stop an adult abuser from abusing. Of course, there are anecdotal cases of abusive men who have stopped, either in treatment or on their own. And these cases may, by themselves, justify the use of batterer treatment. However, these are exceptional cases statistically speaking. The vast majority of abusive adult men do not stop abusing within and across their close relationships, and batterer intervention programs are generally not very effective. Given these sobering conclusions, it seems reasonable to direct attention to other possible ways to prevent partner abuse, e.g., intervention during adolescence.

Intervention in Adolescence for Abusive Teens

Peer dating violence has significant negative consequences on the mental health of victims. For instance, Banyard and Cross (2008) recently found that victims of dating violence tended to experience more depression and diminished academic performance. (This relationship appears to be further complicated by substance abuse, though the causal pathways are as yet unclear.) Regardless, for these reasons alone, it is important to prevent or stop partner violence between teens. However, intervention with abusive adolescents may have the long-term effect of helping prevent abusive behavior in adulthood.

It stands to reason that if most abusive adult men will not or cannot be made to stop abusing, that there might be an earlier developmental period during potentially (or actively) abusive men's lives when the abuse could be prevented or stopped. Several investigators have made this argument based on sound theory and research (Avery-Leaf, Cascardi, O'Leary, & Cano, 1997; Banyard & Cross, 2008; Ehrensaft et al., 2003; Magdol, Moffitt, Caspi, & Silva, 1998). The following paragraphs describe these arguments as they developed (i.e., in chronological order) and conclude that intervention with abusive and potentially abusive male teens may be a more effective short- and long-term approach to preventing (at least) some abusive behavior during and after adolescence.

Avery-Leaf and colleagues (1997) reported on a five-session dating violence training program that they developed and tested among 192 New York high school students. The program focused on changing the students' attitudes toward acceptance of partner violence, and the program resulted in a significant reduction in the male students' acceptance of and justification for dating violence. However, on the one hand, there is a psychologically murky and unreliable relationship between peoples' attitudes and their actual behavior (see Albarracin, Johnson, &

Zanna, 2009, for a recent and well-written overview of this topic). So, it would be a shaky leap of logic to conclude that the five-session program resulted in less *actual* partner violence.

On the other hand, Schwartz, O'Leary, & Kendziora (1997) found a significant relationship specifically between young males' attitudes toward aggression (i.e., their justification of aggression) and actual aggression. This does support the conclusion that the program developed by Avery-Leaf and colleagues. (1997) does effectively reduce teen dating violence. By extension, and based on the relationship between teen and adult partner violence described above, it is reasonable to conclude that this brief five-session intervention will result in at least some reduction in adult partner violence for the students who participated.

As part of the longitudinal study discussed earlier in this chapter, Magdol and colleagues (1998) looked into the possible early childhood, late childhood, and adolescent markers for partner abuse in adulthood. Among the significant predictors, a close relationship between the adolescent and his parent was negatively associated with adult partner abuse. Further, having parents with higher-status occupations while a boy is in middle school and having both parents living in the household were negatively associated with adult partner abuse. Positive childhood predictors of adult partner abuse included dropping out of school and delinquency in adolescence.

Considering that it is possible to identify potential adult abusers during their middle school years, it may be reasonable to argue that identifying at-risk middle school males and intervening with them while they are in middle school would be a good approach. However, the reliability of the middle school predictors is somewhat less than that of high school–age predictors. In other words, it is more difficult to predict a person's behavior the longer the time between the prediction and when you anticipate the behavior occuring. Therefore, identifying at-risk boys during middle school and intervening may not be cost effective, because one would have to intervene with a very large group of boys in order to expect to bring about results. Based on this, Magdol and colleagues (1998) argue that early adolescence (early high school age) would be a better time to intervene, because as time lengthens between an intervention and the focal outcome behavior, the efficacy of the intervention wanes (Caspi & Bem, 1990). In other words, intervention when the early adolescent males are closer to exploring and entering close relationships would be more effective in preventing teen partner abuse and, theoretically, adult partner abuse.

Ehrensaft and colleagues (2003) argued on the basis of their findings from the Children in Communities Study that partner violence prevention strategies should focus on children with a history of abuse by parents and other adults and that these strategies should focus on avoiding escalation of behavioral problems. They cite social learning theory and research to conclude that children who witness abuse between parents can be helped to understand that violence is not an acceptable or effective means of handling conflict in close relationships. In other words, children who grow up learning that violence is a normal or acceptable means to conflict resolution can learn nonviolent conflict resolution methods. They further suggest that these prevention programs could be coordinated with courts, law enforcement, and services for abused women and children.

However, in contrast to Avery-Leaf and colleagues (1997) and Magdol and colleagues (1998), Ehrensaft and colleagues (2003) argue that prevention should occur earlier than adolescence (in late childhood) so that abusive responses to conflict do not become entrenched in the child's psyche and behavior patterns and then later emerge in adolescent and adult close relationships. They base this argument on their clinical observation that excessive punishment by parents is difficult to extinguish by the time a child becomes an adolescent. Therefore, intervention should occur while the child is younger and has not necessarily been taught to resolve relationship conflict through extreme coercive methods.

In summary, there are both theoretical arguments and a few empirical findings that support the conclusion that partner-abuse intervention with adolescent boys should occur sometime earlier than in adulthood. However, the optimal time for such intervention is under debate in the research literature. Some researchers argue that early middle school (preadolescence) would be optimal. Other investigators argue that intervention in early adolescence, when the boys are first exploring close relationships, would be better. Further research is needed in this area to assess the effectiveness of adolescent abuse intervention and to better pinpoint the optimal developmental stage for such intervention.

Summary

In summary, there is some direct evidence that an abusive teen will mature into an abusive adult. The research to date tends to suggest that an abusive adult man will continue to be abusive to his partner, whether or not he ever undergoes a batterer intervention program. However, there is some preliminary evidence that intervention with abusive and potentially abusive boys will reduce the likelihood that they will be abusive toward their partners in adulthood. Taken together, these results suggest that partner abuse prevention might be more effectively focused on adolescent males, before they become adult abusers who are highly resistant to non-punitive intervention. Future research should focus on the development of early interventions for young men. More distal research should longitudinally explore the short- and long-term effectiveness of such intervention programs.

References

Albarracin, D. Johnson, B., & Zanna, M. (2009). *The handbook of attitudes.* Mahwah, NJ: Lawrence Erlbaum Associates.

Aldarondo, E. (1996). Cessation and persistence of wife assault. *American Journal of Orthopsychiatry, 66,* 141–151.

Archer, J. (2000). Sex differences in aggression between heterosexual partners: A meta-analytic review. *Psychological Bulletin, 26,* 651–680.

Avery-Leaf, S., Cascardi, M., O'Leary, K., & Cano, A. (1997). Efficacy of dating violence prevention program on attitudes justifying aggression. *Journal of Adolescent Health, 21,* 11–17.

Babcock, J., Green, C., & Robie, C. (2004). Does batterer treatment work? A meta-analytic review of domestic violence treatment. *Clinical Psychology Review, 23,* 1023–1053.

Banyard, V., & Cross, C. (2008). Consequences of teen dating violence. *Violence Against Women, 14,* 998–1013.

Bratton, I., Roseman, C., & Schweinle, W. (in press). Educating teens to discriminate abusive from nonabusive situations. In M. Paludi (Ed.), *The psychology of teen violence and victimization.* Santa Barbara, CA: Praeger.

Browne, K., & Saunders, D. (1997). Process-psychodynamic groups for men who batter: A brief treatment model. *Families in Society, 78,* 265–272.

Campbell, J. (2004). Helping women understand their risk in situations of partner violence. *Journal of Interpersonal Violence, 19,* 1464–1477.

Caspi, A., & Bem, D. (1990). Personality continuity and change across the life course. In L. Pervin (Ed.), *Handbook of personality: Theory and research* (pp. 549–575). New York: Guilford.

Centers for Disease Control and Prevention. (2009). Youth Risk Behavioral Surveillance System. Retrieved on October 13, 2010, from http://apps.nccd.cdc.gov/YouthOnline/App/Results.aspx.

Dutton, D. (1998). *The abusive personality: Violence and control in intimate relationships.* New York: Guilford.

Ehrensaft, M., Cohen, P., Brown, J., Smailes, E., Chen, H., & Johnson, J. (2003). Intergenerational transmission of partner violence: A 20-year prospective study. *Journal of Consulting and Clinical Psychology, 71,* 741–753.

Feld, S., & Straus, M. (1990). Escalation and desistence from wife assault. In M. Straus & R. Gelles (Eds.), *Physical violence in American families: Risk factors and adaptations to violence in 8,145 families* (pp. 489–505). New Brunswick, NJ: Transaction Publishers.

Foshee, V., Benefield, T., Ennett, S., Bauman, K., & Suchindran (2004). Longitudinal predictors of serious physical and sexual dating violence victimization during adolescence. *Preventive Medicine, 39,* 1007–1016.

Geffner, R., & Mantooth, C. (2000). *Ending spouse/partner abuse: A psychoeducational approach for individuals and couples.* New York: Springer.

Gondolf, E. (2002). *Batterer intervention systems.* Thousand Oaks, CA: Sage.

Gottman, J. (1994). *Why marriages succeed or fail.* New York: Simon & Schuster.

Herrenkohl, T., Huang, B., Tajima, E., & Whitney, S. (2003). Examinig the link between child abuse and youth violence. *Journal of Interpersonal Violence, 18,* 1189–1208.

Jacobson, N., & Gottman, J. (1998). *When men batter women: New insights into ending abusive relationships.* New York: Simon & Schuster.

Loza, W., & Loza-Fanous, A. (1999). The fallacy of reducing rape and violence recidivism by treating anger. *International Journal of Offender Therapy and Comparative Criminology, 43,* 492–502.

Magdol, L., Moffitt, T., Caspi, A., & Silva, P. (1998). Developmental antecedents of partner abuse: A prospective longitudinal study. *Journal of Abnormal Psychology, 107,* 375–389.

Morse, B. (1995). Beyond the Conflict Tactics Scale: Assessing gender differences in partner violence. *Violence and Victims, 10,* 251–272.

National Institute for Justice. (2003). *Batterer intervention programs: Where do we go from here?* (NCJ Publication No. NCJ 195079). Washington, DC: U.S. Government Printing Office.

O'Donnell, L., Stueve, A., Myint-U, A., Duran, R., Agronick, G., & Wilson-Simmons, R. (2006). Middle school aggression and subsequent intimate partner physical violence. *Journal of Youth and Adolescence, 35,* 693–703.

O'Leary, D., Barling, J., Arias, I., Rosenbaum, A., Malone, J., & Tyree, A. (1989). Prevalence and stability of physical aggression between spouses: A longitudinal analysis. *Journal of Consulting and Clinical Psychology, 57,* 263–268.

O'Leary, K. (2000). Are women really more aggressive than men in intimate relationships? *Psychological Bulletin, 126,* 685–689.

Paymar, M. (1993). *Violent no more: Helping men end domestic abuse.* Alameda, CA: Hunter House.

Pence, E., & Paymar, M. (1993). *Education groups for men who batter: The Duluth Model.* New York: Springer.

Quigley, B., & Leonard, K. (1996). Desistance from marital violence in the early years of marriage. *Violence and Victims, 11,* 355–370.

Roberts, A. (Ed.). (2002). *Handbook of domestic violence intervention strategies.* New York: Oxford University Press.

Schaefer, J., & Caetano, R. (1998). Rates of intimate partner violence in the United States. *American Journal of Public Health, 110,* 1702–1705.

Schwartz, M., O'Leary, S., & Kendziora, K. (1997). Dating aggression among high school students. *Violence and Victims, 12,* 295–305.

Schweinle, W., & Ickes, W. (2007). The role of men's critical/rejecting overattribution bias, affect, and attentional disengagement in marital aggression. *Journal of Social and Clinical Psychology, 26,* 175–199.

Schweinle, W., Ickes, W., & Bernstein, I. (2002). Empathic inaccuracy in husband to wife aggression: The overattribution bias. *Personal Relationships, 9,* 141–158.

Schweinle, W., Ickes, W., Rollings, K., & Jacquot, C. (2010). Maritally aggressive men: Angry, egocentric, impulsive, and/or biased. *Journal of Language and Social Psychology, 29,* 399–424.

Stosney, S. (1995). *Treating attachment abuse: A compassion approach.* New York: Springer.

Straus, M., & Gelles, R. (1990). *Physical violence in American families: Risk factors and adaptations to violence in 8,145 families.* New Brunswick, NJ: Transaction Publishers.

Wexler, D. (Ed.). (1999). *Domestic violence 2000: An integrated skills program for men.* New York: Norton.

Woodward, L., Fergusson, D., & Horwood, L. (2002). Romantic relationships of young people with childhood and adolescent onset antisocial behavior problems. *Journal of Abnormal Child Psychology, 30,* 231–243.

About the Editor and Contributors

The Editor

Michele A. Paludi, PhD, is the series editor for Women's Psychology and for Women and Careers in Management for Praeger. She is the author/editor of 38 college textbooks and of more than 170 scholarly articles and conference presentations on sexual harassment, campus violence, psychology of women, gender, and discrimination. Her book *Ivory Power: Sexual Harassment on Campus* (SUNY Press, 1990) received the 1992 Myers Center Award for Outstanding Book on Human Rights in the United States. Dr. Paludi served as chair of the U.S. Department of Education's Subpanel on the Prevention of Violence, Sexual Harassment, and Alcohol and Other Drug Problems in Higher Education. She was one of six scholars in the United States to be selected for this subpanel. She also was a consultant to and a member of former New York State governor Mario Cuomo's Task Force on Sexual Harassment. Dr. Paludi serves as an expert witness for court proceedings and administrative hearings on sexual harassment. She has had extensive experience in conducting training programs and investigations of sexual harassment and other Equal Employment Opportunity issues for businesses and educational institutions. In addition, Dr. Paludi has held faculty positions at Franklin & Marshall College, Kent State University, Hunter College, Union College, and Union Graduate College, where she directs the human resource management certificate program. She is on the faculty in the School of Management. She was recently named "Woman of the Year" by the Business and Professional Women in Schenectady, New York. She is currently the Elihu Root Peace Fund Professor in Women's Studies at Hamilton College.

The Contributors

Craig A. Anderson is a Distinguished Professor of Liberal Arts and Sciences in the Department of Psychology at Iowa State University. He received his PhD from Stanford University in 1980 and has served on the faculties of Rice University, the Ohio State University, and the University of Missouri–Columbia. He has been awarded Fellow status by the American Psychological Society and the American Psychological Association. Anderson's 150 plus publications span a wide range of areas, including judgment and decision making; depression, loneliness, and shyness; personality theory and measurement; and attribution theory. In recent years, his work has focused on the development of a General Aggression Model designed to integrate insights from cognitive, developmental, personality, and social psychology. His pioneering work on video game violence has led to consultations with educators, government officials, child advocates, and news organizations worldwide. His recent book *Violent Video Game Effects on Children and Adolescents,* published by Oxford University Press in 2007, describes the effects of playing violent video games, explains how these effects occur, and explores possible actions that parents, educators, and public policy creators can take to deal with this important social issue. His 2010 meta-analysis article published in *Psychological Bulletin,* psychology's top review journal, combined the results of all relevant empirical studies (over 130,000 participants) and conclusively demonstrated the harmful effects of violent video games.

Bethany Ashby, PsyD, is a postdoctoral fellow in adolescent medicine at Aurora Mental Health Center and the Children's Hospital in Aurora, Colorado. She received her doctorate in clinical psychology with an emphasis in family psychology from Azusa Pacific University. Her research and clinical interests include adolescent pregnancy and parenting, family systems, and cross-cultural issues.

Marios N. Avraamides is an assistant professor of cognitive psychology and the director of the Experimental Psychology Laboratory at the University of Cyprus. He has a BA degree in psychology from the University of Texas at Austin and MSc and PhD degrees in cognitive psychology from Pennsylvania State University. He has previously worked as a postdoctoral scientist at the University of California–Santa Barbara and at the Max Planck Institute for Biological Cybernetics, Tübingen, Germany. His primary research interests lie in the field of spatial cognition, although he is also involved through collaborations in research projects on attention and media violence.

About the Editor and Contributors

Shelly Bloom is currently a master's student in education at the Ohio State University. She completed in her BS in human development and family studies in March 2010. For the past four years, she has been engaged in research on youth violence prevention. She is a coauthor on a peer-reviewed journal article. She plans to teach middle school next year.

Imelda N. Bratton received her doctorate in counselor education and counseling from Idaho State University in 2008. Dr. Bratton has been a professional school counselor for 12 years and has published several articles relating to childhood disorders, school counseling issues, expressive arts, clinical supervision, and sandtray. She is currently a professional school counselor in Spearfish, South Dakota, and an adjunct faculty member at South Dakota State University, where she trains future professional counselors.

Brian D. Christens is an assistant professor of human ecology at the University of Wisconsin–Madison. His research focuses on efforts by nonprofit and grassroots organizations to effect change in policies and systems and on the predictors and impacts of voluntary participation in these efforts. He is also interested in young people's involvement in change efforts and is a member of the editorial board of the *Journal of Youth and Adolescence*.

Jessica J. Collura is a doctoral student in human ecology at the University of Wisconsin–Madison. She formerly served as a Teach for America corps member, and her interests include community leadership, youth engagement in community networks, and youth organizing. She recently coedited (with Shepherd Zeldin and Derick Wilson) a special issue of *Youth and Society* on promoting restorative cultures and shared societies in Northern Ireland and the United States.

James Crosby is an assistant professor of psychology at Sam Houston State University (SHSU) in Huntsville, Texas. He received his PhD in educational psychology with an emphasis in school psychology from Oklahoma State University in 2008, following the completion of his doctoral internship with the Devereux Foundation's Institute of Clinical Training and Research in Villanova, Pennsylvania. At SHSU, James teaches graduate courses in behavioral and academic consultation, psychometric theory, and psychopathology, among others. His primary research interests include peer victimization, psychometrics, and rural psychological service delivery. He lives with his wife and two sons in southeast Texas, where he spends an inordinate amount of time trying to be a drummer.

Christina M. Dardis is a graduate student in the clinical psychology doctoral program at Ohio University. Her professional interests include prevention and recovery processes for sexual assault and domestic violence, as well as perceptions of abuse and intervention efforts.

Billie Wright Dziech is the primary author of *The Lecherous Professor* (Beacon Press, 1990) and coauthor of *On Trial: American Courts and Their Treatment of Sexually Abused Children* (Beacon Press, 1991) and *Sexual Harassment and Higher Education: Reflections and New Perspectives* (Garland Series on Higher Education, 1998). She has authored numerous book chapters and articles in scholarly journals and publishes regularly in the *Chronicle of Higher Education*. Her work has been reviewed and quoted in sources as diverse as the *New York Times*, the *Wall Street Journal*, the *Chicago Tribune*, and *People Magazine*. She has lectured and consulted at higher education institutions and businesses throughout the United States and Canada and has appeared on television and radio, including *The Today Show*, CNN, *Phil Donahue*, and *Oprah*. Dziech is a professor of English and comparative literature at the University of Cincinnati, where she has served in both administrative and faculty positions. She is the recipient of the university's A. B. "Dolly" Cohen Award for Excellence in College Teaching and the Honors Scholars Program's Faculty Teaching Award.

Katie M. Edwards is a fifth-year doctoral student in clinical psychology at Ohio University. She is currently completing her predoctoral clinical internship at the Vanderbilt University–Veterans Affairs Internship Consortium in Nashville, Tennessee. Her area of programmatic research focuses on understanding women's leaving processes in abusive relationships, ethics of interpersonal trauma research, and interpersonal trauma recovery. She is also engaged in violence-related advocacy work.

Kostas A. Fanti is a lecturer of developmental psychology and the director of the Developmental Psychopathology Lab at the University of Cyprus. He has a BSc degree in psychology from the University of New Orleans and MA and PhD degrees in developmental psychology from Georgia State University. He is interested in the development of various types of externalizing problems (overt aggression, delinquency, bullying, proactive and reactive aggression, and conduct and oppositional defiant disorder) and how generalized and specific types of externalizing problems relate to contextual (family, peers, school, community, media) or individual (psychopathic traits, temperament, cognitive functioning, internalizing problems) factors. He is the principal investigator of different funded projects investigating desensitization to media violence, the development of aggressive and depressive problems during adolescence, and the development of attention deficit hyperactivity disorder.

Roseanne L. Flores is an associate professor in the Department of Psychology at Hunter College of the City University of New York. She is a developmental psychologist by training and was a National Head Start Fellow in the Office of Head Start in Washington, D.C., in 2009–2010. She has expertise in both quantitative and qualitative research methods, statistics, testing and measurement, and linguistic, cognitive, and social development of children across various ages and cultural groups. Some of her current research examines the relationship between environmental risk factors, such as community violence, socioeconomic status, and food insecurity, on the health and educational outcomes of children. She recently received an NIH grant to examine the relationships between poverty and nutrition and African American and Latino preschool children's early learning skills. She has published a number of peer-reviewed journal articles and book chapters on children's exposure to community violence.

Alice Fok-Trela, MA, is a PsyD candidate in clinical psychology at Azusa Pacific University. She is registered as a provisional psychologist (Alberta) and has trained in cognitive-behavioral therapy at the Harbor-UCLA Medical Center and British Columbia Mental Health and Addiction Services. Her research and clinical interests include cognitive-behavioral therapy in challenging populations, systems theory, cross-cultural adjustment, and assessment and treatment of families and children.

Christine A. Gidycz is a professor of psychology and director of clinical training at Ohio University. Research interests include the evaluation of sexual assault prevention and risk reduction programs and correlates, predictors, and consequences of various forms of violence. Her work has been funded through the Centers for Disease Control and Prevention and the Ohio Department of Health. She has served on various state and national panels that address violence-related issues.

Marjorie Graham-Howard, PhD, is an associate professor at Azusa Pacific University and a licensed clinical psychologist with a private practice in forensic psychology. Her private practice includes both court-referred and attorney-retained referrals for evaluations in the juvenile and adult court system. Her research interests are focused primarily on juvenile forensic psychology, specifically the evaluation of juvenile trial competence, waiver to adult court, juvenile sex offender risk assessment, and treatment of adjudicated minors.

Ashley Hicks is pursuing her doctorate in the Department of Human Development and Family Science at the Ohio State University. She earned her BS from the Ohio State University in sociology and Spanish. Her research interests include adolescent development, urban communities, trauma-informed intervention, and ecological models.

Beth M. Housekamp is a professor of clinical psychology at the Los Angeles campus of the California School of Professional Psychology at Alliant International University. Her research and clinical interests include exploring neurodevelopmental contributions to challenging behavior in children and adolescents and assessing and treating those who have experienced traumatic events.

Ann Booker Loper, PhD, is a clinical psychologist and professor at the University of Virginia's Curry School of Education. Her research focuses on mental health and adjustment of prisoners, with a particular interest in understanding the experiences of women in the criminal justice system and incarcerated parents. Dr. Loper has collaborated with prison, jail, and community partners in the development of a parenting program for incarcerated mothers. She has consulted with local and state agencies concerning the rehabilitative needs of returning prisoners, particularly as related to family reunification. Dr. Loper has also conducted research concerning the needs and characteristics of female juvenile offenders.

Emily B. Nichols, MEd, is a doctoral student in the clinical and school psychology program at the Curry School of Education at the University of Virginia (UVA). She is involved in a wide range of research activities concerning incarcerated parents and affected children, with a particular interest in educational outcomes for children who experience incarceration of family members. Prior to coming to UVA, Nichols worked with children with pediatric bipolar disorder and their families as a predoctoral research fellow at the National Institutes of Mental Health.

Caitlin M. Novero, MEd, is a doctoral student in the clinical and school psychology program at the Curry School of Education at the University of Virginia. She has previously conducted research regarding adjustment patterns of prisoners who were themselves children of incarcerated parents, and she continues to examine the long-term impact of parental incarceration. She has also worked with forensic populations in prison rehabilitation programs in Boston, Massachusetts, and central Virginia.

Sara Prot completed her master's degree at the University of Zagreb and is a graduate student at Iowa State University.

Christopher P. Roseman received his doctorate in counselor education and supervision from the University of Toledo. His research has focused on deficiencies of shame, guilt, and empathy of individuals who are charged and/or convicted of physical and sexual abuse. This research has spawned innovative interventions and treatment modalities in the field of sex offender treatment. He is currently a faculty member at the University of South Dakota in the counseling program, where he trains future professional counselors and counselor educators.

William E. Schweinle received his doctorate in 2002 from the University of Texas at Arlington in social and quantitative psychology. He received postdoctoral training in quantitative psychology at the University of Missouri–Columbia. He has studied men's maltreatment of women for 14 years and has published several articles and book chapters on the subject of abusive men's social cognition. He is currently an assistant professor of biostatistics in the University of South Dakota School of Health Sciences.

Robert L. Thornberg is an associate professor in the Department of Behavioral Sciences and Learning at Linköping University in Sweden. He received his master's degree in educational science (including psychology and sociology) and doctorate degree in educational science from Linköping University. His current research is on school bullying and peer harassment, with a particular focus on social processes, morality, and students' perspectives. His second line of research is on school rules, student participation, and moral practices in everyday school life. Robert has published reviewed articles in international academic journals, such as *Educational Psychology, Educational Studies, Psychology in the Schools, Child and Youth Forum, Journal of Moral Education, Teaching and Teacher Education,* and *Social Psychology of Education,* and he serves on the editor review board of the journal *Nordic Studies in Education.* He is also a board member of the Nordic Educational Research Association (NERA) and a coordinator for the NERA Network for Empirical Research on Value Issues in Education as well.

Deanna L. Wilkinson is currently associate professor in the Department of Human Development and Family Science in the College of Education and

Human Ecology at the Ohio State University. Dr. Wilkinson is a criminologist and expert on urban youth violence, community processes, and violence prevention. She earned her PhD from the School of Criminal Justice at Rutgers University, her MA in criminal justice from the University of Illinois at Chicago, and her BA in sociology from Cornell College in Mt. Vernon, Iowa. Her primary research and teaching interests are adolescent development, risk and problem behaviors, youth violence, evidence-based practice, firearm use, prevention, event perspectives, community-police partnerships, citizen participation in social action, collaborative processes, program evaluation, and urban communities. She is the 2008 recipient of the Society for Research on Adolescence Young Investigator Award. She received the Les Wright Youth Advocacy Award in 2009, the College of Education and Human Ecology's Dean's Distinguished Service Award in 2010, and the Fire and Focus Scholarship Service Award in 2010.

Shepherd Zeldin is Rothermel Bascom Professor of Human Ecology at the University of Wisconsin–Madison. His research explores the impact of youths on civil society. He is also an outreach specialist for Wisconsin Extension. He provides research and consultation to youth and community initiatives across the United States. His most recent publication, coauthored with Jessica J. Collura and published by Cornell University's ACT for Youth Center for Excellence (2010), is titled "Being Y-AP Savvy: A Primer on Creating and Sustaining Youth-Adult Partnerships."

Index

abuse: adolescents' attitudes toward, 90–92; behavioral problems and, 203; definitions of, 92–95; history of, 203; in the literature, 92–97; patterns of teenagers/adolescents, 99; prevalence of, 89; research on adolescents' experiencing, 89–90
abused children, risks for, 25
abused teens, risks for, 25
abusers: adult continuation of, 239–241; educators as, 152; future predictors for, 242; identification of, 246; males as, 146, 148; recidivism rates for, 244; sex abuse and characteristics of, 154; treatment programs for, 241
abusive behaviors checklist, 99–100
abusive relationships involvement, 97
abusive situation: mental health issues, 90; recognition, 97–99
abusive vs. nonabusive situation discrimination: abuse in the literature, 92–97; abuse patterns of teenagers/adolescents, 99; abusive behaviors checklist, 99–100; abusive relationships involvement, 97; abusive situation recognition, 97–99; adolescents' attitudes toward abuse, 90–92; research on adolescents' experiencing abuse, 89–90
Achtman, R. L., 58
addictionlike behavioral disorders, 61–62
adolescence: changes described, 138–140, 190, 222; definition of, 138; developmental stages of, 91; firearms and, 191; harmful behavior during, 163; intervention programs during, 239–240, 245–247; intimate partner violence (IPV) and, 29; physical dating violence during, 74; physical perpetration in, 75; post-traumatic stress disorder (PTSD) diagnosis, 8; victimization experience during, 72, 74, 79; young women's use of aggression in, 73
adolescents: abuse intervention, 246; adults views about, 222–223; girls' victimization and subsequent perpetration of dating violence, 73; gun homicide situations, 173; idea of violence, 91; incarceration of, 22; intimate partner violence (IPV), 28–30; persecution venue, 222; rape victims problems incurred by, 26; victims of physical and sexual assault, 25–26
adolescents and firearm suicide: prevalence, 184; trends, 184–185
adolescents and firearms: about, 171–172; adolescent gun violence epidemic, 172–174; adolescents and firearm suicide, 184–185; fixed factors, 186; gun availability and carrying, in disadvantaged urban neighborhoods, 179; gun availability and carrying, patterns of, 178–179; gun availability and carrying, suburban and rural patterns of, 180–181; guns and the

peer context, 181–182; personal factors, 188–189; prevention, 188–189; qualitative study of adolescents and firearms, 182–184; reasons for weapon carrying, 181; risk factors for adolescent suicide, 185–186; social/environmental factors, 186–188; survey about youth violence and firearms, 175; violence-related risk, 175–177; conclusions, 190–191

adult partner abuse, childhood predictors of, 246

Adults and Children Together Against Violence (ACT) (American Psychological Association), 168

Advocacy Center and the Domestic Abuse Project, 93

affect dysregulation, 25, 27

affect theory, 78–79

African Americans: firearm suicide by, 186; homicide rates, 172; homicides as cause of death, 221; male suicide by firearms, 189

agency orientation to violence reduction, 226

aggression and related variables, short- and long-term effects on, 49–56

aggression in dating relationships: research evidence, 73–75; role of victimization experiences, 71–73; theoretical explanation, 75

aggression in dating relationships, theoretical explanation: about, 75; developmental traumatology theory and affect theory, 78–79; self defense, 76; social learning theory and inter-generational transmission of violence theory, 76–78; summary, 79–81

Aggression in the Schools (Olweus), 4

aggression scores, 125

aggressive affect, 50–51, 54–55

aggressive behavior: aggressive cognition and, 53; chronic desensitization, 56; dating violence and, 56; depression and, 206; factors determining, 50–51; GAM (model), 43, 53, 127; Internet violence, 129; knowledge structures, 121; learning, 43; media habits and, 48; media violence, 127–129; mental pathology, 206; probability of, 45; trait aggression, 121; violent video games and, 50, 52, 56–57, 62, 121, 126, 129

aggressive cognition, 50–51, 53–54

Aisenberg, E., 32

Alexander, J., 7

Altman, I., 230

American Indian/Alaskan natives: suicide rates, 186; violent crime rates, 17–18

American Psychological Association, 168

amusement as cause of bullying, 112–113

Amy and Isabelle (Strout), 142–145

Anderson, C. A., 53, 54, 57, 59, 122, 123, 124, 126, 127, 128, 129

Anderson, Jess, 141–142

anger management, 244

Archer, J., 71

Arcuri, A., 209

Ariga, M., 206

arrests: by gender, 200; rates by race, 225

Arsenault, L., 5, 6

assessment: elements of, 23; of treatment of adolescent victims of violence, 22–24

attention and cognitive control effects: attention deficits, 58–59; benefits to visuospatial attention, 57; disruption of cognitive control:, 59–60

attention deficits, 58–59

attention related problems, 58

Augimeri, L. A., 211

Avraamides, M. N., 123, 128

Azrael, D., 179, 187, 188, 189

Babcock, J., 95

BAI test, 24

Bailey, K., 59

Baldacci, H. B., 53

Bandura, A., 43, 117, 123

Banyard, V., 90

Barber, C., 188, 189

Barlett, C. P., 55

Bartholow, B. D., 54, 56, 125, 126, 127

batterer intervention program (BIP), 243, 244

Bauman, K., 76, 91

Bauman, S., 9

Baumgardner, J., 53, 123

Bavelier, D., 58
BDI test, 24
Bechtoldt-Baldacci, H., 123
behavioral changes, 212
behavioral problems, history of abuse and, 203
behavioral scripts, 43, 53
behavioral theory, 147
Belknap, J., 202, 203
Bell, K., 98
Bellmoff, L., 110
Berkowitz, L., 128
bidirectional abuse, 99
bidirectional violence, 94
Bijvank, N. M., 52
biological theory, 147
Birckbichler, L., 110
Birckmayer, J., 187, 190
Birnbaum, H. J., 147
Bjerregaard, B., 182
Black, B. M., 92
black youths homicide rate, 17
Blackburn, A. G., 207
Black's Law Dictionary, 93
Bloom, S., 184
Boat, B., 154
Bobo doll paradigm, 43
Bonanno, R. A., 116
Bosacki, S. L., 112
Bostic, J., 208
Bowes, L., 5, 6
Boyle, J., 11
boys: dating aggression, 79; dating assaults by, 72; family violence influence on, 204; firearm availability to, 178; firearm ownership of, 181; future assault predictors, 205; grade point average of abused, 90; in abusive relationship, 97; juvenile arrest statistics, 200–202; on bullying, 109, 110, 117; parental monitoring, 205; physical and sexual victimization, 202; power and control, 72; psychological distress, 29; rape, 28; risk factors for, 29; self-defense by, 76; victimization risk factors for, 29; video games rating, 41–42; youthful sexual activity by, 146
Bradford, J., 147
Bradley, J. F., 107
Bradley, M. M., 124
Bradley, Michael J., 139
Bradshaw, C. P., 10
Braga, A., 178
Branch, O. L., 55
Bredekamp, J., 110
Bridge, J., 185, 190
Briere, J., 18, 25, 26
Brown, G., 116
Buchanan, P., 106, 112, 114
Buchanan, R., 214
Buckley, K. E., 57
Buka, S., 179
bullies: moral disengagement of, 116; teachers perception of, 10; view of, 114–116
bullying: as harmless fun, 115–116; at schools, 9; benefits of, to bullies, 115–116; blame for, according to bullies, 117–118; gender considerations, 117; interventions for, 30; peer pressure as cause of, 113–114; power and status from, 110–111; prevention and intervention, 117; reports of, 3; self-esteem levels and, 111–112; teenager motivation for, 109–111; victim attributing, by gender, 109; vs. peer victimization (PV), 5; workplace, 7
bullying causes, young people's representation: about, 105–106; amusement, 112–113; deviant victim, 106–109; disturbed bully, 111–112; from bully's view, 114–116; peer pressure, 113–114; power, status and friendship, 109–111; practitioners' implications, 116–118
Burnette, M. L., 203
Burns, S., 116
Bushman, B. J., 52, 53, 55, 57, 122, 123, 124, 125, 126, 127, 128, 129

Caldwell, A., 175
Callahan, C., 175, 178
Campbell, D., 154
Campbell, J., 91
Campo, J., 185, 190
Capaccioli, K., 7, 8, 10, 11
Capaldi, D. M., 78
Carlson, K., 107, 180

Carnagey, N. L., 122, 123, 124
Caspi, A., 71, 73
CDI test, 24
Centers for Disease Control and Prevention (CDC), 163, 175
Chamberlain, P., 215
Champion, H., 175, 181
Charles, D., 76
Chauhan, P., 203
Child Access Prevention (CAP) laws, 189, 190
Child Behavioral Checklist, 24
childhood physical and sexual abuse and assault treatment, 24–25
childhood predictors of adult partner abuse, 246
children: maltreatment of, 24. *See also* adolescents; boys; girls
Children in Communities Study, 246
Clarke, Naomi, 141
Clayton, R., 180
Cline, V. B., 122
Codispoti, M., 124
cognitive desensitization, 123
cognitive-behavioral approach, 27
cognitive-behavioral theory, 148, 211
cognitive-behavioral therapy, 32, 244
cognitive-control disruption, 59–60
cognitive-functioning elements, 23
cognitive-neoassociation theory, 43
cognitive-processing therapy, 27
Cohan, A., 140
Cohen-Kettenis, P. T., 206
community interventions, 163–169
community violence, 33–34
Community Violence Exposure Survey, 24
comorbid diagnoses, 26
competitive reaction-time (CRT) task, 125
complex post-traumatic stress disorder (PTSD), 18–19
complex trauma, 23
concealed weapons in safe areas, 179
conduct disorder (CD), 212
Cook, P., 172, 173, 174, 178
Cornell, D., 201
Cosby, R., 149
couples: mutual violence, 94; physical abuse after marriage, 241–242

couples counseling, 244
couples therapy, 244
Courrier, S., 122
Court TV, 149–151
Cram, F., 25–26
Crawford, E., 73
Crick, N. R., 105
crime displacement, 228–229
Croft, R. G., 122
Crosby, A., 185
Crosby, J. W., 7, 8, 10, 11
Crosby, L., 78
Cross, C., 90
Cross, D., 116
cross-sectional correlational studies, 47
Cullingford, C., 110, 113, 114, 116
cultivation theory, 43
Cuthbert, B. N., 124

Dane, A. V., 112
date rape incidence, 25–26
dating aggression, 73
dating violence: risk factors for perpetration of, 72; role of girls and women in, 71; training program, 245–246; victims' academic performance, 245
David, J., 107
Davidson, L. M., 11
Davis, E., 54, 56, 127
Decker, S., 175
DeGarmo, D. S., 214
Del Rio, A., 9
delinquency: reductions in, 215; substance use by girls, 208
delinquency and violent behavior in girls: about, 199; intervention for violent and aggressive girls, 210; mental illness and emotional distress, 205–207; multidimensional treatment foster care, 213–216; risk factors for juvenile female offending and violent behavior, 202; sexual and physical victimization, 202–203; snap-girls connection, 210–213; substance abuse, 207–210; trends in female juvenile offending, 199–202; troubled family life, 203–206; conclusions, 216

delinquent girls: mothers of, 204; physical and sexual abuse among, 203; post-traumatic stress symptoms, 206; substance abuse and victimization, 209–210; substance use by, 207; suicide and, 206
Deluca, Ken, 152
Demaray, M. K., 11
Demetriou, A., 129
Denson, D., 154
Department of Justice, 227
Desai, A. D., 72, 74
desensitization: about, 121–122; at psychological level, 124–126; behavior correlates to, 126–128; definition of, 122; empathy and, 50–51, 55–56; future directions, 129–130; individual differences, 128–129; mechanisms, 122; to media violence, 122–124
desensitization theory, 43
developmental concerns, 28
developmental traumatology theory, 78–79
deviancy vs. difference examples, 107–108
deviant victim as cause of bullying, 106–109
DeVille, J., 182
Diagnostic and Statistic Manual of Mental Disorders (*DSM*), 61
Dill, K. E., 127
Ding, C., 179
displacement hypothesis, 61
distal factors, 43–44
disturbed bully, 111–112
Dixon, A., 206, 208
Dodge, K. A., 105
Doll, H., 206
domestic distress homicides, 201–202
D'Onofrio, B. M., 204, 205
Doreleijers, T. A. H., 206
double standard for offenders, 151
Drabman, R. S., 122
Duluth model, 243, 244
Dunn, D. W., 59
Dyer, E., 154
dynamic theory of personality, 228
Dziech, B. W., 140

Eckhardt, C., 97, 98, 99
ecological levels of intervention, 233

education of teens to discriminate abusive from nonabusive situations. *See* abusive vs. nonabusive situation discrimination
Educator Sexual Misconduct: A Synthesis of Existing Literature (Shakeshaft), 136
Edwards, K. E., 72, 74
Einarsen, S., 7
electroencephalography (EEG), 125
Elkind, D., 138
Elvevag, B., 139
emotional desensitization, 123
empathy: bullies and, 111, 118; described, 56, 126; desensitization and, 50, 55, 56; diminished, 53; prosocial video games, 57; protection factor of high levels of, 49; reduction of, 126; therapeutic, 28; violence and, 79; violent films impact on, 56
Entertainment Software Rating Board (ESRB), 42
Entertainment Tonight, 149–151
environmental interventions, 229, 233
Erling, A., 106, 110, 114
Esposito, L. E., 7, 8
Evans, W., 180
Everson, M., 154
experimental studies, 47

Fabio, A., 185, 190
facial electromyography, 124
Fagan, J., 71, 174, 175, 183
Fairbank, J. A., 5
family violence impact, 204
family-of-origin abuse effects, 75
Fanti, K. A., 123, 128, 129
Fazel, S., 206
FBI Supplementary Homicide report, 201
Federal Bureau of Investigation (FBI), 199
Fedoroff, J., 147
feminist theory, 79–80
Feng, J., 58
Finkelhor, D., 25–26, 137
firearm availability, 187–188
firearm homicide rates: by race and ethnicity, 174; of inner-city adolescents, 175
firearm selling, 172

firearm suicide: adolescents and prevalence of, 184; adolescents trends, 184–185; by African Americans, 186, 189; by ethnicity, 186; by females, 185; Child Access Prevention (CAP) laws and, 189; trends of, 184–185
firearms, adolescent accessibility to, 187
five C's of positive youth development, 228
Foehr, U. G., 61
Foshee, V., 76, 91
foster parents, 214
Fredland, N., 91
Frisén, A., 108, 111, 114
Fualaau, Vili, 148–149
Funk, J. B., 53, 123

Gainer, P., 175, 181
galvanic skin response (GSR), 56, 124
gaming addiction, 61–62
Gang Resistance Education and Training (GREAT) program, 227–228
Gary, N., 154
Gavazzi, S., 208, 209
gender bias theory, 151
gender variations in dating violence, 80
gender-neutral vs. gender-specific programming, 80
general aggression model (GAM), 43–46, 127, 128
general learning model (GLM), 43–46
Gentile, D. A., 57, 59, 60
Get Out of My Life, But First Could You Drive Me and Cheryl to the Mall (Wolfe), 138
Giauque, A. L., 59
Gidycz, C. A., 72, 74
Giedd, J., 139
Giordano, P. C., 204, 205
girls: arrests rates of, 200; dating aggression, 79; dating assaults by, 72; family violence influence on, 204; future assault predictors, 205; grade point average of abused, 90; in abusive relationship, 97; juvenile arrest statistics, 200–202; on bullying, 109, 110, 117; parental monitoring, 205; physical and sexual victimization, 202; psychological distress, 29; rape, 28; risk factors for, 28; self-defense by, 72; stereotypes of, 199; victimization risk factors for, 28; video games rating, 41; violent behavior of, 200–201; violent offending among, 204; youthful sexual activity by, 146. *See also* delinquent girls
Grasley, C., 78
Graves, K. N., 75
Green, C. S., 58
Greenhouse, J., 185, 190
Greenwald, M. K., 124
Groth, A. N., 147
Gruber, M. L., 124
gun violence, 172
gun violence decline, 172
gun-carrying data, 176

Hamarus, P., 108
Hamerlynck, S. M. J. J., 206, 207
Hamm, A. O., 124
Hara, H., 116
Hardy, M., 190
Harris, R. H., 55, 56
Harris, W. H., 5
Harrison, P., 231
Hassle Log, 211
hate and bias incidents against LGBTQ victims, 18
Hawa, V., 129
Hazler, R. J., 111
heart rate, 55, 124
helpful and prosocial behavior, 57
Hemenway, D., 178, 187, 188, 189, 190
Henrich, C. C., 123, 128
Hepburn, L., 187
Herrera, V. M., 201, 204
Hilkene, B., 167
Hoffman, M. L., 117
Holmqvist, K., 108, 111
Holsinger, K., 202, 203
homicides: adolescents and guns, 173; African Americans rates of, 172; age groups risk of, 221; as cause of death of African Americans, 221; domestic distress, 201–202; firearm homicide rates, 174, 175, 185; records of, 201
Hoover, J. H., 111
Hopf, W. H., 54
Horowitz, J. A., 107

Index

Horowitz, R., 179
Horton, R. W., 122
Howard, J., 209
Howie, P., 205
Huber, G. L., 54
Huesmann, L. R., 43
human brain, changes in, 139
Hunsaker, D., 187
Hunsaker, J., 187
Hunter, S., 11
Hwang, C. P., 106, 110
Hymel, S., 116

identity disturbance, 25
Ihori, N., 53, 55, 57
imminent risk treatment, 20
impaired-self capacities, 25
impaired-self disturbance, 25
Inciardi, J., 179
individualist bias, 228, 229
individual-level interventions, 233
inner-city adolescents, firearm homicide rates of, 175
integrative treatment of complex trauma (ITCT), 26–28
interdependence theory, 77
intergenerational transmission of violence theory, 76–78
internalized distress, 4, 6
Internet violence, 129–130
Internet-related sex crimes, 26
interparental violence, 73
intervention focus, 227
interventions: categories for youth violence reduction, 227; conclusions and implications, 11–13; effectiveness of, 31–32, 241; family-based, for community violence, 34; for bullying and school violence, 30; gender sensitive programs, 210
intimate partner violence (IPV): causes of, 98; mental health issues and, 29; prevalence of, 28
intimate terrorism, 96

Jackson, S. M., 25–26
Jamison, T. R., 97–98
Jansen, L. M. C., 206

Jenkins, P., 181
Joe, S., 186
Johnson, A., 114
Johnson, M., 96
Jones, D., 154
Jones, L., 137
Joseph, S., 7
juvenile justice detention center, 21
juvenile justice system, 21–22, 224–225

Kahn, D., 179
Kaikkonen, P., 108
Kalamas, A. D., 124
Kaplan, M., 186
Karch, D., 185
Kasian, M., 90
Kazimi, M., 179
Keenan, K., 204, 205
Kegler, S., 185
Kelleher, K., 185, 190
Kennedy, D., 178
Kenny, D. T., 209
Kercher, G., 148
Khoo, A., 57
Kirsh, S. J., 53, 127
Kline, Heather, 155
knowledge structure changes, 127
Knutsen, S., 110, 113, 116, 117
Konijn, E. A., 52
Krahé, B., 53
Kronenberger, W. G., 59
Krugman, R., 154
Krull, R. A., 124
Kub, J., 91
Kubrin, C., 187, 189

Lafave, Debra, 149–151
Lahelma, E., 116
Lahey, B. B., 204, 205
Lang, B. J., 124
Lang, P. J., 124
Langhinrichsen-Rohling, J., 94–95, 99
Langstrom, N., 206
Lanktree, C. B., 18, 26
Larsen, J. L., 59
Lassonde, C., 179
Laub, J., 172, 173, 174
Lauer, M., 149

Layne, C. M., 32
Lennings, C. L., 209
lesbian, gay, bisexual, transgender, queer, or questioning (LGBTQ) victims, 18
Letourneau, Mary Kay, 148–149
Leve, L. D., 215
Levene, K., 211
Lewin, K., 228
LH Research Survey, 181
Li, T. Q., 59
Liau, A. K., 57
Lim, J., 208
Linder, F., 76, 91
Linder, J. R., 60
Lippincott, E. C., 122
Lippmann, S., 187
Lipsey, M. W., 31–32
Lizotte, A., 181, 182
longitudinal studies, 47
Loper, A., 201
Lopp, E., 110
Lorenz, Konrad, 4
Lowe, M. J., 59
Lower, R., 90
Lubell, K. M., 185
Ludwig, J., 178
Lurito, J. T., 59
Luster, T., 90
Luthra, R., 74
Lynch, P. J., 60

MACI test, 24
Mackdacy, L., 209
Magdol, L., 71, 73
Makepeace, J. M., 89
Male Perpetrators of Child Maltreatment: Findings from NCANDS (National Child Abuse and Neglect Data System), 146
Manganello, J., 189
Mansfield, Troy, 155
Marini, Z. A., 112
Marquart, J. W., 205
Marsh, S., 180
Marshall, M., 110
maternal abuse vs. paternal abuse, 73
Mathews, V. P., 59
Maupin, J. R., 231
Maycock, B., 116

Mays, G. L., 231
McBryde, M., 184
McCloskey, L. A., 201, 204
McCullough, B., 107
McGee, Z., 182
McGraw, J., 154
McKinney, C., 34
media violence: bidirectional relationship view of, 128; causal links to aggression, 121; desensitization to, 121–130; imitative behavior source, 123; mechanisms and effects, 122
medical centers and hospitals, 20–21
Meichenbaum's anxiety management procedures, 27
mental health issues: dating violence, 90; intimate partner violence (IPV) and, 29; risk factors for adolescent firearm suicide, 186–187
mental illness: abuse and, 203; among incarcerated adolescents, 206; depression and, 206; emotional stress, 205–207; family dysfunction, 209; female offenders and, 202; substance abuse and, 207; suicide attempts, 206
mentors, 168
Meyers, J., 110
Mikkelsen, E., 7
Mikuni, M., 207
Miller, M., 178, 179, 187, 188, 189
Ming, L. K., 57
Mitchell, K. J., 25–26
MMPI-A test, 24
mobbing, 4
Moffitt, T. E., 71, 73
Mohler Rockwell, S., 204, 205
Molidor, C., 76
Möller, I., 53
Molnar, B., 179
Montoya, C., 107
Moor, A., 28
moral disengagement, 116, 118
Moretti, M. M., 203, 204, 205
Morrison, J., 110, 113, 114, 116
mother-daughter relationship, 204
Mulhall, P., 182
Mullings, J. L., 207
Multidimensional Treatment Foster Care

Index

program, 213
multiple trauma experiences, 18–19
multiple treatment modalities, 27
Mulvihill, M., 179
Murphy, C., 98–99
Mynard, H., 7

Nakano, R., 207
National Center for Health Statistics Mortality, 184
National Center for Victims of Crime, 17, 93
National Center of Juvenile Justice, 203
National Child Abuse and Neglect Data System, 89
National Coalition of Anti-Violence Programs, 18
National Family Violence Survey, 241
National Institute of Justice, 244
National Longitudinal Survey of Youth, 205
National Survey of Adolescent Males, 178
National Youth Risk Behavior Surveillance System (National Youth Risk Behavior Survey) (YRBSS), 175, 188
Naugle, A., 98
Neff, J., 209
Nelsen, E., 179
New York City Youth Violence Study, 182–184
Newman, D. L., 71
Noonan, R. K., 76
Norris, F. H., 6, 12

Oates, R., 154
O'Brennan, L. M., 10
Obsuth, I., 204, 205
odd student repertoire, 106
Odgers, C. L., 203, 204, 205
Oehler, J., 7, 8, 10, 11
Okeefe, M., 73, 74, 76
O'Leary, D. K., 76, 77
Olweus, D., 4–5, 20
One Hundred Black Men of America, Inc., 168
opposition defiant disorder (ODD), 212
orientations of intervention, 233
Oscarsson, D., 108, 111

Owens, L., 110, 113

PAI-A test, 24
Painter, S., 90
Paradise, M. J., 75, 76
parental monitoring, 205
parental rights, 22
parental violence factors in father relationships, 91
partner-abusive behaviors, 239
Pasold, T., 53, 123
paternal abuse: perpetration of physical dating violence and, 74; vs. maternal abuse, 73
pathological gamers, 62
pecking order process, 111
Pedlow, S., 204, 205
peer juries, 230
peer pressure as cause of bullying, 113–114
peer victimization (PV): about, 3, 4; adult perception, 10; as traumatic experience, 4; behaviors, 9; definition, 4–5; forms of, 5; post-traumatic stress disorder (PTSD) and, 7; post-traumatic stress disorder (PTSD) symptomatology and, 8; social support relationship, 10–11; vs. bullying, 5
peer victimization (PV) and post-traumatic stress disorder in children and adolescents, 3–13; intervention, conclusions and implications, 11–13; peer victimization and post-traumatic stress disorder, 6–9; peer victimization and post-traumatic stress disorder in children and adolescents, 10; trauma and ecology, 9–10; trauma in children, 5–6
peer violence intervention, 92
Pennell, S., 175
People (magazine), 3
Pepler, D. J., 211, 212
perpetrators, subtypes of, 95
person factors, 44–45
personal factors: life experiences, 188–189; mental health problems, 188
personality assessment tools, 98
Persson, C., 114

Peterson, Robert, 135, 140
Phillips, C., 110, 111
physical aggression in dating relationships: by women, 71; motivation for, 72
physical and sexual abuse among delinquent girls, 203
physical and sexual victimization among delinquents, 202
physical victimization, 11
physiological arousal, 50–51, 55
post-traumatic stress disorder (PTSD): definition of, 5; peer victimization (PV) and, 7; rate of, 18; severity of exposure for symptoms, 22–23; violence as cause of, 6. *See also* peer victimization (PV) and post-traumatic stress disorder in children and adolescents
post-traumatic stress disorder (PTSD) symptomatology: as violence perpetration predictor, 78; peer victimization (PV) and, 8; peer victimization (PV) behaviors, 9
Pottieger, A., 179
power, status and friendship as causes of bullying, 109–111
Power and Control Wheel, 243
practitioners' implications, 116–118
Pratt, J., 58
prevention strategies, 225
primary care providers, 20–21
primary preventions, 225
probabilistic causality, 48–49
prolonged exposure therapy, 27
prosocial (helping) behavior, 50–51, 57
protective factors, 49
proweapon socialization, 181–182
proximate factors, 43–44
psychiatric hospital settings, short- or long-term, 20
psychodynamic abuser therapy, 243
psychodynamic theory, 147
psychodynamic treatment, 243
psychological abuse prevalence between teens, 90
psychological aggression in dating relationships, 72
psychological trauma, 18
punitive policies vs. restorative justice, 32

Putnam, Adam, 156
Putnam, F. W., 5
Pynoos, R. S., 32
pyschoeducation, 27

rape: date rape, 25–26; problems incurred by adolescent rape victims, 26; statutory rape, 26; trauma, 27
Rathouz, P., 204, 205
recidivism rates, 222, 231, 244–245
Reebye, P., 204, 205
Reid, J. B., 214
relational disturbance, 25
relational victimization, 9
Rembusch, M. E., 59
Renk, K., 34
Reppucci, N. D., 203
residential treatment settings, 20–22
Resnick, M., 167
restorative justice principles, 231
restorative justice vs. punitive policies, 32
Ricardo, I., 91
Rice, J., 76, 91
Richardson, Clive, 141
Rickards, S., 25
Rideout, V. J., 61
Riggs, D. S., 76, 77
Ris, J., 182
risk factor approach, 48–49
risk factors: by gender, 29; for adolescent suicide, 185–186; for aggression, 49, 52; for juvenile female offending and violent behavior, 202; for perpetration of dating violence, 72; victimization, for boys, 29; victimization, for girls, 28
Rivara, F., 175, 178
Roberts, D. F., 61
Robertson, C., 154
Robins, Sydney L., 152–154
Rochester Youth Survey, 181
Rocke-Henderson, N., 116
Rodeheffer, C. D., 55
Rodgers, J. L., 204, 205
Roethke, Theodore, 137
Rogoff, B., 230
Rojas-Vilches, A., 34
Romero, M., 184
Ross, D., 43, 123

Index

Ross, J., 95
Ross, S. A., 43, 123
Rothstein, H. R., 53, 55, 57
Rountree, P., 180, 181–182

Safe Dates Program, 29, 80
Sakamoto, A., 53, 55, 57
Saldana, L., 214
Saleem, M., 53, 55, 57
Salmivalli, C., 106, 110, 114
Saltzman, W. R., 32
SAMHSA (Substance Abuse and Mental Health Services Administration), 207
Samper, R., 98–99
Sawyer, A. L., 10
Schackner, R., 188, 189
Scheer, S., 208
school gun carrying rates, 175
school performance, 60–61
school settings, treatment in, 19–20
school violence: common forms of, 30; prevention program elements, 31
school-based group therapy, 32
schools: bullying at, 9–10; student's weapon carrying at, 176–177; youth safety in, 223; zero-tolerance policies at, 174
Schubiner, H., 179
Scott, K., 78
Scott, R., 179
screen time, 60
script theory, 43
Sechrist, S. M., 75
secondary preventions, 225
Seiger, K., 34
self defense, 72, 76
self-blame, 27
self-devaluation, 27
sentencing, 149–151
Sestir, M. A., 54, 56, 125, 126, 127
setting-level interventions, 229
sexual abuse: about, 135; definition of, 136; prevalence of, 137
sexually transmitted disease (STD) risks, 25
Seymour, F. W., 25–26
Shain, B., 188, 190
Shakeshaft, C., 136, 140, 156
Shakoor, S., 5, 6

Sharps, P., 91
Sheftall, A., 185, 190
Sheley, J., 178, 179, 182
Sheppard, D., 181
Shibuya, A., 53, 55, 57
Shields, L., 187
Shute, R., 110, 113
Sidwell Friends school, 135
Silva, P. A., 71, 73
Sirotnak, A., 154
situational couple violence, 96
situational factors, 43–44
Slee, P., 110, 113
Sloan, L. B., 6, 12
Slovak, K., 178
Small, S., 90
Smith, M., 179
Snyder, H., 137, 145
social cognitive theory, 42–43
social environment, 18
social information processing (SIP) models, 105
social learning theory: feminist theory, 79–80; intergenerational transmission of violence theory and, 76–78; social cognitive theory and, 42–43
social support: access to, 12; definition of, 11; effect of reliance on, 11
social victimization, 12
social/environmental factors: firearm availability, 187–188; geographic location, 186–187; socioeconomic status (SES), 187
socioeconomic status (SES): social/environmental factors, 187; weapons carriers, 181
Spence, I., 58
Stark, E., 95–96
Starling, J., 206, 208
State-Trait Anger Expression Inventory (STAXI), 97–98
statutory rape, 26
Steinberg, A. M., 32
stereotypes: about adolescents, 222; of girls, 199
Storch, E. A., 7, 8
Straatman, A., 78
Strengthening Families model, 168

stress inoculation training, 27
Stroop effect, 59
Stroop tasks, 59–60
Strout, Elizabeth, 142–145
Student Protection Act of 2009, 156
student's weapon carrying at schools, 176–177
substance abuse: about, 207–210; adolescents, 22; aggressive behavior, 51; bully victims and, 30; by female delinquents, 207–209; childhood abuse and, 25, 26; dating violence role, 81, 99, 245; parental involvement, 164; personal factors, 188; psychiatric hospital settings, 20; residential treatment settings, 21; risk factors for, 168, 202, 209–210; treatment facilities, 20, 21; victimization and, 209
Substance Abuse and Mental Health Services Administration, 30
Substance Abuse and Mental Health Services Administration (SAMHSA), 207
substance use: by delinquent girls, 207, 208; fighting and, 207
suicide: delinquent girls and, 206. *See also* firearm suicide
suicide rates: by gender, 186; mental health problems and, 188; rural vs. urban, 186–187
Swart, E., 110
Swing, E. L., 53, 55, 57, 59
symbolic interactionism, 105
systemic interventions, 20

teachers: abuse identification by, 99–100; intervention by, 9–10; perception of bullying by, 10; responsibilities and actions of, 153–155; social support from, 11
teachers, abuse by: as educators, 140; DeLuca case, 149–150; fiction about, 142–145; Lafave case, 149–150; Letourneau case, 146; male adolescent student response to, 146; Mansfield case, 155–156; Mary Kay, 148–149; Peterson case, 135; prevalence rate of, 137; reporting of teacher misconduct, 145; reporting problems, 154–155; Richardson case, 141; school investigations regarding, 152–154; sexual victimization by, 135; Sidwell Friends school, 135; Student Protection Act of 2009 proposal, 159
teen pregnancy risks, 25
teenage victims of violence: community interventions, 167–169; protective factors for, 167; scenarios of, 164–166; support for, 163–164
television and television watching, 58
television violence, 123
Teräsahjo, T., 106, 110, 114, 116
tertiary preventions, 225
"The Adolescent Brain: A Work in Progress" (Weingberger, Elvevag, and Giedd), 139
theoretical frameworks, 41–46
Thomas, M. H., 122
Thornberg, R., 107, 110, 112, 113, 114, 116, 117
Tolman, R. M., 76
trait aggressiveness, 125, 128
transactional interventions, 233
transactional strategies for youth violence reduction, 230
trauma: ecology and, 9–10; in children, 5–6; integrative treatment of complex trauma (ITCT), 26–28; psychological trauma, 18; rape trauma, 27; severity of exposure for, 22–23. *See also* post-traumatic stress disorder (PTSD)
trauma-specific measures, 24
traumatic events, 6, 17
treatment: court ordered, 22; for aggressors, 32; for individuals, 32–33; interventions for adolescents and community violence, 33–34; types of settings, 19
treatment of adolescent victims of violence: about, 17–19; adolescent intimate partner violence (IPV), 28–30; adolescent victims of physical and sexual assault, 25–26; assessment of, 22–24; childhood physical and sexual abuse and assault, treatment of, 24–25; community violence, 33–34; integrative treatment of complex trauma (ITCT), 26–28; interventions, effectiveness of, 31–32; interventions, for bullying and school violence, 30; juvenile justice system, 21–22;

medical centers and hospitals, 20–21; psychiatric hospital settings, short- or long-term, 20; residential treatment settings, 20–22; school settings, treatment within, 19–20; school violence prevention programs, common elements in, 31; treatment for individuals, 32–33; treatment setting types, 19; summary, 35
triggers, 211
Trulson, C. R., 205
Tzelepis, A., 179

Van, Hulle, C. A., 204, 205
Vandiver, D., 148
Vanman, E., 123, 128
VanWynsberghe, A., 72, 74
Varjas, K., 110
Vaughan, A., 212
verbal victimization, 12
Vermeiren, R., 206
Vernick, J., 189
Vessey, J. A., 107
victim attributing, 109, 116
victimization: dating relationship aggression, 71–73; dating violence, 73; delinquent girls and substance abuse, 209–210; physical, 11; relational, 9; risk factors by gender, 29; risk factors for boys, 29; risk factors for girls, 28; sexual and physical, 202–203; social, 12; verbal, 12. *See also* peer victimization (PV)
video games: popularity and usage of, 41; rating, 42; types of studies in research, 47–48. *See also* violent video game effects
violence: acceptance of, 91, 92; adaptive role of, 183; agency orientation to reduction, 226; as cause of post-traumatic stress disorder (PTSD), 6; as outlet for traumatic experiences, 78; cessation by adult males, 242; functional material and symbolic meanings, 183; initiation of, by gender, 92; race and ethnicity, 223; resistance to, 96; surge of, 5
violence-related risk factors, 174
violent crime rates by racial groups, 17–18
violent video game effects: about, 41–42; aggressive affect, 54–55; aggressive behavior, 52, 56–57, 62, 121, 126, 129; aggressive cognition, 53–54; desensitization and empathy, 55–56; effects on attention and cognitive control, 57–60; gaming addiction, 61–62; physiological arousal, 55; probabilistic causality and the risk factor approach, 48–49; school performance, 60–61; short- and long-term effects on aggression and related variables, 49–56; theoretical frameworks, 41–46; types of studies in video game research, 47–48; summary, 62–63
visuospatial attention benefits, 57
Vittes, K., 178

Wadsworth, T., 187, 189
WAIS-IV or WISC-IV measures, 23–24
Waite, D., 203, 209
Waldman, I. D., 204, 205
Walsh, D. A., 59, 60
Walsh, M., 211, 212
Wang, Y., 59
Watt, J. H., 124
Watts, K., 97–98
weapons carriers: gender, ethnicity, and economic status of, 180; peers of, 182, 184; socioeconomic status (SES), 181
Weaver, A., 5, 7, 8
Webber, J., 212
Webster, D., 175, 181, 189
Wechsler Abbreviated Scale of Intelligence (WASI), 23
Weiner, L., 140
Weingberger, D., 139
Weisz, A. N., 92
Wekerle, C., 78
West, R., 59
White, J. W., 75
white youths: firearm homicide rates, 174; homicide rates, 17–18; weapon carrying, 180
Wilcher, R., 76, 91
Wilcox, P., 180
Wilkinson, D., 174, 175, 183, 184
Williams, B., 184
Williams, S., 182
Wilson, S. J., 31–32
Wintemute, G., 184

Winzer, M., 106, 112, 114
Wolak, J., 25–26
Wolfe, Anthony, 138
Wolfe, D. A., 78
Wolpe J., 122
Wood, E. A., 59
workplace bullying, 7
World Health Organization, 186
Wright, J., 178, 179, 182
Wright, M. O., 73

Yarcheck, C., 208
Ybarra, M. L., 25–26
Yes, Your Teen Is Crazy! Loving Your Kid Without Losing Your Mind (Bradley, Michael J.), 139
Yonas, M., 91
young women: dating aggression, 79, 81; mental illness and emotional distress, 205–207; sexual abuse experience, 78; victimization and subsequent perpetration of dating violence, 73, 74, 77–78; youth organizing by, 232
youth agency, 224, 226, 227, 230
youth courts, 230
youth development program, 228
youth engagement and violence prevention, 232
Youth Relationship Project, 80
youth violence: decreases in, 163, 169; prevention strategies, 224; rates of, 223; reduction methods, 223–224
youth violence reduction: from youth agency, 230; intervention categories for, 227; transactional strategies for, 230
YRBSS (National Youth Risk Behavior Surveillance System), 175, 188
Yuile, A., 212
Yukawa. S., 57

Zeoli, A., 189
zero-tolerance policies, 32, 174